Curiosity drives John Blashfc
With eccentric animals at he
to defend Herefordshire agai

German tunnels. Sandhurst taught him leadership; he already had the personality and flair.

Epic expeditions, interspersed with spells of active service, have since dominated his life. At Haile Selassie's request he led a sixty-strong Army team to make the first descent of the infamous Blue Nile. Combating exhaustion, stress and health hazards, he then tackled an even tougher obstacle: the Darien Gap, eventually getting his battered vehicles through after 100 days of unrelenting toil under appalling conditions. The Scientific Exploration Society, which he chaired, then set off in the steps of Stanley, being the first to navigate almost all the 2,700 miles of the great Zaire River whilst seeking a cure for a terrible eye disease.

So stimulating and worthwhile were these expeditions that John was persuaded by the Prince of Wales to launch Operation Drake and, later, Operation Raleigh. Recruiting dedicated experts and generous sponsors, he masterminded the most ambitious and successful youth leadership programme ever devised. It doesn't stop there. In the tracks of Genghis Khan his team tackled vital community aid and conservation tasks in the Mongolian Gobi. Then he discovered giant elephants in a Himalayan valley...

Full of wit, thrills and excitement, these memoirs enter a world of adventure and discovery. They will inspire you to reach for your pith helmet and, in the words of Kipling: 'Go and find it. Go and look behind the ranges.'

Colonel John Blashford-Snell was educated at Victoria College, Jersey and the Royal Military Academy, Sandhurst, then commissioned into the Royal Engineers. He has been on over 100 expeditions in almost every part of the world, and in recognition of his leadership has been awarded the Royal Geographical Society's Patrons Medal for 'encouragement of exploration by young people'. He was also honoured with an MBE in 1969 and OBE in 1996.

Now President of the Scientific Exploration Society, he continues to explore non-stop.

By the same author

Weapons and Tactics (with Tom Wintringham)
Expeditions, the Experts' Way (with Alistair Ballantine)
Where the Trails Run Out
In the Steps of Stanley
A Taste for Adventure
In the Wake of Drake (with Mike Cable)
Operation Drake (with Mike Cable)
Mysteries: Encounters with the Unexplained
Operation Raleigh: The Start of an Adventure
Operation Raleigh: Adventure Challenge (with Ann Tweedy)
Operation Raleigh: Adventure Unlimited (with Ann Tweedy)
Something Lost Behind the Ranges (autobiography)
Mammoth Hunt (with Rula Lenska)
Kota Mama (with Richard Snailham)
East to the Amazon (with Richard Snailham)

SOMETHING LOST
BEHIND
THE RANGES

John Blashford-Snell

To Amanda

I'm told that you are an amazing lady and a truly seasoned traveller. I hope that this book will remind you of your journey to date and inspire you to keep travelling and see those parts of the world you have not yet seen.

John Blashford-Snell

7/11/15

Live Wire Books

Dedicated to my parents, Gwen and Bish,
and my parents-in-law, Lal and Tommy Sherman.
Great supporters.

First published in Great Britain by HarperCollins*Publishers* in 1994

First published as a paperback by HarperCollins*Publishers* in 1995

This new paperback edition published in 2014 by

Live Wire Books,
The Orchard, School Lane,
Warmington, Banbury,
Oxfordshire OX17 1DE
www.livewirebooks.com

ISBN: 978-0-9553124-7-2

Printed and bound in England by Short Run Press Ltd

Contents

Maps

Illustrations

ILLUSTRATIONS

Acknowledgements

Writing by candlelight in the Gobi and trying to stop the sweat dripping all over the paper in the jungle or the winds of the high Altai blowing the manuscript away, I have struggled to put down an account of some of the events of my first fifty-six years. It is also a story of the endeavours of an army of people all over the world who have befriended and helped me.

I am especially grateful to Eddie Bell and Michael Fishwick of HarperCollins, the original publishers of this autobiography, who didn't even blink an eyelid when an elephant accidentally mucked up my right hand, forcing me to have an operation before I could continue writing.

Over the years I have had expert help from my chums, including the late Ann Tweedy Savage, Mike Cable, Andrew Mitchell and Richard Snailham in recording the events of many of the expeditions described: I trust they will forgive any plagiarisms.

I am indebted to the Council of the Scientific Exploration Society for their kind permission to use some material from the books on Operations Drake and Raleigh. The photographs have come from numerous sources, but there are some really good ones by Chris Sainsbury, who accompanied us for twelve years. I am especially grateful to Nick Wilcox-Brown, who provided the cover photograph for this new edition of the book, Nick Turner, who snapped the dramatic back cover shot, and John Edwards, who also helped with photography in Nepal. My thanks also to Jane Harvey of Canon UK and to Jeremy Gilbert of Nikon UK for keeping my own camera operational and to Jessop's for their generous help with photographic gear.

I have been most fortunate over the years to have had the support of a number of most efficient and charming PAs, including Sue Fyson, Rosh Allhusen, Pam Baker, Betty Starling, Sara Everett, Margot Baker, Sally Harris, Sue Farrington, Melanie King, Peta Lock, Nadia Brydon, Barbara Carlisle, Sally Cox, Carol Turner and now Anne Gilby. Their contributions have been enormous and their friendships have meant much to me.

The assistance and backing of the late Harbourne Stephen, formerly Managing Director of the *Daily Telegraph*, was immensely valuable and the advice of my friend, the late Jennifer Watts, on literary matters was always greatly appreciated. I'm especially indebted to Sally Cox who worked at the word processor in sand and hailstorms in Mongolia, whilst Anne Cooke and Judith, my wife, typed and prepared a huge amount of the transcript back in Britain. My late mother-in-law and supporter, Lal Sherman, and my son-in-law, Julian Matthews, also did much to help as 'readers'.

There has simply not been space to mention all those who have played important parts in the various activities I have described and I ask their forgiveness. However, I must record my special gratitude to two outstanding friends, sadly no longer with us, Ambassador Walter Annenberg and General Sir John Mogg, for their marvellous support and wise counsel over many years.

It is largely due to the encouragement and expertise of Mike Cable that this revised edition has been published and, hopefully, it will be followed in the near future by a new volume covering the numerous expeditions with which I have been involved since 1993. Meanwhile, my thanks also to designer Dick Malt for his work on this book, to Jude Gray, who typed the revised text at lightning speed, and to Dave Smith, who skilfully scanned all the maps and photos.

John Blashford-Snell
Motcombe
December 2013

Something Lost Behind the Ranges

Happy Days

Clutching the Maori war spear alongside, Jacko and I wormed our way through the long grass, still damp with dew. The great cat must be very close and we hardly dared to breathe. Inching forward with the spear forward and with the sun rising behind, I lifted my head very slowly over the stalks. There, only ten feet away, crouched our quarry, his evil green eyes fixed on me. Changing my grip on the spear, I rose and hurled the heavy weapon with all my strength. But the killer leapt sideways and the blade thudded into the ground. In a trice, Jacko, my pet monkey, was in hot pursuit. Alas, the enormous ginger tomcat that had so recently devoured one of my mother's rabbits escaped.

The spear had come from New Zealand where my parents spent their early married life. Jacko was an ex-regimental mascot, whose tail had been shut in the NAAFI canteen door, making it permanently crooked, thus he detested anyone in khaki. We had much in common; like me Jacko was mischievous, loved eggs, hated cats, pulled little girls' hair and screamed with rage when he couldn't get his own way. Together we went on safari through the 'jungle' of orchards and rose-gardens. The long grass behind the church became our Serengeti in which lurked a fearsome lion, obligingly played by the over-fed tom. On sighting our prey, Jacko would chatter excitedly and, with Tarzan-like whoops, we would give chase. Sometimes we both got too near and were badly scratched for our pains, but it added greatly to the realism.

At this time the family lived in a Herefordshire rectory, but maintained strong links with Jersey. My father had been born there in 1903, the son of a sea captain. He had a good brain and during his time at the island's public school, Victoria College, had intended to try for a commission in the Indian Army. In his final year, however, he decided to enter the Church and in due course attended a theological college in Essex. Here he met the beautiful daughters of the squire, George Sadler, and in July 1924, at a dawn ceremony in St Helier Parish Church, Jersey, he married the elder, Gwendolen, and they took ship to join the pioneering population in New Zealand, where he was ordained.

My mother, like all her family, was a great character. Full of fun, loving life and adventure, she claimed a strange assortment of forebears that included Louis XV, Oliver Cromwell and Judge Jeffreys. My father's ancestors were largely seafaring people and their graves are found in the West Country and the Channel Islands. I believe our name originated from a family of Snells, from the village of Blashford in Hampshire. Indeed there is a Snell Lane in the village today.

After twelve years of travel, father became rector of a busy parish on the outskirts of Hereford and here it was that I arrived in October 1936. Father was a leading figure in local affairs, the council, the RSPCA, the Territorial Army and, of course, the Church. Our home was the centre of parish activity, and everyone who called, be he duke or dustman, was given a cheerful reception.

At first, I was a shy child, but this temerity rapidly disappeared and I learned to make friends easily. My babyhood was marred by a shrivelled left arm, the result of a difficult birth, and it was only the attention of our old family doctor and my mother's persistent strapping of the offending limb that eventually induced it to grow properly. Gwen had a great love of animals, which we all shared, and seeing her bandage up a sparrow's broken wing in later years, I could imagine her treating me in exactly the same way. She certainly had plenty of opportunity to practise her healing because, in spite of being well-built, I suffered from a host of ailments.

Father's involvement with the Army had originated in the OTC in Jersey, and during his time in New Zealand he had been the padre of the Southland Regiment. As war clouds gathered over England, Pa, or 'Bish' as his friends knew him, foretold the coming conflict, and made himself unpopular in many quarters amongst those who refused to face facts. However, his reputation as a fiery, forthright preacher was well-known and this, coupled with his infectious good humour, won him a wide circle of friends, especially amongst the more radical. As a boy, I met many dashing soldiers, who told of hair-raising adventures so it is not surprising that from my earliest days I longed for a life of travel and excitement.

At home we were surrounded by animals: horses, donkeys, cows, dogs, cats, foxes, rabbits, guinea pigs, tortoises, pigeons, chickens, budgerigars, a parrot and the monkey. Today, it would probably be classed as a private zoo and, to the local children, it was just that. The dogs usually included Alsatians, which at least twice saved my mother from serious injury. The first occasion was at night while driving down a narrow Jersey lane. She came upon another car blocking the road, with its headlights blazing. Hooting produced no reaction and Gwen was about to reverse when a hand came through the open nearside window and switched off the ignition. The black Alsatian bitch, sitting on the back seat, caught it in her mouth and it was only with some difficulty that Mother managed to prise the teeth apart. A day or two later, a farm worker was admitted to hospital, severely mauled, saying he had been bitten by a dog in a field. The police thought otherwise, but no charges were pressed. He lost the hand through gangrene.

Another time, Mother was mistaken for the St Helier Prison governor's wife and was attacked by a demented escaped prisoner. The faithful Alsatian almost killed him and Father then arrived in the nick of time, breaking a priceless antique vase over the rogue's head. Bish was the prison chaplain at the time and much liked by the inmates and on discovering his dreadful error, the would-be murderer wrote Gwen a letter of apology and complimented her on her guard dog!

Without doubt, she had an extraordinary power over animals. As the years went by I saw her calm a mad, half-starved dog that had been locked in a caravan without food for a week, and she mended the broken limbs of countless small creatures that people brought to her, often after a vet had pronounced them beyond help. Accepting these cures as being perfectly normal, it was not until I reached manhood that I realised many of them were almost miraculous. Perhaps they were. She seemed to know just the tone of voice to use to each particular animal, the right expressions, where to touch or hold them and never to show fear, although at times she must have felt it. 'They smell fear, you know,' she would say. 'Dogs immediately sense someone who is frightened.' My attempts to imitate her methods have been fairly successful, although my skill could never compare with hers.

It is to my deep regret that I did not know my maternal grandmother, Ferdie. By all accounts she was a great personality with many attributes that included being an accomplished shot. One summer afternoon the village ladies had gathered for tea on the terrace when Ferdie spied a large carrion crow perched vulture-like some seventy yards away on the pheasant pen. With accustomed nonchalance, she summoned her butler, Wootton, and asked him to bring the rook rifle. A few minutes later, hardly interrupting the conversation, she raised the weapon to her shoulder and despatched the predator!

My grandfather, George Sadler, was a large, jolly man and reached 300 pounds in his prime. His house was always full of wild men, who, by all accounts, were the scourge of the county. The stories of their escapades are legendary: George killing an escaped circus python with a tractor or collecting a runaway bull on the bonnet of his new Armstrong Siddeley as the enraged beast fled down Braintree High Street; or, returning from a hilarious shopping spree in London with a trick truncheon (one side of which was sorbo rubber) and, happening upon the vicar, a nervous introvert who was taking sherry with my grandmother, raised the club and bellowed, 'The Philistines are upon you,' and struck the cleric over the head. Unfortunately he had neglected to use the soft face and the poor man was downed on the spot!

One night during the Great War, Wootton tapped on the door of my grandparents' bedroom and announced that an enemy dirigible was hovering over the park. The household was immediately woken and while the governess led the ladies to the summerhouse, George climbed to the roof with the keeper. There, for all to see was a Zeppelin, poised like a giant cigar 1,000 feet above the hall. Possibly to aid its navigation, it was dropping flares that illuminated the surrounding countryside with an eerie green light. The opportunity to strike a blow for England and defend his heritage was too strong for even George, who had not seen a day's military service, to let pass. Rifles and ammunition were passed from the gun room and, encouraged by the ladies, he engaged the enemy. History does not relate whether it was the squire's gunfire or some whim of the

German airman that saved the village from destruction. However, on learning that the raider had eventually been destroyed by the Royal Flying Corps, George wrote to the Secretary of State inviting the brave aviators concerned to join him for a celebration of their joint victory. To everyone's joy the visit was arranged and instructions given for the large paddock to be used as a landing-ground. Alas, the field was a little short and the biplane ran into the fence, snapping its propeller.

'Never mind,' cried grandfather, 'Wootton will go to London and get you a new one.' The squire's teenage daughters had already caught the eyes of the handsome pilots. 'Don't hurry back,' urged Gwen, slipping Wootton a half sovereign. A great party was enjoyed by all and I still have half a propeller as a memento.

During World War II, the Hereford rectory became a centre of activity and was the local Air Raid Precaution (ARP) Headquarters (HQ). Sandbag blast walls were built across the front of the house, an Anderson bomb-shelter was installed and the study became the control-room. Nearby, an RAF station had opened and a regiment of Indian Cavalry with horses camped on the racecourse. At night, a band of portly gentlemen armed with shotguns and pitchforks patrolled the parish on bicycles. The Home Guard, as it was named, was led by our churchwarden, the redoubtable Captain Faulkner. For a small boy it was very exciting and I wished I could grow up quickly and rush off to fight, but, if the posters that adorned the walls were anything to go by, it was likely that the Germans would come to me anyway.

I cannot remember exactly the date that it happened, but I recall a summer's afternoon in my playroom. Hereford housed an important ammunition factory and air-raid alarms were not uncommon. The sirens had wailed on and off all day and the thump of anti-aircraft guns was clearly audible to the east. A new sound caused me to stand on a bench and peer out of a high window. Low over the fields a green-and-grey, twin-engined aeroplane was gliding earthwards. A trail of black smoke streamed from one engine and the other was emitting a spluttering roar. Above, in close formation, two spitfires followed, the red-and-blue roundels on their wings standing out clearly. Through the smoke I saw emblazoned on the fuselage of the bomber a black cross. I did not see it crash, but the ting-a-ling of the fire engines and the Home Guard speeding by on bicycles told me the bomber was down nearby. In the study, Bill Bailey, the duty warden, picked up the phone. 'By the Canny Brook,' he shouted, 'they've got one of the Jerries alive.'

Only a short time elapsed before I confronted our prisoner. He was a tall, slim warrior, although, in retrospect, he was probably barely out of his teens. Dressed from head to foot in a black flying-suit with a silver eagle and a swastika on his breast, he looked impressive. A mass of straw-coloured hair fell untidily over his pale face. By the door stood Captain Faulkner, his twelve-bore levelled menacingly.

'Were you in that bomber?' I enquired.

'Yes,' he said without emotion in perfect English.

'Now you'll go to prison,' I pointed out.

'But not for long,' he smiled.

The significance of the remark was lost on me, but the men in the room stiffened. At that moment a khaki fifteen-hundred-weight utility vehicle full of burly military policemen swept up the drive. 'Auf Wiedersehn,' said the German, with a sad look, as he was escorted away.

Everyone was terribly cross that I had even spoken to him. There was no love of the Boche in our house. Jersey was occupied and, for all we knew, everything that Father's family had possessed was now German loot. My godmother, Aunt Jess, had served as a Red Cross nursing sister in France in 1914 and her aged father and brother were still in Jersey. Cut off from her beloved island, Jess nursed wounded troops and spent her spare moments filling bombs with TNT at the armaments factory. After the war I learned how Father Le Brun had defied the enemy. When their military band passed beneath his window, the cantankerous and supposedly bedridden old man had emptied his chamber pot over them, shouting as he did so, 'Les sales Boches'. His arrest was only averted by his housekeeper's protest that he had TB and was insane.

Mother spent much of her time helping welfare organisations and ran the parish whilst Pa was abroad with the 53rd Welsh Division. Granny was left to run the house and attempt to keep me in order. She was a grand little lady, very Victorian with a stubborn Jersey personality. Married twice, first to John Blashford-Snell, she was again a widow and thought to be on the lookout for a third husband. The war years were hard, but she managed to relieve the tension with a wee nip of Scotch from a bottle concealed in her boot cupboard. I discovered that she also kept her false teeth in a weak solution of brandy.

Early education at Miss Gibson's School for Girls and Young Boys became a nightmare when we were forced to go through 'wedding ceremonies' every break-time with the older pupils. Nor did I enjoy acting. In the school play, Robin Hood, being of ample girth even at such a tender age, I was cast as Friar Tuck and had to prance on stage addressing Maid Marian with the words, 'Behold I am the brave Friar Tuck'. Strangely, even now I sometimes mix up my Fs and my Ts. On this occasion it caused great embarrassment to my mother.

Sadly, Jacko had now developed a liking for birds, which he feathered and ate alive. As he aged, long fangs protruded from his mouth and, one day when teasing him, I was bitten to within half an inch of my jugular vein. Wisely, Mother decided he must live in a cage, but he frequently escaped and still managed to terrorise our neighbours. His exploits were renowned, but eventually he rather overdid it by climbing into the machine-gun post outside the ARP HQ. He swivelled the ancient Maxim at the curate, who did not approve of Jacko anyway and liked him even less when he was forced to dive for cover into the freshly-manured rose-garden. Ironically, my erstwhile chum was shortly despatched by a local farmer in, of all things, a monkey puzzle tree.

However, I had other animal friends to console me. There was Brutus, the huge St Bernard, who adored being dressed up and always won the prize for the best-attired dog at the church fête. He did not travel well and I will never forget one epic journey from Hereford to Tenby, moving in the wake of a long military convoy. Bish was chaplain to the unit and the presence of German aircraft added excitement to the trip. However, in the small green Hillman car was Granny, her cat and parrot. The bird was green, swore, belched and bit. Neither Aunt Jess nor Brutus, who were with us, liked the revolting creature and to show its distaste my canine pal vomited over everyone. At this moment some bombs fell nearby and we dived into a ditch. The huge dog landed on top of my grandmother, who was clutching her cat, and the parrot escaped, sadly only temporarily.

Back home I set about turning Brutus into a gun dog. Unfortunately, he couldn't differentiate between rabbits, cats or small dogs and once ate a poor, deaf, old Pekingese in the act of cocking its leg on the war memorial. I tried to comfort its grief-stricken mistress, pointing out that the end had been both quick and painless and, anyway, the Peke had had a good innings. Furthermore I mentioned that my 160-pound pal, who now sat dejectedly beside me, dribbling in dismay, felt strongly about dogs of oriental origin desecrating a British war memorial. My reasoning was not appreciated.

By now the rectory was being used to house twenty attractive nurses and Mother, seeking to add a little sparkle to their lives, invited the Commanding Officer of a nearby American Air Force unit to send along some of his men for Sunday afternoon tea. It was my duty to welcome them at the front door and, as such, receive the copious quantities of candy that our gallant allies carried. The scarcity of chocolate made this a highly-prized trade good. Tea was served in the drawing room and soon the airmen were fascinating the ladies with tales of America. One huge sergeant named Tex came from Texas, where, he informed us, everything was larger, faster, stronger and better than anywhere else in the whole wide world. He was a very big man and I feared for Mother's bone china tea cup, which was completely encompassed by his vast hand. I noted that no one contradicted Tex. When the hot crumpets, a special treat, were produced, the door rattled. Brutus had a passion for crumpets and had learned to open doors by seizing the doorknobs in his great jaws. Tex was in full flow when it swung open to reveal the awesome sight of a massive St Bernard, strings of saliva hanging from his cavernous pink mouth.

'Gawd, what a dog,' cried the Texan.

'Oh, that's only the pup. You wait until you see his mother,' said Gwen, refilling the tea cups.

One crumpet later the enormous creature sat obediently, its bloodshot eyes fixed upon the rapidly emptying plate. The girls were now exchanging sly glances with our guests so I felt I should provide a little distraction. A stock of pheasants' feathers were kept by the fireplace for cleaning Father's pipe. Deftly slipping one along the carpet I was able to flick it back and forth across Brutus's testicles (a little trick I had learned from the verger's daughter). Within a few minutes conversation began to die away as all became aware of the St Bernard's enormous erection. Then my Mother caught sight of the offensive item.

'Filthy beast,' she shrieked, hurling a cushion and ordering him out. 'Hey kid, do that next Sunday and we'll double the candy ration,' said Tex as he left.

Meanwhile my faith in the Home Guard had diminished and, unable to play a more active part in the war other than run messages for the ARP, I decided to raise a small private army to defend the parish. Recruiting was easy. Before the war Mother had laid in a plentiful stock of tinned pineapple and other mouth-watering delights. These, plus our fruit orchards and the abundance of cuddly pets, attracted hordes of children. From this host I was able to select some thirty loyal followers of both sexes. We had our headquarters in an old stable, shared with a pet fox, and from here would sally forth against the enemy, which, in the absence of German paratroopers, was provided by a rival organisation of uncouth lads, whose main occupation was to raid the apple crop. Epic battles involving dozens of children raged back and forth across the countryside. Our weapons included catapults, grenades, Molotov cocktails and even a ballista (copied from a history book) with which to hurl evil-smelling dead cats.

By the time I was fourteen, the need to defend the parish from Hitler had long receded and my schooling was making serious inroads into the conduct of the campaign. However, early scientific education and a patriotic local chemist gave new impetus to our activities. We had managed to construct a lethal cannon, mounted on an old invalid carriage, and, worse still, a great mortar, fashioned from a brass church candlestick, that could hurl a one-pound projectile 200 paces.

It was a bright summer's afternoon when our heroic little band, already suffering depletion as some members, whose voices had broken, showed more interest in the choir girls than their military duties, made its last stand. After the first engagement, the scrumpers, as the fruit-thieves were known, used all their low cunning to draw us to one side of the churchyard, whilst a nimble group scaled the eight-foot garden wall and wrought havoc amongst the Cox's Orange Pippin. These were similar tactics to those used by Prince Rupert at Marston Moor to raid my ancestor, Oliver Cromwell's baggage train. We were not unprepared. Concealed in a yew hedge was the invalid carriage cannon and in a trench by the rhubarb bed sat the mortar. The two possible escape routes through the allotments were liberally sown with mines, consisting of Kilner jars filled with a fearful mixture of chemicals and acid. Leaving a handful of archers and air riflemen to deal with an enemy feint, I joined the artillery and catapulteers. There were now some fifteen scrumpers looting the best fruit. 'Now, Hitchen,' I hissed in the ear of my master gunner, who applied his illicit cigarette to the touch-hole. The cannon roared, hurling half a pound of dried peas across the kitchen garden. Even as the carriage was careering backwards, I heard the screams of the enemy, but noted with some dismay that we had at least one innocent victim. Meredith, the gardener, rose phoenix-like from the spinach patch, clutching his posterior and mouthing a dreadful oath. But he who hesitates is lost, and having gained the advantage of surprise, we followed it up with a volley of missiles and charged the enemy. As expected, they ran into the minefield. At least half turned back, were seized and dragged to the potting shed for unspeakable torture by the choir girls. Meanwhile, the mortar came into action to cut off the survivors. With a loud crump, it fired a bundle of fizzing fireworks inside a tin can high into space. Alas, the senior chorister's aim was hasty and the bomb overshot, to explode immediately behind an old lady, who, along with her little dog, was hidden in the long grass. Scared witless, dog and owner fled, clearing two stiles with extraordinary ease. The next shot landed on the rectory roof and brought down an avalanche of tiles. I accepted the chorister's resignation, apologized to Meredith, released all my prisoners unharmed and offered to pay for the roof as soon as I could negotiate a loan from Mother. It was to no avail. Father, now a JP, spent a week calming the populace and my private army was disbanded.

It is ironic that much of my military service was spent at the receiving end of missiles very similar to those with which I had disturbed that peaceful shire. Father decided that the Church was not my vocation and thereafter encouraged me to join the Army, where my destructive nature might be put to good use. But this was some years off, and in the hope of keeping me out of trouble in the meantime I was despatched to the sparsely-populated Welsh Mountains, where lived an indulgent, nature-loving aunt and uncle. Here I, too, learned to appreciate wildlife and the countryside. However, I had been taught to shoot at the age of nine and, when Father returned from the front and, in spite of family protests, thrust a .45 Service Revolver into my hand, I roamed the hills blazing away at rabbits and collecting wildflowers to my heart's content. It was not long before I shot both myself and the village idiot and learned a useful lesson on gun safety.

I sometimes longed for the sea, and so we regularly visited our relatives on the south coast. I met retired ship's captain, great-uncle Albert, in his garden by the Solent. As I was brought forward to be introduced by a timorous cousin he sat, enormous in his deck-chair, a flowing grey beard cascading over his massive chest. Raised to his eye was a naval telescope. The old sea dog growled with a voice that had sent fear through a thousand square rig sailors. 'So it's young John, is it?' and, without looking down he asked, 'What ship's that?', swinging the lens in the direction of a sleek destroyer seaward bound. 'Nice lines,' he muttered, 'I like nice lines.' His telescope had focused on some scantily-dressed girls bathing on the far shore. 'See the world,' he roared, fixing me for a moment with a twinkling, reddened eye, and then turned his attention back to the ladies.

My 'Just William' existence progressed throughout prep school in sleepy Worcestershire, where my voice broke early, enabling me to learn poker in the commoners' stalls. At home for holidays, my musical enjoyment was confined to playing a drum, which made Brutus howl, a ghastly and unsociable noise. So I turned my attention to the church organ. The organist was unsympathetic and, in a mood of sullen revenge, I took a dead rat that Granny's cat had been gnawing and popped it down one of the organ pipes. With evil glee, I sat in the choir stalls next day, awaiting the awful note that would result from the rodent rattling on the reed. There followed a very strange sound. Then, oh horror, it flew out and landed in a choir girl's lap. 'Eeeek,' screamed the maiden and, unseen, I seized the carcass and secreted in it my hassock. They scolded the poor girl, no-one believing her innocence, but I was encouraged because the rat had lasted to be played another day.

Father, believing that I was a useless waster, encouraged me to do something positive to help at home. I therefore rather reluctantly agreed to rise before dawn on Wednesdays and ring the church bell for mid-week communion. The searing cold in the unheated rectory bit through me like an Arctic wind as I stumbled through the snow to open the heavy vestry door and tug the aged bell-rope. Even a nip of the sideboard brandy failed to fortify me and I knew that if I were to survive, I must find a better solution.

It came to me like a vision – indeed, it may have been divine prov–
idence that showed the way. The great bell was within view of my
bedroom window and a round of .300 rook rifle fired from my bed
would produce a ring to waken the dead. Twenty shots and we had
filled five pews, but, alas, the resultant ricochets may have had more
to do with it. As the last of the faithful scampered into the cover
of the church porch, Father, in a biblical rage, reminded me that it
was a house of peace. Nevertheless, he realised that we must move
forward with the times and thus, by the next holiday, a gramophone
and loud-speaker system had been installed to give a rendering of
a slightly tinny version of 'Bow Bells' and other well-known peals.
Not only did this increase the congregation, but when I turned the
volume up to full power we even pulled in a few of the rival vicar's
flock. Whilst fellow clerics muttered disapprovingly in the cathedral
cloisters about progressive parsons, Pa enjoyed a full house.

By now I had become friendly with the milkman's dark-eyed
daughter. This temptress dared me to put a certain disc on the
machine. And so it was that the parishioners were greeted one
morning with a jolly ballad, 'Captain Brown, Captain Brown, he
played his ukelele as the ship went down'. In a final defiant gesture,
I turned up the volume to the deaf-aid system for the last few bars,
which sent the rows of pensioners bouncing in their seats.

It was perhaps understandable that my parents should send me
to secondary school as far away as possible. Thus, in 1950, I arrived
at Victoria College, Jersey. Granite-built, it stood fortress-like
above St Helier. In the high-windowed classrooms, generations of
Channel Islanders, including Father, had studied hard to gain places
in the establishments of the Empire and also, for the chosen few, a
venerated position in the dignified local government, the States.

Studies at Victoria were made tolerable by the many unofficial
extra-mural activities available for the adventurous. Some of my
contemporaries preferred to gain early experience of the French
maids, but, for me, the great attraction was the maze of underground
tunnels left behind by the German army of occupation. The island
abounded in a liberal quantity of ammunition, mines and weapons.
Years later, during my training as a sapper officer, I discovered
how lucky we had been to survive our experiments with assorted
explosive devices.

Bish had made his mark at Victoria and had become its first Scout

Master. I joined his old troop, but soon found the attractions of the Combined Cadet Force irresistible. Joining the brutal and licentious military, I was able to indulge my love of shooting, and, with the school team, made the annual pilgrimage to Bisley.

While Hans Hass and Jacques Cousteau were making headlines in the new world of underwater adventure, my friends, Adrian Troy and Tony Titterington, and I were seeking the great grey conger eel amongst the seaweed and rocks of Jersey's treacherous coastline. Our adventures were numerous, and when I regaled my mother with them she must have been horrified, but she simply smiled encouragingly and helped me to buy a powerful harpoon gun to continue the battle.

Tony was the mechanical genius and he converted German submarine escape apparatus into underwater breathing equipment. We should have used soda lime to re-purify the air, but, being short of funds, employed caustic soda. To test the device I was lowered off St Brelades Harbour wall, a net full of house bricks tied to my waist for ballast. 'Give two tugs when you want to come up,' said Tony, as the sea closed over me. After a few minutes the oxygen tasted awful so I pulled hard on the safety line. To my horror it came snaking down from the surface. It wasn't tied to anything and the attention of my handlers had been distracted by a couple of girlfriends. In desperation, I fought to untie the net, but the knot was immovable. With head spinning I therefore climbed the harbour wall like an underwater mountaineer. It took a terribly long time and when I had scaled the fifteen feet, I emerged blue in the face! 'Oh well, back to the drawing board,' grunted Tony.

To turn our minds to safer activities, our headmaster created a compulsory debating society. Thus, all sixth-formers had to learn to speak in public, a valuable training that has stood many an Old Victorian in good stead. To liven up our debates, a mock election was held. At once an evil bunch of us formed the 'Neo-Fascist' party. 'Nellie' Le Geyt became poet laureate and composed party political ballads, while Adrian, Bungle Colson and John Gwyther became henchmen to myself as 'Blashford von Schnell', the dictator. The population of Jersey was more than mildly surprised to see our Nazi uniforms, armbands and steel helmets. However, it was not until our stormtroopers raised a fourteen-foot German banner over the school that the patient head intervened. Nevertheless, for weeks the election campaign raged with its incredible dramas and satire mainly centred on the controversial problem of the emancipation of the mole. Mass meetings were held and hecklers dragged off screaming by my black-shirts to the showers, where they were treated to a cold dousing, fully clothed! Party songs were sung at midnight sessions in a secret beer cellar. It was all great fun and, to everyone's horror, we almost won the final election.

I loved schooldays, but my great failure was with the opposite sex. Girls did not seem to appreciate bombs, guns, underwater fishing or my dancing. The ones that did were singularly unattractive.

Much of the school holidays I spent with the Territorial Army. Father was chaplain of a Monmouthshire gunner regiment and thus I learned the intricacies of anti-aircraft defence. Most members, having served in the war, regarded the time at training camps as holidays. Regular officers, who had the misfortune to be posted to the various gunnery stations we visited, lived in dread of our arrival.

Of course there were occasions when the regiment excelled. One such was the visit of the Lord Lieutenant. By the time he arrived, monocle in eye, thrashing his breeches with his riding crop, we were feeding heavy shells into the guns. With deafening noise, our twenty-four 3.7s hurled tons of high explosive at a red canvas sleeve being towed half a mile behind an RAF Mosquito fighter-bomber. Rich Welsh voices screamed orders, while acrid brown smoke drifted over the firing point, obscuring the bright summer sun and glimmering sea. The Australian pilot of the aircraft encouraged us with a running commentary over a loudspeaker system.

In the hot stuffy radar wagons, the operators followed every move of the little green blips, indicating the path of aircraft and target. It was the operator's job to 'lock on' to the rearward blip, which was the moving sleeve, and thus direct the gunfire. We were a mixed-sex unit and it was not uncommon for the male controllers to arrange their shift with a female soldier of their liking. By coincidence, a red lamp glowed outside each wagon during firing, prohibiting sudden entrance which would spoil the operator's night vision. Under these darkened conditions and with a pretty girl beside you, it is easy to imagine how even the most ardent gunners attention might wander. 'You're dropping short, cobber. Wow, that's a good 'un!' came our pilot's voice, as his Mosquito droned to and fro.

The Lord Lieutenant, enjoying the sun, and clearly happy

to smell cordite, watched the regiment sweating in the heat. Everything was going terribly well and it must only be a matter of time before someone actually struck the sleeve. The beer tent was sited conveniently near and ice-cold ale awaited the traditional celebration that would follow a direct hit. Perhaps the temperature in the radar wagon was too high or Private Jones too passionate; we shall never know. Suddenly the Mosquito disappeared amidst a welter of shell bursts.

'Cease fire, cease fire,' shrieked the safety officers, as the plane began to spiral downwards.

The loudspeaker system had gone silent. Then, to our intense relief, the Australian pilot spoke. Most of what he actually said is unprintable. But he ended, 'Remember I'm pulling this f ... ing thing, not pushing it.'

'How about some gin, sir,' suggested our quick-witted colonel.

The official party stomped off to the mess, whilst we gunners tittered and the Australian managed to land his plane, full of holes.

Our camp was plagued with rats from the tip on the outskirts of a small town. I was appointed the rodent NCO and, armed with Sten gun and torch, did nightly battle against the loathsome creatures on the stinking dump. Although I expended a fair quantity of ammunition, it was to little avail, and so I decided on more drastic action. Approximately sixty pounds of old explosive had been lying around the magazine for several years and the quartermaster sergeant was delighted to be rid of it. I spent a whole day burying it in the centre of the tip. With all the noise of gunfire, I reckoned another bang would go unnoticed and, as the rats were most active after dark, awaited a night exercise before touching off the charge. To my consternation, the blinding flash and thundering roar were much more spectacular than any gunfire. Refuse and rats rained down for half a mile. Passing the village chapel next morning, I found the preacher pointing to dead rodents on the roof. 'A message from Heaven,' he proclaimed with religious fervour.

Those fortnights at firing camp were the times when I really grew up. And it was from here that I mounted my first expedition, into the Welsh mountains. A schoolfriend, Cliff Le Quelenec, and I set out from my uncle's cottage at dawn one August morning, carrying rucksacks bulging with camping equipment. The packs were badly balanced and it was almost impossible to stand upright. On our heads were Australian-style bush-hats and we each carried a four-foot ash-staff. I had a revolver with which to shoot rabbits when inevitably our rations had gone and starvation threatened.

The first day was sheer hell and by afternoon our feet were raw and shoulders aching. A mountain mist dropped suddenly upon us and within minutes we were utterly lost. So we camped for the night, but next day visibility was just as bad. By late afternoon we were following some sheep along a narrow track when, to my astonishment, I saw my colleague sink waist-deep into a pool of bright green slime. The sheep scattered and ran back to dry ground, leaving us in the middle of a very treacherous bog. There was no point in looking around for help – we had seen no one all day. Cliff, in spite of his considerable strength, was quite unable to move. Slipping off my cumbersome rucksack, I unwound the eight-foot toggle-rope we both carried. 'For God's sake, hurry,' was all Cliff said as I tossed him the free end. The ground shook like a jelly, so to spread the weight I lay face down. We both pulled hard, with the result that I began to slide towards him. 'It's no good,' he shouted, a note of fear in his voice. 'I can feel the bloody stuff sucking me down.'

'Can't you get your own rope off?' I asked, but I realised that if he took his arms off the surface, he would probably sink right under. Overhead a lone buzzard circled, oblivious to our plight, and the sheep baa'd contentedly. 'Wait,' I said, 'I've got an idea.' Crawling back to my pack, I undid the waist and shoulder straps and buckled them together. It gave an extra six feet of line. Sliding back across the oozing surface, I joined it to the toggle-rope. It was just sufficient to enable me to get behind a hummock of grass that stood like an island in the swamp. Now we had an anchorage and I began to pull. I'll swear nothing happened for ten minutes. The sweat was being forced out of our pores and neither of us said a thing, but went on pulling. Suddenly it was a little easier and to my great relief I realised that, inch by inch, Cliff was beginning to move towards me. Thirty minutes later we lay laughing together on the mountainside. For a further ten days we marched on, exploring ancient ruins, crossing fast-flowing streams, being chased by bulls and getting lost time and time again. When eventually we emerged, we were thinner, fitter and wiser for our experience. I managed to pass the entrance exam to Sandhurst and, with a year to kill, took every opportunity to broaden my knowledge, whilst remaining at school to debate, shoot, swim underwater and take a few A levels. By the time I left Victoria I had grown to love Jersey and have regarded it as home ever since.

Sandhurst meant going to the bottom of the ladder again. However, Britain still had an Empire and we hoped for a life of adventure and travel, engaging in the numerous bushfire wars. The basic training brought one down to earth with a bump and we did all those useful character-building activities like floor-scrubbing, book-bulling, spud-bashing, bed-packing and cutting grass with nail scissors. Cursed, chased and screamed at by baying drill sergeants, we learned and re-learned our military skills for sixteen weeks until, suddenly, we were officer cadets, fit to enter the Academy proper. Now we were cursed, chased and screamed at by more senior officer cadets and thus the process started again. But if we survived, and most did, we came away from that famous establishment with its motto 'Serve to lead' firmly fixed in our minds. It was a grand finishing school, often likened to a third-rate university, where the Officers' Training Corps had been allowed to run wild.

The two pleasant years at the Academy passed quickly. I had to work hard to get into the Royal Engineers, but nevertheless I had time to make hundreds of new friends and enjoy the lighter side of life. There were the famous Sandhurst rags, such as when we chained the cannon wheel across the London road causing traffic jams. Doubtless today we would be prosecuted. The bright lights of London were a great lure and in our senior terms there was increased freedom to visit the capital. By working hard one leave, I managed to buy a Triumph motorcycle, which worried my parents so much that they quickly helped me purchase a bone-shaking old BSA sports car. 'Rigormortis' was far more lethal than the motorbike but, because it had four wheels, was considered safer. 'Don't laugh, Madam, your daughter may be inside,' proclaimed a notice in the boot. Indeed, some of my girlfriends' parents were so horrified by the machine that they gladly lent me their own cars for evenings out. A family friend with a reputation for wild living was quick to understand the pressing needs of a Sandhurst cadet. 'Wouldn't it help if you had a flat in town?' he enquired after a good dinner. 'My company has one in Jermyn Street. It's always free at the weekends.' I accepted the offer with alacrity and thus began a splendid era of parties that the late Rosa Lewis, in whose famous Cavendish Hotel the apartment lay, would have approved.

I now found the opposite sex more receptive. One in particular, a lady soldier, was more so than most and we saw a lot of each other. On the night of her Commissioning Ball I set out with a friend in Rigormortis. It was a crisp, clear March evening as, bedecked in black tie and silk scarves, we sped past Frensham Pond. Because the headlights gave out such a poor light, it took me several seconds to realise that my front wheel had mysteriously become detached and was proceeding in front of us towards the pond. Out of control, the car ran down a sandy bank and stopped abruptly in a pool of black mud. Fortunately a convoy of Austin 7s and sundry wrecks belonging to other cadets saw our plight, and within a few minutes we were on our way to the ball once more, this time seated less comfortably on a spare tyre attached to the boot of an aged Riley. Even so, I was a little late for the dinner and my first meeting with the dignified and upright colonel, whose daughter I was escorting. He was clearly not impressed by my dishevelled appearance and an immediate request to borrow his car.

2

Travel and Adventure

'Christ,' gasped Lieutenant Joseph N Beerbecker Jnr, 'We're on fire.'

This was my opinion too, but it was only when my curiosity about the black smoke belching from an engine had got the better of me that I had woken my fellow passenger.

The pilot's loudspeaker cut in: 'Hear this, hear this, we have a malfunction in our starboard engine and are returning to base.'

Aboard the USAF transport plane we sat tensely as the grey Atlantic waves swept by beneath, and felt a huge sense of relief as the American coastline appeared. Fire engines racing alongside stifled the fire with jets of foam as the plane halted.

Back on terra firma I said a short prayer of thanks that my career in the Royal Engineers had not ended before it had really begun. Indeed, it was not a year since our fresh-faced batch of young officers had gathered at Chatham to learn the black arts of sappering. For nine months we had built bridges, laid mines, dug trenches, fired demolitions, surveyed roads, driven bulldozers and pumped water.

'By the time we have finished with you,' stated the mild mannered, pipe-smoking warrant officer, 'you will be fit to tackle any obstacle in the world.'

'Sappers', we were informed, 'are all mad, married or methodist' and there was certainly a number of Royal Engineer officers who lived up to this reputation. Such men, we noted, were often well-decorated and would have blushed had they heard some of the legends told of their deeds. It was they who encouraged us, possibly because they felt that even we might go on to invent some fiendish engine of war or maybe act irrationally, but courageously, in battle.

Mess nights beneath the portraits of Gordon, Kitchener and Napier reminded us of the illustrious heritage of eccentric generals. Determined to live up to our reputation, we once derailed an army train by accident and blew up a row of washbasins in the mess. The authorities were amazingly patient, although we drove one instructor after another beserk. 'There has never been such an ill-behaved course,' stated the adjutant. But discipline and self-control did not seem to go with independent thought and the practical application of unconventional ideas.

Being only thirty miles from the West End, the austere barracks did nothing to dampen our spirits. My Jowett Jupiter sports car had a fine turn of speed, with torsion-bar suspension that enhanced its cornering, and I enjoyed trying to beat the record from London. My twenty-first birthday party was celebrated in a cellar in Gray's Inn Road. It was a well conducted orgy and so impressed were the police, when inevitably they arrived, that they returned later, off duty, to join in the fun. Although some superiors regarded us as irresponsible, immature idiots and told us so frequently, there were others who tended to encourage our exploits.

A posting to a field squadron on active service in Cyprus came at the end of the course, and we had six weeks' leave, which I was determined not to waste. My girlfriend from Sandhurst days was in Singapore and her letters gave vivid descriptions of Malaya. Coupled with my deep-seated desire to travel, I decided to head for the Far East.

Forty-two days were quite enough to get there and back. A friendly MP said he knew someone in the Royal Air Force who might help, if I would carry out a few despatches. Thus, early on a July morning, I boarded a glittering silver RAF Comet and set off on a trip that did not turn out quite as planned.

Firstly, the flight was prolonged because of mechanical problems and I experienced my first tropical heat. Then, on arrival in Singapore, we learnt of a revolution in Iraq and the RAF air route's closure. Ours had been the last plane through. This was tricky. The civil airfare was £350, over a year's pay. I just had to catch that troop-ship to Cyprus. However, after several enjoyable weeks and the failure of all attempts to get home westward, I turned my attention to reaching England via America.

The US consul in Singapore was sympathetic. He said that if I could get to Clarkfield in the Philippines, there was a chance that the USAF might lift me to the States. Thus it was that I found myself, drenched to the skin in a leaking Royal New Zealand Air Force freight plane butting through a heavy tropical downpour over the South China Sea. Eventually we reached the jungle-clad mountains of the Philippines. The resident RAF liaison officer explained my plight to his taciturn opposite number.

At last the heavily-built American major spoke. 'You've a problem, boy,' he said, drawing hard on his cheroot, 'but maybe we can help. You come to the party tonight and tomorrow we'll figure what we can do.'

In the morning I learnt that the first difficulty was for a non-US national to remain on the air-base for more than seventy-two hours without contravening some greatly-respected regulation. The resourceful Major Harry had solved this even before I met him at 0730 hours.

'You've just become a UN observer,' he exclaimed, passing me a large cup of black coffee. My 'papers' bearing the crest of the House of Commons had impressed our allies far more than they had the RAF. 'We'll always try to help guys on a special mission for the Pentagon,' he said, 'and I guess that's the sort of duty you're doing.' I did not contradict him.

The Americans overwhelmed me with kindness. But after ten days I was still there and, despite all efforts, some red tape still blocked my progress. It was at the end of the morning when the office staff was leaving for lunch that Liz, the secretary in the outer office, invited me to her twenty-first birthday party that night. She had left before I realised that I knew neither her surname not where she lived. Hearing my predicament, Major Harry gave a low whistle and then very slowly said, 'Man, you've just struck gold. She's the general's daughter.' Arriving at the residence wearing my tropical dinner jacket, I was greeted by the commander of the 13th Pacific Air Force in his braces. His huge hand gripped mine as he skilfully manipulated a barbecue spit with the other. To the strains of Sinatra, he told me with relish of the wonderful times he had enjoyed in London during the war.

'How long are you staying, young man?' he said, filling my glass with a liberal quantity of 'Old Crow'. I told him my problem and he promised to sort it out.

The fifty-six sets of orders that I was handed next day authorized my travel from Clarkfield Air Base, Philippines, to Burtonwood in England via America. It was a long flight in the comfortable Constellation with stops at Wake and Guam Islands, where, thanks to the general's signals, I was ushered into the VIP lounges and entertained royally. I could only assume that the wartime parties in London must have been very good. At Honolulu the aircraft was diverted to the civil airport, where an impressive array of grass-skirted girlies and Hawaiian bands greeted us. On discovering that we were not the anticipated tourist flight they disappeared, grumbling, into the night.

The last leg was passed in oblivion, thanks to a monumental party and I still felt slightly jaded when we arrived late at night at Travis Air Force base, California. To my dismay the general's liberal supply of signals had dried up. However, there was a plane flying east in two days' time and, if I cared to stay at the officers' club for a couple of nights at ten dollars a time, I could catch that. Stringent British foreign currency restrictions and the total inadequacy of a second lieutenant's pay had reduced my ready cash to three dollars, ninety-five cents, hardly sufficient to keep one in essential body liquid for forty-eight hours. At this point a kindly sergeant mentioned that a giant C130 transport plane was en route for New Mexico and, what was more, the pilot was an RAF officer on secondment. Flight Lieutenant Hicks was sipping grape-juice at the bar when I acquainted him with my problem. He seemed delighted to meet another Brit and readily agreed to add me to the load of pineapples being flown to some highly secret destination in the desert. Soon after take-off I climbed into a bunk and slept soundly until we reached a place that really sounded like the wild west – Albuquerque.

On landing I was invited to join the crew for breakfast and Hicks persuaded his merry men to part with their loose dollars in exchange for my British cheque. Whilst we were doing this a man in white overalls approached and asked about the C130's radio. Without paying him much attention, the operator said it was 'all fine', but that the aircraft was open if he wished to inspect it. The crew then went off to change, leaving me to finish my coffee. The white overalled technician returned and said in an angry tone, 'That radio's not working and you know it! How in hell's name am I going to speak to the President of the United States?'

I looked up in bewilderment and tried to explain that I was not a member of the crew. He stormed off, clearly very angry, muttering that I was a spy from Russia.

When Hicks got back I said, 'That chap was here about the radio again – he wants to speak to the President.'

'Oh well,' said Hicks, only mildly interested, 'I expect he'll come back.'

Obviously the whole matter was of no importance and due to my lack of comprehension of American terminology and vocabulary, quite above my head.

At the flight operations desk they attempted to get me a lift eastwards, and while we were enquiring about aircraft timings the over-alled gentleman reappeared.

'I want to speak to the President,' he boomed at the sergeant who was helping us.

'You wait your turn, man – jeez, sit right over there and wait your turn.'

The fellow turned puce with rage, went over to a drinking fountain and pressing the knob, yelled, 'Get me the President.'

Conversation in the flight operations ceased. Even Hicks looked surprised and the desk sergeant said. 'Excuse me, sir, I think we may have a problem.' He picked up the telephone and said, 'Air Police.' The man was still in consultation with the President (down the water pipe) when the police seized him.

'Who is he?' I asked Hicks.

'Oh! Just some nut escaped from the local lunatic asylum.'

There were no Air Force planes going east that day, so I decided to buy a ticket to Denver in Colorado where I might pick up a USAF flight to Washington next day. I was about to leave the air base when the desk sergeant thrust me a piece of paper. 'You'll need that to get out of the main gate,' he said, 'our security is pretty tight here.' Outside the civil airline office, legs crossed and smoking a pipe, sat the first Red Indian I had ever seen. He eyed by brown shoes, long stockings, khaki shorts and stared fixedly at my officer's cane. 'How,' he grunted.

Unconsciously raising my hand in the sign of peace, I replied, 'Very well, thank you,' and went outside.

I sat in the shade awaiting the plane. The Indian watched me, sucking and puffing at his empty pipe. The temperature rose. At last he spoke. 'What that stick for?'

Could I say a symbol of authority? A British Army tradition, we exchange them for a baton on promotion to Field Marshal, or the bloody dress regulations say I've got to carry it? 'You may have heard of General Gordon?' I enquired. The Indian nodded solemnly. Perhaps the Americans had a Gordon too, so better be careful what I say, I thought. He may have butchered the Blackfeet or whatever tribe this gentleman belongs to. 'Well, General Gordon led an army of Chinese soldiers many years ago. A stick like this was the only weapon he ever carried in battle. The enemy believed it to be magic, and it so inspired his men that they never lost a fight.'

The Indian nodded. 'Plenty good wood,' he wheezed.

At Denver, I followed the usual procedure of telephoning the nearest USAF Base. In this case it was the Air Force Academy. Within minutes a car arrived and a major ushered me into an office to await the arrival of the colonel. Coffee was produced, my papers checked and we began talking about England.

'Say, who won the FA Cup last year?' he asked. I am not a keen disciple of football and simply could not remember. 'How about cricket? How's the Test Match going?" he went on. I only played rugby and he looked a little disappointed.

Suddenly the door burst open and a large red-faced man in a shortsleeved shirt and Bermudas stepped in. 'Well, what do you think?' he demanded.

'Oh. I think he's genuine, Colonel,' said the major.

The colonel pumped my hand and apologized for the 'interrogation'. 'Can't be too careful,' he emphasised. 'Now, James here will see you have all you need and we'll hope to get you on that flight tomorrow. Any friend of General Morman's is a friend of mine.'

Hurray for General Morman, I thought as I tackled a giant T-bone steak with James. Unfortunately he had arranged for me to attend an all-night 'orgy' at the nearby nurses' home and so I was not in the best condition as I waited for my plane. I decided Old Crow really lived up to its name! A buckskin-clad six-gun-toting sheriff with two bloodhounds arrived to hunt for a deaf-mute child, lost in the Rockies. Someone introduced me.

The sheriff, with a grip like a gorilla, shook hands and said, 'Howdy. Partner.'

'Do you think you've a good chance of finding the boy?' I asked.

'Yep,' he drawled. 'If the bears don't find him first.' Everyone around nodded and muttered, 'bears'.

When the plane finally arrived it was a special, plushly furnished aircraft of the Presidential Flight. Most of the passengers were members of an army golf team returning from a tournament. They had a high-stake poker school in progress, but I declined their offer of a game. Next to me sat an enlisted man, reading a comic.

'Do you play golf too?' I asked.

'No, I'm going home on special furlough,' he replied.

'Oh! Compassionate leave,' I said.

'Yes, you might call it that,' he replied. 'Papa attacked Momma with an axe last night.'

'Really? How awful! I am sorry. Is she badly hurt?' I asked.

'Yep, I guess so, he chopped her head clean off, darn it', he said sadly.

At Washington the general's signals had done their stuff and I was taken on a conducted tour of the capital by night, before flying on to Macquire Air Base, near New Jersey. With luck I would arrive in Britain two days before the troop-ship left for Cyprus. I sent a telegram to my depot regiment and settled down to write my diary as the four-engined transport lifted off. We had only been airborne for twenty minutes when the engine caught fire. Back at the base I discovered that a plane was leaving for Paris that afternoon, which would be better than waiting another twenty-four hours whilst our aircraft was repaired. A helpful movements officer said that he would try to get me transferred and went off to see his supervisor. He returned with an uneasy expression. 'The major says you've to see him,' he said.

The major, a harassed man, looked as if he carried the troubles of the world in his briefcase as he flicked through my papers. 'The 13th Air Force can't issue orders for you to travel to England,' he said, his voice rising. The phone rang – he answered it – 'You're – ' he started but the phone rang again, and whilst he spoke the light on a silent red phone glowed.

Two aides bumped heads as they seized it. 'Yes, sir,' they said four times. It was obvious that war was about to break out so, apologizing for being a nuisance, I gathered up my documents and was backing out when the major screamed, 'Not so fast – I know what you are – you're a deserter – and those orders of yours are no good here.'

The movements officer looked embarrassed. 'It's been a busy

day,' he said.

'Do I look like a deserter?' I asked him.

'Well, I couldn't say as I've never met an English deserter,' was his slightly unhelpful reply.

I felt very much like Alice in Wonderland. However, I guessed that the overworked staff officer would be off-duty the next day, if he had not suffered a coronary beforehand. I was still on the passenger list of the original plane and, keeping well out of sight, hopped aboard at the last minute.

Our only stop was Goose Bay in Labrador, where, contrary to my expectations, I was not arrested. It was bitterly cold, sleet was falling and I felt rather foolish in my khaki shorts and shirt, so headed for the transit lounge. A fur-clad figure shuffled past with a trolley. He stopped suddenly, spun round, looked and said slowly, 'Gee, you must be British.'

When we got to Prestwick I found that by chance a USAF Dakota was going down to Burtonwood. As I climbed aboard the pilot said. 'This bird's got a sick engine. You'd better wear this,' handing me a parachute. However, we arrived safely and the Yanks couldn't understand my profuse thanks. There wasn't time to tell him how the USAF had devoted so much effort to getting a very junior officer 12,000 miles to catch a boat.

The band was playing on the quayside as I staggered up the gangplank with numerous items of hastily packed luggage. I waved goodbye to my parents, remembered to shout a brief word to my father about a parking summons that I would not be there to receive and bumped into several chums from Sandhurst days.

'Hello, Blashers – you look brown, where have you been?' 'Let's have a beer and I'll tell you.' I was fortunate to join a Cyprus-based unit in September 1958. The 33rd Field Squadron was commanded by an energetic, unconventional major, who gave his subordinates a free rein with the minimum of supervision and the maximum support. Our regiment was in a tented camp on the foothills above Limassol. My troop consisted of fifty-four sappers, mostly National Servicemen with no great love of the Army, but they were a tough, spirited and hardworking gang who got into trouble continuously.

'Why did you throw the NAAFI juke-box at the manager?' I asked one of my sinners.

'Well, sir, I put a five-piastre piece in and nothing happened.

"You've been done", my mate told me. At that moment up comes the manager bloke. So I hands him the juke-box to see if he can get me five piastres out.' The manager, allegedly struck by a flying 200-pound music machine, was in hospital with multiple injuries.

We usually supported one or more infantry battalions, and roared about in our own little fleet of trucks and armoured vehicles, armed to the teeth with a variety of weapons and explosives. Like all small units acting independently on active service, we had our fair share of adventure.

One dark night a patrol discovered a hole that had been cut in the rock surface of a mountain track. Obviously it was intended that a mine should be placed here later. It was decided to booby-trap the hole to give the EOKA bomber a rude shock and I was ordered to lay a suitable device. Accordingly, I fashioned a fiendish little bomb and placed it in position. Being aware that if it did not function someone would have to remove it, I marked the place with a strand of green plastic-coated wire, bound round a tree five paces away, and then made a detailed sketch map of the area.

Unfortunately, when the campaign ended some months later, I was ordered to dispose of it. It was after dark when we reached the area. With no need for secrecy, we drove up the moonlit track. Since my last visit, a great many trucks had used the road and the surface was hard-packed. To make matters worse, I could not see any sign of the green wire. Nevertheless, I found the area and my driver, Corporal Cutler, began to search with a mine-detector.

'Nothing,' he grunted. 'Not a thing, sir.'

'Not surprising,' I replied. 'There's very little metal in it anyway and we put it eighteen inches down.'

There was one slight depression that fitted my bearings and distances, so I ordered the vehicle to back off and, whilst Cutler held the torch, I probed the soil. It was solid rock, but suddenly my prodder penetrated something rather soft.

'I think we have it,' I murmured. 'Feels like the edge of the hole that the terrorist cut.'

Cutler's face was, as usual, expressionless. We had been through a number of anxious moments together and he never showed any emotion. I located a slab of rock the size of a book. 'It's under here – I remember this stone,' I remarked.

The wind rising from the Mediterranean sighed in the fir trees and I felt a shiver of excitement run down my spine as my fingernail touched something metallic. Must be the release switch, I thought.

Now I've got to get hold of the tongues and hold them together whilst Cutler lifts the slab. Then he inserts a safety-pin and, hey presto, we are home and dry. But I couldn't get at the tongues, the soil around the bomb was packed solid. 'Not worth fooling with this,' I said. 'Let's blow it.'

A moment later the corporal returned holding one miserable stick of the almond-scented explosive. 'That's all there is,' he said, handing it to me together with a detonator and a length of fuse.

'Oh! Well, that should do,' I replied and tamped the charge carefully into the hole about the bomb. We sheltered round a bend in the track whilst the fuse burned. 2,000 feet beneath us the moonlit ocean glittered and the lights of the coastal towns twinkled amongst the olive groves.

The explosion was not very loud and, as soon as the debris had stopped falling, I walked forward. The stone slab had gone and there was no evidence of the bomb. Funny, I thought, expecting to find something and thrusting my hand deep into the warm soil at the bottom of the crater. To my horror Cutler's torch revealed a hideous string of mechanism, fuse and explosive dangling from my hand. Our charge had failed and, as I watched the release switch, shifted a fraction. It was only held together by the glutinous soil and now the tongues were opening.

'Down!' I yelled, pitching the whole thing over the cliff.

A split second later the explosion shook us. 'You all right?' I said. 'Sir,' said Cutler.

'Have yer done then?' asked my batman, Rampling, as we reached the Land-Rover.

Rampling was one of the most amusing and yet courageous soldiers I ever met. A born comic from Preston, where his mother made confectionery, he was also the troop medical orderly. I reckoned that even if a chap were dying, Rampling would make him laugh.

A few days later I was on reconnaissance in the Troodos mountains. My party consisted of the Land-Rover, driven as usual by Corporal Cutler, and the Daimler armoured scout-car, driven by Sapper Oran, with Rampling as his crewman. We rounded a bend and saw a Royal Marines Commando vehicle parked on the verge.

The driver was punching out the remains of a smashed windscreen and an officer was tying a dressing around a gash in his forehead.

'What's wrong?' I asked, pulling up.

'I wouldn't go through that village if I were you,' he said, indicating a cluster of red-roofed buildings nestling in the foothills beneath us.

'The road's barricaded with huge earthenware jars and when you try to move them they stone you to blazes from the roof-tops,' he explained.

'Did you open fire!' I asked.

'No, not a man in sight. The usual trick. Just women and children.' To avoid the village would mean a detour of over sixty miles and I had another job to do that evening. Explaining the situation to my group I said, 'Oran, you lead the way in the armoured car. If the road is blocked, don't stop, just smash through. We'll be right behind you in the Land-Rover.'

'Good luck,' nodded the commando officer, as we sped off down the dusty road towards the village. We were still half a mile away when the chanting of 'Ee-oo-ka, Ee-oo-ka' reached our ears.

Cutler pulled on his goggles and I drew my revolver. Turkeys, dogs and chickens scattered as we roared into the narrow street, flanked by the vine-bedecked coffee shops. Not a soul in sight. At the narrowest point in the road, an unbroken line of earthenware jars formed a solid wall. 'Keep going,' I roared, as the brake lights on the armoured car flickered, but Oran needed no encouragement and, with a loud crunch, hit the jars. The Daimler disappeared momentarily in an explosion of pottery, olive oil and grain. The bits were still falling as we followed through the gap. From the roofs astonished faces peered down. We sped on and were still in the village when, to my consternation, Oran stopped. At once I realised why. We had taken the wrong turning and were now in a dead end. There was hardly room to turn round but, as I leaped out Rampling was there directing the driver.

In record time we were facing outward. A huge crowd of villagers were moving slowly towards us. My stomach felt very queasy and I remembered the awful stories of similar incidents when troops had been caught by hostile crowds. There were four of us and at least a hundred of them. The crowd was silent, grim-faced, determined. Not a man in sight. Just dark-skinned women in the traditional black dress of the Cypriot peasant. The fact that we had just destroyed a large amount of their winter food stock did nothing to endear us to them. Their leader was a wrinkled old woman, carrying an axe in her bony hand. She knew she had us cornered and like a cat with a mouse was enjoying the scene. Even if we fired, we couldn't stop more than half a dozen before they seized us. My only other thought was to charge them with the vehicles. The consequences were too horrible to contemplate.

'You must disperse or we shall open fire,' I said in a voice as stern and authoritative as I could manage.

The old woman, standing twenty-five yards away, spat a long stream of filthy green phlegm in reply.

'Oki,' roared her comrades edging nearer.

'Here, will you hold this?' Rampling thrust his rifle into my hand. 'What on earth ...' I began to ask, but he was already ambling towards the crowd.

He reached the old crone and, looking forever like an English Bobby on duty at a football match, placed his hands on his hips and said loudly, 'You can't do that here, Mom.' The witch looked bewildered.

'Come on. I'll take ruddy axe,' said the lad from Preston and grasping the razor-sharp weapon, turned to the crowd and waving them back said, 'Now I've got to get back to camp for tea so if you'll just clear the road, we can all go home.' To my astonishment, they obeyed.

'Come on,' yelled Rampling and signalled us forward. 'Tata, sorry about the oil jars. But thou shouldn't park them on busy highway you know,' he grinned, as he leapt aboard the armoured car.

We got almost fifty yards before the crowd recovered and ran screaming after us with sticks and stones. Thanks to the cool courage of this extraordinary soldier, we escaped.

Back in camp two hours later I called him over. 'You did well, Rampling, thank you very much,' I said.

'Ay, it were a good laff, weren't it?' He grinned and shuffled off to persuade the cooks to give him a late tea.

Years later, instructing at Sandhurst, I tried to impress on cadets how fortunate they were to lead men who would be untroubled by disaster, unflattered by success, who would face adversity and anger with the same cool courage, sparkling with a unique brand of ready wit.

As the winter set in I was ordered to support the 3rd Battalion, Grenadier Guards, who had been sent to quell the terrorist-infested Panhandle district. Thus, on a wet evening we found ourselves harbouring in broken country. Our sections were quickly deployed to the rifle companies whilst I established my small headquarters near Battalion HQ. The first thing to do, a matter of great importance, was to site the thunderbox.

'Where would you like it, sir?' asked my transport corporal.

'That spot by the trees looks well drained, nicely concealed and has a pleasant view,' I replied. So my fine oak portable lavatory was erected under a Karib tree so that, when enthroned at dawn, I could survey the mountains of Turkey, forty miles' distant.

The next day the corporal reported that the thunderbox must be moved as it was 'full up'.

'Full up?' I gasped. 'With only five of us here?'

'Fraid so, sir. It's them Guards sergeants been using it.'

This was an insult of the highest order. An officer's thunderbox is a very private thing; although I allowed my own soldiers access to it, it was a gross insolence for outsiders to intrude. The proximity of the device to the Guards sergeants' mess was clearly too great a temptation. Regretfully I ordered it moved westward, some sixty paces. Alas, next morning it was found to be 'full' again. This really was too much, and I was of a mind to report the matter when the corporal, a devious but ingenious man, suggested an alternative plan to dissuade trespassers.

'You may recall, sir, we captured some home-made explosive yesterday,' he smirked. 'Might I suggest that we place a minute quantity, with a simple booby-trap switch, beneath the toilet, to be operated by anyone seating himself thereon?'

The idea appealed. 'What about us?' I inquired.

'We shall leave a safety pin nearby. All Engineers, before seating, must replace the pin,' he replied.

It was an hour after dark and I was on duty in the battalion operations room when I heard a dull 'boom' followed by a cry of 'Medical orderly, medical orderly'. When the padre relieved me, I asked what the medic had been called for.

'Oh! One of the sergeants sat on a stove; bit singed, I gather!' replied the vicar.

Back at our lines, I found my men grouped about the thunderbox or the remains thereof. The hessian screen lay on the ground and the shattered timbers were scattered around. The black plastic seat was fifteen feet away and the roll of soft white paper trailed sadly across the field. The pungent smell of explosive was heavy in the night air.

'About 2100 hours, sir,' reported the corporal. 'Rampling and I perceived a light bobbing across the field. "Stand to lads," I says, "Here comes the enemy". We sees the light go behind the screen and a few second later there is a blood big bang.' The wreckage told the rest. 'Then there's t'bloke rolling about in t'smoke,' said Rampling, in his strong Lancashire accent, continuing the tale. 'He can't get up quick like, cos 'is trousers is round 'is ankles and 'e's lost 'is belt.'

'Was he badly hurt?' I enquired with concern.

'Well, 'e was making bit of fuss like, but I think it were just shock,' replied Rampling.

It took all next day to rebuild the thunderbox but it was never quite the same. A week later, after a long cordon and search operation, most of the battalion regrouped at the main camp. My sections came in and, having arrived in the middle of the night, were not familiar with the layout. Unfortunately a sapper was discovered on the Grenadiers' commanding officer's thunderbox by the battalion adjutant, with whom I had already crossed swords on other matters. 'One of your wretched men is on the Colonel's thunderbox,' he screamed. I was tired and considered that there were more important things to worry about at that moment. 'I'm sorry,' I grunted, but the adjutant continued to rave. 'For Pete's sake,' I retorted, 'I am always finding Guardsmen on my thunderbox and I have a way of dealing with them.'

For a moment I thought he would have a seizure. 'You, you, you have a way of dealing with a Guardsman?' he stammered.

'Yes, said I, 'We blow them up.'

Then the colonel entered.

'Sir, Blashford-Snell has been blowing up Guardsmen,' blurted out the adjutant.

'Really?' said the CO, looking mildly interested.

I explained what had happened, hoping that I sounded more confident that I felt.

'Hmm,' muttered the senior officer, looking stern. 'Can't have that, can we?'

'Certainly not,' snapped my tormentor with obvious satisfaction. Poking me with his walking stick the Colonel said slowly, 'Your punishment, young man, is that you must write the story for your regimental magazine.'

My next assignment was to help a gunner regiment sent out from Britain in the infantry role. Their commander was a great character and insisted that I run a course on terrorist weapons. This was designed to teach all ranks the techniques employed by EOKA and one lesson was devoted to homemade bombs. We had with us a quantity of captured chlorate. The class, consisting of most of the officers and NCOS from regimental headquarters, had gathered around as I showed them how simple it was to mix the chemicals to produce an explosive.

The lesson was adjourned for lunch and we found afterwards that, owing to the heat, the chlorate had solidified from a fine white powder into a number of solid lumps. I needed powder to make up a small bomb and without thought I picked up a safety-match box and used this to pulverize the lumps. The phosphorous particles on the striker surface at once combined with the powerful oxidizing agent and I saw a thin wisp of smoke – just in time to hurl the entire box, containing about twenty pounds, behind me. With a great 'whoosh' and a brilliant yellow flame, it ignited. I sat down rather heavily, my NCOs scattered in all directions and the class dived for cover – all, that is, except the colonel.

'Get up, get up, you idiots,' he scolded. 'Don't you know every sapper demonstration begins with a bang? Come on, Blashers, stop fooling around and get on with it.'

My face was blackened, my eyebrows had disappeared and my trousers were full of small holes; however I attempted to smile and continued as if the whole thing had been intentional.

In 1959 EOKA surrendered and peace descended. Now was the time to create a friendly atmosphere. The Underwater Section that I now ran was sent to the ancient city of Paphos to seek evidence of an extensive port, thought to have sunk beneath the waves during an earthquake.

So it was that I stood with a group of soldiers in the Paphos museum, whilst the curator recounted the history of this famous area. The men shuffled, sniffed, coughed and scratched; archaeology was not a subject close to their hearts.

'So you see, each year many, many ships came from all over the Mediterranean bearing young maidens.' The men's eyebrows raised.

'He's on about skirt,' whispered a lad from Leeds, waking his pal with a nudge in the ribs.

'Ough!' grunted Sapper Robins, taking an instant interest in the lecture.

'The young women were unmarried,' explained the curator, 'it was necessary that they should be virgins.' Even Rampling was awake now. 'They left their ships at anchor in the port and walked up through a place we call the beautiful gardens, where they made offerings of terracotta figurines. At Kouklia there was a great temple, in the centre of which was a fifteen-foot phallus. This is a model of the original,' said the curator, tapping a four-foot black monolith. 'It is said that so many maidens came to be initiated that some had to wait here until the winter.'

'Bet there weren't no shortage for ordination in them days,' muttered Rampling.

Complete with a 100-ton flat-bottomed open-decked Royal Engineer Z craft, thirty-five soldiers, piles of diving equipment, plus an eager Army Public Relations Officer, the expedition arrived at Paphos. The introduction of a spot of ancient sex into the task was a splendid catalyst and the men set about their work with enthusiasm. Thus, for a few weeks during four summers, the army surveyed the seabed and brought up tons of pottery, marble, glass and metal.

One of our earlier finds was the wreckage off the Moulia Reef of a man of war, whose carronades lay scattered in shallow water. We had just raised the last of five large cannons and the wind was freshening as I took a last look round in case we had missed anything. Flipping along over the rocky bed, I came to a ravine and peered down. Something smooth, grey and round, like a metallic cylinder lay across the sandy floor of the cleft. I turned round slowly. What on earth .... ?, I thought and, jackknifing my body, I slid down into the crevice.

On the seabed I found myself staring into a low cave. The cleft was simply a large crack in the roof. The grey cylinder now looked about twelve inches in diameter and got thicker as it disappeared into the gloom. Grasping the rock, I pushed myself down and under the ledge. For a few moments all seemed black then, as my eyes grew accustomed to the dark, I perceived movement. A small cloud of sand billowed up. To my left the cylinder moved, or I should say twitched, and, at the same time, the floor of the cave slid forward several feet. Still puzzled I stared in and it was another few moments before I realised I was hovering between the roof and the back of a giant stingray. An arm's length in front, I could make out the gentle mound of its head, and behind me stretched the huge tail that had first attracted my attention. I guessed it was ten feet across. Why did it stay so still? Perhaps it had been stunned by the explosions earlier that day? Hardly daring to breathe for fear that the rattle of my valve would disturb it, I inched backwards from the black hole. Before I reached the ravine it twitched again, but at last I was back in the light and speeding to the surface.

'What's that in the crack?' shouted Corporal Jones, who had been watching my descent.

Tearing out my mouthpiece I yelled back. 'The monster of the Moulia Rocks – it's a bloody great ray.' Only a couple of evenings before, we had listened to the fisherman of Paphos telling us of a terrible creature that lived on this reef, destroying their nets and threatening boats.

'If you kill it,' they promised, 'we'll buy everyone a beer.' 'Prepare a five-pound charge,' I shouted. 'Tell Christos to come and see. We'll need him to give evidence if we're to get that beer!' Christos, our Cypriot boatman, swam over and, donning a mask, kicked his way down to the monster's lair. He came back ashen and convinced. Five minutes later the sea erupted as the charge detonated.

'It is far too big to be killed by you,' laughed the fisherman, in spite of Christos's assurances. We never did get our beer.

In August 1960 I returned to England and married Judith, now home from Singapore. My new partner was an excellent swimmer and became the general manager of the underwater expeditions. Solving the mystery of Paphos became an obsession. We searched and searched and then, towards the end of one particularly gruelling day, I made a discovery that sent the adrenalin racing through my bloodstream and almost led to disaster as I struggled to bring up a heavy, inscribed marble slab.

The needle on the pressure gauge was approaching the danger zone. After a few more deep breaths the air supply would stop abruptly and I knew the aqua-lung had no reserve. I cursed my stupid stubbornness for causing me to neglect a basic safety rule of diving that would now probably cost me my life.

Letting go of the slab, I fought to control my breathing and watched the precious artefact twirling down into the tangled seaweed. For ten minutes I had struggled, using up far too much air, to bring it up from its watery grave forty feet below. I had found it jammed between rocks near the infamous Moulia Reef and felt certain that the inscription would provide a valuable clue to the origin of the great port.

Above me the late afternoon sun glittered on the waves. And as I rose quickly to the surface still the air held out, although the needle was now right against the top, I hardly dared to glance at the gauge. I had ditched my fourteen-pound weight belt on the seabed, so I tried to control the ascent with my breathing. 'Too fast, too fast,' I kept thinking as I rose in the cloud of bubbles. I felt a twinge in my leg but, thankfully, I had not been down long enough to be at risk of the dreaded bends. As I surfaced, the valve went clunk, signifying the end of the precious supply. Tearing the mouthpiece out, I sucked in air and sea water. The sun was blinding and the strong wind blew the short waves into my face. Looking down, I noticed with interest that the seabed was sliding past. Two more mouthfuls of water left me feeling horribly sick and an awful rattling noise came from my chest. A red film was clouding my vision. 'Don't panic, think'. I repeated my own advice, but I felt terribly tired and even thought was an effort. To get a good mouthful of air, I turned over on my back and, at the same time, tried to release the useless aqua-lung. One shoulder strap come off at once, but the other was stuck. Now I was drifting with the current straight towards the foaming outline of the reef. How ironic that the rocks, whose earlier victims I had been investigating, should claim me as well.

Suddenly the strap came undone and the tanks dropped away, leaving me free to swim with what strength I had left. Rolling over, I noticed that the seabed was only twelve feet below. I still had a chance, and in the far distance the bridge of our Z_{11} flagship was rising and falling in the swell. Any instinctive cry for help would have only wasted valuable energy, so I tried to swim, my leaden legs doing little against the current. The waves breaking on the jagged rocks were clearly audible. Each second their boom grew louder. Two hundred yards, I thought. Five minutes if I'm lucky. What a damned silly thing to do, leaving the other divers and going off alone after some antique tombstone. Again I tired to swim, but my legs refused to answer. 'Conserve your energy for the reef. There's still a chance of clinging onto a rock, if you can get through the outer breakers,' said optimism. 'Some hope! You've seen the dragon's teeth, they even slice you open if you touch them in calm conditions,' replied pessimism and realism together. 'You're a bit off course,' said another voice and I turned my head to see one of the expedition's boats about thirty yards away. Kneeling in the bows was the public relations officer, who had come out to cover the story. Drowning men are supposed to relive their past in the last few seconds, but I must confess that I had been too busy trying to survive.

However, the evidence of the existence of the port was found inconclusive and, before I had to return to Britain in December 1961, I decided to have one last thorough look to see if we could unravel the mystery. Operation Aphrodite II consisted of a task force of boats, vehicles, light aircraft and the Z 11. Almost a hundred soldiers and civilians were involved. The Royal Navy made some preliminary soundings for us and the RAF flew special sorties with infra-red cameras. The people of this quiet corner of Cyprus were awe-struck by the incredible effort that the British, who had now given them independence, were putting into solving some ancient legend. The press was also interested and the expedition needed a special public relations section to deal with the growing number of enquiries.

At last I was told someone was coming to help and, to the joy of our merry men, a delightful and very attractive lady arrived. Whether it was her charming personality or her undersized bikini I'm not sure, but productivity increased tenfold and the deck was soon piled high with ancient artefacts. A few days after the start of the venture, I realised that at least three of our members were vying with each other for her favours, which, in fairness, I must say she kept to herself. Even so, at the end of the first week, I had to rebuke two of my colleagues for quarrelling over her, and that evening asked her as discreetly as possible if she wouldn't mind wearing a one-piece costume. Giving me a delicious smile, she said in her husky voice, 'Well, John, which piece would you like me to wear?'

Although we never did solve the mystery of the lost harbour, we made one important discovery. Many of the older folk at Paphos had told me a tale of a great cannon believed to have disappeared in the sixteenth century. When the Turks had ruled Cyprus, they had a garrison in the square fort on the harbour wall. It was said that on top of the battlements they placed a huge cannon. Reportedly this piece was able to hurl a ball to any part of the town and thus the Greek Cypriots lived under constant threat. Eventually there was a revolution during which the Greeks captured the castle and butchered the garrison. Like many before it, this revolt eventually failed, but when the Turks returned to Paphos, the great gun had gone. With customary ruthlessness, they took numerous prisoners and, in an effort to discover its whereabouts, tortured and burned them to death, but the cannon was never found.

Everyone thought that it had simply been lowered over the battlements into the water but we had already made exhaustive searches of the seabed beneath the fort and although we found a few cannon balls, there was no sign of the gun. To throw a shot into the town, it must have been a sizeable piece and would probably weigh several tons, not easily moved over land. If the cannon were not in the immediate area of the fort, the Greeks had probably dragged it away into the town, but then it was most likely that the Turkish inquisitors would have located it. Where on earth could it be hidden? Everyone in the port had his own theory. One thing was sure; the great gun had vanished without a trace; perhaps it was all a myth.

When two local police officers then came to me claiming to know exactly where it could be found, I was pretty sceptical. However, it was a hot night, Greek music echoed from the bar and overhead the cloudless sky glittered with twinkling stars, and I was in a benign mood. They sat down, the barman brought ice-cold Keo and we toasted each other. After a long pause, one said slowly, 'You know about the great gun?' I nodded, passing him the dish of salted nuts. 'I have seen it,' said the other, looking very solemn.

'Where?' I enquired, still unconvinced.

'It is near here, on the other side of the headland, very close to the shore,' he gestured. 'I can show you the place, sir.'

It was 1600 hours next afternoon with the worst heat of the day over when we boarded our tug and set out on yet another quest for the long-lost cannon. I was not very hopeful, but the sea on the Moulia Reef was too rough for diving and it seemed a useful way of keeping in training. Rounding the headland, we followed the constable's directions to the sheltered beach. 'Getting pretty shallow,' cautioned the helmsman. Fifty yards ahead the waves rolled over a reef. 'We can't go in much closer,' I said over my shoulder to the policeman. 'Where do you reckon it is?'

'There, just beyond the rocks,' he said pointing at the line of black shadows. The tug rolled in the gentle swell.

'Drop anchor, we'll swim in.' With a splash, half a dozen divers jumped in and, fanning out in an extended line, began to flipper slowly towards the shore. For about ten minutes we searched. There was nothing but bare rock and sand. Suddenly Corporal Jones's excited voice rang out above the sound of waves. 'It's here, it's here,' he yelled, 'a damned great gun.' And there indeed it was. At first, all we could see was the breech sticking up about eight inches above the sand. It was lying in four feet of water and, within a few minutes, we had uncovered two feet of it. It was certainly big. Protected by the sand, the heavy black metal bore no growth nor encrustations. I was surprised to see it was so plain and, seizing the boss, I pulled myself down for a closer examination. There were no inscriptions, but it was obviously an iron cannon – and so large that it was unlikely to be a ship's gun.

'What a monster,' said the excited public relations officer. 'How are you going to lift it?' That was the problem – it was buried at an angle of forty-five degrees. Landward and seaward were low reefs. It must weigh at least two tons, I calculated, and would need strong lifting tackle to move it. To get our landing craft above it was out of the question.

Walking onto the beach and standing in the warm white sand, I looked around. Just inland rose the massive natural rock slabs in which were carved the 'Tombs of the Kings' and running down from them was a narrow pathway. This track was very old and made a relatively smooth route through the rock formations. Did the Greeks drag the gun down this, I wondered, and then somehow manage to push or float it out to its grave. 'We'll blast a channel through the inshore reef, then we'll bring the recovery vehicle ashore from Z11 and try to get it over the headland to this point. Next we'll run out the winch cable for divers to fix to the gun, then heave ho and it should be like pulling a tooth,' I explained to the team.

So at dawn next day, our divers laid the charges. The wind was up and a heavy swell made work difficult. Several sappers had to be treated for lacerations after being swept against the reef. On shore, the massive Scammell recovery vehicle had already run out its heavy steel cables. Z 11 lay 200 yards out, providing communications and refreshments. By 0800 we were ready to fire the first demolition; the police cleared the area and the fuse was ignited. Suddenly, low overhead, came an Army Auster aircraft containing several senior officers who had flown down to witness the operation. It banked sharply over Z11 and came straight over the beach. Frantically I waved it away as the spluttering fuse burned down. With a dull roar the charges exploded, sending a column of spray straight upward at the Auster, which, none the worse for a drenching, flew straight on! One more bang, then the cable was fixed and the winch took up the strain. The explosives had done the job and in a few minutes the onlookers could see the great black, iron cannon in the surf. Inch by inch it was dragged like a stricken whale to the beach. 'Can't find any sign of a carriage,' said Corporal Jones, emerging from the surf as I took a closer look at the gun. How many poor devils were torn apart or roasted alive to preserve this secret, I wondered. Eight feet long and weighing over two tons, our prize was carried in triumph to Paphos port. That night Cyprus Radio credited us with solving the mystery. I knew, however, that to leave the metal exposed to the air would ruin it in no time, so we lowered it into the harbour to await the construction of a special preservative bath.

Eight years later Judith and I went back and walked amongst the ruins on the headland. Some spectacular discoveries had been made since our expeditions and, to our amazement, we found that we had been camping only inches above the wonderful mosaic floor of a villa. But although Paphos had gained much in its knowledge of the past, the present political situation had greatly deteriorated. Now Turks and Greeks lived behind barricades, and the houses bore the signs of civil war. Takis, the museum curator, found us in the Crusader Castle overlooking the harbour. 'Welcome, welcome,' he said, embracing me. 'Have you seen your great gun? It is in a place of honour on the quay.'

We strolled into the little port and at once saw the cannon, mounted on a carriage in front of the local Cyprus Navy HQ. I raised my camera. A sentry rushed over. 'It is forbidden to photograph military weapons,' he explained politely.

'Things have changed', apologized Takis.

Elsewhere in Cyprus we had made other discoveries, but, of course, there was also the military side to the diving that usually meant hard work under difficult conditions. One morning the military port office rang. 'John, we're in trouble,' said the commandant. 'Some idiot has run our mobile crane into the harbour. It's effectively blocking the slip and we've no crane big enough to lift it.'

It seemed the only way to move it was to pass a cable underneath and then partly sink Z craft on either side, fasten the cable to them and re-float the two craft. The only snag was that the machine was lying in liquid mud. Securing the crane's jib to the dockside, Sapper Ellis and I slid into the chilly water. I used a hosepipe to 'tunnel' through the mud. Ellis handled the steel-wire cable that we were to pass beneath the mobile crane. The mud closed about us as we felt our way through the tangled mass of struts and cables. It was pitch black.

Communicating by hand signal we descended slowly and I hosed away the solid lumps. I guessed we were right beneath the crane when I felt a slight increase in pressure on my ears. I could not see my depth gauge, but I realised at once what was happening. The machine was sinking deeper into the mud, pushing us down with it.

I held my breath. The clatter of Ellis's valve stopped also. The slow, relentless movement of the steel-work was obvious. Only our efforts beforehand had masked it. We had to get out of this deathtrap with all speed. I tried to go forward, but came upon an impenetrable barrier that was probably a wheel. I could either go down and try and come up beyond it or retreat the way we had come. At least I knew the way back was clear. The mud was getting thicker and movement against it was an effort. I touched Ellis and gave the signal for 'going back and up'. He seemed to understand. I remembered that I was still clutching the hose, and it was now vital for survival. Suddenly the crane gave a jerk, which frightened me stiff. I must move faster, I thought, so I slid one shoulder under the hose and passed the nozzle down towards my feet. Then, gripping it between my knees and hands, I began to tunnel backwards, following my lifeline. Something tightened around my thigh. It felt like a small octopus but I couldn't move against it and as I struggled it tightened. I felt it, coarse and rough. It was simply a loop of rope into which I had stuck my foot. Laboriously I went forward, freed my leg and started back again.

It seemed like minutes, but was probably only a few seconds before I found my nylon lifeline rising. Feeling above me all the way, I began to ascend. Once I hit a loose cable and a surge of panic returned. Was I still under the crane? The water was jet-black and I saw nothing until I surfaced. As the mud drained from my face-mask, Ellis came into view beside me. 'Bloody hell!' was all he said.

''Sorry about that,' shouted the port officer. 'One of the stops slipped on the jib, but you'd have been all right – we had another one anyway.'

'Thanks for telling me.' I murmured into my mouthpiece.

We got the cable under at the second attempt and I went home. Judith was waiting. 'Come on,' she smiled. 'Don't look so fed up – let's go underwater fishing this afternoon.'

Our Mediterranean diving activities also extended to examining the ancient harbours of Apollonia and Leptis Magna in Libya. However, it was not the African shoreline that attracted me, but the desert. The desolate, magnificent Sahara had not changed in 4,000 years. The population was still largely coastal or located at the few oases. Maps bore the tempting words 'relief data incomplete'.

Libya stretched over 500 miles deep into this wilderness. All one needed was time, a few Land-Rovers and fuel to be able to explore areas where few, if any men, had trodden before. We quickly learned to navigate by sun compass, to de-bog vehicles with pierced metal planks called sand channels and to mend every possible breakdown. Our forays into the dun-brown wasteland were enlivened with visits to oil-rigs, where rare and glorious hot baths, ice-cold beer and inch-thick steaks were available. The oil men had not yet penetrated far into the desert, but they always seemed glad to see us at their lonely, but well-stocked camps.

Near the coast where our predecessors, the Desert Rats, had fought desperate, but finally victorious battles against the Afrika Corps, one moved with caution. Much of our work here involved clearing mines that still remained in abundance.

It was late one afternoon and we hadn't seen a mine for miles. I was impatient to get back for a swim in the warm sea, so, instead of walking slowly ahead of my Land-Rover, eyes peeled for evidence of a deadly device, I'd decided to sit on the bonnet as we drove slowly.

'If I shout, stop immediately,' I told my sapper driver. We had been going for almost an hour when a movement right in front of the offside wheel caught my eye. 'Stop,' I yelled and shot off as the brakes slammed on.

The baby tortoise tucked his head in his shell as I reached for him. It was then I spotted something else. He was on top of a set of three rusty prongs. 'Back off very slowly and keep in your own wheel tracks,' I ordered the mystified driver, my heart pounding. Once the Land-Rover was away I pocketed my little friend and gently cleared the sand from around the German S mine. Slipping a safety pin into the igniter, I checked for booby traps and lifted the heavy pot. It was in perfect condition.

'Cor, what's that?' asked my soldier.

'Anti-personnel Jumping mine,' I replied. 'Step on it and it bounces up six feet, explodes and showers ball-bearings for a hundred yards.'

'Charming,' he muttered. It had been a close call. Back in Cyprus, I planted a special spinach patch for my tiny friend who was christened 'Churchill'.

In 1961, on an expedition deep in the Sahara, we had been held up awaiting spares for a broken-down truck. At last they arrived and we headed home. 'Do you mind if I go on ahead?' I asked the expedition leader.

'No, by all means,' said Bob in his usual cheerful tone.

'I'll keep to the main track and come up on the radio schedules as usual,' I assured him. So saying, I set off in my well-laden Land-Rover with Sapper Smart at the wheel and Corporal Smith as navigator. We made good time and by noon had cleared one hundred and thirty miles when, suddenly, our nearside tyre collapsed with a hiss. Smart swore.

I unbuckled the spare tyre, then ran it towards the punctured wheel. The driver was standing silent and grim. 'Well,' I said, 'let's get on with it.'

He looked very dejected as he uttered the awful words. 'I lent my box spanner to Higgins last night.'

It took several seconds for the full meaning of this statement to become clear. The desert Land-Rovers were fitted with a special hub to which a rope could be attached and provide the vehicle with a simple capstan. However, with these on, it required a long box spanner to undo the wheel nuts. 'There must be another way,' I protested. We turned out our kit, but there was no way to unscrew even one nut. We were stranded.

'Four gallons left,' said the corporal and I knew he was talking about water.

'Plus the water bottles,' I added.

Silently and trying to avoid unnecessary activity, we laid out the fluorescent air identification panels in the form of the emergency signal, prepared flares, made a shelter along the side of the Land-Rover and crawled underneath it. Our radio was not working well and therefore it was no surprise when we failed to make contact by dusk. After the day's scorching heat, the blissful cool of the night was a welcome relief.

When the first flush of panic passed, I had wanted to call Smart every name under the sun. However, eight hours later my anger had subsided and I concentrated on trying to evolve a plan that would save us. We had broken down on the edge of the mile-wide track and it was quite possible that the convoy would find us. But they only had to be 500 yards eastward and they would pass behind a low ridge, missing us completely.

That night, lying in the depression I had dug in the sand, I awoke to hear a rattling metallic noise nearby. There was no wind, yet when my eyes opened to peer out across the moonlit desert, I could see nothing. That's strange, I thought. And there it was again. I instinctively drew my Walther pistol from my bedroll. As I scanned the desert, from behind a low hillock, one of our discarded tin cans rolled into view. It was rolling over and over as if propelled by a strong wind, but the night was still. As I pondered this, the can suddenly stopped and then rolled back the way it had come. I'm going mad. I thought. Then it changed direction and came towards me. My God, a haunted tin can, probably something they put in the rations.

The shining object was only ten feet away now, rolling this way and that, when I raised my pistol. The sharp crack rang out in the still air. The bullet threw up a spurt of sand a couple of inches from the can, which instantly accelerated away. I fired again. The can stopped rolling and, to my amazement, a desert rat hopped out – clearly annoyed at having his feast disturbed.

At daylight, I rose stiffly to find the radio still silent and, although I went through all the drills a dozen times, I could get nothing; altering the setting of the aerial didn't help either. However, just in case others could hear us, I sent an SOS signal giving our position. The sun was up when I gave up fiddling with the knobs.

'What shall we have for breakfast?' asked Smith.

'I don't mind,' I replied, 'but let's have it quickly before the heat hits us.'

Lying under the shelter I made a mental check of our emergency actions. Flares ready, ears alert for noise of aircraft or vehicles, air identification panels out. Remaining water, now down to two-and-a-half gallons, carefully stowed in the shade. All other sources of liquid checked, we lay in silence, the beads of sweat growing on our filthy skin and turning into rivulets, which ran into the sand. God, how we smelt! On the move we had not noticed it, but now it was becoming unpleasant to be near anyone else. Somehow one's own odour was bearable, almost fascinating, but anyone else's was disgusting. Sleep was impossible, so I tried to read, but a voice in my head kept saying 'there must be a way out'. Rather like shipwrecked sailors on a raft, I mused. It's the waiting that is the worst.

At noon the sun was right overhead, and to reassure ourselves we took a fix with the bubble sextant. It simply confirmed that we were about 120 miles south of the coast. The nearest water was seventy-five miles away. We discussed walking out, but realised this was hopeless. Stay with your vehicle, was the great cry.

Smart was looking very sorry for himself. After all, it was his fault we were in this predicament. But then I had asked if we could go on ahead and alone. Corporal Smith was truly without any blame and looked the most cheerful of us all. We delayed lunch until mid afternoon to avoid working in the full heat. 'These boiled sweets certainly help to lessen the thirst,' I remarked. Smart passed me another, and I began to remove the paper. We all heard it together, a sound like a distant rumble of thunder.

'Three-tonners,' yelled Smart. 'It's the convoy, I knew they'd find us.' Our flares streaked upward, but I still couldn't see the trucks, the noise of which was quite clear. Oh God! They must be just the other side of the ridge. The Corporal was already tearing towards it, when I heard another engine and, spinning round, saw a Land-Rover bearing down on us.

The goggle-clad face grinned. 'Having a spot of bother?' our rescuers enquired.

We had all learned a lesson.

3

.

Adventurous Training

On 28th May 1962, a terrible tragedy occurred in the former German Army storage tunnels in Jersey. Two teenagers from my old school were killed by a concentration of poisonous gas, reported as a mixture of cyanide and methane, set off by decomposition in the damp tunnel.

Eventually it transpired that the boys had been overcome by carbon monoxide produced by the smouldering remains of some old pit props set afire underground by youngsters who had visited the passages the previous day. The victims died as they struggled to reach the open air through a narrow passage dug beneath the concrete plug that had sealed the tunnel. Would-be rescuers were struck down by mysterious vapours wafting from the entrance. Rumours of wartime cyanide gas were soon circulating, holidaymakers cancelled bookings and hoteliers screamed for action.

The local government – The States of Jersey – quickly called upon the Ministry of Defence to investigate. There were few Jerseymen in the Royal Engineers and thus I found my time at the Junior Leaders Regiment interrupted by this unusual and exciting job. Our task was to examine all the old German underground works on the island and, equipped with the original maps, my small team sailed from Weymouth on a ferry loaded with apprehensive tourists.

As we had expected, the German map had been drawn with Teutonic thoroughness and, guided by my pal, Tony Titterington, with whom as a boy I had spent hours exploring some of these very tunnels, we set to work. The mysterious shafts were rumoured to contain everything from Nazi treasure to Luger pistols.

Several tunnels were as large as a London tube station and, lined with ferro-concrete, looked very similar. However, others had bare granite walls, dripping with water and often blocked by roof falls. There were stories of Russian prisoners being cemented into the walls when they died at work. There was no doubt that the piles of jagged rock that we found hindering our exploration had almost certainly entombed workers and soldiers alike. However, many of the tunnels had been completed and were now filled with untidy heaps of military hardwear – helmets, anti-tank guns, bazookas, machine guns – everything lay scattered by the hands of generations of small boys seeking souvenirs. There were more lethal items – the occasional shell and drums of flame-thrower fluid. Working our way forward over the debris, we surveyed, checked roofs, examined equipment and searched for any unknown passages that might conceal especially dangerous items.

'I feel just like a bloody mole,' said my cockney sergeant, stripping off his emergency oxygen breathing-apparatus, miner's helmet and lamp after six hours underground. 'Funny smell in the place, ain't there, sir?'

'Yes,' I admitted, pulling a crumpled packet of filter tips from my pocket.

'I'm not sure what it is – it smells familiar, but I can't place it.'

'Well, it didn't show up on the test papers,' said Tony, who'd joined us.

One of the soldiers had found something. 'Do you think it's this stuff that's smelling?' he asked, handing me a grey rocklike lump. One sniff confirmed that it was. 'There's barrels and barrels of it in one of the side tunnels,' he remarked.

We passed the lumps around and eventually tossed one away. It landed with a soft plop in a pool of rainwater. To our amazement, the puddle began to bubble and boil, giving off a pungent vapour – I flicked my lighted match at it. 'Pop' went the gas, igniting with a bright orange flash. 'My God!' said the sergeant, still holding a lump. It was calcium carbide and the tunnel was full of highly inflammable acetylene gas. We stubbed out our fags and moved away from the entrance rather speedily. The Germans had obviously used this for emergency lighting and, in case any other little nasties turned up, I decided to get some expert local advice.

A number of Jersey quarrymen had been forced to work for the Germans. Virtually enslaved, they were given a little potato soup and black bread at dawn each day, then marched under armed guard into the growing labyrinths. Together with prisoners of war, and anyone else the Hun could press into service, they laboured in the darkness with pick and shovel until well after dusk. Many who had survived the ordeal were now dead, but those who still lived would never forget the years in this underground hell, the terror of the roof falls, the screams of the injured and the endless passages down which they shuffled, half starved and cold, knowing that, if they as much as paused, a jackboot would come crashing out of the darkness to drive them on.

'You know, you could smell a German and you learned to step out when you passed him,' said my visitor. Charlie was a small quarryman who had spent two years there. He and several friends had come to advise us on a particularly difficult tunnel, where a massive rock fall had blocked progress. Scrambling together over the fallen granite and rotting pit props, we reached a dead end. 'Reckon they gave up here,' grunted my guide. 'I can't say exactly what happened 'cos I was working in the main passage when this lot came in – but I'll never forget the rumble when she went – then the dust and the yelling.' The pale yellow beam of my lamp lit the lined faces of the grim-looking men.

The next day, I was already in the tunnel when the two quarrymen – Charlie and his mate – groped their way towards me. 'I've found an air-shaft that we may be able to squeeze through and get behind the rock fall,' I told them. With much grunting, we heaved ourselves forward on our stomachs inch by inch through the narrow passage.

Not the place to suffer from claustrophobia, I thought, moving aside a fallen pit prop and worming my way into the shattered passage behind the rock fall. The wood, sodden and rotten, broke away in my hand and I cast a furtive glance at the unsupported roof. The tunnel was littered with debris: a bottle, a broken spade, a rusty drilling rod, then our lamps shone down the passage and we saw another rock fall. Tree roots hung from the roof like giant fingers.

'Must be pretty near the surface,' said Charlie and I nodded, looking round. The other quarryman stood watching with us and said nothing, but nodded in agreement. He was slightly shorter than Charlie and I guessed a little older, but I was hardly in the mood for conversation and we only exchanged a few words.

Having inspected the chamber into which we'd crawled, I said, 'Well, that's it – let's get out of here.' So we wriggled back through the ventilation shaft into the main tunnel and I led the way to the entrance. Just as the welcome blast of fresh air hit us. I remembered my maps that I'd put down before entering the narrow passage. 'Blast!' I swore. 'You go on Charlie – I'll just nip back for my millboard.' A few minutes later, when I emerged, the soldier, whose job it was to check everyone in and out ticked me off on his list.

'Everyone out then?' I asked.

'Yes, sir,' he replied, swinging back the metal grid over the entrance.

'Oh! Which way did Charlie and his mate go?' I asked, thinking I should buy them a beer.

'He's gone off on his bike,' said the sentry, 'but I didn't see no mate.'

'You must have,' I remarked tetchily. 'You know, the chap who came in with him.'

'Charlie went in alone, sir, and no other civilians have been in this afternoon.' The hair stood on the back of my neck. Yet I knew there'd been a second man. Hell. I'd spoken to him!

'Are you sure?' I questioned.

'Quite sure, sir,' replied the soldier pushing his notebook towards me to emphasise the point.

Five minutes later I found Charlie in the pub. 'Where are your chums today, Charlie?' I said, trying not to seem concerned.

'Couldn't get away from work,' he muttered, wiping the frothy beer from his cracked lips. 'Like a drink?'

'Yes,' I said' 'I would very much.' I had several!

Back at the Regiment, trying to train young sappers in the face of an ever tightening defence budget was a frustrating business but it did bring me into contact with the Outward Bound Organization with whom I spent some time as a temporary instructor at their Ullswater School. It was while there that I found myself trudging around the Lake District in the middle of winter, trying to prevent twelve young boys from smoking, talking after lights-out and reading pornographic literature. The only way to do this was to work the little blighters so hard that they practically fell asleep on their feet. As part of the process there was a rather insane tradition at the school that demanded you rose before dawn, stripped naked, ran through the woods onto a jetty and plunged into the freezing lake. There was a limit to everybody's patience, I explained to the warden. I would be lashed helpless into a mountain-rescue stretcher and dangled upside down over a thousand-foot drop; I would survive without cigarettes or whisky for ten days; I would collect moss and lichen on the nature trails and even press flowers in books; but I quite categorically refused to be seen belting down a woodland path starkers, pursuing a dozen naked little boys.

The warden thought me unreasonable, but I stood my ground. I agreed that if it would satisfy him, I would enter the water in military uniform and with dignity! So, next day, I waited whilst long lines of youngsters, hell bent on improving their characters, dashed screaming into Lake Ullswater. Then, at a regulation quick march, dressed in full combat kit and fortified with four swigs of illicit cherry brandy, I marched off the jetty. I felt I had registered my protest and won my point.

It was something that the warden wrote about me that caught the eye of a well-known sapper, Colonel (later Major General) John Cowtan. He was then the senior Royal Engineer at Sandhurst, and in 1963 I was invited to return to my former haunts as an instructor – poacher turned gamekeeper! The Army had started a new scheme, and on arrival I was appointed as an Adventure Training Officer. The Commandant, then Major General John Mogg, explained my task, 'Your job is to get as many as possible of these young men overseas for the benefit of their character and the least possible detriment to the Empire.'

'Yes, sir,' I said and went away to try to find an office.

The helpful College Sergeant Major provided me with the old boot room, and placed a world map on the wall, sticking the title TRAINING AREA above it. By 1400 hours he'd produced tables, 'sixfoot, with blanket army grey' to cover it and a chair 'folding flat'. When I explained that my visitors might be invited to sit down, a second chair arrived. By tea I had cabinets, 'filing, grey, one', and I enquired about a telephone. For the first time the Sergeant Major looked worried, but eventually produced a field telephone with handle which I turned to attract his attention in an office seventy-five yards away. I would give the number required and he would hold the field telephone to his GPO device. I planned global expeditions in this way for several weeks until my own phone arrived. In the summer of 1963 I went along to help fellow sapper, David Hall, who was leading an expedition of cadets in the far south of the Libyan desert. Historically, this is a fascinating area, for it was here that a famous British Army Unit, the Long Range Desert Group (LRDG), had fought a magnificent hit-and-run campaign against the Italians during World War II. Our task involved important mapping and scientific work directed by David, who was already a legendary figure in desert exploration. He was happy to leave me to handle the administration.

On one re-supply run from our remote base to the oasis of Kufra, I had a strange experience. There were three of us in my Land-Rover when we set out before the glowing orb of the sun rose to destroy the glorious cool of dawn. How I loved those blissful couple of hours! Quite why we went with only one vehicle I cannot recall, but it was an easy run on what was by now a well-trodden trail, and we had a radio. We made good progress and in the afternoon were bowling along at about seventy mph on the flat, hard sand. The cars were always piled high with kit, and panniers of wire-mesh hung out of both sides. In these we carried our rations, sleeping-bags and personal belongings. The back of the Land-Rover was fitted with a dozen tightly-packed jerry cans of petrol. Water, not petrol, would be carried in the jerry cans at the front – in case of a collision. Smoking in or near vehicles was strictly forbidden for obvious reasons. The good old army-issue boiled sweets were great thirst-quenchers and John, my navigator, turned to get some from a pannier.

'Fire!' John had screamed the dreaded word. If you stop a moving vehicle that is on fire, suddenly the flames may come back and – woomph! – that's the end, but by keeping going, one might just keep the fire away from any fuel cans. 'In the pannier – the bedding's alight!' he yelled.

The wind, such as it was, was blowing from behind so I pulled the wheel over to the left to keep the flames from the cans and we halted gently enough to avoid spilling any fuel. Hurling survival gear away from the car, we leapt out, tearing at the burning bedding. The other crewman had already dragged to safety a can of precious water in case the vehicle blew up with all our supplies. Using the pathetic little fire extinguisher and some hastily-dug sand, we smothered the fire. A hard bump had bent our exhaust pipe upwards, pointing at the bottom of the pannier. Fortunately the only loss was a sleeping-bag, but it had not been a pleasant experience. We stopped shaking, repacked, had a few good gulps of water and drove on in silence.

I'd wanted to make Kufra by dark, but now we hadn't a hope. At dusk we reached some low rocky hills, really just big piles of jumbled broken stones with numerous narrow passes running through them. The map wasn't very precise so I chose one at random, which turned out to be a little west of the usual route. The sand was soft, and in the failing light we bogged down several times. Heaving the sand channels back aboard for the third time I said, 'We should be able to get some shelter amongst these rocks,' and my weary crew readily agreed that it was none too soon to call it a day. None of us felt like cooking, so we munched a few hard-tack biscuits smothered in raspberry jam and washed them down with a mug of coffee. The night was clear and before turning in I went to commune with nature.

Squatting beneath the stars I swore I heard the sound of a voice. The first time, I looked back towards the dull outline of the Land-Rover. The second, thinking one of the crew had called, I said loudly,

'Just a minute.' Back at the car, I asked, 'What's the matter?'

John was already asleep, his colleague looked up and said, 'Nothing, why?'

'Didn't you call?'

'No,' he replied.

'Funny,' I yawned, 'must have been the wind.'

I woke just after dawn, with a shiver and a bursting bladder.

Standing up, I shook off the sand, rubbed my eyes and stretched stiff limbs in the half-light. I was only partly awake when I saw something odd. About sixty yards away was a truck, or rather the remains of one, and all around it were scattered bits of equipment, dark against the white surface. I walked over to the Chevrolet, for even at this distance I recognized the familiar shape of the LRDG raiding vehicle. The debris consisted of cartridges, grenades, mortar bombs, broken rifles and parts of a machine gun. Thirty feet to one side by a low mound lay a small wooden cross and pieces of splintered wood that had probably been another. Similar vehicles were 'parked' along the rock walls of the pass. Some had engines missing, all appeared to have been blasted apart by a single explosion in the back. A self-destruction charge, I guessed.

Combing the area, we made an interesting discovery high amongst the rocks; a faded canvas British Army haversack, containing a rusty Kodak camera and a toothbrush. Nearby was scattered a pile of empty .303 cartridge cases. I now believe it was here that the LRDG's T Patrol was destroyed by its Italian opposite number, the Auto-Saharan Company based at Kufra. According to W B Kennedy Shaw in his book *Long Range Desert Group* (HarperCollins), a running fight developed on 31 January 1941, when the Italians, with a heavily armed motorized patrol and three aircraft, caught T Patrol advancing on Kufra, in the valley of the Gebel Sherif. Following the battle a New Zealander, Trooper R J Moore and three colleagues had remained undetected amongst the rocks of the waterless hills. Almost everything they needed for survival had been destroyed. They were wounded and all the wells within 200 miles were either in enemy hands or filled with stones. The situation seemed hopeless. However, they managed to salvage a two-gallon tin of water and, scorning any idea of walking a mere eighty miles north-east to surrender at Kufra, they buried the dead, then turned and marched south towards their allies. The Free French Army's positions were known to be several hundred miles away across almost waterless desert. Their remarkable and heroic escape, over an astonishing distance, was typical of the soldiers of one of the finest Special Forces ever raised. Three survived and their leader, Trooper Moore, was found by the French walking steadily after ten days, having marched 210 miles. He was awarded the DCM for his leadership and courage.

We tidied up the grave, re-erected the crosses, saluted, stood silent for a moment and drove off towards Kufra. I reported the matter in Benghazi and later heard that the Imperial War Graves Commission had visited the site. But I never discovered the origin of the strange voice.

Since childhood my godparents, Lord and Lady Forester, had encouraged my adventurous spirit with tales of big-game hunting and excitement in distant lands. Cecil Forester had commanded the Royal Horse Guards. When I asked him the origin of the German Maxim gun, mounted at Willey Hall, he always smiled and just said 'Something my regiment picked up in the Great War.' After his death I learned he had captured it single-handed. He had lived a wonderful life in the days of the Empire, hitch-hiking from Cape to Cairo, exploring the Congo and, above all, devoting himself to the service of others. He was much respected in Shropshire, where he helped many and pursued his hobbies as a naturalist and sportsman. He lived out his final years in the other land he loved – Africa – and finally died peacefully in Rhodesia in 1977. The patience and understanding this kindly man showed me as a small scruffy schoolboy were to be a lasting inspiration.

During World War II the Foresters had been hospitable to His Imperial Majesty, Haile Selassie, Emperor of Ethiopia, during his exile in Britain. The Emperor never forgot this kindness and thus a door was opened that changed my life. When my godfather wrote requesting his support for a Sandhurst expedition, there followed four highly adventurous visits to this little-known land of mountains, bush and desert.

Meanwhile I continued with my other duties at Sandhurst. Cadets were first given theoretical tactics training in the model rooms, where toy tanks and symbolized units could be moved about with little chance of making some costly and irrevocable error. It was here that I was the unwitting perpetrator of a near disaster. The chief instructor was to lecture on the nuclear battle and asked if I could make a miniature atomic bomb that could be exploded on the model.

'Certainly,' I replied, 'a small charge of powder fired electrically should do the trick.' So, pouring the contents of army fireworks known as thunderflashes into a flowerpot, I disguised it with a paper house and connected it by cable to a switch on the lectern. I explained the firing procedure to the delighted chief instructor, who felt sure it would impress several visiting officers. I wedged a round tin lid firmly in the top of the flowerpot in case anyone should knock it over before it was required, and I instructed the clerk to remove this obstruction before the lecture. Unhappily he was taken ill on the day.

When some seventy officers and cadets had seated themselves on the tiers of chairs overlooking the cloth model, the chief instructor began. 'Before you, gentlemen, you see the 1st Battalion, the Loamshires, and their vehicles,' he stated, indicating a cluster of Dinky toy tanks and plastic symbols. 'They are holding this ridge,' he continued, his pointer stabbing at a sausage-shaped bump, where the hessian had been raised with balls of newspaper. 'The enemy, the Fantasian Army, are here,' he went on, dumping a pile of ominous looking red tanks at the edge of the model. 'They may use nuclear weapons at any moment.'

Allowing the full impact of his words to sink in, he paused before pressing the firing button. The effect was devastating. With a blinding flash and a deafening bang, the innocuous looking 'village' in the centre of the battlefield exploded. Cadets were struck by a barrage of toy tanks and plastic soldiers. Shrapnel from the flowerpot peppered the audience and the colonel seated in the front row had the fluff scorched off his battledress trousers by the resultant fireball, which also singed the black labrador curled up at his feet. A mushroom cloud of white smoke rose quickly to the ceiling, then, like atomic fall-out, descended, choking the shell-shocked spectators. Coughing and spluttering, cadets hurled open windows, the dog fled and the stand-in model room clerk, a civilian of timid appearance but with unquestionable initiative, seized a stirrup pump and extinguished the burning hessian. It was ten minutes before the smoke cleared sufficiently to allow the lecture to continue. There can be no doubt that the demonstration was a success, but I was not asked to repeat the performance.

Sandhurst encompassed every conceivable type of activity. One of my responsibilities was the pistol club, where I was able to teach aspiring marksmen. An aspect of the training was the combat course, which was designed to enable cadets to engage fleeting targets under battle conditions. It was extremely realistic and one of the noted shots was a young man called David Bromhead, whose acute accuracy was to be useful on many occasions.

Preparations for the 1964 Ethiopian expedition were progressing well. Cadets were trained to catch and preserve various scientific specimens. Under the direction of Natural History Museum staff we pursued adders and grass-snakes over Army training areas and caught small rodents in box traps. One over-enthusiastic cadet, trying to anaesthetize a shrew held by a colleague, drove the hypodermic needle clean through the animal and paralysed his friend's arm for several hours.

In early August we set out. One party, which included a number of overseas cadets, went ahead on the first available RAF aircraft.

It flew to Aden in South Yemen, leaving the rest of us to follow a week later. In spite of the impending arrival of Emma Jane, Judith was determined to come with me. The Aden brigade commander offered to find useful employment for the early arrivals and despatched them up country to see some action.

At one small fort a group of dissidents opened fire from the hills. As the garrison took posts, bullets pinged and ricochetted amongst the stone sangars. The range was at least 1,000 yards and no one could see the enemy. Suddenly the machine-gun on the watchtower opened up with uncanny accuracy, flushing the tribesmen from their position and sending them scampering away amongst the rocks.

'Jolly fine shooting,' commended the commanding officer, who happened to be visiting. 'Who's on the gun?'

'A Sandhurst cadet,' replied the company commander.

'Must congratulate him,' said the colonel, climbing the tower. Reaching the platform where the cadet lay behind the machine-gun, he said, 'Glad to see they're teaching you to shoot so well at Sandhurst.'

'Thank you, sir,' murmured the cadet turning about. His ebony face and flashing teeth set in a broad grin.

Slightly taken aback, the CO asked, 'Which regiment are you joining?'

'Oh,' smiled the young man. 'I'm not in the British Army.'

Arriving in Aden a few days later, I was greeted by an impressive array of rather worried staff officers, who hastened to explain the terrible oversight that had caused them to employ a member of another army in the cause of what local propaganda would call 'British Imperialism'. I promised to talk to the cadet.

'Oh! I enjoyed it,' smiled the African when I explained the problem, 'but our President will never know!' He then added rather wistfully, 'I suppose I can't get the campaign medal now?'

In Addis Ababa I found my godfather's letter had paved the way and we were invited to the royal palace. His Imperial Majesty stood erect behind his desk. One by one we entered and shook his outstretched hand, murmuring 'Votre Majesté', and giving a short, formal bow. There was something very powerful about the tiny figure, who could only have been just over five feet tall. His alert, brown eyes seemed to penetrate my innermost thought. Not a man to be misled, I felt. Closely-cropped wavy hair led down to a grey moustache and a short, neat beard. His skin, a light brown, was paler than many of his countrymen. Described as the mouse with the jaws of a lion, his gentle, kindly appearance did not deceive me.

I knew I was standing before one of the most supreme Christian warrior kings the world had ever known.

'How is your godfather?' The soft voice and perfect English took me by surprise.

'Very well, Your Majesty, and he sends you his good wishes,' I spluttered.

'He has a beautiful house in Shropshire. Are the rhododendrons in flower?' mused the Emperor. I was amazed how much he remembered of his stay at Willey Park. 'What do you wish of me?' he enquired, becoming more formal and addressing us through his interpreter.

'Permission to collect scientific specimens in your country, Your Majesty,' I replied.

His answer in Amharic was made without waiting for the interpreter to translate. 'His Imperial Majesty says it shall be so and he will send with you a liaison officer from his army.'

We bowed out of his presence. Outside one of the cadets muttered, 'Well, he's the nearest thing I've ever seen to a deity.'

Captain Marcos Berhanu Haile sat silently beside me in the early morning as we bumped over the water-filled potholes on our way south. Leaving the city behind, we came to open country. Marcos slipped a shining revolver from beneath his greatcoat and held it in his lap.

'Expecting trouble?' I asked.

'In this country I always expect trouble,' he replied ominously, but by evening we had seen nothing worse than several bad traffic accidents. There were few vehicles on the gravel roads, but the previous week Ethiopia had changed to driving on the right. It appeared that only half the drivers had heard the news!

After two days the road reached the town of Soddu. Here we refuelled and drove down into the rift valley. I hoped the road would take us towards the Kenya border, but our information was poor and I had been unable to discover how far it actually went. We did not have to wait long for the answer. Quite suddenly the gravel surface deteriorated and our heavily laden one-ton Land-Rover supply truck came to a grinding halt, axle-deep in mud. It took half an hour's pushing, shoving and towing to free it from the grip of the black cotton soil. Then another vehicle got stuck, then another. Local villagers looked on in amazement. They could not understand why we should make so much effort to press on – around the next bend was the impassable Hamasa River in full flood.

We camped in a small clearing near the road, where a stream flowed down to Lake Abaya and from here began our exploration of the rift valley. The Hamasa had still to be crossed so we attempted to build a raft. Alas, the available wood was too heavy and the device would not even support one man. There were crocodiles nearby and we learned that two Italians had been swept away in the swift currents recently. It was therefore with some trepidation that we piled our clothes and rifles on our heads and, clutching a fixed line, inched our way through the rapids. Marching into the bush on the far side we soon found tracks of lion, pig, antelope and hyena. Splitting into small parties we each took an area of country-side and began to seek the animals that the Museum had listed.

Mid-afternoon we spied a greater kudu browsing a quarter of a mile away. A short, easy stalk got me to within 200 yards. It was not possible to get closer so, taking careful aim, I sent a high velocity round crashing down the valley.

Breathless, I reached the antelope. It was down but not dead. Oh, hell! I thought. Why did I have to shoot it at all? My second bullet killed it instantly and, in order to take a perfect skin for the museum we worked with great care. It was not a pleasant sight and soon the trees around us were heavy with hideous black vultures. Various parts of the body were required to be retained and the skull was removed intact. Inside the beast we discovered a complete foetus, apparently of considerable biological value, which we preserved in formalin in a large plastic tub. Finally we cut a haunch for our supper and then stood back to allow the vultures to clean up. Carrying the bloody items back across the Hamasa that night was a little worrying. Crocodiles were supposed to go for blood!

The local governor, His Excellency Wolde-Semait Gabre Wolde, was a most progressive man. Educated in Britain, he was striving to build up the province and with determination and energy seemed to be doing a good job. He was always helpful and so I was delighted to be able to do something for him. 'There's a lion killing the cattle near here,' he told us. 'I should be grateful if you could get rid of it.'

So that afternoon we drove to the area and met a local guide. Dressed in a blue sports jacket and loincloth, he also wore a large gold ear-ring, indicating that he had killed a lion single-handed. Following him closely, we soon came on fresh spoor, which led into dense bush. Marcos and I were ahead with the guide. Two cadets, David Bromhead and Andrew Penny, were ten yards behind us.

We reached some thick bushes, from which came the sound of a low cough and the guide gesticulated wildly, pointing and shouting, 'Oola. Oola!' I could see nothing, nor could Marcos. Turning, I made a silent sign to David to discover what was happening. As if to answer, he flung up his rifle and, at the same moment, a great yellow shape leapt over me! 'What on earth...' I gasped.

'A bloody great lioness,' replied David. 'She looked round one side of the bush, whilst you looked round the other.'

The guide and Marcos were already in pursuit, but our quarry had disappeared and, after a fruitless search, we headed back to our Land-Rover.

'Look on the track!' whispered David. We stood rooted to the spot. For there, by the vehicle, lay the lioness, stretched full-length in the evening sun. A few feet away in the grass two cubs played. Cunning old thing, I thought, she's doubled back. I raised my rifle, but the sight of this beautiful beast and her young was too much. We sat down cursing that no one had a camera. Even Marcos, an experienced hunter, agreed we should not kill her, so we decided to have a cigarette and then, if she had not moved, we would try to out-flank her and reach the Land-Rover.

But suddenly a shepherd boy appeared strolling nonchalantly up the path towards us, oblivious of the great cat obscured from his view. Jumping up, Marcos yelled. 'Ambessa, ambessa!' The boy stopped with an expression of surprise. He saw nothing wrong and then, peering round the Land-Rover, caught a glimpse of the hind quarters of the lioness. Like a Walt Disney character, he leapt with one bound into a tree and scrambled to its highest and rather precarious branch. The lioness eyed him with mild interest.

'Keep together, safety-catches off, and we'll walk towards her,' I said, trying to sound confident. We were twenty-five yards away – which is not far when one remembers a charging lion can do 100 yards in four seconds – before she moved. Then, with a yawn, she stood up and ambled to the roadside. The guide flung up his rifle, but luckily his shot was wild and in a flash the lioness and her cubs had gone.

'You are extraordinary people,' said the governor, shaking his head sadly. 'How would you feel about killing a fox in England that had taken all your chickens and left you with nothing to eat for four months?' I felt like explaining the British attitude to foxes, but we apologized for our failure and went out to cull some bush pigs that were destroying crops. No one minds shooting an ugly beast!

The thorn scrub was teeming with pig. I managed to get close to one small herd and shot a good eating-size sow, when unfortunately the bush around erupted with pigs, running in every direction in mad panic. Tek Negussie, a handsome Ethiopian cadet, pushed Judith up a tree to save her from one – a deed which she has never forgotten and, as a result, regards all Ethiopians with the uttermost gratitude. Elsewhere, Marcos had shot, in the nick of time, a monster boar that had ambushed him and our other lady, Kay Thompson. Kay, ever intrepid, was left sitting on the carcass with Marcos's pistol while he went for assistance to carry the beast out. He was gone several hours, night fell, and the pig twitched once or twice, but she was still sitting on it when we eventually reached her. She did admit to smoking several cigarettes!

There was one part of our mission that was of great importance. The British Museum had charged us to find Osgood's swamp rat. Only one specimen of this strange black-and-white rodent had ever been collected and this was kept in America. The Museum badly wanted one of their own. Pictures of the creature were reproduced and distributed all over the suspected locality, near Lake Tana, North of Addis Ababa. Through the driving rain of the wet season, we headed up into the highlands. Around us, the bleak plateau was populated by tall, proud Amharas, who lived in neat, round tukuls.

The only real break in the scenery came at Shafartak, when we reached the Blue Nile Gorge and in the space of three miles dropped 4,000 feet. Lunching at the bottom, we watched the Blue Nile, heavy with brown silt, swirling by beneath the bridge. Climbing back on to the plateau, we drove to Debra Marcos, the capital of the province of Gojjam. There we were guests at the governor's palace and were treated to gigantic feast of raw meat, enjerra and wat. Enjerra, the traditional unleavened bread, has the appearance and consistency of a dirty rubber bath mat. The wat is a very hot meat sauce. The Ethiopians believe that by adding peppery spices to the raw meat it will cook in your stomach!

Dressed in tweed jacket and cavalry twill trousers, the governor plied us with Black Label whisky. That night I lay awake listening to raw meat and Scotch churning over in my stomach and also in Judith's! 'What did you think of the Blue Nile?' I asked her.

'Not very blue' was her sleepy reply.

'No one has ever really explored it, you know. There are supposed to be some terrible rapids and the world's most aggressive crocodiles.' She yawned. 'I wonder if it could be navigated with rubber dinghies,' I mused. Judith was already asleep.

Our base camp was set up in a community centre by the Piccolo Abbai River, said to be the origin of the Blue Nile or Great Abbai, and it was to here that the local people came in response to our offer of fifteen dollars reward for an Osgood's swamp rat. We combed the countryside, laid hundreds of traps and dealt with dozens of snakes, antelopes, small mammals and birds that were brought daily to our camp. Many were interesting and we purchased these, but there was no sign of Osgood. We had failed and felt miserable about it.

One day I awoke as dawn was breaking to hear something rustling in the corner of our cell-like room. Sliding the heavy Smith & Wesson from its holster on the bedpost, I levelled it at a biscuit packet in the corner. Maybe a cobra, I thought – one had been seen near the building. The roar of the revolver in the confined space was deafening. Judith shot up with a yell and a surprised rat hopped out of the biscuits. Alas, it was not Osgood's and the bullet, penetrating the wall, ricochetted down the corridor giving the expedition a rude awakening.

On Lake Tana our fishermen had been very successful and made a fine collection. Our dispirited band of rat-catchers needed an outing, so we all went up to Bahadar, partly to fish, but also to view the great falls of Tisisat, where the Blue Nile tumbles 150 feet into its canyon. The mist thrown up by the falls may be seen for miles, hence the name Tisisat – 'smoke of fire'. I watched the great river cascade over the polished black basalt with a mighty roar, while a fish eagle called and brightly-coloured birds flitted amongst the luxuriant green growth swaying gently in the drifting clouds of spray.

The power and majesty was awe-inspiring. 'I know what you're thinking," said Judith, who had been watching me.

'Do you?' I smiled, adding slowly, 'It might be possible with rubber boats.'

On returning to England, we took our specimens to the Museum. Everyone was delighted with them and I had just started to apologize for our failure to obtain Osgood's swamp rat, when the mammalogist cut in. 'After you left, we looked into the question of Osgood rather more carefully and we've decided that the rat he discovered in Ethiopia is exactly the same as one that is found in the Congo, so it isn't really a rarity after all. It was just an unusual distribution.' I stared in blank amazement. How could I tell him of the days and weeks spent searching every inch of the swampy marshland! How could he understand our feelings of failure at not discovering the bloody rat?

Ethiopia had some hidden tricks that did not emerge until after we had returned, when eight of us went sown with malaria in spite of taking the regular dose of Paludrine. Nevertheless, the expedition was highly successful and I immediately began planning a follow-up. The following year I had to do my staff college exam, but in 1966 I could perhaps get beyond the Hamasa.

The Sandhurst Expedition of 1966 was designed to be a joint-service venture. Over fifty officer cadets and scientists of many nations would take part in a study of the archaeology, veterinary and zoological aspects of the rift valley between the Hamasa River and the Kenya border. We would leave after the summer term.

As adventure training officer this was my busiest term. Twenty expeditions were going off and as their departure grew nearer, so the urgency for administrative arrangements to be finalized increased. My office grew chaotic as cadets staggered in and out with animal traps, underwater equipment, mountaineering gear, rifles and mosquito nets. There was very often a good piece for the local press and the Camberley News often rang on Monday mornings to enquire if there were any interesting stories. On one particular day I had to confess that nothing special had happened in the previous week. As I was speaking my yellow Labrador, Kinder, waddled in. To my amazement, she was carrying a stuffed mongoose in her mouth. On the telephone, the reporter was pleading, 'Are you sure there is nothing we can write about?'

'Well, my dog has just brought in a stuffed mongoose.' I said, laughing.

'Where did she get it and what does it look like?' he asked. He was most anxious to photograph the unusual sight, admitting that they were very short of news. The idiotic dog, terribly pleased with herself, continued to waddle round and round the office, snorting. The reporter and a photographer duly arrived and took copious pictures of Kinder parading on the lawns. I had no idea where she had found this trophy – probably in a dustbin. 'What are you going to do with it?' he asked.

'Oh! I'll probably stick it up on the training area and teach cadets how to recognize different animals,' I joked.

When I returned from an overseas trip a week later, our public relations officer (PRO) greeted me in great excitement and explained that, following the Camberley News story of my dog and the mongoose, almost all the national press now wished to descend on Sandhurst and photograph the expedition in a mock jungle. They supposed that I would have sewn the woods with a liberal quantity of stuffed animals.

'But I only said that as a joke?' I protested.

'Never mind. But now you must carry it out. It will be a wonderful thing for Sandhurst,' ordered the PRO.

For several weeks I searched desperately for stuffed animals and, in the end, all I had was a leopard's head, a pair of pottos and the mongoose. It was a warm Sunday afternoon when the media descended en masse. I had laid on all sorts of interesting demonstrations. A special raft was constructed to ferry a Land-Rover over the lake. A light mortar fired a line and grapnel into the dense vegetation on one of the islands, demonstrating how to get a rope over a crocodile-infested river. The fact that the grapnel broke away from its cable and landed in Camberley was fortunately overlooked. But my efforts were all to no avail, they simply wanted photographs of the stuffed animal safari. We duly obliged and bewildered cadets crawled through the trees looking for the leopard and the pottos.

The following Monday almost every national newspaper gave it wide coverage, which strangely the staff at Sandhurst regarded as a good thing to enhance the Army's image! Also, to my great surprise, funds began to come in, helping to make the expedition solvent. So perhaps Kinder's mongoose had been worthwhile after all. And I'd learned that in the silly season the press love an unusual tale!

The plan was to make the expedition main base in the rift valley at the southern end of Lake Abaya, near the developing town of Arba Minch. At this point, the valley is extremely narrow and clearly defined. It is almost exactly 4,000 feet above sea level, with mountains rising in steps on either side to a height of over 13,000 feet. It contained many lakes, swamps and areas of dense jungle, and in 1964 I had noticed that the flora changed rapidly with altitude. The new expedition was going to encounter areas of scrub, grassland, rain forests and, in the highest regions, a topography not unlike Dartmoor.

Reliable weather information was scarce, but I made plans to deal with the worst situation, where ; heavy rain on the mountains causes a rapid rise in the water level of the many rivers that flowed into the lake. The only motor track in the valley ran from north to south along the west side of Lake Abaya, and was dissected by numerous rivers. One of these was the Hamasa.

It was clear that we would have considerable engineering problems and so I appointed Officer Cadet Bill Bullock as the 'chief engineer' and he formed a small team of potential sapper officers. One way to get the vehicles across the river was to fit flotation bags to their sides. These could be pumped up by a device fitted to the exhaust system. The disadvantage of this method was the vulnerability of the bags and the fact that the wheels of the vehicle hung down into the river and could catch on boulders or rocks beneath. I also investigated something called the Bubble. This consisted of a fabric hemisphere connected by a trunk to an industrial compressor, which filled it to slightly above atmospheric pressure and caused it to hover. A vehicle could be suspended on wire strops inside the Bubble and, provided some directional force could be applied, it should be able to cross rivers. However, the problem was where to put the compressor and, although this method was considered seriously, we felt the need for more research and development before taking a Bubble to Africa. There were various swimming vehicles, including an amphibious Land-Rover with a boat-shaped hull, driven along by a propeller running off the rear differential. Inflatable bags gave additional buoyancy, but once again the wheels hung down in the water to catch snags. It was also extremely difficult to get it out of the river and up a steep bank.

Finally we turned to the well-tried idea of a raft. There were various methods involving oil-drums, ground-sheets stuffed with grass and even tarpaulins wrapped right around the vehicles. Boats were too bulky to carry and so I managed to persuade the Daimler Company to build us a light, air-portable raft of fibreglass and polyurethane. This was designed by Bill and the material only weighed two pounds per cubic foot. With its cellular construction, it floated well. The raft consisted of five pontoons made up of the polythene blocks bolted together and coated with a strong, fibreglass skin. Wheel channels were moulded on top, outriggers were fitted to either side, connected to the structure by reinforced fibreglass tubes. It was designed to carry a laden, quarter-ton Land-Rover plus three people. Ramps were made of hard wood. The raft could be carried on the roof of two Land-Rovers and assembled in forty-five minutes by six people. Light-weight nylon rope, aluminium anchorages and blocks enabled it to be used as a ferry.

The sixty-strong team that set out in July 1966 included a zoologist, a young vet and a doctor, who specialized in gynaecology! In the field we were joined by an escort of some fifteen local police. The bulk of the stores and vehicles had come over from the army-base in Aden.

To our relief we found that the rains at the Hamasa River had not been heavy, and the vehicles crossed the wide ford with little difficulty. In the late afternoon of the second day we established our base camp as planned beside the Lake. The weather was excellent, with a noon temperature in the eighties and no sign of rain. But the mosquitoes devoured us at night.

We had been in the camp for a few days when, to our amazement, a certain officer cadet strolled in. He had missed the plane in England, having overslept, and we had left without him. On his own initiative, he had got himself to Aden, had hitched a lift across the Red Sea on a dhow and had come by rail to Addis Ababa. There he had managed to beg some money from the Defence Attache and had flown to Arba Minch. Along the way he had discarded almost all that he had, except one of the special water filter pumps with which he was entrusted. It was a splendid show of initiative and I forgave him for his late arrival!

From our base we explored the rift valley, and usually found the people friendly. However, we were once confronted with what might have been a nasty situation. We had camped near a large village. Supper had been served when suddenly the silence was broken by the sound of drums. In a flash, Negussie was on his feet and disappeared into the surrounding bush. The noise got louder. He returned and whispered 'I'm not happy, the last white men they saw were the Italians, who dropped the chief out of an aeroplane over the village. We must find out what is happening. Will you come with me?'

Clutching our rifles, we set off into the night. I earned a quick rebuke when I tripped, but most of our sounds were drowned by the thunder of the drums. Clearly the villagers were getting worked up. At the stockade, leaving the police corporal and myself to cover him, he went forward to the gate. Through the fence we could see a huge fire burning with half-naked figures leaping about and jumping through the flames. Around them the crowd ululated and the drums beat faster and faster. Negussie paused for a moment listening intently. He came from the north and I doubted he would understand the language. Like most Ethiopian officers, he was smartly dressed and even when working for long hours, in the rain and the mud, always managed to look as if he had just come off parade. Suddenly we saw him push open the gate and stride in. The drums stopped at once and the ululating ceased. He held up his hand, his pistol still in its holster. I could understand a little of what he was saying. 'I am an officer of the Emperor. His Imperial Majesty's friends are camping near here. What is all this noise about?'

A wizened elder in a leopard's skin shambled forward and in a whining, pleading voice talked for several minutes. Eventually Negussie nodded, said something in Amharic, turned and strode out of the compound. At once the drums thundered louder than ever and the ululating began again. I thought it a pretty cool act for, had they been hostile, he wouldn't have lasted long.

'It's all right,' he smiled, 'they're having a celebration for the return of their chief, who is expected back tonight with a new wife.' This was not the only time that Negussie's courage impressed me. Early one morning he came with Bill and me to examine the shores of Lake Abaya. It was barely light when we left camp and at the water's edge walked out along a partly-finished jetty to get a better view. I led the way. We carried oddments of reconnaissance kit as we hopped from the top of one timber pile to the next, never more than a couple of feet above the water. Almost at the end of the jetty I saw what I thought was a tyre, with the tread just on the surface of the water.

'Is that a tyre or could it be a crocodile?' I asked. As if to answer, Negussie used a surveyor's pole to press down in the centre of the object. It sank without movement, and bobbed up again. A tyre, we all thought, and took another pace forward. At that moment, he repeated the process. With a crash a leviathan rose from the depths. It was just like St George's dragon! The tail came crashing round splintering the timber just beneath my feet. At the same time it launched itself at Negussie, who, being extremely agile, leapt to the top of a convenient pile. The beast then turned on me and with his mouth wide open, displaying serried lines of yellowing teeth, tried to get my leg. In one hand I held my rifle and in the other a theodolite. There was no time to aim. Flicking the safety catch off with my thumb, I thrust the weapon into the gaping mouth and pulled the trigger. The jaws closed about the barrel as the gun went off. Blood spurted at me, and at that moment the others pumped more shots. Bullets flew everywhere and, with an awful gurgling sound, the slimy beast slid back into the black water.

'Grab it,' yelled Negussie, and seized the tail. It took us nearly an hour to get the carcass ashore and carry it to camp in triumph. It was a lesson I'm not likely to forget. Crocodiles will very often attack after you have stepped over them and not when you are about to.

The scientific work was going well. The zoologists captured and preserved a great number of species, including fish, snakes and many large mammals. The field laboratory had the appearance of a witch's cave. The collection of smaller animals was also growing steadily. Indeed in the world of zoology these were probably more important because they were less known. Everyone who had a spare moment was sent out to catch frogs, toads, mice and rats.

We had located an isolated area of grassland alive with large game. Behind it rose a steep escarpment, and on the other side was the lake, while elsewhere swamps and rivers cut it off from the rest of the country. It was part of our programme to survey new areas for wildlife conservation, which included this district. To get there we had to cross a difficult little river called the Cullufu. The raft was quickly constructed and we were about to ferry a vehicle across, when downstream, some hundred yards away, a large herd of cattle had come to water. Suddenly the cattle gave startled tongue and scrambled back up the bank, as the herdsmen rushed down, screaming and waving spears. I was mystified. What was wrong? The centre of attention seemed to be a great white bramah bull, now standing with its tall heavy horns raised at the water's edge. His legs were set deep in the mud and he seemed to be struggling to draw something out of the river. The muscles of his powerful body contorted in effort.

'He's got something in his mouth,' gasped a cadet. Through binoculars I saw there was something, but it was not in the bull's mouth, it was round it – the jaws of a huge crocodile. Remorselessly the reptile was dragging the animal into the river. I put up my rifle but, with the demented herdsman dashing round the struggling beast, dared not fire. If we crossed the river, we might have saved it, but the sight of the massive croc did not encourage quick dips. While we watched impotently, the reptile won the dreadful tug of war and, with its thick, squat legs working like pistons and its scaly tail thrashing the water into foam, pulled its victim into the shallows. Suddenly the bull was down and, still kicking frantically as the froth turned red, it disappeared in the turbid brown stream. The rest we could imagine. The croc would place the carcass in its underground lair or beneath a rock on the riverbed until it had putrefied sufficiently for its liking.

A rare species of mongoose was believed to exist several days' match from the end of the road and I decided to leave the Land-Rovers and proceed on foot. Two army drivers would remain with them and I guessed that as soon as we disappeared they would indulge in an orgy of sunbathing and drinking. To keep them gainfully occupied I handed out two large plastic tubs and indicated a nearby mosquito-ridden swamp.

'The British Museum is in urgent need of small green frogs. By the time I return I expect these to be full,' I said.

'Sir,' they replied in a tone verging on dumb insolence.

Three days later I marched into camp and, as expected, the soldiers were dozing in the shade. 'Frogs,' I bellowed.

'In tub,' said one.

To my astonishment both containers were crammed with writhing green frogs. 'How on earth did you do it?'

'Oh, was nuffin really, just a bit of hard work,' they replied with assumed modesty.

My opinion of these two rogues mellowed and I recommended them for promotion! It was long after the expedition that I discovered their method. They would go to a native village with a copy of Playboy. As soon as the local men had gathered round, they would open the centre pages and permit a quick peep and then say 'Three frogs, one look'. Thus encouraged, the natives would rush off to collect as many frogs as they could to earn another look.

The expedition over, we had to get all our zoological specimens back to England. Although we had done our best to preserve them, the presence of some large, slightly putrefying reptiles in a hot, stuffy aeroplane en route from Aden to UK did not endear us to the RAF, and one of the planes had to make an unscheduled landing at Malta when the stench became overpowering. There can't be many pilots who can claim to have been forced down by a crocodile!

We returned via Addis Ababa, where we were greatly honoured to receive an invitation to meet His Imperial Majesty once again. The invitation was extended to everybody, and I wondered whether the court realised just how many of us there were. In Ethiopia protocol demands one bows to the Emperor three times. Once when you enter, again halfway up the red carpet and finally when right before him. On leaving his presence one repeats the process in reverse. No problem, you may think, for well-drilled officer cadets, but Haile Selassie had a population of lions roaming the throne room and I could imagine a terrible incident that might result if a cadet, walking backwards, should fall over one of the royal beasts. I consulted Tommy, an Ethiopian working at the British Embassy, who gave me the solution.

'You will notice,' he said, 'that we cast ourselves down very low when bowing to the Emperor, pressing our foreheads upon the carpet.'

'Steady on,' I said, 'we're British you know – a stiff little bow is all that is usually required.'

'I'm not suggesting you be obsequious,' replied Tommy, 'but if you cast yourself down low you can look between your legs and see the lions lurking behind you.' By this means sixty officer cadets and two ladies in skirts successfully entered and left the presence of His Imperial Majesty.

4

.

The Everest of Rivers

The Emperor's eyes twinkled. 'I should like you to explore my Great Abbai,' he said in a firm, quiet voice. Who knows what animals and minerals you might find there?'

This was like asking an average hill walker to climb Everest.

Playing for time I replied, 'I will look into the possibilities, Your Imperial Majesty.'

Back in Britain I was posted to the Royal Military College of Science at Shrivenham to do fifteen months' technical training. The fiery commandant, Major General Napier Crookenden, had heard of the Emperor's request. 'Quite a challenge, good for morale, just what the Army needs,' he enthused. 'Of course we must do it. We'll need a committee. I'll be Chairman and you can be Secretary. I see no need for anyone else.' So Haile Selassie's challenge was accepted and I embarked on the expedition that changed my life.

The infamous Blue Nile, or Great Abbai River, cuts a 5,000 feet deep gorge through the highlands of Ethiopia, forcing its way through the mountain wilderness to spill out into the sun-soaked plains of the Sudan. Until 1968 this sinister canyon had remained virtually unknown, although the actual source of the great river is a spring that bubbles up in a bog south of Lake Tana.

The first Briton to view this source was the adventurer, James Bruce. Visiting Ethiopia in 1771 he wrote of 'people who anointed themselves not with bear's grease or pomatum, but with the blood of cows, who instead of playing tunes upon them wore the entrails of animals as ornaments and who, instead of eating hog meat, licked their lips over bleeding living flesh'. For my part, whilst seeking Osgood's elusive swamp rat, I had tramped many miles and been eaten alive by mosquitoes in this region.

For its first eighteen miles after Lake Tana, the Blue Nile is wide and shallow, flowing through swampy water-meadows and around numerous islands. But there are long stretches of dangerous white water and several small waterfalls. At Tisisat the river suddenly drops with a thunderous booming over the second-biggest falls in Africa. There, the huge volume of water is compressed into the narrow sheer-sided gorge and, for almost a hundred miles the torrent races through this cleft before the valley opens out. However, the river is still at the bottom of a great gutter in the Ethiopian Highlands and 10,000 feet above it towers the cloud-swathed Mount Choke. From here on, the river alternates between rocky cataracts, dangerous shallows and stretches of flat water populated by hippo and large, aggressive crocodiles.

As far as I could find out, the first attempt at navigation was made in 1902 by an American big-game hunter with three especially designed steel boats. After only three miles these were swamped in a cataract and the expedition abandoned. In 1905, a Swede called Jesson came upstream from the Sudan. He only got his boat as far as the Azir River, where he met hostile natives and retreated.

In 1926, Major R E Cheeseman, the British consul in North West Ethiopia, tried to follow the course of the river by foot. His survey work was invaluable but, due to great difficulty experienced in moving along the banks, he was soon forced up onto the high plateau. In 1955, Herbert Rittlinger and his wife, with a small party of Germans, attempted to canoe down the river. They had with them a number of ladies who, by all accounts, were rather attractive and liked to paddle along in the nude. However, crocodiles are no respecters of persons. Their canoes were attacked and the party driven from the river.

One of the best organised expeditions was mounted in 1962 by the Canoe Club of Geneva. Six experienced canoeists set out in two large Canadian-style boats. They started, as many have, from the bridge at Shafartak and after much effort reached a point near the Sudan border. There they camped on an island and whilst asleep were fired on by bandits. Two died but the rest escaped in one canoe. The next attempt was by Arne Rubin who became the first man to travel along the Blue Nile from Shafartak to Rosiares. During our research, we corresponded with this plucky Swede, who, in

1965, had navigated this stretch in a Kleeper canoe, alone! It was a splendid achievement. The next year, he returned with a friend to attempt the upper reaches of the river, but after fifty miles of hair-raising adventure their canoe was smashed on jagged rocks in the Northern Gorge and they had to walk out.

There have been other expeditions; in March 1968, a small British team, attempting the river in rubber boats, came to grief early on after the bottoms had been torn off their craft. It was a salutary warning, and I realised that if one were to navigate this river it must be done when there was plenty of water.

None of the previous explorers had been able to examine the banks or carry out any scientific research, so we hoped that our expedition would be of value both to science and to the people of the region.

Much of this fearsome river was unmapped and there was little reliable local knowledge, but on an early reconnaissance visit to Ethiopia I met numerous 'experts', who had told me some of the elements of mystery that surrounded it.

There was said to be a great swamp, alive with crocodiles – *Crocodylus niloticus*, the most terrible man-eater of all Africa! Had not the Queen of Sheba sought the advice of Solomon because of the depredations of a monster croc? And it was a fact that an Austrian gentleman had recently been seized by one of these powerful reptiles and dragged down into the Nile, bleeding and screaming, under the eyes of his wife. The crocodiles were said to reach ten metres in length, but this I considered an exaggeration. However, if there were such giants, where did they hide? Where was the legendary swamp, infested with mosquitoes and leviathans? There were many who told tales of radioactive gas, claiming that the intense sun heated the black basalt so much that radioactive vapours oozed out and, being heavier than air, dropped to the bottom of the canyon. There the gas was thought to collect in pockets, bringing a slow death to every living thing it touched. Animal corpses were reported to have been found in such places. If the Blue Nile Gorge had such gas, might it have radioactive minerals? Were there great deposits of uranium awaiting discovery?

Geologists told of extensive lakes being formed when landslides of rock, loosened by erosion and earthquake, crashed into the river, forming instant dams and creating waterfalls over which a frightening volume of water cascaded, making it totally unnavigable. Yet if valuable minerals were present in the gorge, it would be extremely useful if mining companies could use the river for transport.

Doubtless this thought had occurred to the Emperor when he asked us to explore it. Apparently wildlife was plentiful and dangerous. As well as giant crocs, there were rumours of huge leopards, and the lions, Ethiopia's national beast, were said to be the largest in Africa. Herds of buffalo and elephant were reported to abound to such an extent that the Ethiopian Wildlife Department was eager to see if there really was a mysterious untouched natural nature reserve.

Snakes were another hazard. One especially venomous species, a small grey viper with a bite producing a neuro-toxin that caused immediate paralysis and painful death, was thought to be present, in millions! Local hunters advised that we should wear strong breaches and high leather boots whilst smearing our legs with an ointment of dubbin and tar! I had come across an island in a swamp near Lake Tana in 1964 on which we'd captured several dozen little grey snakes so perhaps there was something to this tale. Giant pythons were said to thrive in the Northern Gorge and an earlier explorer had apparently grabbed one by the tail in error whilst following a path beneath the Tisisat Falls.

The legend of the Queen of Sheba popped up all the time. It was said that following the First World War, an ex-Royal Engineers officer had discovered an amazing cave system full of gems that could only be reached by overcoming a forceful underground river. The Ethiopians are well-known for carving churches and dwellings from solid rock and one tale told of a 'lost' tribe of white people living in a subterranean town, somewhere in the gorge. There were also stories of apemen who attacked travellers. Everyone talked of the canyon as the home of the most murderous bandits, and several travellers reported hearing spine-chilling screams echoing about within the walls during the hours of darkness.

My friends at the Natural History Museum reckoned that hippos might be the greatest threat. 'Give them a wide berth my boy,' cautioned one scientist.

'How far away should we be?' I asked.

'Oh! About a quarter of a mile,' he suggested. As the river is rarely more than 150 yards wide in its upper reaches, this would not be easy.

'And avoid them in the mating season, they might mistake your rubber boats for an attractive female,' my friend advised. But he wasn't too sure when that would be, and added that he would be grateful for any information on the sex life of the Nile hippo!

The water was said to carry the dreaded bilharzia, which the river brought down from Lake Tana, but no one was sure if it really did exist in the turbulence and that was something else we had been asked to investigate. Rumours of alluvial gold and vast copper deposits all added to the reputation of the area and I wondered why the Ethiopian police had made such an effort to prevent a small British expedition from entering the Northern Gorge. All this only served to heighten my curiosity; there must be something there.

No accurate information on river conditions was available. But as up to eighty inches of rain falls annually in the mountains, mainly in the summer, I expected the Nile would be in flood in August, the level beginning to drop in September. On the plateau the rain would be heavy and vehicle tracks extremely difficult, to say the least. At the higher altitude the temperature would be around 60°F at midday, but down on the gorge bottom it would rise to at least 80°F. We could expect nights in the mountains to be extremely cold but the great advantage of attempting a navigation at this time was that the higher water should cover the rocks.

Chris Bonington, the British mountaineer, who was to accompany us as photo-journalist on behalf of the *Daily Telegraph Magazine* described the area as 'the last unconquered hell on earth' and 'the Everest of Rivers'. This caused some mirth at the time, but we were later to discover that it was not so much of an exaggeration after all.

To organise a scientific investigation of the area presented me with something of a dilemma. It would cost a great deal of money to get the scientists into the difficult region, enable them to work, keep them alive and get them and their specimens out again in one piece. It would also mean sending a lot of people there just to back them up. To get the money, the resources and the necessary assistance for the project we had to catch the imagination of the Army, the press and Industry. At the same time, I would have to recruit servicemen and civilians who understood the needs of the scientists, their idiosyncrasies and demands.

My first recruit was Richard Snailham, a Civilian Lecturer at Sandhurst. I knew him well and found him one of the most amusing and likeable men I had met. It was Richard who was to become the Chief Nilographer, reading up everything he could find about the area and helping to write the prospectuses and begging letters that we put out to gain sponsorship and support. He would also write the official history of the expedition and act as Treasurer.

My second in command was to be Nigel Sale, of the Royal Green Jackets. I believed that this thorough, slightly serious officer would be a good antidote to my own character. One of the most important people would be the Chief Engineer. Here we required not a fresh-faced, Sandhurst-trained subaltern with bags of enthusiasm, but an experienced, bold and imaginative engineer who would be prepared to tackle any obstacle with the minimum of resources and manpower. For this post I selected Jim Masters, a quiet, forty-year old officer from Somerset whom I knew I could depend on at all times. Having served with him in Cyprus I respected his depth of experience and expert knowledge. To lead the White Water Team, I chose Roger Chapman, an instructor at Sandhurst. A Captain in the Green Howards, he possessed boundless vitality and dogged determination. He would have the unenviable task of navigating the most difficult stretches.

In total the team would consist of seventy servicemen and civilians from Britain and Ethiopia and the scientists were to include an archaeologist, an ornithologist, the medical officers and a host of zoologists. I was simply the conductor of a large, highly-motivated orchestra. Now we had to play.

Shrivenham was an ideal place to launch an expedition. Judith and I moved into a tumbledown camp nearby, took over a host of buildings and, together with the amusing Lance Corporal Henry of the Royal Engineers, who had volunteered to accompany me, we made up the expedition headquarters. The excellent scientific and technical facilities at the College were of great value.

The expedition was divided into two phases. The plan was to set up a base at the hill town of Debra Marcos, roughly at the centre point of the expedition area. From here we could radiate outwards attempting to navigate the river first from Shafartak to Sirba, when the water level was at its highest. On that phase we should use alloy assault craft powered by forty horsepower Johnson outboards.

For the second phase, from Lake Tana back to Shafartak, we needed boats that would stand up to the tumbling white water in the narrow gorges at the head of the river. Arne Rubin told me he believed that only inflatable craft could survive these terrible rapids. So I planned to use Avon rubber yacht tenders. The company thought I was insane but kindly agreed to provide six, payment being deferred until the publicity value was assessed. In the end they were delighted with the result and charged us nothing.

Re-supply would be by small overland parties dragging mules through the mud on the high plateau, before descending into the baking hot gorge. More supplies would be dropped by parachute from an Army Beaver aircraft.

Months of training and preparation now followed. Every spare moment was taken up by the expedition and the thankless task of raising £15,000 in cash. We tested boats on fast-flowing Welsh rivers and trained with Army packhorses on the sandy areas of Aldershot. Boats were selected, boats were rejected, boats were modified and finally, with days to go, boats were packed.

In March, 1968, I was able to visit the river and carry out an air reconnaissance. Flying low in a single-engine plane, I went the length of the lower gorges. Seeing it in the dry season I was impressed and, although we found no large swamps, I observed whole regiments of crocodiles rushing into the water as the aircraft roared overhead. There did not appear to be any obstacles in the river itself that we could not overcome in the wet season, although there would be some challenging rapids. However, weather did not permit an air recce of the unknown Northern Gorge.

We returned to England in time to explain the whole thing to Her

Majesty the Queen and His Royal Highness Prince Philip during their visit to the Royal School of Military Engineering at Chatham. 'You will have to be very careful,' cautioned Her Majesty, looking at the photographs of the cataracts. Meanwhile the Prince was advising Jim Masters on modifications for the boats.

Very sadly my mother, Gwen, my staunchest of allies, died suddenly in April. Apart from family upheavals, the expedition problems seemed to multiply but whenever I became depressed I forced myself to go on, because that is just what Gwen would have advised. Throughout all this, Judith, my jolly, supportive wife, had a great deal to put up with, but she, too, urged me forward.

Our preparations were complete by the end of July. Then, at the eleventh hour, I had an accident that almost knocked me out of the expedition. During the boat training in Wales, I fell heavily onto my right knee. It was excruciatingly painful and I could hardly walk. 'Rest it for a month and then start taking gentle exercise,' said the doctor. I acquired a stout walking stick and a supply of crepe bandages and prayed hard. We flew into Addis Ababa on 31 July.

Our advance party had already achieved administrative miracles. Considerable help was forthcoming from the US Army Mapping Mission and various Ethiopian Government Departments. We were able to move our personnel and stores to Debra Marcos on 2 August and set up the base in pouring rain. Flying ahead of the main column, I went forward with our chief pilot, Major Alan Calder, in the Beaver, reaching the grassy airstrip above the town at the same time as a tropical squall. High winds and rain clouds were sweeping across the flat green landscape as Alan fought with the controls and tried to land. Six times he made his approach and six times pulled away at the last minute. Fuel was beginning to run low and there was not enough to get us back to Addis Ababa. 'Here we go!' he yelled through the intercom as we went in for the seventh time. Ahead, strolling slowly across the strip, a herd of white cows appeared. Alan swore and the next moment we were over the top of the cattle by a hair's breadth and, with a bump, our wheels hit the ground. The crosswind swung the Beaver from one side of the strip to the other, but fortunately there was nothing in the way and we slid safely to a halt.

The true violence of the storm was apparent as we tried to open the doors; they were almost wrenched off in our hands. At the end of the airfield sat a silver and red Ethiopian Army helicopter, rocking in the heavy gusts. Climbing out to meet our allies, I ran through the torrential downpour. Huddled inside the chopper were half a dozen soldiers, with bandaged heads and limbs. The pilot, a young Amhara in a bright orange flying suit, grinned and slid open a small panel of perspex.

'Good morning,' I shouted above the noise of the wind.

'Hi,' he replied, with an American accent, 'who are you?' I explained that we were a British Army expedition, come to examine the Blue Nile Gorge. 'Gee, I thought you were reinforcements.' He added. 'Say, don't you guys know there's a war going on?' He pointed to the wounded soldiers whom he was about to evacuate once the storm abated.

I had heard that there was some minor internal problem in the province of Gojjam, but I had not been informed of the serious nature of the conflict. It seemed that the people of the region had risen up with one accord against what they considered the dastardly imposition of something called Income Tax. Clearly, we had some sympathy with the rebels. But in protest they had turned to slaughtering the tax collectors and now the Army was trying to sort out the rebels. We had landed in the middle of a small civil war.

As soon as the rest of the party arrived, I went down to visit my old friend the Governor. I had last seen him four years ago in his mud-walled palace. On arrival I noticed how few people were around, there was not even a guard on the main gate. Walking up to his office I found the door open and to my surprise saw a police corporal seated at the Governor's desk smoking a cigar. 'Ternastlin,' I greeted him.

He looked up equally surprised and said in halting English. 'Good morning.'

'Where's the Governor?' I enquired.

'He's gone,' said the corporal, 'and I go too.' He hastened to explain to me that the town was soon to be attacked by some 3,000 heavily-armed rebels who were out for the Governor's blood and, indeed, that of anyone connected with the administration.

'Well, before you leave,' I asked him, 'will you be so kind as to let me have some letters that I can send out to the various chiefs to grant us assistance and passage through their tribal areas?'

'Ah, yes,' he said, 'the Governor left these for you.' And, to my astonishment he produced a sheaf of letters which he proceeded to hammer with the official rubber stamp. Messengers were summoned and each was handed a letter for an appropriate chief. Bowing their way out from the corporal's presence, the runners made off at high speed towards the great river. I was given more letters of authority and assured that all would be well.

Back at camp, I explained to the bewildered expedition that we were in a very hostile area and that the town was likely to be surrounded by a large number of armed tribesmen, hell-bent on blood, who would undoubtedly sack it and, having done so, might turn their attentions to us. 'Ah well,' said the quartermaster, 'we'll build a zorib – that'll keep them out.' The zoriba, all of two feet high, was made of thorns and even the small boys who plagued us had no difficulty in hopping over it. The effect was undoubtedly intended to be psychological.

The final preparations and air reconnaissance took a few days. Polaroid photographs of the obstacles were used at the briefings. Mules and donkeys for the re-supply teams had been made available as a result of the Governor's letters, stores were packed, the aircraft flying schedule was detailed and all was made ready. The die was cast. We moved down into the gorge to meet the Nile.

On 7 August, twenty-two of us in four assault boats started on the 275-mile voyage from the great bridge at Shafartak to Sirba. There was no turning back, our engines would not overcome the current. For three weeks we battled through the cataracts, stopping at selected points for scientific investigation. Specimens were taken out of the gorge by mule parties, who likened their journey to the ascent of a never-ending ladder in a Turkish bath. The steep slopes were covered in loose rocks, concealed by elephant grass up to twelve feet high. Midday temperatures could soar to around 90°F and the humidity could go to eighty-five per cent. At night we shivered as the temperature dropped thirty degrees and on many mornings low cloud hung in the gorge blocking out the early sun.

The cataracts were certainly pretty challenging and we found places where enormous rocks, weighing thousands of tons, had crashed into the gorge, but there were no waterfalls. Jim's modified assault boats got us through. Although the crocs were large, they never exceeded twenty feet and only displayed aggression on one occasion. Beaches littered with mica and 'fool's gold' caused momentary excitement, but we found no caves full of gems. The tribesmen were generally friendly and even a couple of bandits we found spying on us turned out to be amicable.

It happened at the first camp at the junction with the Guder River whilst our scientists ranged about their demi-paradise on the sides of the gorge. Two tall, upright, bronzed men stalked one of our patrols for several hours until our people, tiring of the game, reversed the process and herded them down to our camp. Attired in old Italian Army tunics festooned with accoutrements of leather worn over faded loin cloths, they spoke no English. On his right shoulder each of them carried a blanket and in his left hand a thin five-foot staff. On the other shoulder was slung a heavy Russian rifle (circa 1898), almost certainly captured at the Battle of Adowa. Their hair was anointed with rancid butter, which smelt revolting.

Taken off guard, I couldn't think of anything suitable to say to a couple of inefficient bandits. So I offered them a Mars bar. They eyed it suspiciously, as a pair of black Carrion crows might examine an unusual but possibly tasty morsel in an English field. I urged them to eat and eventually one of them shot out a long scrawny hand and grasped the confectionery. He sniffed it without expression and handed it to his comrade who did the same. They looked at each other and then, eyeing me, nodded their approval before handing the bar back again. I broke it in half and gave them a piece each, at the same time eating some myself. They tasted it with care and then nodded again. So I gave them the rest of the bar.

In the middle of the interview Lieutenant Telahoun Mekonnen, our liaison officer from the Ethiopian Navy, came in from a reconnaissance. Immaculately dressed in his uniform he stepped ashore and, sighting our visitors, his jaw dropped noticeably. 'I must speak to you,' he whispered, and leading me to one side explained that it was his painful duty to shoot these men immediately. Could I lend him my revolver as his own pistol had not yet arrived from Naval Headquarters. I felt sorry that we should need to despatch our two visitors so soon, as it was quite possible we would learn much about the river and the flora from these two wanderers in this lost world. Telahoun insisted that he should shoot them and one of our police guides urged him to take off their ears to return as evidence to Addis Ababa. But in the end I prevailed on him to spare us the embarrassment of an incident so early in the expedition. The two policemen who had accompanied us from the bridge looked positively terrified by our visitors and I noticed that the swarthy bandits regarded our other Ethiopian friends with nothing short of contempt and scorn. Anyway it was time to sail so I took the opportunity of shaking them both by the hand and giving them some old plastic bags. They bowed politely and, thanking me in Amharic, strode back up the slope, smiling and clutching the gifts.

We scoured the precipitous sides of the canyon, but detected no smell of any gas, radioactive or otherwise. However, the zoologists made many important discoveries and although we saw no giant leopard or lions, we heard these cats roaring at night. As far as any lost tribes were concerned, all the rumours pointed to the Northern Gorge.

Plans for the second, most difficult and longer phase of the expedition from Lake Tana to Shafartak were already under way. Perhaps the answers to many of the Blue Nile's mysteries lay in those unmapped, vertical-sided canyons which no white man had seen. The first fifty miles were obstructed by raging white water cataracts and the river party would move in the inflatables. We were all novices at this game, learning as we went. Looking back on those days it is interesting that all our river-exploring techniques developed from that expedition.

Meanwhile the archaeological team were making an exciting discovery. On the southern shore of Lake Tana they found a small fortress that defended a peninsula from the mainland. The moat, ramparts and gatehouse were soon revealed from beneath the tangled growth that had gradually crept over them in the passing years. It had undoubtedly been constructed at about the time of the Portuguese arrival in Ethiopia. But the inhabitants had long gone – there was no lost tribe here.

The White Water Team, anxious to get started on their journey into the Northern Gorge, quickly formed a small corps *d'élite* of nine men in the three specially-constructed boats aptly named Faith, Hope and Charity. Flying over the route, Alan Calder reported that there were many more crocodiles than expected, some of them 'huge', and therefore we decided that Captain John Wilsey, a tall, handsome officer in the Devon and Dorsets, should take an assault boat and come upstream from the Blue Nile bridge to meet us somewhere near the Bascillio junction. He could then escort us in his alloy craft through the most heavily-infested area.

The way ahead of the Avons was foaming white water for many miles. By the first afternoon they had met the full force of the cataracts and realised that, with only paddles to hand, they were powerless to do more than keep the bow head-on to the waves. The fury of this untamed river was more powerful than anyone had imagined and very soon the team were battered, bruised and often half-drowned. To make life more difficult, there were parts of the river where it widened out and flowed through hundreds of channels. The problem was to know which one to take. The edge of the river was a swamp with no firm ground for some distance and this meant that setting up camp for the night was a long and tedious business.

While the team continued downstream, I flew to the hilltop shanty town of Mota and prepared a new group to meet them at the fifteenth-century Portuguese bridge deep in the sinister Northern Gorge. In contact by radio, I discovered that they were having more than their fair share of thrills and spills. Far from being stimulated, some were becoming very frightened. Dividing themselves into hawks and doves, some wanted to go on, others to pull back and they argued amongst themselves nonsensically. All I could do was to make one or two unpopular decisions and try to help them sort themselves out. Having done this, they then pressed on with much more caution towards the great falls at Tisisat, where the boats were roped over.

In the Northern Gorge the cataracts became even more dangerous so Nigel went ahead to run the re-supply groups who were now stationed along the lip of the canyon. It was soon found that the boats could not stop and therefore they needed early warning to pull into the bank before a cataract. Then, if there were sufficient water, they would ride it down, whereas if the rocks showed through they had to portage the boat round the side, a laborious and difficult task, especially in the depths of this narrow, vertically-sided chasm.

Leaving Mota in the cool of early morning we went down into the gorge, a long straggling column of mules and men taking with us fresh boats, engines, stores, weapons and ammunition needed for the final part of this epic journey. The last couple of miles' descent proved to be an interesting example of how mules can be used successfully in this terrain. The path was barely wide enough for a man to walk and yet these sturdy beasts plodded on with their heavy loads. Suddenly we came to the edge of a cliff and saw a narrow little path plunging down to the river. I could see beneath me the rickety structure of the old bridge. The central stone arch had been replaced with local timber and as I watched, a small herd of cows was driven across.

Some masonry tumbled away into the swirling brown water and I was amazed that it had stood so long. There was something eerie about the gorge at this point. It was damp, dark and silent, except for the swish of the river racing under the bridge. We had been forced to come here because it was the only place for many miles where there was a track that led down to the Nile and a bridge across it, however, rickety. Here I awaited the arrival of the white water team.

Each evening the radio brought news of the various sections and I knew that Roger Chapman's men were only a few miles away. They were very tired and many were suffering from infected bites and cuts. It would be a relief to have them back with me as I felt that one or two, lacking imagination, were allowing their courage to lead to rashness.

However, at the old bridge we had plenty of problems to occupy our time. The tribesmen obviously resented our presence and each day grew more insistent that we should leave. Stores were in short supply and money was running out. I was more than a little worried about the rains, for if they stopped early, the river would dry up rapidly and maroon us. Time was not on our side.

Everywhere the expedition was showing signs of nervous strain. Whilst working a simple flying-ferry across the torrent, I was swept overboard and came close to drowning. 'Our luck seems to be running out,' muttered one of my friends that night. I slept badly and at dawn was blowing the fire into life when I heard running feet on the trail down the gorge.

Scattering pebbles, Roger rushed in. 'Ian's dead,' he gasped.

Strangely the words did not surprise me. 'Swept away, nothing we could do.'

It was early and the sun had not yet reached us. Teeth chattering, we gathered around to hear the terrible news. I took Roger aside and we sat quietly on a great, black basalt slab in the shade of the high cliffs, while he told the story. He spoke in a low voice, his tanned, muscular body glistening with sweat: he had run most of the way to bring me the news, when he could not get through on the radio.

Late on the previous day the battered, exhausted members of his team had reached the Abaya Canyon. Here the mountain torrent carves a thousand-foot-deep gash in the highlands and cascades down a tortuous rock-strewn path to join the Blue Nile near the ancient bridge. For weeks they had struggled against the mighty river and, at last, in the Northern Gorge, had come upon a stretch of rapids too fearsome for even these stalwarts. On my orders they had let the boats go through the raging water unmanned, to be collected by my own group a short distance downstream, at the crumbling, old bridge. The towering, vertical cliffs had forced them to march west to find a route to my position. Alas, this narrow track had led across a tributary to the Blue Nile – the Abaya. Now it was a racing brown torrent, swollen by the rains, cascading over black eroded rocks, swirling and eddying with an ominous hiss.

They had started to cross in the late afternoon. Alastair Newman, known for his nerves of steel and lack of emotion, had been the first in and, taking a great leap, had swum with fast, powerful strokes to the far side. He carried with him a line of red climbing rope and, clambering out onto the rock ledge on the far bank, called out for another man to assist him. It did not look difficult and they were anxious to be over before dark. After all, they knew that I was only a few miles ahead with fresh men, new boats and supplies.

Corporal Ian Macleod of the Black Watch and SAS volunteered to go next. I had taught him to swim underwater in the sheltered coves of Cyprus years before: this wiry and popular Glaswegian was one of our toughest and most resourceful members. As well as being a thoroughly professional soldier, he had a scholarly air and was an accomplished linguist. Ian was a man who spoke no ill of anybody and no one spoke ill of him. He had not been well, following a narrow escape and bad battering in the rapids above Tisisat a week earlier.

However, apart from a bandaged knee, he showed no sign of his ailments. It was typical of this rugged Scot that he would always volunteer for the dirtiest job. With a rope lashed securely to his waist, he lowered himself into the rushing water and struck out for the far shore, only forty feet away. On the warm rocks his colleagues rested their aching limbs and waited for the ropeway to be completed.

At first all went well, but suddenly, as Ian was about to reach the bank, the rope went taut and he disappeared beneath the surface. Seconds later he bobbed up. His friends, aghast and realising his plight, gave more slack to enable him to reach the far side. But at once the line went taut again. The rope was being carried downstream by the speeding current, or perhaps a submerged tree had struck it and was dragging it along the river bed. Whatever the cause, Ian was drowning, being pulled under by the lifeline. His friends tried to play out more rope praying he could reach the far bank. For a moment it seemed as if he had made it. But then the river washed over him and he disappeared, still struggling for his life.

Roger was already ripping off his clothes. Someone hurled a semi-inflated life-jacket to Ian, but it missed and floated away, tossing in the turbulent waves. Others, aware that he desperately needed just a few feet more of slack line, yelled, 'Cut the rope.' A jackknife was tossed across the river to Alastair and he began to saw through the tough fibres. Roger dived in and reached Ian, forcing the drowning corporal above the surface. Still the rope anchored them against the jetting current. Then it parted and at once the two men spun downstream through the tossing brown waves of the cataract. Roger, fighting with all his massive strength to gain a grip on the bank, could be seen struggling as he was swept along beside the polished, ebony boulders, one arm, muscles bulging, crooked around Ian. Dashing along the bank, the men leapt from rock to rock trying to keep pace. Now Roger had an arm around a finger of rock and was trying to pull Ian from the water. But the current pounded them relentlessly and by now Ian was unconscious. Ahead was a small waterfall, only a ten-foot drop, but with jagged rocks at its base; their chances of survival would not be high if they were swept over. Roger's face was red and contorted with effort, Ian's ashen and grey. Suddenly his limp body was seized by some unseen force and he was dragged relentlessly downward. In a second he had gone. Once his head bobbed above the surface, but after that he disappeared over the waterfall and was never seen again.

On the bank the exhausted men summoned every last ounce of energy and raced down the narrowing, boulder strewn ledge, desperately hoping to catch a glimpse of Ian and to be able to reach him. It was all in vain. The ledge soon ended and they were forced to stop. Ahead they could see the river disappearing into a black abyss, into which the water tumbled with a terrible roar.

Chris Bonington, his voice broken with emotion, said, 'We can't get any further, he's gone.' Gulping in the warm humid air, his weary companions nodded agreement and all turned back. As darkness fell, they rigged up an aerial ropeway and crossed, to spend a damp, cold night huddled amongst the rocks. Their minds and bodies had reached a point of exhaustion, which sleep would barely alleviate. To make matters worse, the deep canyon prevented radio contact with the rest of the expedition. Roger knew I was only five miles ahead, but he also knew that we were virtually captives of the tribesmen. To the dispirited white water men, it seemed that the bottom had fallen out of their world. Any hope of continuing the expedition seemed out of the question, indeed some even wondered if they would survive.

This was the story Roger told me. I found myself issuing the orders for an emergency helicopter search. I seemed to do it almost mechanically and, after a moment, realised that my mind was running on two tracks at once. One of the signals officers was already calling base and the intelligence officer was asking me short, sharp questions, to which I gave automatic answers that must have been subconsciously thought out minutes or perhaps even days before. The other part of my mind was saying, 'Poor Ian, a search is hopeless.' I remembered my own desperate struggle in the grip of the river only the previous morning. Having finished giving orders I stood deep in thought, looking at the milk chocolate coloured water racing under the old bridge. How many disasters had this awful place seen, I wondered.

In the early afternoon a small US Army helicopter landed on a broad ledge above our camp. This caused a great stir amongst the locals, but we were extremely glad to see it. Leaving his crewman at our camp, the American pilot flew me up and down the gorge, travelling as slowly as possible so that I could scan the innocuous looking water and the rocky banks for any sign of Ian. Once something did catch my eye. It was a football bladder, obviously released from a wrecked Redshank. It could only have escaped if the tube had been torn open and this could only have been done by a crocodile. There were several huge log-like reptiles sleeping on the sandbanks.

Turning up the Abaya Gorge, we saw the terrible conditions into which Ian had disappeared and there, still camped on the ledge, were Alastair and Garth. They waved slowly, as if to say, 'It's no good, you're wasting your time.' We made a final sweep of the immediate area and, with fuel running low, turned for Mota. As we rose out of the chasm the engine gave an unhealthy cough. We dropped a few feet and the pilot started to sweat profusely, although it was quite cool in the aircraft. We were too low for safety, only 100 feet above the ground that was now rising rapidly to meet us. The engine coughed again and the American grunted something unintelligible over the intercom. By his actions I gathered we were going to land. Skilfully he brought us in on a small patch of grass beside a low bluff, and whilst the rotors continued to thrash around, he sprang out and began to tinker with the motor. Satisfied, he climbed in again, grinned and gave a thumbs-up. We flew up to Mota without further incident.

On the bumpy little airfield outside the tin-roofed town that nestled amongst the eucalyptus trees, I saw the twin-engined Otter aeroplane. This was also from the US Army and had carried the fuel for the helicopter up from Addis. Time was precious if I wanted another flight before dark, so as soon as the chopper was re-fuelled, we flew down to the gorge again, dropping over the lip of the plateau as if it were the edge of a coral reef, into the abyss beneath. More crocodiles were in evidence but more alarming was the increase in the number of tribesmen gathering about our camp at the bridge. All were well-armed and waved their rifles excitedly. Was this the vanguard of the force of 3,000 rebels that local chiefs had assured us would attack unless we moved away quickly? I had dismissed this as gross exaggeration at the time but now I was not so sure, and wondered how long forty of us with sporting rifles, shotguns and revolvers could hold out in the exposed bed of the canyon against an attack by so many. Nigel Sale and his party, with one injured man, were still out in the Abaya region, making their way to the bridge. The problem of searching for Ian was rapidly being overtaken by a far more desperate situation involving the safety of the whole expedition.

The river was running too high for comfort and I did not want to sail on until it had dropped another two feet. We only had enough boats to take ten men and their equipment. Many of the survivors of the white water team were injured or sick and quite unfit to proceed by river. Ahead lay the worst crocodile-infested stretch yet and I wanted John Wilsey to reach the Bascillio Junction with his relief force before I set out to study the one part of the Blue Nile that was unmapped, unexplored and unknown. It would be a difficult enough stretch of water without interference from rebels and, as we had our last look for Ian, I felt I was sitting on a powder keg with the fuse burning shorter each second.

By the time we landed on the ledge above the camp, my plan was made. Get the walking wounded, sick and other persons up to Mota as quickly as possible. Gavin Pike, a robust young cavalry captain, who had been with me before in Ethiopia, would take these men out; I prayed the rebels would let them pass. Nine of our fittest would sail on with me to survey the last stretch and meet John Wilsey at the rendezvous. I would tell Nigel by radio to make for Mota direct and not come to our camp. All I needed was about four hours to organise this. As I clambered out onto the short grass I noticed two young warriors with their rifles unslung and pointing vaguely in my direction. Trying to appear unconcerned, I thanked the pilot and said just loud enough for him to hear, 'I think we've got trouble here. I'll get your crewman up, but keep your engine running.' A precipitous goat track, a foot or so wide, led down the cliff face to the camp. One of the warriors followed me, his rifle aimed at the small of my back. Mesfin, our Ethiopian Government liaison officer, came over and whispered quickly, 'I cannot do anything more with them.' In camp, everyone looked worried and watched with drawn faces. The tribesmen were in a truculent mood.

When in doubt, confuse the enemy! 'Good,' I said loudly. 'Thank you, Mesfin, please tell the Chief I have been to Mota and I bear important news for all the tribe, but first I must prepare some notes then I will come and tell them all about it.' Hoping the interpretation of this white lie and ensuing questions would keep the warriors busy for a few minutes. I seized the confused American crewman.

'You've got problems, Captain?' he asked.

'Yes, but with luck you can get out as soon as I start speaking to the tribesmen. Go to the Chief of Police at Mota and get him to come here as fast as possible and sort out these old gentlemen and their people. You are our only hope, so do all you can. Also, please tell my headquarters what is happening.' With that I turned, and, replacing my beret with the pith helmet, I strolled over to the stone bridge and, whilst Mesfin interpreted, gave a long harangue about Ian's death, the search, our scientific work, the medical aid I had brought from Mota for the treatment of all ills, and how grateful we were to the tribesmen for looking after us. I threw in the names of Haile Selassie, Churchill and Wingate for good measure, and I was still speaking when the helicopter lifted off the ledge and soared back towards Mota. My audience barely seemed to notice.

To endorse the speech, I announced that there would be a sick parade in ten minutes' time for the tribesmen. Then, grabbing Ian MacLeod's medical kit, I told Corporal Henry to gather together all the spare pills and potions he could find. Together we set up a clinic on the bridge.

The queue of evil-smelling patients stretched fifty yards. They jostled for places, and minor punch-ups took place between the warriors to get to the head of the queue. Our meagre resources were totally inadequate for anything more than token treatment. Our proper medical officer was himself sick at base and Ian, who had been our best medical orderly, was dead. Treating the tropical sores and eye diseases as best we could, we gave out aspirins for tummy aches, while Henry's remedy for the numerous malingerers was a Horlicks tablet sellotaped over the painful area. In the case of a particularly unpleasant brave, he administered two dozen powerful laxative tablets with a drink of water. He then told the young warrior to run home as fast as possible, lie down and await results! He never saw him again.

As night fell we held a simple memorial service for Ian. Many a tear rolled down tanned faces. We had lost a good friend.

I then gave the orders for the next day. Gavin would take out the overland column. Nigel had already been diverted. I would lead the new group down river to investigate the last unexplored part of the gorge and eventually meet John Wilsey. We would take most of the guns and ammunition from the others. I had a feeling our need might be the greater. However, everything depended on the tribesmen letting us leave. But I had sent out word to the muleteers of Mota to bring their beasts to the bridge the following morning.

At it grew dark the chiefs and their followers retired to the top of the gorge and fortunately there was so much preparation to carry out that our minds were fully occupied until sleep took over. Once during the night our sentries woke me. A noise had been heard twice on the track above the camp, but the early warning necklace of stone-filled cans strung across the path had not rattled; probably a hyena.

The misty dawn was cold and damp when the tribesmen returned. Hardly had the sun appeared over the cliff when we heard the helicopter. The Police Chief of Mota. Captain Mulena Alamu, strode into view, smartly dressed in a freshly laundered uniform peaked cap, shiny boots, black Sam Browne and bearing a .30 carbine and revolver. He walked amongst the chiefs, smiling and greeting them; a diminutive figure, confident and authoritative, just like his Emperor. Crossing the bridge, he spoke with the Begemir Province chiefs, who had remained on their own side. He then made copious notes in a large official book. In no time, this efficient law officer had sorted out the problem with commendable tact and diplomacy. I spoke to him through Mesfin and, as he left, I followed him up the cliff path to the waiting chopper. Glancing around to make sure he could not be overheard, he said to me in perfect English, 'It is all right for you to continue, but keep your guns handy and a good watch at night.'

'Where did you learn English?' I said in genuine surprise.

'England,' he hissed, and climbing into the cockpit shouted, 'Tanastalin,' and was gone.

At the bridge we remained under guard. However, following the visit of the gallant captain, we were treated with a new respect.

Miraculously, the mules arrived on time and the overland party was soon shouting farewell as it started up the steep ascent to the high plateau. They did not have an easy journey; ambush parties met them throughout the route, and at each stop there was much argument and discussion before they were allowed to pass. The entire province was in turmoil and the rebels were said to be marching on Mota.

Back on the river, we prepared to sail next day. The Beaver made an air drop of supplies, but many of the items that were free-dropped fell onto rocks and were badly damaged. With foresight, the packers had placed the whisky inside new socks, so at least we were able to wring out the remains of a few precious drops! Circling above, Alan told me of more tribesmen massing in the mountains, and added that the Beaver had been fired on. We really were in a boiling cauldron and I wondered if our overland party would reach Mota. My first problem was to overcome the fears and anxieties of the team, who were apprehensive about the conditions ahead. Reconnaissance by air does not always give a true picture of river conditions, and we had been lulled into a false sense of confidence several times. I knew we could do it, but the men needed a lot of persuading. They had not seen the Army recce boats in rough water and, of the six sent from Britain, only two had been found fit for use. Nevertheless, I had no doubt that these craft would manage the rapids.

It was 21 September. The temperature at 0800 hours was 74°F; rain had fallen during the night. We awoke cold and wet on our rocky beds. My knee, injured during the pre-expedition training, was stiff and the pain under my armpits told me that the poison from infected rope burns on my hands was spreading. Somehow the antibiotics had ceased to work, and, anyway, we had only a few left.

My helmsman was Sub-Lieutenant Joe Ruston, Royal Navy. Joe, a rugged, amiable person, was an engineer, and his quick wit and good humour made him an ideal companion under such arduous conditions. He and I were to scout ahead in the recce boat *Semper*, warning the two engineless Redshank inflatables of any forthcoming hazards. An ingenious mechanical engineer, John Fletcher, brought up the tail of the fleet with the second recce boat, *Ubique*, and with him was our crocodile expert, a young zoologist named Colin Chapman.

The recce boats were both equipped with nine-and-a-half-horsepower motors and could hold against the current, which enabled them to manoeuvre more easily than the Redshanks. Even so, they were not as robust as the Avon. But if anything went wrong, the recce boats would come to the rescue, and if we were attacked by crocodiles, they had the heavier weapons necessary for defence. Colin was certain that the crocs would not attack, but I remembered he had said there were none north of Tisisat and yet one had strolled into our camp above the falls!

Many tribesmen were still with us, having spent an equally wretched night wrapped in their voluminous shammas. As I dipped the blunt razor into a mess tin of tepid water, a fish eagle screamed its yodelling call into the canyon of the Blue Nile. The river simply hissed and bubbled as it swept on its way. Our guards, seeming to sense our imminent departure, eyed us suspiciously and shuffled nearer like optimistic vultures, hoping for gifts of surplus food. I wondered if they would really let us go.

5

A Close-run Thing

'Go, Go, Go,' I shouted as we pulled into the current, and in seconds our little fleet was borne away by the swirling flood.

One or two of the guards raised their rifles as if to fire, but our sudden departure had taken them by surprise and we were out of sight before they recovered.

Rising early, we had gone about our usual chores as if everything were normal. Most essential items had been stowed in the boats under the cover of darkness and we left a pile of boxes, which had given them the impression that we were not going anywhere. The river gave us an exciting ride and at times I judged it prudent to come into the bank to use the roping technique past a particularly difficult cataract. We shot through most rapids in grand style! Hitting big waves, we were drenched, but the old recce boats did remarkably well and our confidence grew.

Antelope stared from the banks and birds rose in dismay as we flashed by. The crocodiles were well hidden for we saw none. Perhaps the engine noise drove them to shelter in the murky depths. High on the hills white-robed figures gave shrill cries, announcing us from mountain top to mountain top. At water level the black basalt was so polished that it looked like marble. Scribbling in my log I recorded that the river width varied between thirty to fifty yards, and in the rapids we were moving as fast as nine knots. The Redshanks paddled on steadily and it quickly became apparent how useful the powered boats were in escorting, guiding and towing the paddled craft.

We were able to inspect a place where Major Cheeseman believed the river had changed course. There was every sign that this happened, but the water level was sixty feet below the old bed so it must have happened long ago. In fact, Cheeseman's original map was correct, but the copies and reproductions showed the river in the earlier course. We updated the map and passed on, looking all the time for evidence of minerals and people. As we journeyed on into the most fantastic, vertically-sided gorges the water hissed between the cliffs like a stream of liquid brown mud. These sheer walls, which rose from the water for 100 to 200 feet, appeared to be limestone, capped with volcanic rock. Towards late afternoon we reached some vertical lava pillars, standing in mid-river. This gave me our exact position, as I recognized them from the air reconnaissance. I felt instinctively that if we were to find a clue to the mystery of the Northern Gorge, it would be in these sinister canyons, through which I knew no white man had sailed.

Suddenly we caught sight of a roughly-built dwelling, perched high on a cliff on the Gojjam bank. This was a niche in the rock, closed off by a stone wall. A doorway in the wall had a timber frame. Was this evidence of a lost tribe? Waving our Ethiopian flag, I signalled the other boats to pull in to the shore. Stumbling along the rock-strewn beach, we sought a route inwards, but then Joe called out, 'Hey, there's a man there.' At the top a lone figure stood watching us intently. He did not return my wave, but regarded us in sullen silence.

Then, without warning, he became agitated, shouting and waving us away. I thought this unusual as Ethiopians are most punctilious about returning greetings. However, it could be that he lived alone in the dwelling and thought us to be raiders, although I doubt if raiders would bother to fly the Imperial Ethiopian flag! But tax collectors might! So, after a short inspection, we sailed on through the vertical rock walls, our voices echoing unnaturally and for some way we were completely enclosed in the massive slot.

A sharp bark to our left surprised us and there, scampering amongst the rocks, was a party of hideous old men clad in grey fur coats. Or that was what it looked like! 'Hamadryas baboons,' called Colin. The boats slowed, cameras clicked, the baboons screamed with rage and one quite deliberately threw a small stone. They really did look human. My God, I thought, so those are the mysterious ape men! It was easy to see how a legend of a lost tribe could be based on a colony of Hamadryas, living in crevices on these remote cliffs. I was still making notes when Joe said, 'Look at those caves, surely they're man-made?'

On our right as we passed by were two large openings situated in the rock face about thirty feet above the water. At the same time, a small cove containing a stream and some low trees appeared on the left. It was probably the Tammi River. 'Pull in to the beach!' I yelled.

It was the most pleasant site we had found to set up camp so far. The stream had cut a narrow gorge, which ran back some fifty yards behind the beach. The little river formed a beautiful waterfall as it entered the cleft, spurting out from the terrace above and sending clouds of spray to gather rainbows in the last rays of sunlight. The water in the stream was clear and slightly warm. Lichen and ferns grew out from the cliff in profusion. Beneath the trees was a plentiful supply of firewood and a clear area in which to erect our bashas.

Across the Nile the cave entrances gaped at us, one semi-circular, the other triangular. They were partly blocked by a well-built wall of rough stones. That was certainly man-made, but there was no evidence of any inhabitants and, as I studied them through my binoculars, I wondered how we could gain access. There was an overhang immediately above the caves and the only possibility seemed to be to ascend from the river bed. This was a job for our rock climbers. We all felt excited and yet slightly apprehensive. After our adventures of the past weeks I wondered what fate had in store for us now.

In no time our tents were pitched on a sandy ledge amongst the trees. While supper was cooking, Garth and David, our zoologists, went on a lizard hunt. John Fletcher repaired the transom on his boat, which had been damaged during the day. Chris and Roger discussed a plan for getting into the caves on the morrow. Richard filled several more pages of his notebook. Joe was working on the engines. Alastair, Colin and I cooked up an awful mess of sardines and rice. After supper I strolled up the narrow canyon behind our camp and there I made another discovery. Jumping across the stream, something green caught my eye. I stopped and looked back. The bed was littered with bright green rocks. 'Copper,' I thought aloud. Sure enough, the stream bed contained lumps of copper oxide, apparently carried over the waterfall at the end of the canyon. Picking out a few specimens I resolved to return next morning to seek the source.

Darkness fell rapidly but, in spite of our exertions, spirits were too high to sleep and we talked for several hours. It had been a good day. After weeks of painfully slow progress we had covered seventeen miles in five hours and conquered the worst of the rapids below the Portuguese Bridge. We had made these intriguing discoveries that might unravel some of the mysteries of this mighty river. Furthermore, from now on we should have a relatively easy voyage, although there might be the odd sporting stretch of water to keep us on our toes and, of course, there were always the ubiquitous crocodiles!

I did guard duty from 2200 hours until midnight, spending the time writing my log by the light of a guttering candle. The night was quiet, warm and dry and our camp seemed safe from interference. I had much to record and ponder. Were the caves in fact entrances to tunnels leading to an extensive subterranean settlement? Did the Hamadryas baboons live there? How could we get in? Once inside would the baboons attack us? Was the presence of the copper significant? Perhaps the caves were mine shafts? I felt a great surge of excitement sweeping through me – after all these months we seemed on the verge of a great discovery. No other white men had been here which explained the lack of knowledge of the region.

A sudden puff of wind blew out my candle and I was about to relight it when I heard a sound on the beach, so I remained still and listened. There it was again – the crunch of shingle. My fingers eased the long barrelled Smith & Wesson from its holster as my left hand gripped the flashlight. Flicking on the beam, I scanned the beach. Nothing moved and I relit the candle to continue writing. I was in mid-sentence when I heard the voice. Unmistakably it said, 'Be very careful in the morning.' The hairs on the back of my neck rose, but I didn't jump up. In fact I was rooted to the spot. My mother's voice? I heard nothing more, but I was wide awake and alert. That warning caused me to review our plans.

My concern now centred on the crocodiles that lay ahead. From the air I had seen some monsters; certainly many more than we had seen elsewhere on the river. Scientific advice had told us that the crocodiles would now either be far up the tributaries or well down the river beyond Shafartak. But they were still here. This was why I had despatched John Wilsey with three men to come upstream from Shafartak to meet us. However, he'd had a great many difficulties and we had not made radio contact for several days. However, Main

Base had managed to pick him up and had learned that two of his outboards had blown up under the terrific strain of forcing the rapids. A third engine, dropped from the Beaver, had disappeared into the Nile when the parachute failed to open. Unfortunately, this load also contained the team's rations so they must now be pretty hungry. Our last spare outboard was on its way to them by American helicopter. I knew John wouldn't give up and I could easily imagine him straining every muscle to get his boat to the Bascillio Junction.

Base also told me that the assault boat team had reported an alarming increase in the number of crocodiles and strongly advised that we should not proceed past the junction without the alloy boat as escort. Until we met John, I had a simple plan of defence against the crocs. We'd try to avoid them, remembering the bite one had taken at an assault boat the previous month, but each craft was to carry a sandbag full of stones for use as a deterrent. If all else failed, we would open fire with our heaviest weapons and thrash the water with paddles. Colin, who had been working on crocodile surveys in Ethiopia for several years, considered an attack to be most unlikely. Nevertheless, I always had the heavy Mauser rifle ready, just in case. I prayed that if we met an angry thirty-foot croc, this would stop it.

Healthwise we were not in bad shape. Most people's cuts and lacerations were now healing, or at least the infection was not spreading. My own injuries were giving little trouble; the knee hurt occasionally but I could dispense with the walking stick. My torn hands were of more concern. The nylon rope that had cut through to the bone during my earlier rescue from the river had led to an infection that sent a jabbing pain to my elbow joints and armpits, but with constant cleansing and dressing I hoped to keep going for another week. As the moon rose over the gorge I thought again about the voice, 'Be very careful in the morning'.

Heavy rain fell while I slept and at dawn the baboons' barking chorus roused us from our moist sleeping bags. We wolfed down breakfast and, while the air was still cool and with the canyon in deep shadow, started to explore the caves. Joe lightened *Semper*'s load to the minimum and, with his engine racing against the current, took Chris Bonington across the river. Festooned with rope and climbing equipment, the mountaineer stood in the swaying boat. Joe brought his craft with throttle wide open against the cliff and, as we watched apprehensively from the other side, Chris studied the rock face, then he sprang upwards, found hand and toe holds and started climbing. Had he slipped he would have plunged into the turbulent river. In a minute or so he was in the cave and lowered the rope, which Roger, coming across next, secured as a fixed line. Richard was the last to go and soon all three climbers were safely inside the cavern. Quickly, and with some regret, they discovered that there was no tunnel and that the cave was uninhabited. 'The place is full of pottery and basket work,' yelled Chris. Joe ferried their archaeological finds back to camp, while Roger shot a small bat for the zoologists. It appeared that we had discovered some ancient refuge, probably deserted for many centuries. The floor was deep with bat dung giving off a nauseous smell, but the remains of an old leather rope provided a clue to how the former dwellers had got in. Perhaps in the dry season there was a ledge beneath the entrance.

Just before midday the party returned and we spread out their discoveries to photograph. Gazing down at the potshards, bones, fire carbon and aged leather rope, I heard a distant whooping cry. This was the usual way that one Amhara shepherd signals to the next, but it was repeated and sounded excited. I couldn't read the strange language, but I had heard our guides use it often enough to realise that the tone had much to do with the message. 'I think we'll have a quick lunch and press on,' I said.

'What, and leave the caves only half explored?' said my chums with obvious disappointment.

'Yes,' I said crossly, 'just grab a Mars bar and let's pack up and go.' I had intended to continue the exploration in the afternoon. Quite why I suddenly changed my plan, I'll never know. The tone of the shepherd's cry would not have been sufficient by itself. Something made me uneasy. It would take us at least thirty minutes to pack up and load the boats and I simply felt we must move.

I was so entranced by the beauty of the waterfall behind the camp that I decided to take a quick snapshot before we left and record the site of the copper. In the little canyon it was cool and pleasant and I spent a few moments deciding which would be the best angle. The sharp crack and the shower of chippings from the rock face made me duck instinctively. I looked up. There, at the top of the bluff, a hunter, silhouetted against the blue sky, stood clutching his rifle and watching me. 'Look out you idiot, you nearly hit me,' I shouted in anger and, ludicrously, in English. The man opened the bolt to reload and I suddenly realised that was exactly what he was trying to do. Instinctively my right hand flew to my holster, but I had taken off my belt a few moments before when going to commune with nature. My revolver was on my pack in the camp.

My feet hardly touched the ground as I raced back down the gorge, leapt over the stream bed and rushed into camp. I don't think I've ever run so fast in my life. 'Blashers, running?' said the look on the faces of my friends. But before they could speak I shouted, 'Hurry. We must get out quickly. Just grab everything and get into the boats.' We moved fast and I had just loaded my pack on to *Semper* when a horn sounded several short, strident notes. A second later a bullet smacked into the shingle a foot away and I looked up to see the cliff top on the far side of the river alive with some thirty armed tribesmen, their white shammas billowing in the wind. They were only sixty yards away!

A wild fusillade of shots followed, ricochets whined off the rocks and spurts of water sprung from the river. Our attackers waved their weapons and screamed blood-curdling war whoops. Up on high ground beyond the cliff top I could see long lines of tribesmen coming to join them. Obviously the lone rifleman had given the game away too soon. Perhaps my appearance with the camera had surprised him, but what on earth had prompted the attack? This was not the moment for analysis. We ran for cover under the trees.

Army training in dealing with hostile crowds brought to mind the words 'minimum force'. I seized the loud hailer and dashed out on to the beach. One man seemed to be the leader and, addressing him, I boomed out, 'Tanastalin, tanastalin, we come in peace and are your friends.' To my relief, the firing ceased and Geronimo, as he was instantly nicknamed, bowed low in the customary Ethiopian manner. I realised that they had never heard a loud hailer before so I hoped to gain time by keeping him talking. After all, they could not reach me. Having completed his bows, the man deliberately raised his rifle and fired at me from the waist. The bullet came uncomfortably close, showering me in pebbles. In another attempt at appeasement, I again told Geronimo in my few words of Amharic that we came in peace and offered him a Mars bar! As before, the firing and stone slinging stopped and Geronimo bowed.

'John, for God's sake let's fire back,' yelled Garth.

'No,' I said, 'must try minimum force first. Just let me attempt to get them talking.'

'You'll get yourself shot standing out there in your bloody white hat. It's not bullet proof, you know,' said another voice.

But the tribesmen were clearly a little confused and, as I spoke, they held their fire. Meanwhile the team packed vital kit.

As I spoke, I tried to switch my mind on to track two again. To stay and argue would give us time, but we would be slaughtered once we tried to run the gauntlet on the river. Right, if we did not want to end up with squeaky voices, at best, we must escape. Perhaps they would stop shooting and we could slip away. I doubted it. My heavy rifle was securely packed in *Semper* and Garth's shotgun, too, was in his boat. David had a .22 rifle at hand while I had my Smith & Wesson .38 Special, and knew how to use it. We could put up a pretty good show if only we had more ammo and some cover. At 180 feet a good pistol shot will register a fair score on a man-size target. But I did not want to fire.

As the tribesmen argued and the loud hailer impressed them more, I shouted rapid orders to the team. 'We are going out by boat. Redshanks first, keep in under the far cliff for cover. Joe, go upstream and draw their fire. If they start shooting, zigzag. John, escort all the Redshanks down river. Joe, pick me up when the rest are clear, we'll regroup half a mile downstream. Colin, you and I will give covering fire, but only on my order.'

I was interrupted by the sudden arrival of several boulders the size of overgrown footballs crashing through the trees. The cliffs behind us were also alive with the enemy. What coordination! If only they could shoot straight, we'd be dead. Rocks, sling-shot and bullets rained down again as our attackers screamed and yelled. They were not just trying to frighten us. Already the Bejimir tribesmen behind were beginning to descend into the gorge. In a few moments we would be fighting hand to hand. We must leave now.

'Get ready,' I yelled, using the loud hailer to overcome the noise of the gunfire.

'We'll all be killed,' shouted Chris. 'We can't go out there. Call for an air strike. It's suicide.'

'I'm bloody well giving orders here,' I said. 'Shut up and do as you're told.' For many it was a baptism of fire and a frightening experience for all of us.

The rifle fire was now very heavy and it seemed incredible that the inflatables, lying in the open, had not been hit. 'To the boats,' I cried. Joe was out first, showing no regard for his own safety, and as the storm of shot and stone raged about him, he calmly pushed his craft into deep water. Then, shaking his fist, he sped upstream to draw the enemy fire. I watched him for a second and thought, in the best traditions of Nelson, I only hope he survives. I suppose we all assumed that being a naval officer he would be rather good at this.

John Fletcher and Colin Chapman were in *Ubique*, ready to escort the Redshanks on their way downstream. One Redshank was launched and was paddled furiously for the relative safety of the far cliff. The surface of the water danced with plumes of spray from the missiles. At any one time six or seven rocks could be seen in the air and many struck the boats. It will be a miracle if we can come through this unscathed, I thought. The second Redshank was caught up in some reeds by the beach, the crew struggling to get it into the main stream. I was alone on the beach. Around me lay the scattered remains of our camp. Gripping my .38 Special I looked up to the Bejimir cliff. As I did so, a bullet hit the beach between my legs. The firer stood on a rock slab twenty-five yards away in the Tammi gorge, working the bolt of a short Italian carbine. Raising my revolver, I fired whilst he was re-loading. Slightly to my surprise, he doubled up, dropped his rifle and ran up the cliff path. I probably only hit his weapon, but gave him quite a fright. I turned my attention to a group higher up, who carried long barrelled rifles of an early vintage. One shot drove them to cover and, hearing a clang of stone striking metal, I spun round to see a jerry can of fuel standing on the shingle. Nearby lay the precious artefacts collected so laboriously from the caves.

By now Joe was planing downstream, sending pale brown spray up in a fan behind the boat. Weaving in and out of a pattern of missiles, his revolver clutched at the ready, he yelled, 'Get aboard.' Seizing the can of petrol, I regretfully left the artefacts and, racing across the beach, I was up to my knees in the swirling water before *Semper* reached me. Half-falling over the side, I collapsed into the boat. Joe immediately gunned the throttle and we hurtled across the river. The sky above was full of rocks and slingshot. Several lumps, the size of tennis balls, struck the inflatable's tubes and bounced off with a loud 'pong'.

Forty yards ahead I could see the Redshanks now coming under aimed fire. Using his engine, John Fletcher was pushing them downstream. 'Fire,' I cried. And from *Ubique* came the crash of Colin's .45. I swivelled to face the Gojjam bank. Geronimo was there, standing in full view atop a buttress of rock. I saw his rifle kick and a bullet sent a shower of water over me, missing the boat by inches. Joe's tense face was pointed ahead. 'Chris has been hit,' he said. Oh God, what a mess, I thought.

Geronimo was trying another shot as I took aim. 'Hold us steady, Joe.' I yelled. The Smith & Wesson roared and my bullet struck the rock six feet beneath the white robed target while his went towards the Redshanks. In the time it takes to squeeze the trigger, I fired again, this time three feet too low. Rock chips flew downwards towards the swirling current. My last shot came almost at once. Geronomo's head jerked up as he reeled backwards and, with his arms outstretched as if seeking support, fell from sight. I turned to face his followers, but they were now hiding behind the rocks, their rifles silent. Only the odd long range shot whistled after us and splashed harmlessly into the river.

During the battle, Joe had calmly taken Chris's Redshank in tow. The injured photographer was now seated, blood running from a stone wound in his back and trickling down the side of the boat, but he was not badly hurt and he still had his camera at the ready. 'Look left,' he cried. Joe and I, our guns still in our hands, spun round to face the next enemy and 'click' went Chris's camera. I suppose it may have looked authentic! It was 1210 hours. The whole incident had lasted only ten minutes.

For several miles we towed the Redshanks. The gorge gave way to sloping hillsides, plantations of maize and a few huts. Great square blocks of basalt lay like islands in mid-stream, the results of massive avalanches. When I judged we had gone a safe distance, we halted to reorganise. As I dressed Chris's wound, Joe set up the radio and I scribbled a message for Base. 'Sitrep. Attack on camp by forty natives from both banks, with rifles, rocks and slings. Fire was returned in self-defence. No enemy casualties. Bonington minor injury. Do not cause flap over this. Tell Base all OK, but much kit lost. Do not release to press.' I hoped that this statement would keep the whole matter at a very low key and this was the reason why I had not mentioned Geronimo or any other enemy casualties. The

Racal radio was fitted with a twelve-foot rod. Such aerials are only designed for short distances but, to our utter astonishment, Base, almost 100 miles away and with Mount Choke (13,000 feet) between us, answered our first call.

We cruised on throughout the afternoon. Whoops and shouts followed us from the hills. 'Here come the tax collectors,' they probably said. Eventually all was silent, but I knew that dozens of unseen eyes were watching and, sitting with the big Mauser on my lap, I scanned the high ground through binoculars. Crocodiles were appearing here and there on the banks, but they made no aggressive movement. I estimated we had covered twenty-five miles since the ambush and felt that we had probably out-stripped any pursuit. Darkness usually fell at around 1830 hours, so it was as well to stop an hour or so before this. At 1700 we were still some three miles north of the junction, when I saw another canyon ahead. The walls were much wider apart than the previous gorges and I recognized a pinnacle of basalt leaning out from the Gojjam cliff in the far distance. I had noted this on the air reconnaissance and remembered it marked a short stretch of small rapids and also the start of a longer stretch of vertical cliffs. If we got into any difficulties in those rapids, darkness would probably catch us in that gorge. We drifted on downstream coming upon a long, low shingle island. A small patch of trees and scrub grew in the centre. There were a few driftwood logs that could be used for defences and there were no crocs about – as far as I could see. The current was quite fast and even the narrow channel on the right contained deep water. Around the island the river banks were largely devoid of cover and the nearest high ground was at least half a mile back. It seemed a reasonable defensive position and probably the best we should find for miles. It will take a determined bunch to attack us here, I thought. Crunching ashore on the pebbles, we pulled the boats up and established camp under the trees in the centre of the island. In order to get the radio equipment as nearby as possible Joe sailed *Semper* into the narrow channel, mooring to a tree.

We were sipping a brew of hot sweet tea that Richard Snailham had cooked up when we spotted three boys swimming diagonally across the river from the Bejimir side. Any bitter feelings we had felt after the ambush had now abated and we waved a friendly greeting to these brave newcomers, who treated crocodiles and the swift current with such contempt. They came out of the water and stood at the edge of the island, their smooth athletic bodies glistening with water. They stood there shyly, stark naked except for a small silver Coptic cross on a string around their necks. These people had probably known Christianity when our ancestors were painted blue. Unlike most natives we met they seemed timid and hesitant and simply stared at us. Eventually our gestures and offers of small gifts tempted them to come into the camp and, once there, they lost all shyness. I doubt if they were older than fourteen. They spoke a dialect none of us understood and even Colin, whose Amharinya was better than most, could not get through to them. They seemed quite amicable and we presented them with aspirins, plastic bags and Mars bars. Like all Ethiopian young men, they displayed considerable curiosity towards our weapons and, when they swam home a few minutes later, I felt rather uneasy about this interest. Was it the normal respect for guns, which are a status symbol in this wild land, or was there more to it? I was still pondering when Joe called me for supper. We had been forced to abandon some of our rations at the Tammi, but although on a reduced scale, the meal was quite adequate.

As it grew dark I held the usual briefing and outlined the plan for our defence and possible withdrawal should we be attacked that night. We arranged to have two sentries on duty at all times and built a rough zoriba, or thorn fence, around the camp. Colin and I were carrying ministar flare launchers, which we would keep loaded and close at hand. Each man was given his responsibilities and ammunition was distributed. Being Sunday, after orders we held our usual service. Richard selected a hymn from the Army Prayer Book and just then it began to rain. Everyone huddled under my basha and we sang, 'Now thank we all our God, with hearts and hands and voices...' The words seemed appropriate.

The night was very black and, apart from the patter of the rain and the hiss and gurgle of the river, all was silent. I wrote up the log, penned half a letter to Judith and then lay fully dressed on my sleeping bag. I undid the laces but kept my boots on. Positioning my flashlight nearby, I cleaned and checked my battered old revolver and laid it beneath my pith helmet, which served as a pillow. Next, I oiled the Mauser and loaded the magazine before placing it in its plastic tube. This I pushed inside the sleeping bag. The final act was to dress my throbbing, suppurating fingers and swallow an anti-malaria tablet. It was just after 2200 hours when I blew out the candle and sank into a deep sleep, snoring like a pig, as usual!

In the distance I heard yells and shots. A faraway voice shouted, 'Stand to, stand to,' but it was all a dream. Or so it seemed for a long time, which, actually, could not have been more than three seconds.

As I came to, my hands groped for the ministar launcher. The shots and war whoops were very close, and, somewhere, a hunting horn was sounding short blasts. Tearing open my shirt pocket I felt for the pen-sized device and, rolling out of the basha, I thrust it upwards and tried to manipulate my swollen fingers to fire it. 'Crack' went the tiny cartridge as the flare curved through the sky lighting up the island and the river. The shingle beach was alive with shining black bodies advancing on the camp. One figure, carrying a short spear or a sword, was only fifteen yards away chasing Roger towards the zoriba, trying to stab him. My hand was searching for my gun as I saw David, our second sentry, crouched by a tree. He brought up his .45 and its flash and roar came together. In the last light of the dying flare I saw the leading attacker stop as if he'd hit a glass wall, then sink to his heels and roll over backwards. A hole the size of a dinner plate gapped in his back. Another flare rose into the sky almost at once, fired by Colin and in its light I buckled on my belt and drew my revolver. As I put up another ministar, a volley crashed out from the camp. 'They're coming through the trees!' I heard someone shout. 'For heaven's sake, guard the boats.' yelled Chris.

It was now 0105 hours and bullets from the enemy side were hitting the camp. Suddenly a figure came blundering through the scrub. It was pitch black. My gun came up and was about to shoot John Fletcher when I heard him say, 'Joe's down by *Semper*.' It was not until this moment that I realised that the heaviest fire was coming from the river bank on the Gojjam side. The bandits' covering party had been in position there all the time and was now trying to pick us off in the dark. I let go another flare, horizontally this time, aimed at the next rifle flash and, to my delight, saw half a dozen white robed figures scampering away in panic. Meanwhile the raiders were still on the north end of the island and trying to work their way through the scrub.

'I'm firing into the bushes,' I yelled, not wishing to risk the chance of an accident with one of our own men. There was no reply and, advancing a few yards, I waited. Low voices muttered about twenty yards ahead. More firing and whoops on my right showed that Roger and his party were busy by the boats. Then I saw a definite movement a few yards ahead, one or probably two men, I thought. Someone was calling out in the local tongue on the bank. The figures showed again and I blasted two quick shots, deliberately aiming low in the scrub. With much noise of breaking undergrowth and grunts, the bandits fled through the bush.

'Beach is clear,' came the cry from the right.

'Garth,' I shouted.

'Yeah,' came back the faint Australian accent.

'Take David and recce forward up the island. See if there are any of them still here. We'll switch our fire to the covering party.' Alastair Newman had joined me and together with ministar and revolver, we took on the bandits on the mainland. The tactics were simply to watch for a gun flash, put up a flare in its direction and get off a couple of quick shots whilst the target was illuminated. Joe was already packing up the radio equipment. 'The aerial's caught in the branches,' he muttered, 'I'll have to climb the bloody tree and sort it out.' As most of the shots from the enemy were passing over our heads through this particular tree it would be a hazardous undertaking, but the radio was of little value without it. He started to climb up the thorny trunk and I heard hoots of laughter from the bandits. I'll swear there was a clink of a bottle and I realised that the gentle thudding I'd heard earlier was a ramrod being driven down some ancient musket barrel. To confirm my impressions, there was a bright flash, a 'boom', and a cloud of white smoke jetted out from the trees. A six-inch nail or some similar object crashed through the branches near Joe, who swore loudly. A few minutes later he jumped down. 'Got it,' he gasped. 'See you at the RV,' and, clutching the radio aerial and his machete, he staggered down to *Semper*. Then, continuing to ignore his own safety, he pushed off into the channel and drifted silently downstream between the firing lines. Although there was no moon, the night seemed to be getting lighter as my eyes became accustomed to the darkness. It was possible to distinguish large objects, especially on the water, and I saw the bandits only twenty yards away from Joe. The firefight continued for another fifteen minutes and slowly all of us pulled back to the pre-arranged rendezvous at the far end of the island. Roger had brought the boats down the shore and was joined by Joe in his inflatable from the other side.

Alastair and I pulled back to the defensive position last. There was a low shingle bank, but we were close to our boats and had a completely clear field of fire. Everyone was there. Garth reported the island clear of enemy. Ammunition was quickly redistributed. We had just three rounds left for each .45 so although we had more liberal quantities for the other weapons, we were not well off. I checked each man's arc of fire and, coming to Richard, said, 'You cover from that bush to ...'

'John,' he interrupted quietly, 'I feel there is a small point I should raise at this juncture.'

'What on earth is it?' I said tersely.

'I haven't got a gun,' he replied. I found it difficult not to burst out laughing. Richard, as gentle and unassuming as ever, was clutching his Swiss Army penknife. 'Would you like your pith helmet back now?' he said. Guarding it like an Imperial Eagle of Rome, he had carefully concealed it from view throughout the battle.

It was now 0200 hours and I planned to hold out until just before dawn, then slip away when the light was sufficient for us to see the way through the cataract approximately a mile ahead.

The bandits' shooting was as bad as their tactics and field-craft were good, so I doubted if they would be able to hit us as we moved down river. I could probably discourage them from following too closely with my rifle. But it meant holding them off for another three and a half hours at least. They were brave men and, I rather suspected, well-primed with alcohol. It is difficult to estimate the numbers involved, particularly as we were fighting at night, but I believe a reasonable approximation would be forty to fifty, against ten of us.

There was only occasional firing from the bank and this we returned with the rifle to conserve revolver ammunition. Once I thought I saw a figure swimming the channel between the island and the mainland. If indeed it was a man, my shot must certainly have worried him.

At 0300 hours Richard reported a growing movement on the mainland opposite his post. I listened and could hear a lot of muttering and shuffling amongst the bushes. The bandits were probably massing for another attack, so I put up a flare, which revealed nothing. 'If they make another determined attack we shall have to withdraw,' I said. 'Simply not enough ammunition.' No one questioned this, but all wondered how we could negotiate the rapids in the dark. I gave instructions for the withdrawal and, to avoid revealing our movement to an enemy cut-off party who might be lurking downstream, I said that no engines were to be used except in dire emergency.

The silence was broken by the short, sharp notes of a hunting horn, the same as we had heard earlier. I put up another flare and, in its light, I could see groups of robed figures moving forward through the trees on the far bank. They were coming again.

'Right, man the boats,' I whispered loudly and, firing several shots at the massed bandits, clambered into *Semper*.

'Life-jacket,' said Joe, thrusting one at me as he pushed us into deep water. 'By the way, I think we've been hit somewhere up front, we've got a frightful leak,' he remarked, bad news that was confirmed when I tested the forward tubes of the boat and found them soft and squashy. As we pulled away from the island, I rummaged about and found one of the foot-pumps. Fortunately, it was easy to connect to the valve and as I sat I used one foot to keep the pump going, whilst my hands were free to paddle.

We reached the far bank and at once the current forced us against some trees. 'Push clear quickly,' came Roger's urgent warning, 'or we'll be dragged under the branches.'

We had only been on the water for a short time when the whoops and horn blasts announced that our evacuated position was under attack.

'We've got a good start,' I said to Joe, but he was too worried about his craft to notice the events behind us.

'Keep pumping, we're losing air fast,' he said.

To help keep together, each recce boat took a Redshank in tow and it was in tandem that we reached the cataract. Ahead, in the blackness, we could hear its thunder, but saw nothing. As we raced towards it at some six knots it was an eerie, unnerving experience. The terrifying noise got louder and louder. In daylight we could have chosen the best route through the white water, but now we had no idea whether we were coming upon a small waterfall, a huge rock in mid-river or some shallow rapids that would tear our hulls open, like a knife through butter. Straining my eyes ahead, all I could see was inky blackness. To our left *Ubique* and its Redshank were now invisible.

The water hit us without warning. The Redshank under tow was completely engulfed. A second wave swept over and the rapidly deflating front tubes almost bent double. I lost the foot-pump in the chaos and heard Joe yelling, 'Can't go on like this!'

'OK. Let's use the engine to run into the bank,' I screamed back, 'but we'll have to cut the Redshank loose.'

'Can't make it,' called Joe to the boat behind, 'we're going ashore for repairs ... Casting you off, pull in further down. Good luck.' At least they'd have a better chance without us. The tow-line parted and at once they were swallowed up in the darkness and the raging river.

Our outboard started almost immediately and, with superb seamanship, Joe took the sinking craft astern and out of the main stream. We thumped into a shingle bank and I shot out backwards onto the shore as Joe killed the engine. As I landed, something slightly blacker than the pebbles slithered off into the water – I'd almost fallen on a crocodile! For a few moments we sat still with drawn revolvers, listening for any enemy, but the noise of the cataract drowned everything. Suddenly from the darkness, two shapes loomed up. It was *Ubique* and her Redshank. They landed ten yards away and we heard their horrific story of a capsize in mid-cataract. David and Richard had both gone overboard and were only saved by a miracle. Much kit had been lost including the vital box of rations. We were now soaked to the skin and very cold. 'Where's Chris's boat?' asked Colin. As if to answer him, a light appeared flashing dimly down river. The signal, in morse, read 'OK'. So they were safe, too! Back upriver, our camp was still burning, small showers of sparks cascading skyward as our enemies vented their wrath on everything we'd left behind.

Joe had discovered *Semper*'s trouble – a leaking valve that was easily cured. Someone passed round a handful of boiled sweets and we cracked one or two nervous jokes.

Making a quick reconnaissance, I discovered to my relief that we had landed on a featureless shingle bank, separated from the mainland by a fast-flowing stream. However, we dared not show lights nor speak loudly, as the bandits could not be far away. Thankfully cloud still covered the moon. We worked quietly in the dark to refit the boats and it was about 0415 hours when John Fletcher lost the nut that held on the propeller of his engine. It had slipped from his wet hand into the river. Without this, the propeller could not be secured and therefore the engine was useless. John tried everything his resourceful mind could dream up, but it appeared there was no solution. As a last resort he mixed a paste of Araldite in a tobacco tin and glued the propeller on to the shaft.

'How long will it take to set, John?' I asked.

'About an hour and a half, if I can keep it dry,' he replied.

'You reckon that we can sit here in daylight, do you?' I exclaimed. 'No, I realise we must push on, and if necessary I'll lash a plastic bag over the propeller when we go. We'll just have to hope that it will set and meanwhile we'll paddle,' he answered. Fitters, like John, are worth their weight in gold on expeditions!

An hour later the sky began to lighten and, casting off once again, we skirted round the tumbling cataract and picked up the missing Redshank and crew downstream. The dawn was fantastic. The growing light revealed an incredible view of towering cliffs, giant boulders and natural limestone arches painted shades of brown, pink and yellow. The river was like a mirror, much wider now and slower, only a gentle wave or two disturbing the surface. Nevertheless I made sure I had the rifle handy and kept a close watch on the cliffs. We passed Bascillio Junction, but I reckoned John Wilsey must be further south.

Along the banks we could make out the shapes of dormant crocodiles, but it was not until the sun began to reach the gorge that they started coming out to inspect us. We watched warily, occasionally hurling a rock to deter them. However, they kept their distance and at 0700 hours Joe managed to raise Base on the radio. Once again it was a miracle of communication, for he was only using the twelve foot rod.

I had just spoken to Nigel, the deputy leader now safely at Base, when I saw Joe's mouth open. 'Oh, my God,' he said. Looking up, I saw a leviathan of a crocodile literally galloping with its legs extended. The giant reptile plunged into the water and came speeding straight at us, its great head causing a bow wave. I simply yelled 'Crocodile attack!' into the microphone and reached for my rifle.

The huge twitching tail propelled it like a torpedo as I aimed the Mauser at a point midway between his evil yellow eyes.

'Don't shoot,' shouted Colin, 'he's only curious, he'll stop short.' If you're wrong, my friend, I shall kick you off the cloud when we meet in Heaven, I thought. The huge creature closed to within eight feet of the boat, when, without as much as a splash, it dived and passed beneath us, its scales rubbing the hull, only to surface on the far side. It then cruised alongside for about twenty-five yards, giving me a chance to estimate its size, which was even bigger than our boat. At a conservative guess I would have said fifteen feet in length! Suddenly, he disappeared beneath the muddy water again, this time for good.

Base was trying to contact us on the radio. 'Sorry for that interruption,' I said, giving a brief outline of the battle. 'Don't get the authorities all worked up yet. Give me a chance to get well clear before Haile Selassie's jets come thundering in to deal with the bandits.

'They've got troops standing by to be helicoptered in and get you out,' replied Nigel. 'And John Wilsey is twelve miles south of Bascillio Junction.'

'Fine, but we need ammunition and food in that order, so may we have a drop when we meet John?' I went on.

'Our stocks of rations are almost out,' retorted Nigel. 'What has happened to all of yours?'

'Oh, I gave them to friendly people around here,' I replied sarcastically.

We switched off the engine to save fuel and drifted for a while. More crocs swam out to investigate, but Colin was right, they always stopped short. However, I could see how any inexperienced person would assume they meant business and would open fire long before they had got to within eight feet. It was 0815 hours as we rounded a bend and saw the dark green assault boat. A great cry of joy went up and I stumbled ashore to shake John's hand. For several hours crews swapped stories. Cataracts grew bigger, bandits and aggressive crocodiles multiplied. John himself had a great tale to tell. For seven days he had struggled upstream, his boat leaping rapids like a giant salmon. No one had ever brought any form of powered craft so far up the Blue Nile before. It was an incredible achievement.

Having washed, shaved, cleaned our guns and re-fuelled, we ate a meagre breakfast. Food supply was very short, but at mid-morning the Beaver came roaring into the gorge and dropped several bundles. They only had one parachute left and that was used for the petrol and ammunition. The rations came in by freedrop and, sadly, the pack burst as it hit the ground, scattering its contents far and wide. They were all the supplies they had left at base. This consisted of some packets of biscuits, a bag of rice, tins of sardines and cheese, plus a four-gallon plastic container of whisky! 'Well, at least we can lay on a cocktail party,' joked John. The whisky container was leaking, so we had liberal gulps before setting off in an euphoric haze to study the last part of the river.

The remaining time passed quickly and then a new menace hit us: mosquitoes. The dry season was approaching and already the trees were turning brown and the river beginning to drop. We had started picking the chewing gum repair patches off the petrol cans, but the hunger pangs got unbearable and eventually we persuaded Colin to shoot one of his beloved crocs. With a single accurate shot he took out a seven-footer, killing it cleanly with the big Mauser. 'Joe,' I said, 'you're a Naval officer, you're bound to be good at croc skinning.' So my helmsman got to work and we ate the tail. Cooked in some candle fat, it tasted delicious to starving men.

It was 24 September when we sailed from our camp on the Uolaka junction and began the final run to Shafartak. On the radio we heard that quite a reception awaited. It was hard to realise that we had got through, and now, after nearly two months, it was almost over.

Sitting in the boat as we made that last day's run, I began to make notes for my report to the Emperor. No lost tribe, just some unsociable apes and a large population of reluctant tax-payers. No radioactive gas or uranium as far as we could tell, but very likely a good deposit of copper. The crocs were certainly huge, but nothing above eighteen feet had been seen. Although there'd been massive landslides, there were no waterfalls below Tisisat and, in the wet season, inflatable boats could navigate from the Portuguese Bridge to the Sudan if His Imperial Majesty so desired!

At 1620 hours the Beaver came skimming over the river and we knew we were close. Ten minutes later we ran ashore and the champagne corks popped. A large lady from Texas was amongst those who had come out from Addis Ababa to see us arrive.

As we staggered up the beach she turned to her husband and said, 'These guys must be crazy.'

'Hush dear,' he replied, 'they're British.'

* * * * *

It was to be thirty-seven years before I returned to Ethiopia and the Blue Nile in 2005 at the head of a follow-up expedition. Supported by the Scientific Exploration Society, an international team consisting of over fifty British and Ethiopian servicemen and civilian specialists carried out the first successful navigation of the 140-km Beschillo River, a major but little known and rapid-strewn tributary of the Blue Nile up in the Ethiopian Highlands that was believed to be the main breeding ground of the infamous Nile crocodile before again tackling the Blue Nile itself, this time at low water, which actually proved to be much less hazardous than we had anticipated. Travelling for 48 days by foot, 4WD vehicles, donkey and special Avon inflatable boats, we covered some 600kms on water and many thousands overland, carrying out extensive scientific research along the way. A specially designed inflatable tug, sponsored by J.P. Knight Ltd and fitted with an EP Barrus Mariner outboard motor proved a great asset to the flotilla.

An important discovery was an archaeological site that yielded artefacts dating back to the Neolithic period 2-3000 BC and indicating the movement of Neolithic people up the Blue Nile from Sudan. One artefact was identified as the first example of a corn grinder in Western Ethiopia.

Community aid tasks also formed an important part of the programme. These were co-ordinated by Simon Hampel, who lead the Reconnaissance and Support Group (RSG) that kept the flotilla supplied. Four wells – funded by the British Charity 'Just a Drop' and 'The Alan Rivers Charitable Trust' – were constructed. Equipment was provided for a school and a clinic, and the expedition medical team assisted local people. The expedition dentists extracted 320 teeth.

Temperatures rose to over 106°F and the muddy, chocolate-coloured river water had to be laboriously filtered. Many stretches of the river were teeming with crocodiles, fifty were counted in one day and an inflatable canoe was torn open by one aggressive reptile. Hippo were also encountered and over 600 specimens of flora and fauna were documented. An exciting moment was seeing African Wild dogs, which were believed to be extinct in this area. A hydrographic study of the rivers showed parts of the waterway to exceed 50 metres in depth and it is believed that fewer than 70 people have ever sailed much of this route. Many more have reached the summit of Everest!

Earlier in the expedition, we were fired on and held at gun point by bandits until Ethiopian police made a long overnight march in challenging terrain and carried out a professionally executed 'dawn snatch' of the criminals. It seemed just like 1968 again, except that this time we were virtually unarmed. Otherwise, the main problem was malaria, including the dreaded *P. falciparum* type. Eight of the team caught the bug and Yolima Cipagauta, the SES's Latin-American representative, almost died.

However, although it was certainly no picnic, the project, which received much help from the Ethiopian Government and the British Embassy, was nevertheless an exciting and extremely worthwhile enterprise.

6

.

Escapism

The King's Army was crossing the open ground some six hundred yards in front. In the summer sunlight the cavalry, infantry and camp-followers of the Royalist forces were a colourful sight. The breeze carried the sound of drum and fife as well as the oaths of the gunners, sweating on the drag ropes as they heaved the great culverins over the ankle-deep grass. Sir William Waller, my commanding officer, dressed in puritan black, his hand resting on a fine silver-embellished pistol, glanced casually towards the clump of trees, where I sat upon the sixteen-hand grey charger, and nodded. I acknowledged the signal and, turning about, cantered to the rear, rounded a leafy bush and faced my Ironsides.

Sixty or so stood by their horses, their black lobster helmets glinting, orange sashes standing out against their drab leather coats. There was not a cigarette, not a pair of dark glasses, not a wristwatch, nor indeed any vestige of the twentieth century.

'Ironsides, mount,' I yelled, and at once the troopers sprang into the saddle. 'Captain Muir,' I shouted. 'Pray advance thy horse beyond yonder ditch, whence you will see the malignant host. Then thou shalt take them in the flank, for they do presume to cross our front.'

'It shall be so, sire,' replied the young cavalry commander.

'We'll ride with you,' I called, as the horses began to trot.

'On the right, then,' replied the good Captain. Emerging from the trees, the Ironsides shook out into five ranks of twelve. 'Draw swords,' came the order.

Visors dropped as we splashed over a shallow brook, passed through gaps in the hedge and entered a large meadow, at the far end of which the enemy was still moving slowly to the east. They saw us when we were four hundred yards away, trotting forward in good order and they began to run out cannon and form square. I could see Prince Rupert's cavalry behind the Foote, trying to find a way through the confused ranks.

'Ironsides, charge,' screamed Johnnie Muir.

At once every trooper brought the flat of his blade down on the rump of the horse in front. The tight box of cavalry rocketed ahead with the thunder of hooves. We bent forward, grateful for the cooling wind. Even to stand in forty pounds of armour, leather and thigh boots is no joke on a summer's day.

Screaming like banshees, we scattered two gun crews, kicking over powder barrels and slashing down a standard before whirling right to circle behind the enemy and rejoin our friends. What tremendous fun, the wildest schoolboy dream come true!

'Ow!' I spat, as something very hard hit my upper arm a stinging blow. 'What the hell was that?'

'A tennis ball, my lord – one of ours,' said Frances Copping, my ADC, raising her visor and mopping the perspiration from her brow. Sure enough, in the middle distance the line of trees where we had started was masked now by drifting clouds of smoke, as the Roundhead artillery engaged the army of King Charles.

'There,' cried a gunner,' let's see how they like this – fire!' Propelled by a thunderflash, a tennis ball whistled down the meadow. His earlier shots had been high, but this one struck a small enemy cannon, whose fuse was already burning. The gun spun and discharged itself at its crew. A great cheer went up from the Army of the Lord, as we sometimes called ourselves. Cromwell's men were enjoying the artillery duel. Their next shot hit the breech of an enemy culverin and bounced about amongst the gun crew, causing a standard-bearer to drop his colours. Thus encouraged, the Vicar General ordered the Twenty-third Psalm and the Roundheads sang.

The final act of the day was the inevitable head-on clash of the Foote – as chance would have it, on a narrow bridge. The cavalry stood back as the rival mobs, no regimental order remaining, beat hell out of each other! One poor fellow lost his teeth to a pike but – 'Well he shouldn't have joined if he couldn't take a joke,' commented Sir William (alias author and historian, Professor John Adair). Eventually the stentorian bellow of ex-commando Brigadier Peter Young, Captain General of the Sealed Knot, brought a stop to the bloodbath. We all shook hands and limped back to our respective camps. The five thousand spectators trooped home, having had twenty-pence-worth of fun.

Peter had started the Sealed Knot in the spring of 1968 and in no time the brigadier had formed an army. Many of his friends, always ready for a spot of colourful fun, joined. Promotion was rapid and by the time I reached Marston Moor in June 1970, I was a 'General of Engineers'. Beneath all the amusement, there was a serious purpose to our activities. By restaging the battles on the original ground, using authentic equipment, those interested in the history of warfare could appreciate the difficulties faced by the forces from which developed the modern British Army.

Both Roundheads and Cavaliers had regiments of horse, foot, dragoons and traynes of artillery. Our membership included people from every walk of life. Girls fought as men and acted as camp followers: on the Roundhead side, Judith and Kay Thompson organised a nursing corps, known as the Sisters of Chastity! Alas, Judith was later dismissed for drinking wine upon the field of battle.

Recruiting was no problem. Those with the sense of the theatrical obviously preferred being Cavaliers, for the glorious uniforms, if nothing else, although the simple, more modest amour and leather of the Roundheads had a definite appeal and was certainly less expensive. The recruiters for the Army of the Covenant were ever ready to point out that many attractive damsels rode with the Royalist cavalry 'and will be ours by right of conquest, for, as according to history, we always win'.

The battles were usually staged so that a local charity could benefit from the large crowds that flocked to see the carnage. Was this not the attitude of Rome in its decline? However, although casualties were not uncommon, they were rarely serious. Beer flowed like water and demure young ladies cast inhibitions to the wind and flirted outrageously with men whom they scarcely would have glanced at in twentieth-century garb. It seemed that once we donned our costumes, we left today's world far behind. A 'wench' was carried off to hospital at Plymouth with a strained back.

'How did you do this?' enquired the doctor. 'I had to be raped by a Roundhead,' she explained, 'but, whilst trying to catch me, he fell off his horse and squashed me flat.' Officers had no real authority but discipline was surprisingly good, although we always considered the Cavaliers rather unruly and issued strict warnings to our Ironsides against 'brawling, duelling, bear-and bull-baiting'.

At the re-enactment of the first battle of Newbury (20 September 1643), I took the part of Sir John Merrick, whose Parliamentary artillery had played an important role in the battle. I persuaded a dozen fellow students from the Staff College to join in, including a United States Army major, George Smolenyak, who had recently fought in Vietnam. George, dressed as a puritan officer, was in the thick of the fight during which his fibreglass helmet was topped by a Cavalier's sword! Emerging battered, bruised and truncated, he was heard to mutter, 'Gee, Vietnam was never as dangerous as this!'

Judith and I have often given unusual parties, and in 1970, with some pals, we held a Viking Blot (an early Scandinavian drinking 'orgy' and fertility ritual) at Hawley Lake, the Royal Engineers' watermanship training area in Hampshire. Here we set up a marquee, and hired an extraordinary all-electric musical group equipped with a sort of portable water organ. We decked out two thirty-five-foot whalers as Viking ships and moved in a vast quantity of wine.

Whilst we were setting this up, the Sealed Knot was amusing the crowds at the Sandhurst Horse Show. At the height of the battle, our friend Ken Monk, playing his usual part of the Vicar General and extolling the Roundheads to spare no one, but to do the Lord's work and smite the malignants with all their might, was ridden down by a Cavalier. Looking much the worse for wear, poor Kenneth was carried off to a waiting Army ambulance. When he came to his senses he was at the Cambridge Military Hospital in Aldershot.

'Rank?' enquired the orderly.

'Vicar General,' groaned Kenneth.

'Name, sir?' said the soldier with new respect.

'Monk.' replied Kenneth.

'Date of injury?'

'11 September 1646.' said Ken.

'How exactly did it happen?' asked the orderly, more than a little puzzled.

'Ridden down by cavalry,' said Ken, in his soft Welsh voice. Looking at the form, the orderly wrote in the remarks column 'Mind wandering', and sent him off for a head X-ray.

It was nearly 2230 hours before they finished setting his broken arm and Ken was able to change into his costume as the High Priest of Wodon and persuade the army to despatch him by ambulance to the 'orgy'. The dancing girls, a dozen nubile nymphs fresh from being 'raped' on the Sandhurst lawns in the cause of charity, were now attired in sealskin bikinis and cavorting in an erotic dance that set the men's pulses racing. Just as Ken arrived, a duel resulted in one guest being run through the hand with a sword, so the ambulance did not have a wasted return trip.

As the extra strong Danish beer flowed, the party got into its stride. The Viking ships raced up and down the lake. A few guests who had foolishly come in suits of chainmail almost drowned. Finally, we auctioned the slave girls for charity and, when a thick mist descended, the party dissolved into chaos as guests tried to find parked cars and, having done so, attempted to drive them. I will never forget seeing Richard Snailham, dressed as Diogenes and wearing a barrel, trying to climb into his Triumph sports car.

I spent what remained of the night collapsed on a bearskin in the marquee. At dawn, very stiff, with a wicked headache, I stepped over my prostrate friends, and staggered out. There was a terrible scene of desolation, with broken weapons, sealskin bikinis, Viking regalia and empty bottles scattered around. The smoke from the fires drifted vertically upwards in the still air and, beyond, I could see the ships, one demasted, riding at anchor on the misty lake.

Seeking some privacy to attend to the most pressing business of the moment, I strolled off into the rhododendrons. Still dressed as Wodon, with two-horned helmet, beard, cloak, skins and sword, I was eagerly watering the flowers when I sensed I was not alone. Looking up, I saw a wide-eyed, bespectacled fisherman, complete with green waders, landing net and rod, gaping at me from twenty yards off. His Jack Russell, one leg raised, also stared. 'What ho!' I bellowed, waving the sword with my free hand. To my amazement, the poor fellow turned and fled. I often wonder what he told his psychiatrist!

Much of my time at Staff College was unofficially devoted to planning explorations and, although the idea of pushing paper in the MoD did not greatly appeal, I opted for a posting to Whitehall, knowing that it would be immensely valuable to understand the workings of the Civil Service. I found that if handled correctly, this much-maligned body of dedicated people could really be most helpful, especially to expeditioners.

I found myself in trouble early on whilst attempting to oil the wheels of a conference dealing with defence estimates by ordering chocolate biscuits for coffee break. My claim to the finance branch for ten pence was rejected out of hand with the comment, 'Biscuits, chocolate are for generals. Other officers only qualify for biscuits, plain.' However a colleague got £10 from the Daily Telegraph's Peterborough column for the story and took me out to lunch.

There were countless files to be studied, many of which had been in circulation for decades. I was given one concerning a claim for compensation from an irate householder who complained about a wartime concrete bunker, complete with coastal artillery piece, which was still in his garden. He pointed out that as a housing estate had grown up around the weapon, firing it would certainly cause fatal casualties amongst the population of Little Piddling-on-Sea and that we should therefore either remove it or pay compensation. The correspondence had flowed back and forth since June 1945 and one could trace the steady decline in the poor fellow's health. The Ministry letters were sympathetic, but unhelpful. Sometimes they blamed the economy, sometimes another Ministry and, finally, the local council for having erected houses around a gun emplacement. However, positive suggestions were made from time to time, such as: 'The matter is under review by the Engineer-in-Chief and it is hoped that the defences in question may be demolished by explosive charges with the minimum damage to your property', or: 'As the removal of the blockhouse is now considered impractical, perhaps you would wish to make an offer to purchase it.'

There was the usual crop of letters to the Member of Parliament concerned and, about once every twelve months, a really abusive one from the tortured victim himself. When this happened the Ministry rolled itself up, hedgehog-like, in a protective ball and refused to reply, thus forcing the complainant to eat humble pie and write an obsequious plea to obtain an answer. Of course, staff officers changed every two years and so the Ministry was constantly being revitalized whilst the complainant grew more frustrated. When he finally expired, a loose minute on the file suggested that the matter should now be passed to the antiquities department of the Ministry of Public Buildings and Works.

The telephone rang for the hundredth time one morning. Grabbing it, I said, 'One minute, please,' and signed the letter that my sergeant was holding in front of me. Scowling at the aged, chipped, black telephone with barely concealed malice, I wondered which lost cause this call would ask me to support.

The voice sounded polite and hesitant. 'Some friends and I have a small exploration problem on which we should value your advice. Could you lunch with us next Thursday?'

A good meal would be more than welcome. 'Thank you very much,' I said, 'where shall we meet?'

'The Hispanic Council at Canning House' came the reply.

I had heard of this organization: Anglo-Latin-American relations, trade, cultural and economic links. I had become very interested in South America whilst acting as rear-party officer for the Roraima Expedition, which had explored the site of Conan Doyle's Lost World that summer. The mystery of Colonel Fawcett's disappearance also intrigued me, but I wondered why anyone should want to consult me on exploration in South America. I had never been there.

Following the success of the Blue Nile expedition and on the advice of the then Sandhurst Commandant, Major General John Mogg, a group of us had founded the Scientific Exploration Society (SES), to organise and encourage scientific exploration worldwide. This charitable organization was to become the driving force behind many major expeditions.

In 1969 we ran our first project to investigate a strange blindness as well as the fauna and flora of the remote and little-known Dahlak Islands in the Red Sea. The team had returned in triumph. Freddie Rodger, our eye surgeon, decided that the blindness was largely caused by intense ultraviolet radiation and, what was more important, he believed that in many cases a cure might be possible. I felt a deep satisfaction from helping these simple, unselfish people who, possessing few worldly goods, had shown us kindness as great as anyone could expect in our own world. Already the SES was establishing a reputation for tackling challenging but worthwhile expeditions. Lunching at Canning House, Colonel Julian du Parc Braham, eyeing me through his monocle, asked 'Have you ever thought of driving from Alaska to Cape Horn?'

'No, but I do not imagine there would be much of a problem, simply a question of time and petrol.'

'Then you do not know about the Darien Gap,' he said sharply. I didn't!

I learned from the British Darien Action Committee that the Pan-American highway system, 17,000 miles long and stretching from the snows of Alaska to the deserts of Southern Chile, is a bloodstream with many arteries, feeding twenty-three nations with trade, tourism and the exchange of ideas. But it was not complete. In the middle, at the Isthmus of Darien where the Atlantic almost meets the Pacific, there was a tiny block, a thrombosis that stopped the flow of lifeblood between North and South America – a mere 250 miles of hills, jungle and swamp that had so far beaten the highway engineers of both continents. This was 'El Tapon' – the 'Stopper', or the Darien Gap.

Tim Nicholson, the committee's secretary, explained that a bill recently passed by the United States Congress would provide two-thirds of the $150 million dollars needed to build a road across the barrier. President Nixon himself had commended it. But words were one thing, action another. The area was receiving publicity through being the site for alternative projected routes for a new Panama Canal, but the road was a poor relation. A spark was needed to fire men's imagination and translate words into the deeds so desperately needed by the nations concerned.

This spark, the Colonel said, had been lit by the Darien Action Committees of the United States, Panama and Colombia. Now they were seeking support for a pioneering British expedition to try something never before accomplished because of the natural hazards: to drive specially-equipped vehicles all the way from the Arctic Circle to southern Chile, traversing the Darien jungle and swamp for the first time. Other hazards and obstacles it would meet included almost perpendicular razor-back ridges, bridgeless rivers, wild beasts, reptiles and insects in profusion. The expedition, he claimed, would bring a dream a step nearer to completion by providing the publicity and 'spark' needed to get money for the roadbuilders. My hosts explained their plan to send a party of six in two Land-Rovers to tackle the journey in the coming December, and they wanted my advice. There seemed to be no real difficulty in getting from Alaska to Panama and from Colombia to Tierra del

Fuego. The problem was the Darien Gap. Several expeditions had reached the Panama-Colombian frontier, but had then run out of time and were caught by the rains which came in April. The most difficult part of the obstacle was the Atrato Swamp, almost the size of Wales, which nearly severs South from Central America. Clearly the promoters considered the British mad enough to take up the challenge.

It seemed to me that to be successful an expedition from the north must get its vehicles to the frontier in time to cross the swamp before the rains. The team must then have a proven method of crossing the morass and must plan a feasible route. I wondered if it would not be better to tackle the swamp first, by going from Tierra del Fuego to Alaska, but the committee lacked any real information about the swamp and their knowledge of the Darien jungle was pretty sketchy. My advice was that they make a thorough reconnaissance at the same time of year in which they proposed to tackle the obstacle. This meant postponing the expedition for twelve months.

A week later Tim Nicholson telephoned to ask if I knew a suitable person to carry out the reconnaissance, so I began to look for a determined, self-sufficient SES member with a keen eye for observation and the stamina of an ox. Brendan O'Brien, at twenty, was a wild, tough, well-travelled Irish daredevil. His amusing, easy manner and winning smile helped him to get on with people, who rarely took him seriously. Having recently overtaken a police car at enormous speed on the wrong side after a London party and fearing the consequences, he accepted the post without hesitation and, after some rushed training in Spanish and field engineering, set off for Darien in January 1971.

While our stalwart friend was hacking through the jungle, I did a little research into the type of vehicles and equipment that might be used in the Gap, assuming that, as a result of Brendan's reconnaissance, the committee decided that the project was feasible. At this stage I was simply an advisor. Then Tim telephoned me again.

'The leader's been posted to a new job,' he said with apprehension in his voice. 'Would you be interested?'

My curiosity was already aroused and, subject to the Army's blessing, I agreed. I realised this was going to be a tough challenge even with a good team and the best equipment.

Recruiting began at once. Rosemary Allhusen, a charming and

highly competent young lady, with enough self-sufficiency and determination to put half a dozen men to shame, volunteered to be my PA. Rosh, as everyone called her, had a real love of adventure, and experience of handling horses that was to be of considerable value. We worked well together. Even so, I must have driven her mad and I'll never understand how she managed to put up with me.

In April, Brendan returned, thin and haggard. For two hours I listened to his story and examined his photographs. In the end he said, 'Well, there it is. I think you can do it, but don't ask me to come with you.' With that he rushed off to the Hospital for Tropical Diseases, leaving me to reflect on the magnitude of the task.

For several days two voices argued inside me. One said, 'It will be bloody horrible; snakes, insects, heat, rain, jungle, swamp and what's more – very costly. The General Motors expedition, with all their careful planning, well-tried vehicles and generous funding, could not make it. How on earth do you think you can do it? Back out now with dignity.' The other voice said, 'Difficult yes, uncomfortable certainly, but nothing's impossible. A flexible plan, good logistics, sound equipment and a carefully chosen team could do it. What a challenge.'

The weather pattern dictated that we should move from north to south in the dry season, a purely relative term, which could be assumed to run from mid-December to mid-April. To fit this timetable, the vehicles should leave Alaska in early December and they would probably reach Tierra del Fuego in May.

The permission and support of the Governments of both Panama and Colombia would be essential. The help of the US Forces in the canal zone could be extremely valuable and, furthermore, political clearance was required to cross frontiers. Lastly, it would cost at least £25,000 in cash, in addition to the generous support in kind from the British services and other sponsors.

I told this to the organisers, now renamed the British TransAmericas Expedition Committee (BTAE), and added that it would take about six months overall and that my team would be around sixty strong, including scientists. I insisted that the expedition must have a scientific programme. It was of little real value just to get the vehicles through; we must also explore the region as thoroughly as possible. So we planned to undertake important investigations of a zoological, botanical and geological nature in what was, by any standards, a remote and inaccessible area. This task would be an urgent one, in view of the ecological disruption that might result from the construction of the highway. I also believed it was important to study the local people before their lives were changed forever.

My studies of various types of all-terrain vehicles showed that whilst an amphibious tracked vehicle would be best for the Darien Gap, it would not be able to maintain the high speed on metalled roads necessary for the easier parts of the journey. What was needed was a reasonably fast, light-weight, economical and yet robust wheeled vehicle. I talked to Ministry of Defence experts and examined reports on a wide variety of vehicles that might fit the bill. We decided an up-engined Land-Rover was probably the best option. I then asked Captain Gavin Thompson, a cavalry officer with rallying experience in the Americas, to head our vehicle section and he advised that the newly-produced Range Rover might be just what was required. The Rover Company was confident that the more powerful brother to the famous Land-Rover would indeed be the best vehicle and were enthusiastic about the opportunity for some valuable publicity for the new car. They agreed to lend us two Range Rovers, my only worry being that they weighed twice as much as Land-Rovers, but Gavin, whose knowledge of vehicles I respected, was impressed by the power and pointed out that this more than compensated for the extra weight. Jim Masters and Ticky Wright, sappers of the Blue Nile team, had joined the new venture. 'Well, if it won't swim, we'll have to make it float,' they muttered and phoned the Avon Rubber Company to discuss making an inflatable raft that would carry such a load. Jim thought it a hell of a weight to get over the narrow ravines and sought advice from the Royal Engineers (RE) bridge experts on the construction of special alloy ladders that could be carried on roof racks and laid over ravines. Meanwhile, Rover tested a Range Rover with various types of tyres and other fittings that might make it suitable for the expedition.

'We need something else to carry the cordage, tools, explosive, jacks and equipment for the engineers,' said Jim at one of our many meetings. 'We must keep the weight on the vehicles themselves to a minimum.'

'I was hoping to get mules for this,' replied Keith Morgan-Jones, our massively-built Army vet, 'but you can't get them for love nor ruddy money in Panama and because of foot-and-mouth, they won't permit them to be brought in from elsewhere. Only pack-horses are available and they don't carry more than 120 pounds.'

So off we went for more advice. The MoD engineer equipment branch produced details of a tracked, motorized wheel-barrow called a Hill-Billy and it wasn't long before trials of equipment were going on all over Britain. Our experts examined not only the Range Rovers but also Hill-Billys, rafts, power-saws, outboard motors and radios and even foods. The rations were, as usual, Kay Thompson's department and she also took up the reins as general manager and PRO. She and Rosh got on terribly well and were the nucleus of my staff in London. A steady stream of articles began to appear in many newspapers at home and abroad. Television and radio also took up the story, but, alas, having educated Britain to the horrors of Darien, we found that people believed the project was doomed to failure, and were not inclined to give us the support we now so badly needed.

'Look John,' said an old chum in the media business, 'I've put this project of yours to everyone I know and they all say the same – that you've bitten off more than you can chew this time. If it's half as bad as the press reports, it's obviously impossible. Anyway, no one in Britain cares very much about a road through Darien.'

But on the other side of the Atlantic people did care. Ultramar Inc generously offered to supply us with free fuel, the Explorers' Club in New York helped us to recruit scientists and the governments of Colombia and Panama suddenly began to take a considerable interest in the project. The Latin America desk of the Foreign and Commonwealth Office was tireless in its efforts to assist, as were the British Embassies throughout the Americas.

From the United States came a letter of good wishes from President Nixon and from the US Canal Zone came welcome offers of support. I felt we were really getting somewhere at last, and when the Canadian Broadcasting Corporation bought the North American television rights, we reached our minimum fund-raising target. Funds and grants came in from British sources as well. While some learned societies regarded the whole affair as a commercial publicity stunt, certain to fail, it was noticeable that a number of enlightened organizations put their faith in us and backed the expedition to the hilt. Prominent amongst our supporters was the Natural History Museum. I have always found the executives of the museum very keen to take opportunities to further exploration with natural history objectives. Two member of the museum staff, ornithologist Dr Philip Burton and entomologist Mick Baachus agreed to form a scientific section with Jerry Carter, a young geologist, Robin Hanbury-Tenison, sociologist, and Dr Al Gentry, a botanist working in Panama.

Colonel Peter Reid, a cavalry officer with an interest in natural history, would oversee the scientific work. Another keen ornithologist was the Army's Engineer-in-Chief, Major General Caldwell. The General had joined the BTAE committee at the outset. As the senior officer on the committee, he did a splendid job in helping us to get assistance and full-scale support from the Royal Engineers. Captain Ernie Durey, a well-fed, energetic forty-year-old sapper, with much experience of crossing obstacles, joined our team on the General's recommendation.

So the expedition assembled: sappers, infantrymen, cavalrymen, pilots plus an army doctor and his SRN wife. A dentist, a vet, scientists and secretaries, Americans, British, Latin Americans and a Gurkha. In all, fifty-nine men and five women to join another forty or so people in Darien.

In October 1971 we announced our plan. Our aim was simply to take two Range Rovers from Alaska to Cape Horn (or as near to it as it is possible to drive), making a scientific study of the Darien Gap en route.

In early December, a six-man driving-team would set out from Anchorage in Alaska, aiming to reach Panama City in early January. There, they would be joined by the main body of the expedition. Our column would enter the jungle with David Bromhead's recce team scouting ahead, finding a route for Jim's sappers to clear for Gavin's vehicles. My HQ would bring up the rear, with the supplies carried on Keith's horses. Outside the Gap, Major Kelvin Kent, my intrepid deputy leader, another Jerseyman, would organise our re-supply by air and river. Depots were to be established in the Gap or on the coast and a main base would be set up in Panama.

The Avon raft would get the vehicles across the rivers and through the wetter portion of the Atrato Swamp. I intended to airlift recce parties ahead of the expedition so that they might have adequate time to examine the ground, especially the great swamp. The

Colombian Navy promised a gun-boat to act as a floating base on the Rio Atrato and both the Panamanian and Colombian armies would send soldiers to escort us in their territory.

The scientists would accompany the expedition's main body or set themselves up independently in the area, whichever suited them best. Hopefully, their work would contribute to the protection of the environment in the future. I aimed to reach the far side of the swamp by mid-April, when I believed the rains would start. We should all go to Bogota, and, having sent the Range Rovers on to Tierra del Fuego, the rest of us would return to the UK.

Put like this now, it sounds very simple. Basically it was, but, above all else, it was the most flexible plan I could devise. In spite of Brendan's recce and all the information we had gathered, I still felt that there were far too many unknowns. Planning the attack on Darien was like preparing to assault a strong enemy position in war. Staff College training advised a commander to outnumber the opposition three to one. I knew that in this case the odds were very much reversed and the only way we could win was to concentrate our force at one point and maintain it for at least three months.

By December all was ready. The advance liaison officer, Captain Paul 'Arrangement' Arengo-Jones, had already arrived in Panama to make initial preparations and await the end of the rains. Meanwhile, feverish activity had been going on at Rover until the last minute, but eventually the cars were loaded into an RAF Hercules and despatched to Anchorage.

Then, in mid-December, came the awful news that one car had suffered a bad crash on Alaska's ice-bound Alcan highway, which would certainly prevent the vehicles reaching Panama before 10 January. At around the same time there was also bad news from Panama, Paul signalling to report that the rain was still falling hard with no sign of a break. Christmas was beset with worries, and I realised that I had become so consumed by the forthcoming campaign that I was now a real bore to my family.

At the farewell party the Minister of Defence said the expedition was the most ambitious ever undertaken by the British Army. It made me feel terribly responsible. It was a cold, wet dawn when I climbed shivering into the cavernous belly of the Hercules, feeling very tired, unfit and more in need of a week's holiday than three months in one of the most unhealthy regions on earth.

7

·

The Stopper

The turquoise blue sea showed momentarily through the clouds, then, as the Hercules altered course for Tocumen airport, a range of low green hills protruded through the cotton wool. At first the jungle of Panama looked peaceful. Facing inwards again, I fastened my seat belt, gazed across the mound of equipment and awaited the landing.

The belly of the giant freighter was largely filled by the dismembered Beaver light plane, its wings folded alongside, rocking gently on restraining chains, like some giant tethered insect. Around were dozens of boxes and crates, some labelled 'hazardous – with care', others 'fragile – this way up', and all bearing the words 'Operation Darien'. The weariness that had dogged me for the past weeks had gone. I now felt revitalized, alert and ready to go. Perhaps it was the welcome sleep I'd had while crossing the Atlantic, or the long awaited sight of the jungle. Whatever, quite suddenly, everything became very clear.

When the great tail door swung down a blast of humid tropical heat drew rivulets of sweat from every pore. Paul was there, and Kelvin, plus, praise heaven, the two Range Rovers. 'Everything's under control, John,' said 'Arrangement'-Jones. 'The Ambassador's car will take you to his residence where you are staying.' I thanked the crew of the RAF Hercules, which, to the astonishment of our Panamanian friends, was already giving birth to the Beaver.

His Excellency, Dugald Malcolm, was an honorary president of the expedition and, as a one-time regular soldier, the Ambassador understood both the diplomatic and military viewpoints of the project. Sipping whisky in his air-conditioned study, I realised how very fortunate we were to have such an ally and supporter at the startline. Everyone in Panama wanted to know of our plans and volunteered candid opinions about the Darien Gap. I had a strange feeling of being treated with a certain respect, rather as one might regard somebody who had once had a nervous breakdown and would shortly end up in an asylum!

Some say the first few days of an expedition are the worst. However, thanks to the advance party, all went remarkably smoothly. The Guardia Nacional (Panama's Defence Force) was most cooperative, and customs and immigration formalities were waived aside. The US Forces in the Canal Zone bent over backwards to help and provided us with a base, transport, vital jungle boots, hammocks and a one-day course at their Tropical Survival School. Further flights of passengers and freight came in on time and the task force quickly took shape. There were only two problems. Packponies, so necessary as load-carriers, were proving difficult to obtain and, most serious of all, it was still raining hard.

Captain Peter Marett, our intelligence officer, searched Panama for detailed information on the Gap and the weather we could expect. Nothing new emerged, surprisingly little being known of the mysterious forest beyond the city bounds.

As we held a press conference the lightning flickered and the rain fell in sheets. I hoped my replies sounded confident. Luckily, the reporters' attention switched to the ladies. The smartly dressed girls, fresh from swinging London, did not match the conventional idea of hearty women explorers. Did we but know it, they were every bit as mentally rugged and tough as their Victorian forebears.

Our first forward base camp was established in an army training camp on the edge of the actual Gap. Near here, at the 'Wild West' town of Canitas, the Pan-American highway ended as a dirt track. We hung our mosquito nets on the bunk beds and crawled onto the straw-filled mattresses.

Dawn at the Centro Instruccion Militar (CIM) seemed to come very early. I was awoken from a deep sleep by the most hideous din. My watch showed 0430 hours, yet blaring from the camp public address system was a continuous arrangement of martial music. Did our allies realise what they were doing? Heaving myself up, I rushed over to the guardroom. Fortunately I had grabbed my pith helmet, for I suddenly found myself involved in a military ceremony. The guard, immaculately dressed in starched fatigues, presented arms as their national colours were raised. Dressed in a colourful sarong, wearing flip-flops and my white helmet, I was at least able to stand to attention and salute.

The orderly officer marched over and with a smart salute said, 'Buenos Dias, Major.' With halting Spanish and convincing gesticulations, I explained that his music was driving me mad. The officer looked embarrassed and gave a sharp order. The din ceased immediately. Ah! Peace, perfect peace. I thanked him in French and staggered back to bed.

'That was probably their national anthem and they'll shoot you later,' growled the massive Morgan-Jones from behind a pile of saddles.

There was not a moment to spare during those hectic days. The sappers prepared the tools of their trade, the doctor made arrangements for the inevitable casualty evacuations, the scientists liaised with their opposite numbers in Panama and organised the safe custody of specimens, while Kay sorted out the tons of rations and 'goodies'. The vehicle party, helped by an expert from Rover, prepared the cars for the coming ordeal. The team from the Canadian Broadcasting Company arrived, a rugged pair of thoroughly professional film makers who fitted in well.

Peter had arranged an air reconnaissance programme aboard the Beaver and we set off with David Bromhead, our chief recce officer. Soon we were racing along the runway through the cold morning air, the roar of the aircraft's powerful engine taking us up and over our base camp. Now for the first time I saw the Darien Gap. We banked above the airstrip and headed east-south-east. Beneath us was gentle countryside, rolling green savannah, dotted, park-like, with trees and herds of white cattle. The town of Chepo, with its galvanized iron water tower, slid by under the port wing. Beyond, the sun glinted on the thick brown coil of the Bayano river, glistening like a giant snake. Canitas consisted of a scatter of white boxes in a square of red earth.

We tilted down as our pilot, Captain David Reid, turned the Beaver once again. Now the grassland was patchier and the green darkened as it thrust up towards us. A mist that had lain in sausage-shaped clouds at treetop level began to clear. The true shape of our

enemy now showed, yet from 500 feet it still looked innocuous. The steep ridges were thickly forested; in between, the trees appeared to be more widely scattered. All rose straight-trunked, some bearing umbrellas of foliage at their tops, others white and bare, with branches that reached up like spread fingers.

We dropped to have a closer look. The altimeter still read 400 feet even though we seemed to be brushing the tallest trees. I looked again at the green carpet and realised that what we had first seen was merely the primary jungle – the real problem lay below it. The giant trees emerged from undergrowth so thick that even from a modest height it looked solid. This secondary jungle flourished most luxuriantly where the big trees were sparse and let the sun in.

We descended towards the Bayano and flew about 100 feet above the water, over one of the long, narrow outboard-powered canoes or piraguas that serve as river transport in the isthmus. Faces turned up and arms waved. Further on the neat, rectangular, palm-leaf roofs of an Indian village clustered on the bank but, strangely, not a soul was in sight. We climbed to 1,500 feet and headed for the northernmost area of the two mountain ranges that flank the Darien. Our eyes searched the ground for any sign of a track. There was none. From the air the hills did not at first appear to be too steep, but this was deceptive; when we got low we saw that climbing them would be no easy task.

The smaller features, such as the rivers that twisted and turned under the green canopy were hard to distinguish. There were few villages marked on the map; only the occasional dwellings dotted along the riverbanks. I had to discover the best place to cross the Bayano, so we flew up and down the line of the river until our fuel was almost exhausted. Several points looked possible, but all would require rafting and the current was certainly not slack. Then we saw a track deep in sticky black mud leading to the river. So this must be it. We headed home. A further reconnaissance team moved into the Gap on 17 January and eventually located the crossing point.

Our main body was meantime assembling its vehicles, stores and packhorses in Canitas. Two days later, in drenching rain, we loaded the animals. The track ahead was ankle deep in mud but we could wait no longer. So, for the first seventy-two hours we marched in terrible conditions through the heat and mud of the open pastureland. We camped with our hammocks slung between the trees, cooking

Cuddly pets attracted recruits to my small private army at Hereford.
(Guinea pig on JBS's shoulder.)

My parents always visited me at Bisley. (*Daily Telegraph*)

CCF exercises in Jersey were all the more realistic when played out amongst the old German fortifications. (*Jersey Evening Post*)

Judith and I were married in Chester in August 1960.
(The Guard of Honour booby-trapped the exhaust pipe of the car
we drove off in. It was blown off with an enormous explosion an
hour later. We survived!) (*Fotocraft*)

Washing the expedition at an oasis in the Libyan desert, 1963.

'Roaring Meg' in action with a Parliamentary battery of the Sealed Knot. (*Soldier Magazine*)

Captain Jim Masters, the Sapper officer who played such a vital role in many of our expeditions. (*MOD*)

A tricky moment on the
Trisuli river in Nepal.
(*John Edwards*)

The Army Air Corps
Beaver swoops low
over Captain John
Wilsey (now General
Sir John Wilsey) to
drop ammunition and
much needed supplies.
(*Chris Bonington*)

THE DARIEN GAP EXPEDITION 1972
Ernie Durey and his unstoppable engineers forcing the Land Rover
Pathfinder through the Darien jungle. (*Scientific Exploration Society*)

Rafting across the Tuira in a stretch of fast current with the
indispensable Avon M650 rig. (*Daily Telegraph*)

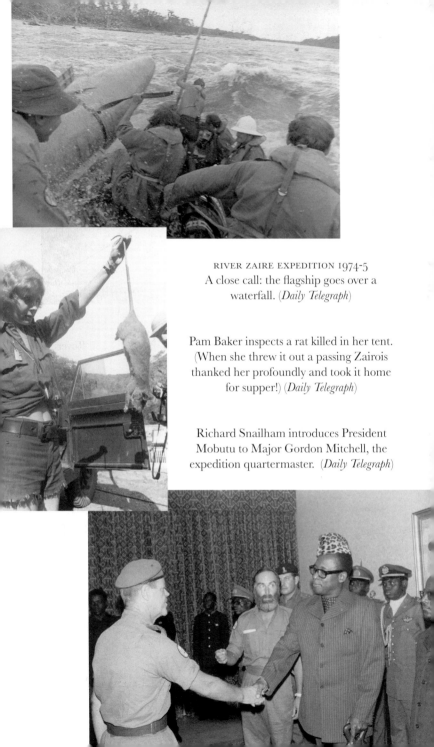

RIVER ZAIRE EXPEDITION 1974-5
A close call: the flagship goes over a waterfall. (*Daily Telegraph*)

Pam Baker inspects a rat killed in her tent. (When she threw it out a passing Zairois thanked her profoundly and took it home for supper!) (*Daily Telegraph*)

Richard Snailham introduces President Mobutu to Major Gordon Mitchell, the expedition quartermaster. (*Daily Telegraph*)

My daughters Victori (*left*) and Emma learr to control elephants during a family expedition in Tiger Tops in Nepal.

Ruth Cartwright (*né Mindel*) finds Monty rather lively at an Operation Drake selection weekend. (*SES*)

on damp wood fires. As yet, the mosquitoes were not a plague but, nevertheless, we always hung nets above our beds.

The Bayano was no mean obstacle, a 150-yard-wide coffee-coloured stream flowing at over four knots between jungle-covered banks. However, the sappers were confident and skilled, and in three hours they had got men, horses, vehicles and equipment all safely to the other side. The Avon inflatable raft again proved its worth. We looked ahead into the darkening jungle of the Bayano valley, the track still fairly clear, but covered in black, adhesive mud. Each day we marched further into the forest in a long straggling column. Our prison, for that is what it seemed, was illuminated by a dull green light, which at times gave an almost translucent appearance to this eerie world. Great trees rose up like pillars reaching for the sun, which beat down on the canopy some 150 feet above. Lianas and vines hung in a tangled mass to catch projecting horse-loads and to trip the unwary. The ground was a mat of leaves, and underneath we found a layer of humus, from which grew thick undergrowth. Visibility was rarely more than thirty yards and, all the time, the jungle resounded to the drip, drip, drip of the condensed humidity and the occasional crash of some giant tree falling at the end of its life. When the rain came it usually fell in torrents, turning the track into an instant quagmire. The thick black mud, ravines, gullies and dense jungle were augmented by the fast-flowing rivers, patches of poisonous palms and stinging plants. Then the sun would emerge, imparting a ghostly appearance under the dripping canopy. This was my first impression of the hot and humid Darien jungle and, after even a week, it seemed that we had been there forever. Our advance along our 300-mile uncharted route was at an average of three miles a day, a gruelling pace. It was easy to see how the ill-fated Scots colony, established on the coast of Darien in 1699, had perished from disease and hunger.

Going to bed was a tedious business. Firstly, we placed a waterproof cape above our mosquito nets to form a shelter and the guy ropes were thoroughly sprayed with insect repellent. Then the procedure involved unpacking a set of dry clothes from a plastic bag: peeling off the stinking wet day-clothes while balancing precariously on another bag; and wringing out the worst of the moisture and popping them into yet another bag to form a pillow. Then we paired up and aided by torch and mirror examined each other's bodies for thorns and septic cuts. We got the thorns out with twee-zers and applied liberal quantities of antiseptic to the sores before climbing into slightly drier night-clothes and ensuring that every item of equipment was suspended by an insect-proof cord above ground level. Now came the hop into the hammock. Great care was essential if one were not to plummet out the other side. Next one pulled on a flimsy sleeping-bag and positioned the pillow so that day-clothes, although soaking wet, would at least be warm in the morning. Finally, I always sprayed inside my net with a liberal dose of insect repellent, which usually put me to sleep as well!

The damp jungle chilled us to the bone by the early hours, I began to notice the effect of the strange environment on my friends and in my log recalled:

I have noted that on previous expeditions people looked for-ward to mail. I think, on this one, it is heightened by the jun-gle's claustrophobic effect, which not only isolates one from civilisation, but also from the sun and light. Daily we advance through a tunnel of dense vegetation.

Our sweat-soaked clothes rotted on us. Leather equipment grew mould, even the special self-draining canvas and leather jungle boots began to fall apart. The mosquitoes, gnats and flies became a constant plague. There were inch-long black ants whose bite hurt like hell for hours, stinging caterpillars and, in the river, electric eels. The heat and humidity were oppressive, and the nights brought little relief. Clusters of aggressive and vindictive hornets nested in hollow tress and swarmed out to meet anyone who disturbed them. I have never seen insects so vicious. Two stallions were among the herd. Randy, a bad-tempered beast, kicked and bit, so I took him myself. I thought he was under control until, without warning, the stupid bugger bit a hornets' nest. I fled and Randy bolted. We both had multiple stings. He didn't do it again! Within seconds a well ordered column could turn into chaos under attack from hornets. Rosh became seriously ill when she developed an allergic reaction to one such assault. She had collapsed, unconscious in the jungle, when Keith found her and it was his rapid action that got her to safety and probably saved her life. Centipedes and black scorpions also took their toll, whilst spiders as large as dinner plates were fearsome to behold.

When brushing against the foliage we constantly picked up ticks that, almost unnoticed, buried their teeth into one's flesh with such tenacity that they often had to be removed by the medical officer. On the other hand, the snakes were usually shy and it was not until later that we came across more aggressive varieties. The larger animals were rarely dangerous but on one occasion we came face to face with a beautiful black jaguar on the jungle track. Other cats included ocelot and margay, and, surprisingly, we saw many large deer.

The white-lipped peccary, a small wild pig, was a different matter altogether. Unlike his timid cousin, the white-collared variety, this vicious beast was much feared and avoided whenever possible. They moved in the twilight areas of the darkened forest in sounders of up to 200. At night in the impenetrable darkness only the noise of their snorting and rooting gave us warning of their approach. A machine gun would have had little effect on the concentrated rush of these ugly-tempered creatures and once they completely wrecked a camp, scattering the terrified horses into the jungle. Our revolvers and shotguns were useless against such an onslaught.

Not surprisingly, Sunday services were well attended and with Keith as choirmaster, the sappers, who loved to sing, would give throaty renderings of 'Guide me, O Thou Great Redeemer' and other appropriate hymns.

These Royal Engineers had been especially selected for their experience and stamina. Many were old hands at jungle bashing, but among them were two seventeen-year-olds from the Junior Leaders Regiment at Dover. Neither had been outside England before but, like other youngsters on the trip, put up a fine show. Also working as an engineer was an eighteen-year-old civilian, Simon Wilson, who had just left school. He obviously enjoyed being with the soldiers because on return to England he joined the Army! Thus started my ideas for later projects.

Our team also included Robin Hanbury-Tenison, an expert on the South American Indian and chairman of Survival International; one jungle expert was Gurkha Sergeant Partapsing Limbu. The Hon Charles Keyes, grandson of the famous Admiral, was an interpreter and navigator and we had soldiers from many regiments.

In the beginning we moved in a complete body with the leading recce team working some five to ten miles ahead. Another reconnaissance team worked about two miles in front marking the trail. Behind this came the first engineer section to cut a track some ten feet wide, using machetes, power-saws and dynamite. They cut their way forward and when they reached a ravine they bridged it with the special aluminium ladders, two of which were carried on each car. These ladders, devised by Jim could be linked together and were vital for bridging and rafting. We used them over 400 times throughout the expedition. The second engineer section used Tirfor jacks, blocks, tackles and the capstans of the cars to their absolute limit to drag the Range Rovers up the steep and slippery slopes.

Finally, the animal transport and Expedition HQ brought up the rear of the column. Rations, petrol, radios and medical supplies made up the bulk of the packhorse loads. Meanwhile the scientists moved independently about the expedition area. From time to time they came in to join the column before once again disappearing into their jungle demi-paradise in their quest for knowledge.

Kelvin brought in supplies by boat, helicopter, parachute, pack-ponies and porters. In all, over ten tons of rations, 15,000 gallons of petrol, 2,400 cans of beer, and 80,000 cigarettes, plus sacks of horse fodder, boxes of dynamite and mail were delivered by these means. These vital items mostly came from our support base in the Pacific coastal town of La Palma. It was not always easy to find us, so to help our pilots gas-filled balloons were launched on the end of a string to come bobbing up above the tree canopy. These fluorescent orange markers were accompanied by a firework display of rockets. Even so, searching for a small party deep in the forest was a difficult task.

Expedition members had been picked for their compatibility, physical fitness and expertise. However, as our problems increased and the going became more difficult the inevitable minor squabbles and signs of nervous exhaustion, more common in mountaineering, began to become apparent. The girls rose highly in our estimation, for, in spite of living under the same trying conditions as the men and being expected to work the same hours, do guard at night, pull the horses through mud, push boats up rivers and beat off the hordes of insects, they retained their good humour, rarely complained and always looked smart. Indeed, they added tone and often brought common sense to cool a heated argument. Kay was a tower of strength, even writing to those who did not receive letters. Limbu, whose wife was in Nepal, got very few. After Kay complained to his regiment he got two mailbags' full, while the rest of the expedition received one between them all! Back in Britain, the 7th Gurkhas CO had issued the order 'all men will write to Limbu'.

The rations designed especially for the project by the MoD were very good and thanks to Kay's efforts, other food was provided by numerous kind sponsors. The climate, with temperatures usually between 90° and 100°F and eighty-five per cent humidity, made us long for fresh, crisp salads, but the dehydrated food, especially the sliced apple, was a fine substitute. To vary the diet we also ate local dishes, which included jungle fruit, iguana, fish, monkey, snake and wild turkey. Just as we were breaking camp one morning two Cuna girls arrived. Earlier our doctor, John Richardson, had treated one of their babies for a skin rash. The child was now cured and they had come to thank us. I could not understand Cuna, but it seemed the young spider monkey they carried was a gift. Intending to release it as soon as they were out of sight, I accepted the little fellow. But one of the girls took it back and, slipping a knife from beneath her dress, smiled very sweetly as she slit its throat. Blood splattered everywhere when she pushed a sharp stick up the monkey's bottom and out of its mouth to enable her to roast it for me on the embers of our fire. She looked terribly hurt when I declined but she and her sister ate it themselves!

By now the rains had stopped and the lack of water became a problem. We had to resort to slicing open vines and drinking from them, filtering the water from slimy pools, or having it delivered by parachute.

A strange recruit was an American hobo who was fleeing the Inland Revenue Service. He had heard in Miami that the British were building a four-lane highway to South America and had decided to reach an aunt in Caracas via this road. Soon he lost our trail and was near starvation when Choco indians found him. Fortunately he had studied their language and, whilst he recovered in their village, learnt what they knew of us. Apparently, we were led by a tall and superior yellow-skinned Indian – that must have been Limbu – and our cars were so light we could toss them over rivers!

But the item they admired most was our magic box through which we communicated with our God. Whenever we needed anything, they said, we simply erected this little green altar in a clearing with a spike pointing to heaven, then we twiddled knobs and spoke to God. If he didn't reply we shook the altar and sometimes kicked it. Eventually God replied and we'd ask for whatever we needed. A great bird then delivered copious quantities of powerful firewater. Some we put in the cars and the rest we drank before advancing with renewed energy. A nice description of a radio call for a para-re-supply!

In the atrocious mud we had only done thirty miles in seventeen days. All our vehicles were casualties. To the sappers' delight, we had abandoned the Hill-Billys: the mud had oozed into their tracks and set like concrete. Then our heavily-loaded Range Rovers, with their immense power, began to break their differentials every few miles, sending gear teeth right through the casing and the floor, just like shrapnel. They ground to a halt at the Piriati River. Determined that the expedition should not fail, the Rover Company fought to solve the problem, flying out an expert from Britain with a massive load of especially manufactured parts. Geoff Miller was lifted by helicopter into the jungle, where he worked non-stop in a makeshift workshop. We were now weeks behind schedule and it was a race against time.

The climate and pace were beginning to tell, and eventually thirty members had to be evacuated by helicopter, light aircraft or boat because of illness. Dr John Richardson and his energetic SRN wife, Suzie, fought a constant battle to keep us fit. To maintain the momentum we needed large numbers of Indians, who, with their long machetes, could continue to hack through the jungle. And it was to the Curie village of Ipeti that I now turned for manpower. My log records the meeting with the chiefs:

> Travelling silently upstream in the dark, skilfully propelled by two braves, we were greeted by others at the entrance to the village and taken up to the council chamber. We entered the low, smoky building, lit only by many glimmering lamps set on little tables, beside which sat the women, embroidering and smoking from conventional looking pipes; olive-skinned children, mostly naked, scampered about the floor. Up towards the roof,

sitting on top of the tiered seats, as in a government chamber, sat the few men of the village who were not out earning their living in some distant part. In the centre of the room was a long bench which faced two hammocks set at right angles. On these swung the wrinkled old chief and his deputy. Our own interpreters, rather like the defence counsel in a court, sat on the right. We felt like prisoners in the dock. With me were Peter and Sergeant Limbu.

After the customary greeting, came the questions – very, very slowly. It was so slow because everything had first to be translated from English into Spanish and from Spanish to Cuna. The chief would then put any major decisions to the entire village and a vote was taken. Eventually we learned that we were allowed to hire twenty men at the reasonable price of $1.50 per man, per day. They asked us how we would communicate with the people who could speak neither English nor Spanish. I must confess I was stumped for a moment, and then said, 'I have a Gurkha!' 'How prudent,' replied the Chief, not really understanding what a Gurkha was. Limbu just smiled.

The Chief then asked about our work and got me to design an airstrip, which I did on the back of an envelope. He was particularly keen that his people should become educated, for he saw this as a means of advancement. He was naturally worried about the Bayano Dam, and what would happen to his hunting grounds and, indeed, to his village if the resultant lake spread up the Ipeti. Finally he questioned us about England. 'Are there Indians in your country. And do they have schools?' I replied that there were Indians and that they all went to school. He said, nodding, his wizened old head, 'Ah, it must be a good country.' They described their political problems and how they had voted for a man who had promised much, including a school, but nothing had happened. I told him such injustice also occurred in Britain.

After dark the jungle, viewed from the river, becomes a towering wall of blackness, broken only by fireflies. At night the creatures of this luxuriant world come forth to hunt and feed and, as we paddled against the current, the noise of the beasts reached an awesome crescendo. Frogs croaked, monkeys screamed and chattered and birds flapped loudly in the tall trees. My torch revealed pairs of red eyes glowing from the bank where small caymans waited expectantly in the shallows.

I placed Limbu in command of a Cuna working party and the column struggled on to Torti. The mud was the worst yet, horses sank in, loads came off, hornets attacked and tempers flared. One horse became so badly stuck that it took Keith and the sappers nineteen hours to extract it, only for the wretched animal to run back in again!

In early February base was set up at Torti. The 500-yard airstrip was the nearest point to the stricken vehicles, where I could air-land the heavy axle assemblies by Beaver. To get them to the Piriati would need a daunting porterage operation. The only real answer was to helicopter the spares direct to the cars. Kelvin would have to use all his ingenuity to achieve this. I had complete confidence in my deputy, but it was as well to be prepared if choppers could not be obtained. So I sketched out yet another contingency plan in my notebook, which was already filled with a mass of illegible hieroglyphics.

Torti had ample grazing and water but beyond this point we would be climbing out of the Bayano valley, leaving behind the sea of mud. The way ahead was, by contrast, dry and almost water-less. By radio David reported several formidable obstacles, many fallen trees and large numbers of aggressive peccary. He said the insects and snakes seemed more plentiful. Even the Indians avoided this region and it was difficult to find guides. We needed water, dynamite, more engineering tools and power-saws to cut the trail through to a ranch on the Gulf of San Miguel called Santa Fe.

It was early morning when, marching ahead of the column, I heard an unusual sound – a heavy diesel! Five minutes later we rounded a bend in the path and came face to face with a gigantic yellow bulldozer. 'Oh, you great big gorgeous creature,' I said, slapping its steel tracks. The operator, a stocky little old man with dirty blond hair, spoke Spanish with a guttural accent. Using the expedition dictionary that Rosh had written, I discovered he was opening a new logging trail and for some of its length would be using our route.

Musing on our good fortune I noticed the operator looking at me in an odd way.

'Americana?' he enquired.

I told him I was a British army officer and he paled slightly. So, for fun, I said, 'You are from Germany?'

He muttered, 'Many years ago, I come here in 1933,' and jumping into his seat went clanking off down the trail. The horses suffered terribly from the vampire bats, which attacked at night, biting their necks and injecting them with anti-coagulant to make the blood easier to drink. The horses' screams kept us awake and they grew weak through loss of blood. Then 'Scouse' Yeun, a Chinese Liverpudlian Lance Corporal in the Royal Engineers, came up with a plan. He cut up a pink parachute and made a protective nightshirt for a badly bitten animal. Eye and nostril holes were cut and the horse hobbled for the night. 'Well done, Scouse', we said after an undisturbed night, but at dawn the horse had gone. Searching for it along the trail, we came upon some terrified Indians who explained that the previous night they had been celebrating traditional fertility rights; the dancing girls had been whirling faster and faster and the purpose of the gathering was about to be achieved when a pink apparition had walked in and ruined everything. They supposed it to be a sign sent by their ancestors to rebuke them for evil and licentious living. When they discovered it was our horse, they were not best pleased so I let them keep it.

On 7 March we reached the dirty old riverside town of Yaviza. While the Range Rovers were being repaired, the column had lengthened to more than 100 miles, so to help speed up the advance we bought a second-hand Land-Rover in Panama for use as a pathfinder. It was flown out in the belly of a giant USAF helicopter, and used to support the leading engineer section.

Time was against us. Every day counted if we were not to be defeated by the onset of the mid-April rains. But by 20 March we were at Boco de Cupé and the Range Rovers were on the move. At the front, the reconnaissance patrol was working over a wide area, desperately seeking the best way through some seemingly impassable terrain known as the Devil's Switchback.

When the rains started again we were lashed with the full fury of the elements to an extent that few of us had ever witnessed. When this happened we were still crossing the Devil's Switchback. Here it was that whilst trying to hurry our reconnaissance we suffered a severe setback by going straight up a 'one-way street'. This led to an impenetrable hilly barrier and, because the Beaver had damaged its tail wheel and was being repaired, we failed to find this out by an air reconnaissance. Thus for ten days we floundered and struggled to conquer the Pucuru heights. I had even hired all the prisoners from the local jail, including several murderers, to cut for me. I guessed they probably feared the Indians more than us and would not flee.

In the wet I turned to Charlie Thompson, a friendly and helpful negro. 'Is this the rains, Charlie?' I asked.

'Rains, man?' Charlie shook his grizzled old head, down which the water cascaded, and smiled. 'No sir – this is jus' hoomidity!' But he told me that the main rains were preceded by a few days of the small rains. Then, some two to three weeks later, the proper rains would start. I looked at my battered map and wondered how much good luck we could count on. And it was at this point that Panamanian Sergeant De Leon told me of a place named Cruso Mono, where the Indians dragged logs down to the river.

If a heavy log could come down, a vehicle might be winched up, I thought. But it could only be reached by river, so we took a gamble and motored the cars up the bed of the river Tuira. This was possible because the water level was still low in spite of the downpours. When we reached deep pools the raft was called in and used to ferry the cars to the next shallow. However, it was not without incident. We were towing the laden raft upstream when, to my horror, I saw it rear up like a stricken beast. A helmsman yelled, 'She's going lads, get away, get away, we're going over.' The tow rope from my piragua slackened as the raft and its swaying Range Rover spun out of control in the foaming water, engines racing and men plummeting over the side. Water was pouring in through a two-foot gash in the hull of one pontoon.

Like a whaler's longboat, my piragua, with which we had been towing the raft across a fast flowing stretch, was dragged backwards by the stricken grey 'whale'. Sergeant Major Ticky Wright, boat expert and formerly a helmsman on the Blue Nile, was still aboard. My Panamanian boatman, Canito, realised what must be done and sliced through the tow rope with his machete. Somehow the raft was still upright. Men were struggling in the water, clearly visible thanks to their bright life-jackets. Downstream it spun, but by a miracle it seemed Ticky was winning control and he rammed the wreck into a shingle bank. The survivors had reached the river's edge and were clinging on to the trees. Few had the strength to climb out:

they had been working for hours in the blistering heat and, for some, every step with their feet raw from 'jungle foot', was agony. With his usual skill, Canito swung the thirty-foot canoe around and we picked them up. Some laughed nervously, some grinned, others looked very shaken and, in spite of a shade temperature of over 80°F, they shivered. Everyone was safe and the vehicle had been saved; but the raft, ripped open by a rock, was crippled and would need extensive repairs.

Nevertheless we got all the cars to Cruso Mono and, winching them up a sixty degree slope, reached the smugglers' trail to the Colombian frontier. A young sapper collapsed with acute appendicitis in Paya the last village, and there followed one of several dramatic night-time helicopter rescues by the USAF 'Jolly Green Giant'.

Half a mile from the border-plinth on the Panamanian side, we found a rusting red car, a sad reminder of the ill-fated Chevrolet expedition that had reached the frontier over ten years before, only to turn back. Now it lay, a rotting hulk, trees growing up through the engine compartment and an ants' nest in the boot. As we poked sticks into the interior a highly venomous coral snake slithered from beneath the remains of the back seat and a large black spider scuttled from the dashboard.

There had been several narrow escapes from serpents. When I was holding our ornithologist on my shoulders so that he could feel in a bird's nest, a coral snake slide along his arm and into his shirt. Luckily, this was not tucked in and the reptile dropped out and fell past me onto the ground. On another occasion, a six-foot bushmaster sank its teeth into the rubber heel of David Bromhead's boot. Its fangs stuck fast and, as it writhed, David blew its head off with his Smith & Wesson. Near the frontier Limbu had a lucky escape when a huge bushmaster reared up behind him. It struck twice, but each time the Gurkha took a pace forward for his next swing at the vegetation and the snake missed. Behind Limbu there was Ruby, a Colombian prisoner who spoke no English and no Gurkhali. Limbu spoke no Spanish and therefore Ruby's timely warning went unheeded. However, he raced up, pinning the reptile down with a forked branch, but could not hold it. Limbu spun round and with a continuous swing of his razor sharp kukri beheaded his attacker.

On 6 April we closed the base at Paya. A Colombian mule-train was joining us and Keith Morgan-Jones, his job done and now four stone lighter, waved goodbye as he set off down river in Canito's piragua. With him went Kay and others to help at Panama City before flying over to join us in Colombia. Charles Keyes took our faithful packponies back to sell them to the kindest homes possible. Many years later I was to see their descendants at Boca.

I presented the young Cuna chief with a splendid all-steel British axe. He looked rather sad and a tear welled in his eye as he gripped my hand. 'Come back one day, Quebracha.' he said.

'What does that mean?' I asked.

'Axebreaker – name of hardest wood in the forest – it's a compliment,' said De Leon.

'Don't tell the sappers that,' I retorted.

This was a significant moment in the expedition. The curtain was dropping on an act; teams welded together by their battle against nature were breaking up after a long time. The old cast had hardly dispersed before the new actors came on stage.

'Buenos Dias,' said the living image of Mussolini in a sombrero. Francisco, muleteer extraordinary, strode into our camp at the head of his column. His massive, muscular beasts dwarfed our ponies. 'If you are ready, my mayor, I will load mules,' said Francisco firmly and we stood back to admire his skill. 'The mules will march by themselves. You go ahead. I will meet you at Palo,' said our self assured friend. Enormous trees soared skyward for over a hundred feet. An occasional ray of sunshine filtered through the canopy, but for the most part the forest floor was a gloomy green world, through which flittered electric-blue butterflies and tiny humming birds. Above us raucous macaws, big-beaked toucans and brightly coloured parrots clucked and called with ear-splitting shrieks. The air was heavy with the scent of blooms that I had not seen when on foot because of the need to pick a path with care.

From muleback I could observe brilliant flowers, beefsteak plants and thousands of tiny creatures that lived in this vast overgrown hot-house. We reached Palo at 1350 hours and, apart from the broken-down concrete plinth that marked the frontier, the little clearing was empty. We were to meet the Colombians at 1400 hours, so I walked forward to photograph our four-man headquarters with the Union Jack, which the American hobo was clutching incongruously.

It was 1400 hours precisely when the jungle around us moved. I looked up to see that we were facing the Colombian Army. A platoon of swarthy, purposeful soldiers in camouflage uniform, their weapons spotlessly clean, watched us in silence. From their midst an officer stepped forward, and said, 'Captain Sierra of the Fourth Brigade Infantry,' clicking his heels with Prussian precision as he saluted smartly.

'Welcome to Colombia.' His sergeant major seized our Union Jack. I was certain that we had committed some unpardonable breach of international law, but he put my mind at rest, saying, 'It is your right to carry your flag into Colombia, according to the Treaty of 1821.' This was true, but I was surprised that our friends were so well briefed. The sergeant major then asked if he might be allowed to carry the Union Jack into his country as indeed the Duke of Wellington's veterans had done when they came to support the colonists in their bid for freedom 150 years before. Thus we marched downhill into the thickening jungle of the Atrato valley.

Kelvin and the Pathfinder group were already a day ahead and going well. And that night we reached the riverside camp of the Colombian Commander, Major Alberto Patron. We ate a communal meal with our allies and enjoyed the first of many cups of superb local coffee. Alberto briefed me on the campaign that was being waged against the communist guerrillas throughout the more remote regions of Colombia. 'I think the Atrato is too unhealthy a place – even for the communists,' said the unusually fair-haired officer, 'but we must take precautions; seven soldiers were killed in an ambush near Barranquillito last week.'

So far the Darien Gap had thrown everything at us except bandits so I checked my revolver carefully that evening. From here on the going got wetter, but a new spirit had come into the team and nothing could stop us now, not even the swamp the size of Wales that lay ahead. I had every faith in Alberto and his soldiers, some of whom were members of the original team sent to meet us when a terrible tragedy occurred. The Colombian gunboat that was to support our crossing of the Atrato was lying off the small port of Turbo. Our liaison officer, Captain Jeremy Groves, was with a party of six Colombian servicemen heading out to join the vessel in one of the ship's boats when it was pooped by a large wave and sank immediately. The only survivors were a Colombian officer and Jeremy. The remaining five Colombians had been drowned or sucked down in the mud of the mangrove swamp that fringed the shore nearby. Nevertheless, our friends produced another team within a matter of days and continued to back us wholeheartedly until the very end. So on 10 April Expedition HQ was established for the last time. By coincidence it stood on a 'peak in Darien' looking out, not across the Pacific, but over the steaming green morass of the Atrato swamp. We were two weeks behind schedule and the promised rains had begun. It was a desperate race to cross the remaining fifty miles that no motor vehicle had ever previously traversed.

Working ahead of us for some weeks, Sapper Captain Richard Summerton had discovered a possible route through. Much of the area was liquid with a coating of water weed, in which lived countless mosquitoes, many snakes and the occasional alligator. To break through we used our raft, which was undoubtedly the most successful single item of equipment we possessed. Forcing a way through the matted weed was a hellish problem. We tried cutting it with machetes, pulling on it with grapnels, and eventually used necklaces of dynamite. The side benefit of this latter method was some good fish breakfasts. Indeed, the swamp was teeming with huge tarpon. As we forced our way through, the foul stench of rotting organic material rose up. In some places logs had mixed themselves in with the weed to form more obstacles and these we smashed with dynamite or sliced through with the outstanding Husquvarna power-saws. Gradually the number of trees began to increase, strange unearthly shapes, growing up out of the swamp around us to form the appearance of a primeval forest, inhabited only by huge birds, lizards and giant otters. At one point my piragua capsized. Luckily it did not sink, because apart from a muddy bank nearby there was nowhere to swim for safety. Whilst bailing out the boat we were supported by our life-jackets and, although we lost some valuable equipment, we managed to re-board the boat and continued our journey, somewhat shaken, very wet and rather smelly.

Eventually the cars were placed on a firmer crust. This slippery surface of matted vegetation and soil would be flooded when the rains reached their height. Now, however, it was about three to four feet thick and would stand the weight of our vehicles fitted with extra wide Firestone tyres. The area, which was forested, had the construction of a giant sponge and you could see numerous holes going down from the surface into the liquid mud. Doubtless it was up these shafts that the water would rise and flood the area. We were told by engineers and surveyors that they had lowered a drum full of concrete on a wire into the swamp and at 1,000 feet they had not yet reached firm bottom. Many parts of this incredible area looked solid, but one day when landing from a float-fitted helicopter I climbed gingerly out onto the surface. Immediately the area within fifteen feet gave slightly and I had the wobbly feeling of standing on a giant blancmange.

On 23 April the sun set with its usual livid orange glow and as it did so a party of ragged, filthy men and women, mules and vehicles emerged on the far side of the vast bog. Their eyes were hollow and their faces drawn, their bodies a mass of bites and sores and their feet were in an indescribable condition, but somehow as they staggered up, dragging, heaving and pushing their vehicles on to the northern end of the southern section of the Pan-American Highway, they managed to smile.

After ninety-nine days in the jungle and swamps of Darien, we had broken through. It was St George's Day. That night a storm surpassing anything we had experienced previously hit the little town of Chigorodo where we slept. As we bailed out our accommodation, Alberto said, 'Now, John, the real rains have come; you made it by ten hours.'

There was always danger round the corner. And on the last day Ticky and a sapper almost lost their lives when returning to Turbo with the gunboat. They were working on the raft tied alongside the ship, which was moving at approximately five knots. Suddenly, something struck the front of one of the inflatables and without warning the bow of the raft doubled up and water swept over it. Both men were hurled into the river and sucked under. They found themselves bumping along the rusty, flat hull and suddenly being spun with enormous force by the screw. Fortunately the gunboat had lost one of its propellers the previous week, which saved them from a horrible death. Nevertheless, they were extremely fortunate to be hurled out into the wake, having lost all their clothing and watches, and to be hauled back aboard with only superficial bruises and cuts.

In Medillin we were received with warm hospitality, and found a message of congratulations awaiting us from Her Majesty the

Queen. More parties, a triumphal motorcade and a ceremony at Simon Bolivar's statue followed in Bogota. Checked and serviced, the Range Rovers drove on.

Complete success came later, on 9 June 1972, when Jeremy Groves sent 'Mission Accomplished' from Cape Horn. In Mexico they had met desert conditions and in Guatemala the Pan-American Highway became a rutted track. They beat the Darien Gap and then climbed into the high Andes. In May 1972 they sped on through South America, crossing more mountains and once again meeting desert in Chile. Here they covered 2,375 miles in four days, and one day made 800 miles cruising at ninety mph on a desert road. In the Gap they had only averaged three miles in a day.

As they neared their goal, they hit snow and ice once more. Many mountain passes were blocked and it took five long days to break through this last obstacle. On one occasion they had to cross a lake on a Heath Robinson local raft to avoid the blocked passes. At Cape Horn the engines were switched off after seven months and 17,000 miles.

We won the special gold medal presented by The Darien Action Committee for being the first vehicle expedition to make a complete crossing, including the Atrato swamp. The project was hailed by governments and sponsors as a notable success, but there had been many moments during the journey when we found it hard to believe that we could win. Common sense and logic should have made us give in a hundred times, but still we had pressed on. Indeed, it had been an incredible adventure, accomplished thanks to determination, flexibility, excellent equipment and good practical engineering, coupled with generous backing from sponsors. Our track has become known by the Indians as the Carretera Inglesa – the Englishman's Road – and they use sections of it to travel to market.

Later we learned the Highway would go ahead and follow our path. However, I sincerely hoped that the road-builders would spare a thought for the animals, the people and the flora of this strange land, whose environment would now be changed forever.

8

The Beavers

'Good Morning, sir,' snapped the wiry Scot. 'Sergeant Major Donald reporting.' Standing in front of me was the erect figure of my new squadron sergeant major. Had I not already heard that he was a very high-grade soldier, I should now have guessed that here was someone with fire in his belly. Although greying hair and weather-beaten features made him look rather older than he was, his twinkling eyes were those of a man young in heart and spirit.

'Do sit down,' I said. 'How do you like the idea of joining 48th Field Squadron?'

'Very much,' he replied sharply, the bristle of his short moustache twitching.

'Any reason in particular?' I asked.

'Well – they say that you're a wee bit of a mad bugger and so am I, so I think we'll get on together,' he said slowly with a broad grin. I decided I liked Sergeant Major Donald.

We both enjoyed being with the squadron. Following the Darien adventure it was time for some conventional soldiering and this was going to be much more enjoyable than driving a desk in the war office. The squadron had been raised in Canada so its symbol was the Beaver; a busy little chap who spends its life eating, sleeping and mating whilst mucking up people's gardens. He epitomized the spirit of our unit.

It was a bitter February morning when we came ashore at Belfast Docks. We were to provide engineer support to the British troops, covering some 2,000 square miles of the Ulster border counties. One of our major tasks was searching for terrorist arms, explosives and equipment and for this purpose we had formed a special search troop. It was a difficult, hazardous and unpleasant task. Houses were often booby-trapped and a 'tip-off' on the robot telephone system could be a lure to get us into a trap. I needed my best leader for this troop and, without hesitation, appointed the sergeant major.

The squadron worked around the clock building defences, hunting for mines, clearing obstacles, manning boats, patrolling the streets and searching, searching, searching. From time to time we got shot at, usually by a sniper, unseen behind a darkened window or a leafy hedge. Mines exploded beneath vehicles and on one occasion it was only a short stop for tea that saved me from being blown up by a 300-pound bomb, placed in a culvert. Tragically it got a Ferret armoured car a few minutes ahead of us, killing a young officer.

However, there were also lighter moments. In one village an old lady had been observed carrying out plates of food, having looked furtively around to place them under an upturned bucket in her garden. Suspecting an IRA gunman was concealed in a hide we raided the property only to find a sleepy tortoise under the bucket.

In Ulster I met the most friendly, hospitable people in the world, but I also met the most bigoted and unreasonable. I saw hatred that I would have hardly believed possible in the United Kingdom, and I saw love and compassion beyond compare. I came away as perplexed as the day I arrived, but sadly I left a good friend behind.

Donald's Goblins, as we knew the search troop, had quickly gained an enviable reputation for their dogged determination and skill. For fourteen weeks the rugged Scot encouraged and led his men from one success to another. In the face of danger, Ian Donald set the highest example of courage, initiative and leadership and his happy manner, devotion to duty and tireless efforts were an inspiration to all. It gave me a tremendous thrill to watch this team at work. One could not help admiring the cool, matter-of-fact way they searched, cheering themselves up with a continuous good-humoured string of obscenities, knowing all the time that they were a prime target for the bomber and sniper.

On 24 May 1973 they had been engaged on a variety of searches since well before dawn. It was a bright, sunny afternoon in South Armagh, when they found the first collection of bombs and booby traps in a post office. Leaving an expert to deal with these, the Goblins moved on to examine a house that was thought to contain another bomb. The infantry had already cleared the council estate

of civilians and children. The semi-detached dwelling was surrounded by a small low-walled garden and stood at the end of the
street. The border was 100 yards away. It all looked innocent, but
Donald trusted nothing. Rightly, he decided to blow a hole in the
rear wall. Doors and windows are likely sites for booby traps. Thus
he deployed his men to minimize the risk and began a methodical
search of the garden.

'No one is to enter the house until I am satisfied that it is safe.'
So saying, he moved forward alone to clear a safe lane across the
lawn. 100 yards away women in curlers, grubby children and sullen men watched in silence. On the hills around, red-bereted paratroopers scanned the hedgerows for any sign of a terrorist, and over
the border the Irish Garda watched too. To the Goblins it was just
another job. There were always these tense minutes when someone
must go forward by himself and it was usually Ian Donald who did
so. Two of the team were circling the house, their cautious movements watched by other sappers from behind the village store. On
the lawn the sergeant major inched his way forward, probing for
the concealed menace and feeling for trip-wires. Only fifteen yards
from the back door, he paused and looked up.

At that moment the house disintegrated into a mass of flying
slates, bricks and splintered timber. The distant roar of the explosion was heard in the sand-bagged police station at Crossmaglen,
where Lance Corporal Szade, one of the search team commanders,
was waiting with his men. Long before the first radio message came
through, they all felt a dreadful foreboding.

At Castle Dillon the rising trout were sending concentric ripples
over the mirror surface of the lake. At my desk as I finished off
some paperwork, the operations room intercom crackled, 'OC, sir
– there's been an explosion near Crossmaglen – we've got Corporal
Szade on the phone.' The hair on the back of my neck rose a little.
I knew Szade would only use a telephone if it was a real emergency.
The line was bad. The NCO had no definite information, but he
could not raise the sergeant major on the radio.

In minutes, I boarded the helicopter, hurtling over the lush green
countryside. The village of Cullaville appeared in the distance and,
as we got nearer, I could see the little estate littered with debris. A
burst water pipe was sending up a fine spray from a pile of rubble
that had been the end house. Donald was lying in the garden, partly

covered by wreckage: he had died instantaneously. In the road out-side, a sergeant in the Parachute Regiment, who had chanced to walk down the street, had been killed by a piece of flying timber, but thanks to the care with which their leader had positioned them, the remainder of the search team had survived.

We waited until nightfall before getting him out, just in case there was a second device, possibly rigged to be fired by remote control. Thus it was 2300 hours, when, crouching behind the garden wall, we carefully pulled aside the wreckage with a length of rope. With my heart thumping I crawled over the lawn and reached out to touch his hand. It was cold and stiff with rigor mortis, but his pis-tol, loaded and cocked, was held in a vice like grip. It took several minutes to prise the fingers apart and release the weapon before carrying the shattered body out of the ruins to the waiting Saracen armoured vehicle. I collected his sheath knife and holster for his sons and then wrapped him in a blanket, before giving him a final salute. I knew that the army had lost an outstanding soldier. Mar-garet Donald had lost a fine husband, and I had lost a friend I was not likely ever to forget.

In June 1973 we handed over to 11th Field Squadron. Its com-mander, my old friend, Major Dick Jarman, waved us farewell. 'Look after yourself, Dick,' I shouted. Three weeks later he, too, was killed by a bomb.

But by now the Beavers were deployed in warmer climes in Belize. On my way back home to Yorkshire, I planned to rest at the Scientific Exploration Society base in Wiltshire. The white-walled Tudor farm was bathed in pale moonlight, the shrubs and trees of the garden cast strange shadows on the concrete patio. As the big Volvo's engine died, I stepped out into the chill English night air. 'Brrr,' I shivered as I strode over to the kitchen door, remembering Jim Masters' instructions: 'Keys in the letter box. We'll be back in the morning.' My friends Jim and Joan were wardens of the base and having just flown in to RAF Brize Norton I was to sleep here; with some snow over much of Northern England, I didn't fancy a long drive after my eight-hour trans-Atlantic flight.

The door swung open and warm air spilled out to greet me. The neon light flickered, revealing a note, a newspaper and a bottle of J&B on the scrubbed kitchen table. 'Welcome, John,' read the mes-sage. 'Help yourself. Please use the bedroom at the top of the stairs.

See you tomorrow.' Pouring a good measure of man's best friend, I flicked open the *Daily Telegraph* and started to catch up on the news. My heavy diver's watch read 1930 (New York time) and, having just caught up five hours, I was not the least bit tired. The glass of Scotch was getting low when I heard the coughing – it was right above me. How odd, I thought, looking up at the oak-beamed ceiling. And then I remembered. Heavens, it must be Michael – and I've woken him up. Michael, Jim's teenage son, slept in the room above the kitchen and although his parents were out, I guessed Michael had come home early, used his own key and gone to bed. So I put away the Scotch and tiptoed up to my bedroom where the long hours of travel quickly had their effect.

Waking up with the sun, I stretched, yawned, climbed reluctantly out of bed and tottered off to the bathroom to shave and bath. The internal walls in the farm were barely partitions and with the creaky, irregular wooden floors every noise was audible. I could hear Michael dressing in his room and later, as I wallowed in the steaming bath, I saw his shadow cross the frosted glass door, followed by the 'clump, clump, clump' as he descended the narrow wooden stairs. As I dried myself, he returned and as he passed the door I called out, 'Morning, Michael,' but there was no reply. Once dressed, I phoned Judith and announced my return. Michael was still moving about in his room.

Suddenly, there was the sound of a key in the lock and in walked Jim and Joan. 'Sleep well?' they enquired.

'Yes – super, and bless you for the J&B. You know my taste.' We chatted for a moment and then, as Joan put on the coffee, I said. 'I'm sorry I disturbed Michael last night.'

She looked at me in a strange way, 'Michael?' Joan asked.

'Yes,' I said, 'upstairs.'

Her brows narrowed. 'John,' she said very slowly, 'Michael has not been here for six weeks – he's away at college.'

'Then who on earth's upstairs?' I said, 'because he's still there.' In a flash we were at Michael's room. The bed was not even made up – there was just a plain mattress on the springs. I felt rather cold and the hairs on the back of my neck lifted. We checked the entire house from top to bottom. All doors and windows were locked from inside. Other than the one in my possession, Jim had the only other key. I must have been alone.

'Leave the coffee – you'd better have something stronger,' said Jim. 'We've got a story you'd better hear.'

The tale they told was all the more amazing because of the personalities involved. Jim and Joan are two of the most practical, down-to-earth people I've ever met. To hear them talking of the mysterious events that had been going on at the farm for the past year left me feeling uncomfortable. It was like finding a life-long teetotaller stoned out of his mind!

For some time the family had experienced strange noises and movements and had finally seen a silver-haired lady in Michael's bedroom. Jim, a stolid West Country man, is not the sort to make a fuss. One of their most dramatic sightings had occurred quite recently. Jim had been alone in his indoor workshop with the door open when he became aware of a cold feeling. He turned around and there stood a man – medium height, ruddy complexion, fifty-ish, dressed rather like a farmer. As Jim gasped in astonishment his visitor wore an inquisitive smile, as if to say, 'What are you doing?' Then he was gone – quite literally into thin air. Jim, an ex-parachute engineer well used to rapid action, reacted at once. Dashing out of the room, he checked the doors and windows. All were locked from inside – there was nobody else in the house.

There was no more to tell. However, the farm belonged to a friend of mine who knew of no previous history of haunting, no accounts of terrible deeds, no tales of unrequited love. However, he promised to ask around. Several months later, I called in on him. 'Oh, by the way, John,' he said, 'I've made some enquiries about the ghostly visitations and something quite interesting has come up.'

'Go on. Tell me more.'

'Well, there was indeed a lady living there once who fits the description; her husband was employed on the farm some years ago and she died in that bedroom, but from natural causes – no murder or anything like that. As for the man Jim saw, that seems to have been her husband. The funny thing is, he's still alive and lives about ten miles away!' I had another whisky and went off to tell Jim and Joan.

Our next destination was rather warmer.

The desert Sultanate of Oman lies in southern Arabia with its province, Dhofar, bordering on the Indian Ocean. This coastal territory separates South Yemen, better known as Aden, from the oil-rich Persian Gulf, where in, 1974, an average of six giant oil tankers would pass through the narrow Straits of Hormuz every hour, carrying the precious lifeblood of the West. Since the British withdrawal from Aden, the former colony had become a Marxist base and was actively supporting a rebel war in Dhofar. The rebels' strategic aim was the Gulf; Soviet arms were sent in and local revolutionaries received training in China and Russia. The oppressive rule of Said bin Taimur, the aged sultan, his long-standing alliance with the Imperial British and the poverty-stricken Dhofaris provided ideal ingredients for Communist propaganda. The People's Front for the Liberation of the Occupied Arabian Gulf was comprised of various rebel groups and initially made good progress. Against them stood the poorly equipped Sultan's army, consisting of barely 1,000 combatants, including a large number of Baluchi mercenaries and a few seconded British officers. In 1970 the situation changed.

It was a quiet July afternoon in Salalah: the still air in the yard of the Sultan's palace was hot and humid. Unnoticed by the household slaves, the local Wali's son, a handful of Omani Askers, plus an amusing soldier of fortune named Spike, entered the labyrinth of passages that led to the private apartment of the charming old tyrant. At first they were unopposed, but suddenly the royal bodyguard discovered the intruders. Shots rang out, ricocheting off the thick stone walls. Dashing through the dark corridors, Spike came to a heavy door, behind which he assumed lay the Sultan's room. Flinging it open and yelling 'Your Majesty?', he found himself looking down the barrel of a tripod-mounted machine-gun with its owner in the act of pressing the trigger. 'Clackety-click' went the weapon as it failed to feed a round into the breech. 'Christ,' swore Spike and, dealing swiftly with the opposition, dashed on to the next room. The door was locked and the answer to his shout of 'Your Majesty?' was a burst of shots through the wooden panels. 'Oh bother,' said Spike (or words to that effect). He was just wondering what to do next when a shot was heard within, instantly followed by a shriek of pain. Bursting in, he found the Sultan hopping around holding his foot! Whilst trying to reload his pistol the ruler had accidentally shot himself. Spike, who knew the old man well, helped him to the courtyard where a Land-Rover rushed him to hospital. Within minutes it was all over. Said bin Taimur signed a letter of abdication in favour of his Sandhurst-trained son, Prince Qaboos, and an RAF aircraft flew him to Britain where he lived out his last few years in a private suite at the Dorchester.

The new Sultan immediately set about strengthening his armed forces and turning the rebel tide, and at the same time the force from the Beavers underwent some hard training on the North Yorkshire moors. In December 1973, in freezing blizzards, we practised our tasks and got fit. 'Just imagine it's sand, lads,' grinned Sergeant Major Cox, Donald's replacement, as we stumbled about in the snow and cursed this new jaunt, which they were convinced was something 'bloody Blashford-Snell' had dreamt up to keep them away from the fleshpots of Ripon.

In a fleet of RAF transports, we left Britain, still in the grip of winter, for the deserts of Dhofar. At last, a hazy coastline loomed ahead. Miles and miles of sandy beaches stretched as far as the eye could see. Breaking waves rolled in from the deep green ocean to pound the shore, upon which we could make out the dun-coloured houses of Salalah. Roaring in low over fertile gardens, the Hercules wasted no time circling the airfield and so risking a burst of enemy fire. In seconds, we were down and taxied quickly between a line of oil drums filled with sand to give protection against shrapnel. The men's eyes screwed up in the intense glare as the sun scorched our skin.

Although the province was largely a wasteland, with barren mountains and just an occasional oasis, the plains of Salalah are an exception. This is because from June to September the southwest monsoon blows in from the sea. Known as the Khareef, it produces clouds that precipitate water onto the Qara Hills, filling the rivers that flow on to the Salalah Plain and giving rise to spectacular waterfalls and raging torrents. When this happens the desert blooms into stunted jungles, lakes and rolling downlands of lush grass.

The Dhofar Brigade, whom we were there to support, was commanded by a tough, dynamic officer with a grand sense of humour. I counted myself fortunate to serve under Brigadier Jack Fletcher. Briefing me in the small headquarters on the edge of Salalah airfield, his sun-tanned hand moved firmly across the map. 'In the eastern and central areas the enemy have been driven back and now we must hunt them out. We also need to convince the tribesmen that we are offering a better life than communism. So that's one of your jobs: to help us win over their hearts and minds. But I also want you to improve our defensive positions and living accommodation on the jebel before the wind and damp of the Khareef hits us in June.' He paused to uncover a separate map and then waited whilst the roar of a departing flight of Strikemasters subsided. The new map showed the mountains to the west. 'Now, this is where you can have a real field day,' smiled Dynamite Jack, as he was known. 'The Hornbeam defensive line runs through these mountains. It's designed to stop the enemy getting personnel and supplies to the eastern and central areas. We've started to wire it, but before the monsoon you must create the most deadly obstacle you can devise. The problem is that the line is thirty miles long. Wire is on its way, but mines are still in short supply. I can't spare many troops to help you and only helicopters can reach the hilltop positions. Meanwhile, the Northern Frontier Regiment is holding the line with a battery of guns in support. I suggest you pop down and see Brian Ray (Lt-Col J.B. Ray, MBE) and then let me have your plan in, say, two days' time. And, by the way, do you know anything about finding water?'

'I'm ready to try,' I replied.

'Good. Well, you'd better see what you can do for Simba.' He pointed out an isolated position where a battalion held a rocky bastion right on the frontier with South Yemen. They were completely surrounded, shelled and mortared daily, and relied entirely on helicopters to lift in their supplies of everything, including water.

As I left the Brigadier's office a staff officer greeted me. 'We're here to help you, but you may be able to assist us,' he said. 'Can you build air-portable ration stores?'

In another room the commander of the Sultan's Air Force handed me a glass of iced lemonade and asked if we could construct landing pads for a squadron of Wessex helicopters that were expected in ten days' time. I got back to my windowless office at Umm Al Ghwarif with enough work to keep an entire engineer regiment going for weeks, let alone a small squadron. Peter Page, my wiry, energetic second-in-command, whose immediate ambition was to get a place in the forthcoming Army Everest Expedition, cleared the layers of freshly blown sand from the operations room table and we sat down to study the map.

As we worked on the deployment plan, Jack Walker, our quartermaster began to list all the nails, timber sheets of 'wriggly tin' (corrugated iron), explosive, cement, hand tools, barbed wire, mines and vehicles that we were going to need. In such an unsophisticated country as Oman the job of obtaining these was no easy task. Everything was 'on order' or 'on the high seas somewhere' or would 'arrive tomorrow, Insh'allah' (If God wills)! On the rocky jebel, even sand was in short supply and if concrete was required in the defensive positions, we had to deliver cement, water and sand to the site by aircraft!

Victory in this war depended just as much on the logistic back-up as on the skill and courage of the front-line troops.

However, before we could serve effectively alongside the Sultan's men we needed to acclimatize, and thus I planned a week's intensive training aimed at getting the Beavers used to working in the blistering heat while building up a protective tan on their skin. We did PT on the beach, swam in the surf and zeroed our weapons on a nearby range. Each day we exposed our bodies to the merciless sun a little longer and rapidly the lily-white torsoes turned a deep brown.

On the fourth day we mounted a simple operation with the aim of building a corrugated iron school at a coastal village seventy miles east of Salalah. The people, mainly fisherfolk, had been resettled on a flat plain separated from the rebels and the rest of Dhofar by the towering peaks of the jebel. Using a fleet of box-like Skyvan transports we flew men, tools, stores and water over the pale brown crags and canyons. The terrain was stark, awe-inspiring and frightening. In this desolate land mere survival against the elements is a battle itself, without the added complication of the deadly human enemy.

Winging our way through the great gorges we rounded a bend to find the green ocean waiting. The mountains fell away in vertical buttresses as we dived steeply onto the short air-strip. Skyvan engines have an unusual characteristic of not changing pitch as they land and it was therefore comforting to realise that we were actually slowing down. Men and children poured out from the shacks to meet us and, without bidding, began to cart all our equipment towards the school site. The area was peaceful and no rebels had been seen in recent times, so the work progressed rapidly. As the school went up, Sergeant Major Eddie McGee of the

Army Physical Training Corps put his knowledge of the area to good use. Chatting up the locals in a Yorkshire dialect of Arabic, he found that one youngster had fallen backwards onto a broken bottle, which had gone right up his rectum. When Eddie arrived the boy was in a terrible state. The villagers, having no proper medical facilities, had covered the dreadful wound with camel dung, believing it to be antiseptic.

Whilst this was going on the leader of these poor people thanked us for the school, presented me with a pair of ibex horns, to which putrefying meat still clung, and asked why we had not provided desks, chairs and a blackboard! Leaving the troop to finish the job I flew back to Salalah, taking with me the prostrate bottle-squatter from whom most of the manure had been removed, and also my rotting trophy. It was not the most pleasant of flights.

As this was a Muslim country, we worked on Sunday, Friday, or Jummah, being the day of rest. On the jebel we actually laboured seven days a week, but when in Salalah the squadron usually spent Jummah by the sea. White women were almost unknown in Dhofar and the Arab ladies lived in purdah, so relaxation was centred around fishing, swimming, boating, football, eating and drinking. The sea yielded up a fascinating array of marine life. Spanish mackerel and crayfish became welcome additions to our menu. Nevertheless caution was advisable when swimming because of the high population of potentially dangerous giant Indian rorqual whales: 100 feet long this dorsal-finned monster is the largest living animal. Lying close beneath the cliffs they blow spouts of water skyward and it was said that at night they utter near-human cries. Sawfish – rays with a long, serrated saw-like shout stingrays, octopus, monster groupers and aggressive moray eels were frequently encountered, whilst the much-feared hammerhead sharks mingled with the playful and harmless dolphins amongst the inshore reefs. However, in spite of such a population of predators no one was attacked. For my own part, I would have loved to explore some of the archaeological sites of this ancient land. Only a few miles east of our base camp lay the ruins of Sumuran. The temple of the moon-god Sin had stood here in 1000 BC, guarding the stores of frankincense that were distributed by camel-train to every corner of Arabia and even to parts of the Roman Empire. Alas, there was no opportunity for an expedition, but I made notes for a future visit.

As the monsoon approached, our ramshackle camp, even with its limited air-conditioning, became a paradise and a cold beer a dream. In the relative cool of the evening we planned our operations, whilst out on the Salalah Plain the artillery thumped as the men of the outer defences engaged fleeting targets located on radar. In the Muscat Regiment mess I was made most welcome and often joined Spike, the soldier of fortune, for a glass of malt and a chance to pick his brains. No one knew more about this complex campaign than he and no one else had survived being blown up in a Land-Rover by a Russian anti-tank mine three times!

On one operation, Mastedon, my faithful bulldozer, hit a mine whilst improving a road. By a miracle, and thanks to the steel anti-mine plates, the operator escaped unhurt. However, this represented fifty per cent of my dozer force so recovery and repair were essential.

Mines were an ever-present threat. Both British models, left behind in Aden, and modern Russian versions were present. However, some were buried too deep to be effective and we surmised that this had been done by a surrendering rebel who, after his conversion to the Sultan's cause, could suddenly 'discover' the mine and claim the generous bounty offered! A favourite place for dreaded Russian anti-personnel mines to be placed was in an old sangar, a rock-walled defensive position. Sangars littered the province but you entered a long-disused one at your peril. Visiting the hospital one day, I saw a Baluchi soldier brought in without legs, hands, face or genital organs after stepping on one of these. Amazingly, he survived!

By the middle of March our men had become experienced desert hands, bronzed and dusty, and they moved from one defensive locality to another providing essential engineer support. We seldom saw the elusive enemy, although undoubtedly they watched us and, when you least expected, there would be the crack of a high-velocity round or the crash of a mortar bomb. They were always 'out there somewhere' in the shimmering dun-coloured hills. Usually, only the eyes of the Firquat – the irregular troops of the Sultan's army, many of them ex-rebels and some with brothers still in the opposition – could pick out our hidden foes. We grew to rely on the Firquat to warn us of an enemy presence, but even they slipped up sometimes, as one of our sections discovered.

A ramp down a steep escarpment was being built by the faithful bulldozers, assisted with liberal quantities of plastic explosive, when an aged tribesman approached some sappers. He jabbered away in Jabali and, when our lads shook their heads and said 'Sorry, Johnnie, don't speak the lingo', he became most excited and appeared to be pleading with them. 'No, Buckshesh, now, go on, push off, will you,' they retorted. Thus the poor fellow went from group to group without success. Eventually he found an Omani NCO of the escorting infantry platoon who certainly did react. The man was a rebel trying to get someone to accept his surrender!

Relations with the Firquat were never easy. Proud men and traditional fighters, they had few material possessions, but believed it their right to have everything provided for them. They seldom carried any water of their own and on operations they would often demand that the Sultan's regular soldiers should give them some. If this were refused they would sulk and become childish, saying, 'You do not like us, you will not give us water. See, you are not our brothers after all.' A jundee (a regular in the Sultan's army) who had carried his precious water for miles could hardly be expected to sympathize. From us the Firquat demanded 'wriggly tin' and building materials for their houses, and even the use of bulldozers to improve their villages! Yet they fought well, so had to be encouraged.

I often met the Firquat at the defended oasis named Tawi Atair. As was the case with most such areas, the occupation depended on a water source, but Tawi Atair was unique in that the precious liquid was brought up from an underground lake at the bottom of a massive sink-hole. One of the first tasks of the Royal Engineers in Dhofar had been to install a submersible pump to raise the water up an iron pipe and thus fill drinking troughs for the livestock. This had been done before we arrived, but we had to maintain the pump.

Access to the caverns was gained by first descending some 300 feet into a huge cavity of rectangular cross-section with the long axis running approximately east-west. There then followed a hair-raising journey down a 270-foot vertical pipe which our predecessors had installed, welding on bars to act as rungs at intervals. Peter Page's mountaineering expertise was extremely valuable here. Descending into the hole, we could see a number of old, dry water-beds running down the sides. Finally, at the base of the shaft, there were many entrances to cave systems, some of which led to huge underground lakes. We explored one of these and found water depths of up to 110 feet. Small, almost translucent fish, which I imagined to be blind, were seen swimming at various levels. With our chums at the British Museum in mind, we tried to capture some but failed miserably. They might be blind, but they always managed to elude our divers.

From the amount of driftwood discovered in the cavern, it would appear that at the time of the rare heavy rains the whole shaft must fill up to a higher level of approximately sixty feet. Running water could be heard falling within the caverns and we decided that even if we installed a second pump there was little danger of running the incredible source dry. There was only one pump in position and, if that failed, the numerous cattle, goats and camels that relied upon it would die. So it was that the sappers set to and installed a reserve. Watched by curious weaver birds nesting inside the rim, we lowered our paraphernalia. The worst part of the whole operation was climbing back up the iron pipe. One rung was missing at the precise point where we had to negotiate an overhang.

Throughout Dhofar water is the key to life. North of the jebel lay the greatest sand desert in the world, the Rubh Al Khali, or 'Empty Quarter'. It stretches for 1,000 miles from the coast of Oman Island to Saudi Arabia. In this harsh region live the nomadic Bedu, whose main interests are camels and simply staying alive.

Patrick Brook's armoured cars prevented the enemy from crossing this enormous obstacle and reaching the jebel from the north. The Sultan's army also maintained one or two small defensive positions from which Patrick could operate and our main job in this area was to find water and build wells. Normally one was not disturbed by the enemy, but on one occasion a section of sappers had been dismayed to discover that the aircraft they had been watching approach was not a friendly supply plane but an Ilyushin bomber. They took cover in their well and luckily the bombs fell wide.

Back at home, things were none too peaceful either and shortly after we arrived in Oman we learned that the IRA had bombed our camp in Yorkshire! However, they managed to get the whole place redecorated far more quickly than otherwise and my quartermaster was able to account for years of deficiencies!

On my recce to the Hornbeam line I was greatly impressed with this amazing terrain. Deep wadis separated the waterless mountaintops on which the soldiers of the Northern Frontier Regiment lived in underground bunkers. After drawing up a plan with Brian Ray and having received the brigadier's blessing, we set to work. Firstly, we had to complete the wiring and then thicken up the mine fields in between the infantry company positions. Thus I moved my tactical head-quarters to a heavily blasted summit named Ashoq. This mountain was occupied by B Company under a delightful Scotsman, Angus Ramsay. His second-in-command was Charlie Daniel, a Royal Marine who, with half the company and the mortars, held the end of a long ridge that stretched north for several miles from Ashoq. Standing on Angus's hilltop, we could look south to the Indian Ocean and north to the skyline beyond which the Hornbeam line ended.

From the air I noticed how white the summit appeared. On close inspection I discovered that this was due to the enormous number of direct hits received from Katyusha 122-millimetre missiles fired from as far away as seven miles by the Adoo, as the rebels were called. Angus kept a small museum of the remains of these onslaughts and an area of ground outside his command post was covered with rows of tail fins, shell splinters and shrapnel that he had picked up in the relatively short time he'd been there. A direct hit by a Katyusha could knock a rock-built sangar clean off the hill. To reduce this hazard we used our electrically driven drills to bore down into the soft rock and blast out deeper bunkers for the troops.

The Katyushas could usually be heard approaching and a lookout would shout 'incomer' on his walkie-talkie. All officers and NCOS carried these and thus would dive for cover. With luck you might have four seconds to act. It seemed extraordinary when considering how many rockets had landed on this position that they never caused a single fatality. Most injuries were due to people banging their heads and shins as they jumped into the holes. However, the enemy rocket crews did suffer (as we learned from Radio Aden), when the Strikemasters bombed the dust-cloud caused by the Katyusha's firing. The Adoo were only about 1,400 yards away across the far side of a deep valley. At night we picked up their radio conversations on our own sets and Ashoq frequently received mortar bombs and recoilless rifle shells in addition to the missiles.

My first night with Angus was an alarming one. He kindly produced a bottle of Scotch which flowed freely while he briefed me on the situation. There was little room inside the rock-walled command post, but I was quite comfortable on the floor. The first interruption of my night's sleep was the feeling that something smooth and warm was sliding over me. It was a small grey sand viper. A few moments later a rat with Mickey Mouse ears bounded over my legs, chasing the snake, and then came fleeing back in the other direction as the viper pursued the rat. Relaxation was not easy under these conditions. But I had just dropped off when there was the most ear-shattering noise. I realised at once that heavy machine gun in the next bunker had opened up. Forgetting rats and snakes, I rushed out to see what was happening, only to hear Angus groan from his pit, 'Bet you it's foxes they're shooting at.' Outside, in the delightful cool of the night, I could see flares alight in the minefield and watched the tracer curving away into the distance. Eventually a somewhat sleepy Angus emerged to see what was going on. But he need not have worried because one of his Arab officers had the situation under control and after ten minutes of fireworks we returned to bed. An hour later the same thing happened again: this time Angus was a little concerned that it might be an attempted intrusion through the line and put down some mortar fire to deter visitors.

The sapper is a very adaptable chap and soon our men were completely integrated with our Arab hosts. Living and eating with them presented no problems although, at best, our men could speak only a little Arabic and few of the Omanis knew any English. I always enjoyed working with the Omanis. They were interesting people and some of their strange ways were fascinating. One soldier, who was said to possess special powers, could take a poisonous sand viper and place its head inside his mouth and then close his lips around the neck with no apparent ill effects. However, before he attempted this he did put a spell, or hesp, on the creature.

The mine laying was not made any easier by the presence of a large number of unmarked mines laid by previous occupants. I soon discovered that the planning figures so religiously stated in our manuals do not apply when you are dealing with live mines. I would recommend multiplying the theoretical timings by five if you are to get the right number of mines per man laid by soldiers who, previously, have only used plastic or concrete ones. One of Charlie Daniel's NCOs accidentally tripped one of our little toys during a skirmish. It was a fiendish device which, when activated, would jump into the air and explode at shoulder height, throwing shrapnel all around it for distances up to 100 yards. Known as 'jumping jacks', these were among the most deadly mines we possessed. Charlie and his NCO were extremely lucky to get away with only minor scratches. Thereafter people treated the minefields with great respect.

A gruesome relic of an earlier attempt by the enemy to get through the line could be seen across the far side of a deep wadi. Through binoculars you could make out the whitening bones of a headless skeleton. Known to the soldiers as Jonah, this unfortunate fellow had been killed by a 'jumping jack' a few months before. Charlie had gone out to investigate and, while approaching, heard some noises and took cover. A few moments later he was able to witness the awful scene when a small pack of Arabian red wolves came stealthily down the track, avoiding the other mines with great care, and feasted on the corpse. Although some valuable papers and documents were recovered after this incident it was not possible to get the body out without risking life and limb in the minefield. This greatly upset our own Arab soldiers who believed that, although a communist, the man must still be a true believer and should be brought back for burial.

There were many nationalities involved in the war and the largest single foreign force was an Iranian brigade. Prior to the start of a thrust against the enemy, I was with an Omani task force passing through an Iranian position. At sunset, as our dishevelled troops prepared supper, we became aware of a ceremony taking place at the Iranian Company HQ. A guard of honour assembled by the entrance to the hillside bunker, an immaculate jeep driven by a cleanly uniformed sergeant drove up and then the smartest major any of us had seen for weeks came out, pulling on white gloves and adjusting his very dark glasses. Inspecting the guard, he said a few words of encouragement. Clearly their commander was leaving for more comfortable night-time quarters elsewhere. The Omani troops muttered darkly that they had little respect for their allies' military prowess. The major then inspected his jeep and, having found it to his satisfaction, decided to drive himself. The sergeant moved quickly into the passenger seat, the major revved up the engine, the guard of honour saluted and their commander then reversed into them! Six hundred Omanis howled with mirth, literally rolling in the sand with tears running down their cheeks. Relations with the Iranians were not enhanced, but their support was pretty important.

Once I knew the mine laying was going well, I flew to the isolated position known as Simba. The cool early morning air left us shivering as we boarded the Iranian helicopter. Packed in with us were some 400 pounds of explosive, two drums of water and three sacks of smelly goat meat. The flight over the sea was as beautiful as ever and it was only a short while before we were approaching the enemy-held coast. Beneath us there were deep shadows in the steep-sided wadis and the stark dry hills stood out clearly in the first rays of the morning sun. Not speaking Persian, I couldn't understand the pilot's conversation with ground control, but he had become rather agitated. Glancing up I was just in time to see two Strikemasters diving steeply past us towards the ground. We swayed in their slipstream and far below I could just make out the defensive positions and the narrow scar that must be the airstrip. The runway was clear, but in the broken ground on either side lay the wreckage of aircraft. Enemy fire had prevented the use of fixed-wing planes and so now all supplies came in by helicopter. I had lost sight of the Strikemasters when something else attracted my attention. Two white streamers were heading groundward and I realised that they were rockets fired from the leading fighter. The flash of the explosion followed almost at once and then I saw the other plane release its rockets before pulling up once again. Now we could see small puffs of smoke drifting about in a haphazard way on the position: we were flying into the middle of a bombardment.

Our pilot was in two minds about landing, but I gesticulated wildly, pointing at my load of explosives and the water, both of which were important for the defence of the garrison. The Iranian smiled again, this time a little nervously, and took us down in a tight spiral towards the landing pad. As the ground rushed up the puffs of grey smoke got bigger, our shadow raced to meet us and the skids were barely on the rock when a Baluchi sergeant came running forward to help me lift down our lethal cargo.

As I jumped out he said in English, 'Good morning, sahib,' and saluted! 'I have a Land-Rover right here,' he added as we dragged the stores away from the helicopter, whilst the pilot yelled at us to get a move on. As the last box was removed, the Huey rose in a cloud of dust and whirled skyward.

Now that we were no longer deafened by the engine noise, the crash of the mortar bombs and the thump of the guns was clearly audible. No time was wasted in loading the battered Land-Rover, and then, with the Baluchi at the wheel and as pebbles and debris rained down, we took off at a frightening pace along a bumpy track towards the battalion headquarters. On arrival, the sergeant insisted on jumping out and opening the door, and saluted once again. A mortar landed fifty yards away as I dived into the cool darkness of the command post. Making my way through the labyrinth of sandbag walls, I came to the open-topped observation post where a British major was controlling the jets, guns, mortars and everything else by radio.

'Hello old boy,' he said with a smile. 'I'm rather busy at the moment – would you excuse me for a few minutes?'

I sat down on an aircraft seat that had been dragged from the wreckage of one of the planes lying by the runway and looked up to see a mess orderly in a white jacket holding a silver tray on which stood spotlessly clean cups and saucers and a pot of coffee. A few minutes later the battle had ended.

'Well, that's this morning's show over,' sighed the acting battalion commander as he joined me for coffee. 'So you think you may be able to find some water for us?'

'I'll certainly try,' I replied.

'Good. Well, I've got a section of men who will go with you. Better have a long drink first, though; it's quite a way and a good climb. And, by the way, be a bit careful – we've mined the wadi bed.'

Thus it was that, within the hour, our small party of engineers was stepping warily over the trip-wires, seeking any patch of greenery or damp sand which might indicate the presence of water. I was just examining a likely spot when there was a loud 'pop' behind me. Certain that it was one of the wretched 'jumping jacks', I hurled myself flat. The Baluchi soldiers roared with laughter. It had only been a trip flare!

On our flight back from Simba we passed over an armed dhow of the Sultan's navy. The crew waved from the deck as the helicopter zoomed homeward. These ungainly looking craft were far more effective than they appeared. They carried recoilless guns on deck and at night would creep in under the communist guns, unseen on the darkened sea. By using their machine-guns they would draw retaliatory fire from the Adoo and as soon as an enemy weapon was pinpointed, the giant recoilless rifle would send its heavy shell whistling shore-ward. The back-blast was enormous and, as soon as it had fired, the dhow would make out to sea with all speed, usually followed by heavy mortaring from the shore.

It was 1130 hours on a June morning when we saw a mine explode in front of Ashoq. Our artillery immediately shelled the area and then Angus helicoptered forward to direct a strike by the jets. Although he was unable to see any sign of movement on the ground, he decided that a rapid follow-up was justified in the hope of finding enemy who might have been wounded. At 1700 hours the swirling mists were low, with visibility down to about 200 yards. Angus sallied forth in daylight and, trusting to the low cloud for cover, he left Ashoq with a thirty-strong patrol, including Charlie and Lieutenant Salim Said. In the fog they came upon a large force of enemy and fought a desperate close-quarter gun battle with every skill they possessed. Angus saved Charlie's life and although they lost several men they eventually managed to withdraw to their mountain top position, carrying their casualties with them. Clashes like that were typical of this bitter campaign.

Working in the Scotch mist conditions of the Khareef was undoubtedly one of the most eerie sensations I've ever had to endure. It is quite different to that of being in complete darkness: somehow one felt that one was always being watched by unseen eyes peering through the drifting clouds.

Just north of Charlie Daniel's position was an enormous wadi called Jizalawt. It was a cleft in the mountains, over 2000 feet deep, and in the early days we suffered a number of casualties due to heat exhaustion simply from walking up and down the canyon. John Hoskinson, one of my troop commanders, had done sterling work in mining this natural route through the line. He was operating from the other side of the wadi with thirty of the toughest sappers you can imagine. Meanwhile I continued to work on the south side, seeding the minefield with a few especially fiendish devices that were designed to be set off electronically from an observation post on the rim of the canyon. It was now a race against time. The monsoon had started early and our task was not yet complete. Thus we could not afford to stop for weather conditions.

One day I was halfway down the wadi side with a small party of sappers and Omanis when the clouds rolled in, reducing visibility to fifty yards. The temperature dropped and I felt a shudder go down my spine. But an even bigger one came a moment later when I heard the familiar 'crump' of mortars. The first bomb landed 100 yards away, showering us with chippings and splinters. I grabbed my walkie-talkie, but couldn't get through as we were shielded from our friends by the wadi rim. To try to climb back up the way we had come was now almost impossible. The rocks, dampened by the mist, were like a skid-pan and a slip could mean falling hundreds of feet. We quickly concealed the rest of our devices under the rocks and tried to climb out, but for every pace we went forward we slid two backwards. There was only one thing to do: we tore up our shirts and, wrapping strips of cloth around our hands, began to pull ourselves up the barbed-wire fence that marked the minefield and led out of the gorge. It was a long, hard, nerve-racking business with the mortar bombs raining down from above. Each time I heard the noise of their descent I wondered where it was going to land. At the top, Lieutenant Salim Said greeted me. They had been his mortars: a sentry on top of the mountain had seen enemy moving into the wadi below us. We had very sore hands but were extremely thankful.

Although we saw rather a lot of B Company, their neighbours, A Company, were also good friends. When we started work on the line the second-in-command, Ian Gardiner, a rugged marine, had been responsible for our escorts and safety and I had many dealings with Major Johnnie Braddell-Smith, the company commander, who advised on the mining of likely places to catch penetrating parties of enemy.

Johnnie was highly respected and beloved by his men, with a quiet manner that gave no indication of the fire that burned within. He was a thoughtful, devoted and tolerant person with whom it was a pleasure to serve. His knowledge and interest in the Omanis was outstanding and in Salalah it was Johnnie's pleasure to go around the barracks, talking to and eating with the soldiers. As a result, he built up an impressive store of knowledge about his men, their families, homes, fears and aspirations. This deep interest in their wellbeing, together with his wisdom and skill as a commander, inspired loyalty and affection such as are rarely seen in a military environment. His outstanding characteristic was his unflappability, which must have contributed greatly towards his courage. But it was his ability to take the sting out of the most formidable situations that we appreciated most. There were many instances of this, but the most notable was an action in the Wadi Sha'ath.

Intelligence had indicated that there were sixteen enemy based immediately east of the Hornbeam line, where they were acting as a reception committee for Adoo who succeeded in getting through our defences. Accordingly, A Company mounted an operation to hunt them out. Thus four platoons, supported by mortars, moved into the area and laid night ambushes. The following morning Johnnie sent Ian and two of the platoons further east to take up new positions, while he remained in ambush with the rest. At 11.30 hours, about ten Adoo appeared and were in the act of walking into Johnnie's killing ground when Ian's half of the company came under heavy and accurate fire further east, at which point the enemy took cover and so avoided being caught in Johnnie's ambush. Meanwhile, his second-in-command's forward platoon had taken up a position on a small hill to the south of their initial position. Ian was moving with the rear platoon on ground that was not to his advantage and he started taking casualties straight away. The soldier on the general purpose machine-gun was killed immediately and, of the party of four who came to assist with the dead man, one was wounded and another killed. In the face of such a heavy attack Ian's group withdrew rapidly, leaving bodies and equipment in open ground. They consolidated their position as best they could with the remainder of the platoon, and Ian called Johnnie for help.

Johnnie had no idea of the enemy's strength, but it was apparent that there were considerably more than the original sixteen. Subsequently, intelligence indicated that up to sixty Adoo had passed through the Hornbeam line very recently. Ian's forward platoon was not in a position to afford direct assistance; it was having trouble of its own, anyway. To make matters worse, communications had broken down. The intensity of the fire steadily increased, despite sterling work by the mortars and jets that had now come up to support A Company. Nothing could be done to prevent the enemy's flanking movements, nor their looting of the bodies. A Company was particularly keen to prevent this, in addition to which the loss of a machine-gun with 500 rounds as well as a radio set would not have been to its credit. By 1400 hours A Company were in the depths of despair. Now low in ammunition, they were being out-flanked and had sustained a further casualty. Ian Gardiner admits he had run out of ideas. If Johnnie did not come soon he would be of little use. But he did arrive. An agitated Ian exhorted him to position his troops with all speed. Diving for cover behind a rock, Johnnie regained his breath and offered his second-in-command a drink of water as Ian frantically explained the situation. Johnnie fumbled in his pocket and produced a crumpled packet of Rothmans and asked for a light. So they lay there, the pair of them, without saying a word, and smoked a cigarette while bullets zipped overhead. Ian knew that everything would be all right.

The combined force now positioned itself where it could at least cover its casualties. Johnnie then organised a small party and, as our jets thundered in to strafe the enemy, led them to a hollow near where the dead lay. On the next air strike, the Omani soldiers ran to the bodies, dashed round them and back again! Patiently Johnnie had another word with the men, led them out again and brought one body back. All this time they were under fire. However, A Company's superior firepower was now beginning to have an effect. Ian felt it was his turn next, he couldn't leave Johnnie to do all the work, so he rushed out and recovered a second body with the help of another party of four. Meanwhile Johnnie, under aimed fire, sprinted forward and recovered both the machine-gun and the radio.

Perhaps one may be forgiven for believing that to risk life for such a comparatively worthless end was nonsensical. Indeed, looking back, Ian admits that his spine shivers. But it must be remembered that they had been told to recover the radio if at all possible and the Northern Frontier Regiment had never left a body for the enemy. To be the first to do so was unthinkable. Apart from anything else, they could never be sure that their friends were dead and the possibility of their being taken alive by the Adoo was a sufficient stimulus to drive anyone to almost any folly. During my last week in the mountains I talked far into a night with Johnnie, sharing a bottle of Scotch. Little did I know that I should never see him again. When the long-awaited advance took place, the Sultan's army, reinforced with Imperial Iranian units, swept forward from the Hornbeam.

The fighting was bitter and there were many casualties. In the forefront was Johnnie. He had been commanding a group of irregulars, the Firquat Tariq Bin Zaid, working with an Iranian task force.

On 10 December 1974 an Iranian battalion sought to establish a position about a mile to the south of its forward base, which was then on the edge of the tree line. With complete disregard for his own safety, Johnnie led the advance through the trees at the front of a column of Iranians. On reaching the objective he discovered the main body had somehow been separated and so he immediately returned along his route and successfully made contact with the missing troops.

Later that day the Adoo attacked the position with heavy small-arms fire and RPG 7 rockets, killing ten soldiers and wounding another. As soon as there was sufficient fire being directed against the enemy, Johnnie went forward to check the position. Moving stealthily around the company perimeter, he recovered the bodies of three Iranians, thought to have been captured by the enemy. Those who watched him operate and organise the evacuation of casualties were greatly inspired by his personal example and tireless vigilance, which eventually enabled the column to withdraw without further losses, in spite of determined enemy attacks.

The next day the Iranian battalion sustained yet more casualties in its forward locations. Because of the proximity of the Adoo it was not possible to evacuate them by helicopter and so the indefatigable Johnnie continued to retrieve the wounded and dead under extremely dangerous conditions.

On Christmas Day he accompanied a patrol moving forward from another defended area to seize high ground near a main enemy position. They had gone 1,000 yards when the leading troops were attacked in a thickly wooded area. The Arab officer of the Firquat died in the opening burst of fire. A soldier picked up his body and attempted to carry it to the rear and, seeing that the man was having great difficulty, Johnnie handed his weapon to another and picked up the dead man himself. Shortly afterwards he was heard to cry out as he fell mortally wounded. The intensity of the enemy's fire was so great that it was impossible to recover Johnnie's or the Arab officer's bodies for some time afterwards.

It was perhaps typical of the man that he should have given his life attempting to bring in the body of a comrade whilst under deadly aimed fire from a ruthless enemy. His action typifies the magnificent courage and complete disregard for his own safety that he always showed and for which he was posthumously honoured with the award of the Sultan's Gallantry Medal. Like so many who died in this little-known war, his gallantry and devotion to duty were actually beyond praise, and it was the deeds of such men that eventually brought victory to the Sultan and peace to this desert land.

In June 1974, as the swirling clouds rolled in from the Indian Ocean to cloak the jebel, I left Oman to face a different challenge: the great Zaire River.

9

·

Dr Livingstone, I Presume?

'Dr Livingstone, I presume?' These immortal words were uttered by Henry Morton Stanley in 1871, and in 1943 they sent a shiver of excitement down my spine as I sat in Sunday school, attentive for once, listening to the gripping story.

David Livingstone, that remarkable Scot, had been found by a successful journalist who went on to become equally famous as a dogged, determined explorer. Their meeting was an historic occasion, which made a deep impression on Stanley and during their four months together he learned much about the old missionary's discoveries and hopes.

When, after his return to Britain, he heard of the doctor's death, Stanley said, 'May I be selected to succeed him in opening up Africa to a shining light of Christianity,' but his chief ambition was to pursue Livingstone's unfinished quest, the search for the source of the Nile. We now know that John Hanning Speke had in fact found the principal source of the Ripon Falls on the northern shore of Lake Victoria in 1862; however, twelve years later this was still disputed by many of his contemporaries. Livingstone was among them; he believed that the Lualaba River, which he had discovered west of Lake Tanganyika, might itself be the source of the Nile. To test his theory one would have to follow the Lualaba's course and Stanley resolved to do just that. Backed by the *Daily Telegraph* and the *New York Herald*, he set out from Zanzibar in November 1874, with three other white men and 356 Africans. They carried an impressive quantity of weapons and the sectionalised wooden boat, which Stanley named *Lady Alice* after his fiancée, a Miss Alice Pike of New York.

Throughout 1875 the expedition pressed on across Africa, circumnavigating and surveying the great lakes, driving off attacks by hostile tribes and marching, marching, marching. In October 1876, Stanley and his now severely depleted party reached the banks of the Lualaba at Nyangwe. Already he had taken heavy casualties and his men were exhausted. He spun a coin saying, 'Heads, I go forward, tails I go back.' Apparently it came up tails twice, but Stanley decided to press on.

They had reached the Lualaba some 550 miles from its source, in the swamps of what is now southern Zaire. The Lualaba is not, of course, any part of the Nile but is instead the headstream of the Congo. Together they form the mighty confluence, which flows across central Africa to the Atlantic. Stanley finally reached the Atlantic in August 1877. Two years later he returned to central Africa to play an important role in establishing what was recognized in 1885 as the Congo Free State. This was annexed by Belgium in 1908 as the Belgian Congo and only in 1960 achieved independence as the Democratic Republic of the Congo. Finally, in 1971, after many internal vicissitudes, both the republic and its great river were given their present names of Zaire.

No detailed scientific work was carried out on Stanley's expedition and, in the years that followed, the vast Congo basin remained largely cloaked in dense tropical jungle and was relatively inaccessible. Then in 1970 Richard Snailham suggested that the SES should attempt to carry out a programme of medical and scientific research here in commemoration of Stanley's epic journey.

So it was that whilst my attention was largely centred on the problems of the Darien Gap, I was also asked to lead the proposed expedition to Zaire. The late Prince William of Gloucester launched the venture at a dinner in the Grocers' Hall on 3 November 1971, the 100th anniversary of Stanley's famous meeting with Livingstone. It was a splendid party and superbly organised, thanks largely to the help of the *Daily Telegraph*. There followed three years of hard, problem-studded planning.

Having digested the reconnaissance report prepared by Martin Romilly and Richard Snailham, we invited Major General Griff Caldwell to chair the expedition committee and battle with the unenviable task of raising the funds. Unlike military operations, the expedition had to pay for everything in advance. It was rather like going into battle, but with the added worry of raising money to buy ammunition.

I could write a book on that subject alone, but in the end we left for Zaire £20,000 short of our target.

Whilst I had been in Oman our London office had been run by my dear friend, Kay Thompson, and her daughter Jill. Without the help of Denis Lowry, Ken Monk and all at Gestetner's , I do not know how we would have coped. But there were literally masses of people who came to our aid and unselfishly gave valuable help to the project.

My first major task was to select the team and its equipment. The Zaire is the seventh longest river on earth and the second biggest in its outflow, which averages 1,483,000 cubic feet per second! The country is the third largest in Africa, approximately the size of Western Europe, and it includes one of the highest rainfall areas in the world. So the team grew, eventually reaching a total strength of 165. We selected our members from all over the world, mainly for their compatibility and industry. People with experience of Africa and those with some knowledge of French or the local languages were especially favoured. Our final complement included Americans, Australians, Belgians, Britons, Canadians, Fijians, French, Nepalese, New Zealanders and Danes. I also asked for a strong contingent of Zairois servicemen.

So many British scientists wanted to join the expedition that we ran a long series of searching interviews, conducted with great patience by Dr Humphrey Greenwood of the Natural History Museum, who had long assisted the SES. The main problem was that, of the fifty scientists, all wanted to go in different directions.

The lady members were particularly interesting. Three were scientists. A charming Australian bacteriologist, Beth Haslewood, was married to Professor Geoffrey Haslewood, another expedition member. We had a French immunologist, and from Leicestershire came Dorothy Bovey, one of the leading painters of botanical specimens, who was to provide illustrations commissioned by Kew Gardens.

There were three nurses, Marie-Therese Guichard, or 'Fifi', was a sister with the British Army of the Rhine and a qualified State Registered Nurse: I discovered halfway through the expedition that this was for mental nursing, but perhaps that was appropriate. A well-built Canadian, Adrianne Damgaard, was also an SRN and a physiotherapist. She was to work wonders on many strained muscles in the months ahead, although one soldier complained that he went to Adrianne with a painful shoulder and came back with a broken neck! A happy-go-lucky blonde nurse called Pamela Baker spoke fluent French as well as some Lingala and Swahili. She was the daughter of George Baker, who as Head of Chancery at the British Embassy at Kinshasa, had done much to help our reconnaissance team. Pam had the ability to work twenty-three hours a day without food and possessed a tremendous sense of humour and sympathy. I reckoned anyone who had known President Mobutu and the people of Zaire would be especially useful, so I made her my personal assistant.

My deputy was ex-Royal Marine Captain Mike Gambier, whom I had known for many years. Major Derek Jackson, a thirty-five year old rugged and ruthless administrator, became commander of the important logistic support group, with Gordon Mitchell, a tough Scots Guards major, as quartermaster. Naturally there were many ex-Darien hands, including Ernie Durey, the inexhaustible engineer who was to crack the land obstacles, and Jim Masters, once again in charge of the fleet. Captain Peter Marett joined in his former position as my intelligence officer. Advanced liaison in Zaire was assigned to a chum from Cyprus days, Major Tom Hawkins, and his able assistant, Jim Winter. Both had been on a British Army training team in Zaire for several years, knew the people and spoke French. A galaxy of experts under Freddie Rodger, a leading authority on tropical eye disease, directed the medical research, seeking a cure for 'river blindness'.

Air support was a vital factor. Here our good friend, Lieutenant General Sir Napier Crookenden, managed to obtain the assistance of the Army Air Corps, who once again provided a Beaver light aircraft. Gordon Mitchell worked long hours to amass over eighty tons of stores and supplies and, together with his aide, Dick Festorazzi, oversaw to its shipment to Africa. Whilst this was going on, the headquarters of the expedition had been established in my Whitehall cellar; in the end there were twenty-eight servicemen and civilians working in the small airless rooms fifty feet beneath the pavements.

1974 was not a good year to launch one of the most ambitious expeditions ever to leave Britain. Money was tight, the RAF was desperately short of aircraft and civil air charter rates were soaring, while the price of petrol was rising daily, as indeed was the cost of almost everything. British Army units were hard-pressed and could ill afford to spare good men for what some regarded as a swan. In Africa, political feelings were running high. The wind of change was sweeping through Angola and Mozambique. President Mobutu had recently nationalised the petrol companies in Zaire and former white settlers were leaving in droves, so the pessimism of Europeans in Zaire about our project was understandable. Nevertheless, we believed it could be done and planning continued. For political reasons, we decided to change our name from the 'HM Stanley Centenary Expedition' to simply the 'Zaire River Expedition', quickly abbreviated by the military to ZRE.

The old SES formula appeared to be working once again: a thorough scientific expedition with the added spice of an attempt to run a dangerous river. A varied research programme made it all objectively worthwhile, and the prospect of heroics on the water attracted the media and the commercial sponsors.

But our use of the Zaire River to move from Shaba (formerly Katanga) to the Atlantic with a vast team, equipment, stores and a variety of nationalities was no gimmick. There were few roads or other means of communication in Zaire and therefore the river was the only option. Indeed, in colonial times the Belgians had inaugurated a steamer service throughout its navigable parts. Where cataracts intervened – below Kinshasa, at the Stanley Falls and the 'Gates of Hell' – they had built narrow-gauge railways around the obstacles. But to move along the river, we had to find a way of getting through these cataracts, where waves could reach forty feet.

After some time on the Colorado River, Jim Masters designed and assembled three giant thirty-seven-foot inflatable rafts. They only had an air pressure of two-and-a-half pounds per square inch and one of the problems that worried us most was how to apply enough power to these flabby craft. In the end we fitted each with two forty-horsepower Mercury outboards. We were also provided with Avon inflatables and two rather unusual Hamilton water jetcrafts, which Prince Philip had very kindly helped us to get from New Zealand. I believed that with this fleet we could tackle almost any rapid and if, in the end, we could not get through, then we should be able to portage. By starting the expedition in October we hoped high water levels would cover the rocks. Two of our giant inflatables were sponsored by companies and were therefore named *David Gestetner* and *Barclays Bank*. Another was called *La Vision* by Mohammed Ali who was in Zaire for a title fight. She became my flagship.

Many of the lessons learned on the Blue Nile were remembered, and it was a great advantage to have some of the old team with us. We could find no suitable river to compare with the Zaire on which to test our craft and no rapids to match its cataracts, so we could only hope and pray that our choice of boat was right. Our lives depended on it! The story of how we got the stores to Africa, through customs, overland and finally to where they were needed, is an epic in itself.

Once there, we would face a river almost as long as the distance from Ireland to New York, and the research groups and boat parties would be split up as if one team were in London, another in Athens and a third in Sicily. The lack of roads, railways, bridges and ferries did not help, but our support group was to work tirelessly to win the logistics battle. We hoped to link the various teams and the fleet on relatively old A14 radios. These were designed with a range of 350 miles and were hardly suitable for the distances anticipated. Nevertheless, great credit is due to the Royal Signals detachment who somehow managed to get our reports through to both the *Daily Telegraph* and the Ministry of Defence, in London. We established a rear base in the capital, Kinshasa, to liaise with the Zaire Army and Government and to run a special expedition post office, set up by the Royal Engineers.

Linking this scattered force were three eight-man, mobile, forward support teams (FST), each commanded by an experienced officer. It was their responsibility to carry out advanced reconnaissance, establish good relations with the local people (who, after their experience of white mercenaries, were highly suspicious) and to move stores, scientists and specimens to and from the river. Each FST was responsible for one sector of the waterway. The whole operation was planned around the requirements of the various scientific parties but, because our experts could not be certain exactly where they would want to work, we had to be extremely flexible.

One hundred years before, Stanley had had a similar system but, lacking vehicles, had been forced to use 700 men, marching parallel to the river, to support him. Nor did Stanley have the Beaver aircraft we possessed. Fitted with the latest Sony video equipment and commanded by Cliff Taylor, a warrant officer in the Army Air Corps who had been with us in Panama, this robust six-seater was used for reconnaissance, parachute delivery of stores and aerial photography. One of its servicing team, Sergeant Ben Cartwright, had also been with us in Central America and had inscribed on its door the proud motto 'Pas de Problème'. Even so, local aviators did not envy them. Flying a single-engined aircraft out from Britain, over the Sahara and then spending four months operating above dense jungle with a countrywide fuel shortage, no diversionary airstrips, poor weather and no rescue facilities is no picnic. 'They'd never find you if you crashed in that cabbage anyway, so why worry?' smiled Flight Lieutenant Steve George, RAF, the second pilot.

In early September the advance parties began to deploy – Tom Hawkins with one group to Lubumbashi and Derek Jackson to Lobito – to extract our vehicles and stores from the hold of a cargo ship and ferry them up the Benguela Railway to Zaire.

The day before the main party's departure, my telephone rang and a voice said in poor English, 'This is Air Zaire, in Brussels.' 'Bonjour,' I replied with relief, for we had not heard anything for a considerable time from the company that was to fly us out, and I was beginning to wonder whether they would turn up.

'Please may we have permission to land in your country?' went the slightly squeaky voice.

General Griff, who was sitting near me, grinned and nodded, so I simply said. 'Yes, when are you coming?'

'In about five minutes,' came the reply.

I was so staggered by this that I forgot to ask them where they were intending to land, so it was Gatwick that got the shock when an enormous DC10 thundered in over their runway completely unannounced!

Gordon had taken great pains to see that all our stores were packed, weighed and listed with meticulous care. Nevertheless we seemed to be considerably overweight. When our convoy reached Gatwick, the Zaire loadmaster rolled back his lips and waving aside any formalities of actually checking the cargo said, 'Stuff it all in, there is plenty of room.' Next morning four hefty guardsmen were still trying desperately to close the cargo doors against the bulging contents. However, we were soon airborne and as we undid our safety straps a smiling Zairois hostess came to me and said, 'Mon Colonel, may I have your permission to serve the champagne?' Warily, I asked, 'Who pays?' 'Oh, it is with the compliments of the company,' she assured me, and proceeded to serve champagne from Gatwick to Lubumbashi. I was reminded of Stanley himself, who, when briefed by his employer, James Gordon Bennett, editor of the *New York Herald*, to go and find Livingstone had also inquired, 'Who pays?' Bennett replied, 'Draw $1000 now and when that is spent draw another $1,000 and when that is finished draw another $1,000 and so on; but find Livingstone.'

We stopped in Kinshasa to refuel with champagne and also to pick up one of our advance party, Captain Paul Turner, and our Zaire liaison officers (ZLOS). Paul, an energetic Hussar, had been in the capital for three weeks making final arrangements. As we flew on into the growing darkness of the African night I questioned the senior liaison officer, a Zaire parachute captain, about the Shaba region. 'It is a very bad place,' he warned. 'They eat people,' he added, tapping his pistol meaningfully. Few of our ZLOs had ever visited the far-flung province; indeed it was rather like expecting a Londoner to know all about Castile!

I spent most of the flight, when not drinking the excellent champagne, learning a speech from Pam. My French is abominable and so I had to write it out phonetically. Meanwhile, the rest of the team enjoyed their last taste of luxury to the full!

It was long after dark when we touched down at Lubumbashi and when the aircraft came to a halt the doors opened to let in a hot blast of African night air. Striding out onto the top of the steps, I prepared to deliver my oration. There was only one problem – the airfield was deserted! Only an attractive Zairois lady stood at the foot of the steps and so, bouncing down, I extended my hand and said. 'Enchanté citoyenne.' As she returned my smile I heard Derek's voice coming from the darkness. He was running towards me and hissed, 'Not her! She's the airport whore!'

'What on earth have you done with customs and immigration?' I said.

'Well, it's a long story, but they have all gone to a Burns' Night supper,' he replied.

'Burns?' I gasped. "I wouldn't have thought they had ever heard of the immortal bard in Lubumbashi.'

'No, no,' he admitted, 'but we are paying for the supper, so they have all gone.

We set off towards our first base at the mining town of Kolwezi. Thanks to the kindness of various expatriates and the authorities, we were made very welcome, and not only that; we were also provided with accommodation in what, by expedition standards, were superb houses. On the first night of our sojourn I was the guest at a dinner given by a local businessman. The meal was excellent and, as the assembled company made their way on to the verandah with their cigars and brandy, my host took me to one side and said quietly, 'Colonel, I have been in Africa a very long time and I know why you are really here. I would not presume to question your orders for one moment but I do hope that when the time comes you will call on me for assistance.'

'But we are here for a long-range scientific expedition,' I explained.

'My dear Colonel, with the utmost respect, when you have been in Africa as long as I, and when you have studied world affairs with the same interest as I, a businessman, have been forced to, you will learn to respect certain people. It is my opinion that for a very long time the British have been underestimated and I congratulate your government on its present plans.'

Nothing I could say would convince him that we were not the forerunners of a massive British army force that was to seize the mineral-rich province of Shaba. I tried, but he simply replied, 'I have looked carefully at your organization: you have a colonel, there are a great many majors, and you have radios, vehicles and a light aircraft. There is no doubt that you have the outline organisation sufficient to raise an army in Africa tonight.' After two brandies I gave up and we joined the assembled company on the verandah.

Two days later Tom Hawkins came to me with a serious transport problem and I instructed him to call upon this gentleman and request the use of his two large trucks.

'But those are the only vehicles he's got,' Tom interjected.

'I know,' I said, 'but just tell him I have need of them.' He did as I bade and came back to me with surprise written on his face. Our friend had provided them without question!

On Sunday 6 October Mike Gambier, Jim Masters and I flew south towards the Zambian border. Here we examined the river and selected a site to launch the boats and start the voyage. As we wheeled over the narrow stream, Peter Marett took Polaroid pictures. There was a slightly tricky fall within a few miles of our starting point that worried me, but not as much as the bumpiness of our ride which made us all violently ill. Jim managed to hold out to the last, but unfortunately the sick-bag was full up by then and when he could wait no longer it was explained that there was no room left in the paper envelope!

At the base morale was high and everyone eager to be off, but there was still a great deal of preparation to be done. Whilst Derek and his team slaved away bringing forward the stores to our depot, the command element continued with reconnaissance.

On 7 October we flew forward to view the rapids immediately north of Kolwezi. The initial expedition recce carried out by Richard and Martin in 1971 had warned that these were very likely to be impassable and I saw two particularly bad falls in an enormous gorge of reddish rock. Peter Marett named it the 'Red Gorge' and marked it on the map. There were many rapids and, of course, the dams themselves, built to provide hydro-electricity for the copper-rich province. Portage would be necessary in a number of places until we came to the great mosquito-ridden swamps of Upemba. Here the problem would be navigation, because it was difficult to locate the river's sinuous course.

Flying low, we spotted hippo, elephant and buck along the river-bank and then, at Kongolo, the foaming Gates of Hell. The water was dangerously shallow and until the jagged black rocks were covered by higher water levels I was doubtful if we would be able to sail through. However, at the local airstrip the people assured me that the water would rise within the month. There was no aircraft fuel available here and we were forced to fly on towards Lake Tanganyika, and eventually landed shortly before dusk at Kalemie (formerly Albertville). Lake Tanganyika, like a vast inland sea, azure blue with long, palm-fringed golden beaches, glimmered beneath us. After a night in the modest hotel we awoke at dawn to find the streets outside lined with armed soldiers. As a flaming orange sun rose over the lake, the troops moved off in vehicles on an operation, but the atmosphere remained tense. It was fortunate that we had a ZLO with us, and another useful asset was our special expedition arm badge, which displayed the symbol of the Mouvement Populaire de la Révolution, indicating that we were on the side of President Mobutu.

Flying back to Kolwezi across the rising hills and savannah we saw magnificent waterfalls and rapid-strewn rivers, all tributaries of the mighty Zaire. Small herds of game dotted the plain, and re-examining the area of the Red Gorge, I decided to deploy a bank reconnaissance group. The vast distances involved in this enormous country and the logistic problems of this expedition had now been high-lighted. This was no Blue Nile or Darien Gap, with a few hundred miles of difficult terrain to be overcome, but a seemingly endless land of mountain, swamp, river and jungle sweltering in equatorial heat. I concluded that wherever possible we must move by water and that, therefore, it would be necessary to increase the size of the fleet we proposed to assemble north of Bukama.

I dozed off at one point during the flight and then, as we prepared to land, awoke suddenly with a searing pain on the right side of my head. My eardrum had burst, undoubtedly due to the rapid descent whilst suffering a mild head cold. The discomfort that followed was a wretched nuisance, especially as we had such a busy time ahead and as I was due to speak that evening at a dinner given by the Lions Club of Kolwezi. Everywhere we went people, both black and white, were friendly and hospitable. In fact, there was a considerable demand for us to show the films of our previous expeditions. Tom Hawkins' deep Scots voice was often heard haranguing the inhabitants in French on the terrors of the Panama Jungle. Indeed, by passing the hat round we were even able to raise some money for our depleted funds!

The first part of the expedition was to navigate the upper reaches of the river. So with our base still at Kolwezi, we proceeded downstream in the Avon inflatables, steered by long sweep oars and the occasional use of small outboard motors. At the Red Gorge some of the younger men wanted to try getting through in the boats. It was the old 'hawks and doves' situation of the Blue Nile and I had to make it clear that we were not here to commit suicide but to get on with an expedition. The hawks grumbled but the doves appreciated this decision.

Meanwhile our whole team was being controlled by Tac HQ (tactical headquarters), which consisted of Peter Marett and Pam, together with Sam Qarau, a Fijian corporal of the Queen's Own Hussars, as signaller.

There were a few minor problems with our Zaire friends, who didn't really comprehend us at this stage and several of the more politically inclined were highly suspicious. There was one in particular, who was wont to stir up trouble. Accordingly I instructed Peter, a prodigious walker, to take him on a forty-mile hike to examine the Red Gorge. Peter set off with our friend and returned two days later, carrying him. We never saw this gentleman again and the political problems ceased.

The river party, with its scientists, went on, crashing and tumbling through the foaming white water in the Katanga gorges. Mike Gambier told of a narrow escape when coming upon a hippopotamus with her calf in mid-river. The hippo did not take kindly to this intrusion on her privacy and charged. With her first bite she destroyed the bow, with her second she got the stern and with her last, she destroyed what was left amidships. After this you don't have a boat and Mike's Marines baled out into another craft. They almost left behind Basil Pratt, our Army padre, who was at that moment in communication with his head office! When they looked back they saw a very perplexed hippo, which, having just eaten an inflatable boat, was suffering from a severe attack of wind. Although many of our number were old hands, we had, as always, brought in fresh blood, particularly junior officers and young soldiers. It was very comforting to see how well the team moulded together in these early and rather trying days.

At the small riverside town of Bukama the river was wide enough for us to launch the giant inflatables. Resembling outsized rubber mattresses, the minimum crew was only three, but each raft could carry up to thirty. In addition, there was fuel, rations, scientific equipment, radio sets, line-carrying rockets, engineer stores and tools, plus television cameras, artist's materials and medical stores to be stowed securely aboard *La Vision*. We also carried a yellow fibre-glass six-wheeled ATTEX amphibian. It was a useful two-seater vehicle, which allowed us to get about more easily in the swamps and along some of the flood plains.

The smaller craft in our fleet consisted of the close reconnaissance section's two Avon S400 boats, twelve-foot inflatables powered by forty-horsepower outboards. The section's task was to scout ahead of the big rafts and find a safe way through the rapids. Commanded by Alun Davies, a cheerful captain in the Royal Regiment of Wales, they were a hard-working bunch who undoubtedly enjoyed the flexibility and speed of their little boats. In addition there was the engineer section commanded by Ernie Durey. This bunch of sappers was the greatest collection of piratical rogues on the river. They moved with their own boats and vehicles almost at will throughout the country. Their task was to ferry Land-Rovers across the rivers, build bridges, dynamite obstacles, transport scientists, collect fresh water and locate stocks of beer. All this they did very successfully, but rather noisily.

From Bukama, I hoped to reach Kinshasa, 2,000 miles away, without taking our rafts off the river. But sailing into the flat, treeless waste of the Upemba swamp I was extremely worried that the water in the Gates of Hell might still be too low for navigation. Stanley's boat, *Lady Alice*, had been built in sections so it could be dismantled. Our giant inflatables were collapsible, but the central float chamber, shaped like an elongated doughnut, weighed 750 pounds. Portaging would be a devil of a problem. I was also concerned about passing through the rocky Gates themselves, even though our padre assured me that, given our many sins, they would probably be wide open! In the still water of the great morass birds wheeled around us and the occasional crocodile slithered from the muddy islets. But the ubiquitous hippo was a worry.

One evening a fearful tropical storm broke as we were making camp. Thunder roared and lightning flashed as the rain drove into every shelter. Crawling under a groundsheet I was soon drenched. The sound of music and the clink of a bottle was heard coming from *Barclays Bank*, moored nearby and, without further thought, I bounded across and landed on a small group huddled beneath a canvas, seeing the storm out with the aid of Neil Diamond and a bottle of Portuguese vinho verde. The shelter was barely sufficient to cover one person, but in spite of the discomfort we fell into a deep slumber. It must have been about four o'clock in the morning when an ear-splitting snort close at hand awoke us. There in the moonlight, only feet away, was the glistening body of a gigantic bull hippo enraged because we were blocking his only exit from the river. Already our ZLOs were rushing from their bashas, cocking automatic weapons, but Dick Festorazzi thrust the loud-hailer into my hand and said, 'Try that, it might have the same effect on him as it does on us.' Pee-eep-pee-eep screamed the device as I flicked the siren switch to full volume. With a startled roar, the beast fled up river. At dawn the sodden, weary fleet continued its voyage

Sailing at night we certainly saved time but it also created other problems. Once, when proceeding after dark, I noticed one of our lady members making her way towards the stern. This had been set aside for privy purposes because we had no loo and to go into the bank would only mean dumping those in need up to their chests in mud! Suddenly the night was split by an awful scream and I thought for a moment that the poor woman had fallen overboard. But when she returned to the 'bridge' I discovered the real reason. A ZLO, unable to understand English and thus the briefing I had given earlier, had chosen to sleep in the scuppers at the stern of the craft.

'What on earth happened,' I asked.

'Oh! How the hell do you expect me to see a Zairois on a dark night?' she retorted.

Each day our scientists would explain their work to us. This was most helpful because on such an adventurous project it is easy to forget that the results of lasting value are those achieved by the experts. Captain Scott had said of his last polar expedition that he believed it was primarily a great scientific project, with the Pole as the bait for public support. Similarly, I believed that, although the navigation of the river was most important, the newsworthy challenge was also necessary to gain funds for the entire operation. Several of our scientists had been unable to obtain financial grants and we thus also needed to raise money for them.

Although immediate results are not easy to obtain, some of the subjects under scrutiny were fascinating. One project concerned the mountain gorilla. These enormous creatures can reach thirty stone and are only found in the high altitude forests of Zaire. Tac HQ had been seeking information on their whereabouts and, one night in a small bar, Pam met a local official who claimed to know all. However, we had no map with us and it was difficult to find out exactly where he thought they resided. The quest was not made any easier by this gentleman having consumed a considerable amount of beer; as he did not speak English, I left him being interrogated by Pam. Later I found her with her back pressed hard against the bar. The Zairois was attempting to describe where we might find the gorillas using the map of Africa on her T-shirt. 'For Gods sake get me out of here before he reaches the Cape of Good Hope!' she hissed.

Jeremy Mallinson, right-hand man to Gerald Durrell at the Jersey Zoo, was eventually treated to a rare opportunity when he spent five days in close proximity to a large family of mountain gorillas in dense forest. Whilst there, one enormous male, who had been named Casimer, suddenly gave a deep roar and, beating its chest, charged to within six feet of Jeremy before calling off the attack! These bluffing tactics are well-known in gorillas and Jeremy stayed just long enough to get a very splendid photograph.

On the river our geologists studied the rocks. Zaire has a great wealth of minerals and in some places we saw whole hills of what looked like solid copper. Meanwhile, the fish team sought their specimens with nets and lines and spent many hours each day trying to collect samples for the study of fish bile, but in desperation had to get the sappers to speed up the project with the aid of a little dynamite! Dr Roger Sweeting, a research fellow at St John Cass College, was concerned with parasites; he also managed to acquire two black kites, which he named Biggles and Cromwell.

At Kongolo there were a great many problems. The giant inflatables were using up to ten gallons of petrol per day and there was simply no more to be had anywhere. Somehow Derek had borrowed a train, filled it with fuel and, doubtless contravening numerous regulations, had got it to the river. So when I arrived I found a base already established with adequate supplies for us to tackle the Gates of Hell. In the meantime, the sappers were still battling to get the overland convoys through on the terrible roads from Kolwezi. To complicate matters, Cliff Taylor had been badly burned when a petrol cooker exploded. He looked a terrible mess, but thanks to Dr Ian Young's skill, he was back in his cockpit within a week.

On our way north we had passed through Mulongo, where we had met two charming missionaries, Mary Goodsell, who had come out from Britain forty-four years previously, and Dolly Mac-Donald from Australia, who had been there for a mere twenty-eight! Together they ran the Protestant mission and were extremely hospitable to us. Everything looked serene and peaceful and there I enjoyed one of those blissful periods of relaxation that are, alas, a rare privilege for expedition leaders.

At Mulongo I became increasingly concerned about the threat from terrorists in the forests near the rapids. The local battalion had suffered many casualties and its CO warned me to be prepared for trouble. He hinted darkly that we were prime targets for ambush as we went through the worst rapids. The Zaire Army, foreseeing trouble, had issued us with a large consignment of arms which Gordon Mitchell had wisely decided to keep under his control in large boxes labelled 'Scientific Instruments'! However, I now decided to issue these 'instruments' and chose another mission as the distribution point. This had been the site of the most horrible massacre on 1 January 1962 when twenty-two priests had been taken out and had their throats cut and, so it was said, had then been cooked and eaten by rebels. When the inhabitants saw us receiving weapons they suspected that retribution was nigh and fled! However, as a result of our gunboat diplomacy, no one had to use a weapon in anger, nor were we fired on at any time. Nevertheless, a few months after we had left the area, Jane Goodall, the chimpanzee expert, had her camp attacked in Tanzania and a number of her students kidnapped and held to ransom So, the terrorists got their publicity after all, but not at my expense.

Despite our misgivings, the Gates were not such a severe obstacle as we had feared. One native, clearly convinced we were going to our deaths, simply stood looking down and made the sign of the cross as we passed through the foaming water between the reefs of black rocks. Our boats proved to be as robust as we had hoped and we sailed on, enjoying a slightly bumpy, but otherwise uneventful, ride in what could have been very dangerous water.

On 10 November we emerged from the final cataract of this stretch. Marc Smith, our young river-runner from the Colorado, was disappointed that the water had not yet really tested his ability and even talked of going home. I was able to persuade him that the dangers and hazards of the Livingstone Falls that lay ahead would test the bravest of us.

As we passed down river, the banks were crowded with brightly clothed villagers cheering and waving excitedly. They had come from miles around to see these, the first boats ever to sail through the rapids, and as it was midday we pulled in for our lunch. Chiefs came on board and were offered lemonade powder and Army biscuits thinly spread with Shippam's paste! The greeting over, they announced that their people wished to sing to us. Squadron Leader Mike Barnard, our musical navigator, found it too good an opportunity to miss and unwrapped his saxophone to give a rendering of 'Sweet Sue', which the people applauded enthusiastically.

That night we camped on a grassy bank looking across a slow moving river, almost 1,000 yards wide, to a low ridge in the east. It was from this point that Stanley had first viewed the river in 1876, when his expedition had crossed almost two-thirds of Africa. As we turned powdered egg into omelettes at breakfast, the chiefs arrived by canoe. These thirty-foot-long craft were each propelled by twenty paddlers who worked in unison, chanting as they dug in their blades. Boats like this had attacked Stanley, but to us the natives showed nothing but kindness. Indeed the fresh rations that they brought were a welcome change from dehydrated food.

On the fleet the pets multiplied. Ken Mason, the expedition's leading humorist and an ace photographer from the *Daily Telegraph*, had bought for Pam a small grey, furry bushbaby named Tiddlypush. Being nocturnal, it was a useless pet, for when, in daylight hours, we wished to play with it, the creature was sound asleep up a tree. At night when we were trying to rest, the wretched beast was bounding about and usually tried to get into one's sleeping bag and do something unspeakable. Thus, to remove Tiddlypush from harm's way, Pam kept it inside her shirt. One day when she was interpreting a rather truculent chieftain, I noticed to my amazement that the man's eyes had suddenly come out on organ stops! The reason was simple: Pam's bosom was heaving up and down in a most remarkable fashion and then the goggle-eyed creature suddenly emerged from her neckline. The chief fled and we had no more trouble!

On 13 November we reached the village of Nyangwe, near where Stanley had launched *Lady Alice* after his march from Zanzibar, and where Dr Livingstone had lived for almost a year, trying in vain to persuade the local people to take him down river. After witnessing a most dreadful slaughter by Arab slavers, the doctor had marched back to Ujiji on Lake Tanganyika where Stanley had found him, sick and weak, in 1871. In the field behind Nyangwe were graves of Belgian soldiers who had died fighting in the Force Publique, which Stanley had set up in the 1880s to defend the new Congo Free State. Ironically, these men had perished whilst driving out the slavers under the infamous Tippu-Tib, who had supported Stanley in 1876. As we stood in the long grass viewing the monument and its simple plaques, there was a movement on the brickwork. A thin green snake rose from the grass and slithered up to the top of the plinth, coiled itself and raised its head to hiss menacingly at us. We left the tombs with their sinister guardian and returned to the river.

Snakes were by no means uncommon. On one occasion, spotting one swimming across the river, I shouted to Bob Powell, commanding a nearby recce boat, 'Catch it!' He did, with the aid of a plastic bag and a paddle, and on getting it into the boat found that he had landed a spitting cobra, which can throw its venom with accuracy for some eight feet. Three men ended up in the water while the snake stayed in the boat!

Thanks to the ever-watchful eye of our fleet's medical officer, John Chapman-Smith, we were always alert for disease. We were riding one of the biggest sewers in Africa, and all drinking water had to be filtered, boiled and sterilized: indeed it was safer to drink whisky. Nevertheless, fevers did occur and Pam, having nursed a Gurkha suffering from chicken pox, caught the bug herself. For days she lay beneath an improvised canopy that Jim Masters erected on the flagship to shield her from the relentless African sun. Others went down with various maladies and for a time we looked like a hospital ship. Meanwhile we pressed on towards Kindu, scene of more tragedies of the 1960s, for it was here that the drug-crazed Simba rebels had started their revolt, through which they eventually seized large areas of the country. The hard-working Commissaire du Zone greeted me with a bottle of Scotch and entertained us royally.

We always made enormous efforts to ensure good relations with the locals when we docked in any small town. Captain Kabe, a Zaire naval officer, would often say to me, 'John, I think I shall go ashore to look into Naval matters.' He normally returned at dawn, usually with two attractive girls on his arms and to the inquiry, 'Naval matters all right, Captain?' would reply with a great grin 'Number one, number one.'

Early one day our 'Orders Group' assembled on the rubbery deck of *La Vision*. I noted the absence of one of our senior ZLOs.

'Slept ashore last night,' muttered Tom Hawkins. 'I'll find him.' A few moments later Tom confronted the concierge at the local hotel.

'Où est le Capitain?' he demanded.

'Numero neuf,' whined the terrified woman.

With barely a tap on the door, Tom thrust it open, revealing our Zaire officer entwined with a lady. His speedy reaction was extraordinary for, leaping out of bed in his underpants, he exclaimed, 'Ah, Major Hawkins. Have you met my sister?' Thereafter, whenever we approached any riverside town, we would enquire, 'Got any sisters here, Captain?'

From time to time in our travels local officials would make the normal gesture of offering me, as commander of the expedition, the gift of a few local ladies. I had learned most of the excuses in the book – 'My religion doesn't permit', 'I am not feeling very well', 'My wife would not approve' – but, in one particular town, when I had exhausted all possibilities, Pam suggested that I hand the matter over to one of our able Zaire sergeants. I explained to him the cause of my embarrassment and asked if he could help out. 'Mais certainement, mon Colonel,' he replied. Next morning the sergeant in question arrived at Tac HQ, saluted, and explained that he was ready to provide his services in the cause of the expedition whenever required. As a result I escaped many a tricky situation and had the most faithful senior NCO of the Zaire Army!

10

In the Steps of Stanley

On 14 November a solid wall of tall trees rose suddenly on both banks of the river. We had passed through bush country and were now entering jungle. At Kindu our entomologists and Gurkhas set up a camp in the tropical rain forest. The scientists were sampling the flying insects at different levels between the top of the trees and the ground. They believed that this would give them the first overall indication of the composition, vertical distribution and richness of the flying insect fauna of the rain forest canopy in central Africa. Such knowledge is essential in order to assess the importance of the forest as a natural resource. Working closely with a team of Zaire scientists, who had been sent on the orders of the president, our experts set electrically-powered ultraviolet light traps to collect the insects at different heights above the ground. In order to get the traps up into the trees a small team of sappers was employed as climbers.

As we approached the site there was an anguished cry. Rounding the bend in the forest trail, I was just in time to see Sergeant Mick Hough hurtling through the air to land with an awful thud at the base of an eighty-five-foot tree. 'Don't touch him,' cried Fifi the nurse when we rushed to his aid. As we gathered round his limp body, Mick stirred. 'F***ing hell,' he said several times and stood up! Given that he was a parachute engineer, no one was surprised at this show of toughness, but we later discovered that he had actually suffered a minor brain haemorrhage and a split liver. The fact that he survived was a miracle.

At ground level they discovered many interesting creatures, including fascinating butterflies, colourful moths and some highly dangerous snakes, including a deadly forty-two-inch gaboon viper, the bite of which gives you approximately three seconds to hand your best friend your wallet!

Supplying these groups in the forest was never easy and usually involved long difficult journeys by Land-Rover or parachute drops from the Beaver. Nevertheless they ate quite well, making up the deficiencies of their diet with monkeys provided by the ZLOs. It was never a taste I enjoyed. Once I bought them a bottle of whisky. The scientists' eyes lit up with glee. It was unfortunate that the water they used to top up the liquor had been tainted with formalin; the lot of them were almost pickled for posterity!

Back at Kindu, Derek's logistic team was working hard to keep the whole show on the road. Many frustrations were overcome, including one when a train started off in the wrong direction and no one could speak the same language as the engine driver. On another occasion a thief stole a video battery and was caught by a Zaire sergeant. Justice was done immediately and seen to be done, for the poor fellow was thrashed mercilessly in front of us before being taken off to the magistrate for sentence. As the battery had expired anyway, I sent a note to the court asking for clemency for the wretched man. The magistrate respected my wishes and only gave him a year's penal servitude.

In a remote village 400 miles away, Freddie Rodger, as senior medical officer, was leading the medical research team investigating many diseases, including river blindness, which afflicts more than two million in Africa. It was a pathetic sight to watch the queues of people outside the head man's straw hut awaiting examination, some blind, many already heavily disfigured by the subcutaneous lumps from which the worms hatch. The only light relief was the arrival of four Pygmies, who politely declined Freddie's invitation to have their eyes looked at on the grounds that he would be able to glimpse their souls! The research was directed at finding clues towards a cure for the disease, which was already known to caused by the bite of a black fly known as *Simulium damnosium*. Freddie was there to find where onchocerciasis was most prevalent, and the background of each person was thoroughly investigated, even down to the number of wives. The results of his work were included in *Onchocerciasis in Zaire*, edited by Freddie and published by Pergamon in 1977.

At Kindu we refitted the boats from the quartermaster's train.

In a railway siding guarded by Zaire soldiers stood a 'wagon-lits' and a collection of closed trucks. Quartermaster Gordon Mitchell paraded up and down with a large stick. Men approached at their peril, but when the custodian of all we possessed decided that an issue should be made, it was a great moment. A huge bunch of keys was produced and, like a medieval jailer, Gordon would stride up to the selected wagon. The heavy steel doors would slide open, revealing a host of goodies. Few were permitted the privilege of actually entering the inner sanctum.

Meanwhile over the radio to Kinshasa I heard that the jetboats had arrived early. The New Zealand team under Jon Hamilton was anxious to get on with the job of reconnoitring the Livingstone Falls. Time spent in reconnaissance is never wasted, especially on expeditions, but I was not yet prepared to have an FST deployed that far ahead. Already our force was spread over 1,000 miles. However, the jets were there and so I reorganised our support groups.

To the west of the Zaire, zoologist Sinclair Dunnett and a tough marine named Bob Hudson were seeking the rare Pygmy chimpanzee on the Lomami River. We would receive faint radio reports from them, but in spite of the most terrible privations they had not yet found the elusive creatures. We supplied them by air and kept our fingers crossed that nothing serious would occur, for they were well outside the range of any immediate help.

In Kindu I met the charming president of the local Luncheon Club, who mentioned that she also ran the cinema, nightclub and brothel. When she invited me to dinner the next day I enquired if I might bring with me one or two friends (for safety!) and went to her house the following evening accompanied by Pam and Captain Kabe. The lady and her sister, their hair arranged in spikes and basted liberally with rancid butter, had prepared a meal of traditional Zaire dishes. We were halfway through dinner when I felt something touch my leg. It was more than that; it was quite clearly a hand, which, very gradually, worked its way up the inside of my trouser leg. I was slightly alarmed and, looking across to the lady's sister opposite, was intrigued by the fact that both her hands were on the table. Eventually when the fingers had almost reached my knee I could stand it no longer and shot my arm under the table to grasp whatever it was. Out came a tiny chimpanzee dressed in a sailor suit and furious at having been disturbed.

'Ah, you have found poor Sophie,' said madam.

'She must be a very young chimpanzee,' I replied.

'No, no, she is very old,' insisted the lady.

Thus it was that whilst Sinclair and Bob were undergoing a most trying expedition, I had found a Pygmy chimpanzee under a table in Kindu!

Whilst the fleet moved to Ubundu under Mike Gambier I went off to see Freddie to cope with the administrative problems that now plagued us. I finally flew on to Ubundu in the Beaver and landed just before half light to be met by Joe Tuwai, another of our cheery Fijian NCOs. Motoring along a forest trail to the town, we came upon a group of large black apes. For a moment I thought we were facing gorillas but they were almost certainly wild chimpanzees and, as I leapt out to follow them up, they disappeared, chattering, into the bush. Their coats of hair were much thicker than is usual with captive creatures.

Near Ubundu was a Christian mission headed by the lively Father Augustine, the only survivor from a Simba attack during the revolt. Everywhere we went on this stage of the journey there were reminders of the civil war: burnt-out tanks, crashed aircraft, destroyed bridges and ferries and deserted hospitals and churches. It was a sad scene although President Mobutu's government was trying to restore this area to its former levels of prosperity.

The Stanley Falls, starting at Ubundu, consist of a stretch of some seven cataracts over a distance of fifty miles. The usual reconnaissance had been carried out by air, land and river and in spite of local stories that the river went underground, we did not expect too much trouble. How wrong we were.

Ken Mason was snapping members of the flagship's crew as we passed through some moderate rapids when, suddenly, all hell let loose.

'Look out,' yelled Peter Marett, who had seen that we were about to plunge into a yawning fourteen-foot-deep chasm that had inexplicably opened up in the riverbed.

Already one of the Avon dinghies was in the boiling pit being hurled about like a cork in a washtub. The giant raft on which I was riding came crashing down the slope and a huge wave swamped our engine, hurling the helmsman off his feet. A wall of water struck the bow, sweeping away stores, including a number of waterproof camera boxes that had been lashed in with 1,000-pound-breaking-strain wire. Decking boards splintered beneath us as the great raft flexed and twisted in the cauldron. 'We're breaking up,' someone cried.

With no engine we were trapped in the hole, being pounded by mountains of brown water that spun us around so that one lost all sense of direction. Then we were thrown clear to drift into slack water. It was a great relief, but behind us the second Avon had already gone into the swirling funnel and I just had time to catch sight of Richard Snailham's bearded face aghast with horror as he held on for dear life. *Barclays Bank*, the second big boat, skilfully avoided the hole, but the *David Gestetner* went straight in. We watched anxiously as she stood on her bow. 'Oh God, she's going over', I thought, but, miraculously, the giant fell back into the pit and escaped.

Next day, we went to a village and tried to send a message offering a reward for the recovery of any lost kit. Although they had no telephones, we found that the local talking drums were quick and efficient and for the equivalent of fifty pence you could get ten minutes on a talking drum during the cheap period! The sweating drummers claimed they could communicate up to thirty miles by night and twenty by day. We thought it compared pretty favourably with our own radios or the GPO!

On Friday 29 November we crossed the equator. At lunchtime we held a small ceremony and drank a toast to mark this epic point in our journey. That night we camped amongst some limestone outcrops. The jungle contained old plantations and wild lemons were plentiful. There were also some interesting caves in the area; in one we found a great many initials which, according to local legends, included some carved by H M Stanley himself!

The recce reports of the Stanley Falls were good. Having met Bill Coleridge's FST in Kisangani, the manager of a local brewery had kindly come out to greet us by road with a large quantity of his products. The party that ensued was memorable and put us in a good mood to confront the Falls next day. Thousands of townspeople crowded onto the bank to cheer the fleet through. As each boat slipped over the six-foot drop into the heaving waves, a great cry went up from the shore.

'Mobutu oyeah,' we shouted over the loud-hailers. 'Mobutu ooy-eeah,' echoed the watchers.

The Avons were hurled high by their impact with the waves, but the big rafts ambled through, all except *David Gestetner*, which delighted the onlookers by demolishing one of the fifteen-foot-high fish traps in mid-river. It was a great day; we had now reached our halfway mark and the brewery kindly saw that the occasion was suitably marked when we came ashore.

In the town our signal section, who had flown ahead, had already set up a high radio mast trying to contact the BBC in London. Sergeant Alan Cobb, our rear base radio operator in Kinshasa, had arranged the details and now we were to attempt the impossible: a link-up from the jungle to Broadcasting House. Early one morning I sat by the set as our signallers fiddled with the knobs. At last there came the clear voice of someone at Catterick in Yorkshire. 'We're connecting you with the BBC now,' it said.

Various pips and squeaks followed and then a clearly audible woman telephonist in Broadcasting House was heard to say, 'I am sorry, dearie, but the number's engaged, you'll have to ring back.'

'Madam, I am in the middle of Africa,' I screamed into the microphone.

'I can't help that, you'll have to call back,' she said. And the line went dead! Thus ended our attempt to communicate with the nation.

Over the next 1,000 miles of wide, slow-flowing river Stanley had fought great battles, but the Zairois were overwhelming us with their traditional hospitality. It was as well that our relations with them were so good for Roger Chapman's life was suddenly at stake. He had been taken ill on the afternoon of Thursday 5 December with what was thought to be peritonitis and Vyvyan Jones, one of our surgeons, was extremely worried about his condition.

'Are you really proposing to operate in this bush hospital?' I asked. 'Well, if I don't, I think he'll die,' he replied.

That night they gave Roger a spinal anaesthetic, which meant that, although he felt no pain, he remained conscious throughout the operation. Roger, with great Yorkshire wit, happened to notice that the two surgeons working on him were John Chapman-Smith, an eye surgeon from New Zealand, and Viv, a gynaecologist from Swindon. He remarked that he hoped they had reached a compromise! However, by morning it was no laughing matter, for Roger was dying; the only chance of saving his life was to get him to a hospital where they could do a full laboratory investigation. The nearest was in Kinshasa, 1,000 miles away and, although our Beaver could have covered the distance in two hops, it was doubtful that there would be fuel at the end of the first 500 miles to get it the next.

At this point our guardian angel intervened and we managed to get the assistance of the local Zaire general. He ordered the nearest airliner to land at Kisangani airfield, which it did. John Benham-Crosswell, a para-sapper, surrounded it with his 'mercenaries' and the French pilots put up their hands in surrender. However, John explained that this was not a coup d'état but simply a question of borrowing their plane for a few hours.

We loaded Roger onto the DC4, which took off for Kinshasa without delay. Also on board was the faithful Sergeant Mulongo, who now needed treatment for VD. It was fortunate that we had Pam with us because she had worked in the President's Clinic in Kinshasa and knew the people concerned. Later, we heard that largely through the good efforts of Dr Bill Close, Pam's former boss and personal physician to the president, they had managed to save Roger's life, although not without a considerable struggle.

Meanwhile our fleet was once again under the command of Mike Gambier. I planned to send the boats on whilst I moved east into the Ituri Forest through which Stanley had marched to rescue Emin Pasha in 1888. In this dark land live the Pygmies and also the strange okapi. Peculiar to this part of Zaire and only discovered around 1900, the okapi is a type of giraffe with a backside like a zebra and a body similar to an antelope. I was keen to see the beast and badly wanted a few days away from the administrative nightmares. Accompanied by our photographers, and after driving 350 miles towards the Mountains of the Moon, we saw two fine bulls in captivity and were privileged to meet the Pygmies who hunt these strange creatures. In olden times the skin of the okapi was much sought after and reserved for chiefs. Apparently it was supposed to bring an endless supply of pretty young girls to those who sat on it!

Guided by the Pygmies we tried to find and film this rare animal. Marching deep into the twilight forest with our tiny, near-naked friends, we searched for days, and, although I was not lucky enough to see one myself, some members did get within twenty yards of them. The only creatures I met were far from gentle. On one sortie two Pygmies, Bongo, a Sandhurst-trained Zaire officer, Val Jones and I were moving along a narrow game-trail in thick jungle. Suddenly the leading Pygmy bounced past like a little chocolate-coloured rubber ball; close behind him was Lieutenant Bongo, who yelled, 'Run!'; and behind him came a very angry jumbo, ears flapping and trunk raised. I leapt aside and just remembered to warn Val. Four irate elephants crashed past, scattering branches and leaves. They looked rather small and it was only later that I discovered they were the very dangerous variety that inhabit the Ituri forest and are much feared by the locals. I couldn't imagine what had caused this unprovoked attack until I remembered that for some 3,000 years Pygmies have been sticking poisoned spears into jumbos' backsides.

The jungle hunts were arduous, but very exciting. To try to follow a Pygmy in the deep forest is not easy, especially if you are over four feet in height. The little warriors were quite superb hunters and very tough. Using their tiny bows they could transfix a cigarette packet at twenty paces with an arrow tipped with coagulant that will clot its victim's blood in seconds. During the search a hunter accidentally shot himself in the foot with an arrow, but luckily it was not poison-tipped; he went on to march seventeen miles with us that day!

When we returned to the village at night our hosts entertained us. We took turns at putting on dances and acts in our own language. Neither really understood the other but it was great fun. Ken Mason's songs made everyone hoot with laughter. Val did a Highland sword dance and Sam Qarau frightened the living daylights out of our tiny friends by drinking the contents of a paraffin lamp and, then with the aid of his lighter, blowing fire all around us.

From my point of view this short interlude was a chance to unwind. On an expedition there is rarely any rest for the leader and under extreme stress I find myself flitting between two characters: the stronger tries hard to defeat the weaker. The only noticeable result of this struggle is that my whisky consumption goes up! However, when the weaker begins to get the upper hand I find I may overreact to situations or exaggerate a problem. The difficulty is, as in war, to know which intelligence to accept. I believe it is essential to keep one's mind as open as possible to avoid blocking out unpleasant information. This is why I enjoy having a small group of trusted aides in my Tac HQ. Peter, with his methodical and cautious approach, was an ideal intelligence officer whilst Pam, with her knowledge of Zaire and its people, was a splendid adviser on the local situation. Sam could be relied upon to make us laugh under the most adverse conditions.

At work in the rain forest was Ken Joysey, a lean and enthusiastic zoologist, who was in hot pursuit of the West African otter shrew. There were no live specimens of this creature in captivity. Aided by the Pygmy bowmen, Gurkha soldiers and Sergeant Major Eddie McGee, Ken and our other zoologists probed deep into the Ituri.

Eventually the Gurkhas managed to capture one. Back on the river our botanists were hard at work, studying amongst other subjects the spread of a notorious water hyacinth. Outwardly it is a pretty violet and green plant that was introduced from South America in 1914 as an ornament, but it is now threatening to block parts of the great waterway.

On returning to our base in Kisangani I was able to review all the problems that faced the expedition whilst Mike sailed the fleet on towards Kinshasa. Ahead, we faced a host of difficulties and our casualties were growing alarmingly as malaria, in spite of regular doses of Paludrine, took its toll. Dysentery, hepatitis, sundry fevers and ear complaints were reducing our force daily. I began to fear that we had too few to carry out the tasks necessary to reach the Atlantic.

On the political front, the Zairois were extremely sensitive and we had to be very careful not to say anything that would cause offence. At Kananga there seemed to be a running problem between the British and the other nationalities in the medical research teams. In minor disagreements the Zairois sided with the Belgians, with whom, of course, they had a common tongue. I was too far away to intervene but the irrepressible Freddie Rodger managed to lead this group effectively. The Zairois said he was 'another Stanley' because he made them work so hard!

The main reasons for success on the river were the thorough reconnaissance and the good equipment. The Sony video was especially valuable and I believe we must have been the first expedition ever to use this equipment in the field.

Although the expedition's discipline was good, I tried to avoid the larger towns wherever possible. It really would have been very useful to have had a regimental sergeant major present to look after the number of soldiers. Officers tend to be rather hesitant about rebuking their men on expeditions, and I was constantly having to remind them about turn-out. The problem is that with the scientists bearded and long-haired it was difficult to enforce. However, there were no really serious personality problems during the expedition. Indeed, I cannot remember an expedition where there had been so few difficulties of this nature. Furthermore, the girls were a cohesive element on the expedition. Whilst Pam was nursing Roger in Kinshasa, Val had taken over as my PA and, with her Cordon Bleu training, was feeding us like fighting cocks. This was just as well because morale was suffering through the lack and delay of mail in spite of the efforts of our army postman to get it speeded up. Another problem was the dire shortage of fuel and Land-Rover spares. Our transport was now virtually worn out. The roads were generally poor and got worse as we proceeded north, and I noticed that the jungle was encroaching at an alarming rate. The railway companies, on the other hand, were extremely helpful and, wherever we could find ferries, the local authorities assisted. However, many of these had been destroyed during the civil war. The weather had been pretty good. We seemed to have dodged the rain along the river and yet had managed to get just enough water to navigate over the rocks. Mosquitoes were extremely rife in places as were the tsetse flies and other nuisances including scorpions.

On the whole the expedition was in good heart, although this was sometimes due to the supply of free beer! Several breweries along the river were about to be nationalized and were thus extremely generous.

Another problem was that having left groups in Kisangani and Kananga, our communications were now stretched beyond range. Nevertheless, the Royal Signals team somehow always managed to get through. The committee in London announced that in spite of our economies they had been forced to raise an overdraft and this we knew would take at least eighteen months in writing, lecturing and selling our philatelic souvenirs to repay once we returned to Britain.

So the whole expedition moved slowly on towards the Atlantic. Pam and I landed at Mbandaka to find our friends being royally entertained by personnel of the Wimpey Company. Alas, we had arrived too late for the party, but the recce section was waiting to take us forward to the giant inflatables, now motoring westwards. Neither of us felt particularly well one morning, waking with a mild fever and feeling very sleepy. I had intended to hold a conference of captains on the flagship, but the river was terribly choppy and we were constantly soaked, so I spent most of the day discussing our future moves with Mike. A great advantage of having such an able second-in-command was that I could bring him in to take over, allowing me to coordinate the whole expedition.

For three days my fever ebbed and flowed and I didn't think too much of it. Indeed, I was more worried and frustrated because our radio communications were being made difficult by constant interference from a Chinese station operating from the Congo Republic. On Saturday 21 December, I decided to move ahead with Alun Davies's recce boat to arrive in the capital ahead of the fleet. At Kinshasa I went straight up to Bill Close's house to see Roger who was then convalescing. Bill gave me a funny look and asked if I felt ill. 'A little hot,' I replied. He took my temperature, which was 104 F! Unemotionally he informed me that I had malaria and in a flash injected me. In spite of feeling reasonably normal I found myself rushed back to the newly-established Tac HQ in the town where Adrianne and Val swabbed me down with icebags, stark naked! It did the trick, for next day I was able to rise and greet the fleet.

Christmas never feels quite the same in the tropics but the European families there threw open their houses and did their utmost to entertain us. It was our only rest in four months. The sick were put into hospital and we prepared to tackle the huge cataracts that lay ahead. It was a time to relax and refit the boats for the battle with the great rapids of the Livingstone Falls. Richard Dorman, a wild Irish Guards ensign, caused a great stir by hurling himself fully dressed into the swimming pool of the Intercontinental Hotel, complete with a packet of soap powder, to get an instant bubble bath that filled the entire pool!

The complete New Zealand jetboat team now arrived and informed me that they did not have a great deal of time left. They were very experienced river-runners and had already done an excellent reconnaissance for us of the Livingstone Falls, which proved extremely useful in planning this last phase. Long discussions went on far into the night. Captain Nigel Warren of the Gurkhas had been left with his PST at Kisangani to support the scientists working in that area and eventually withdraw them to the capital. Freddy was still at Kananga with his medical research team and contact with him was extremely difficult. On Christmas Eve we had a special dinner and after spending a short time with Roger at Bill Close's house,

I returned in time for midnight mass, conducted by Basil Pratt. There were forty-one communicants and as wine and bread were unavailable Basil had to make do with brandy and Christmas cake!

By New Year's Day the boats had been made ready, engines tested and crews briefed and a great crowd gathered on the Island of Mimosa, near the capital, to watch our fight with Kinsuka, first of the thirty-two cataracts of the Livingstone Falls that cover more than 200 miles between Kinshasa and the Atlantic. Assisting us on much of the stretch were the two Hamilton water jetboats. These 220-horse-power, fast and highly manoeuvrable craft were to be a vital part of the forthcoming operation. Stanley had said, 'There is no fear that any other explorer will attempt what we have done in the cataract region. It would be insanity in a successor.' Now I was to discover if he had been right.

At 1100 hours *La Vision* passed easily through the narrows where the river had now been constricted from something like nine miles wide to one mile across. Running down a smooth tongue of water, the inflatables skirted the line of tossing twenty-foot waves that rose and fell in the centre of the river. Acting as rescue boats the jet-craft lay in the lee of weed-covered boulders. Gerry Pass and Eric Rankin, the *Survival-Anglia* television team, had been positioned on one of these tiny islands to get a really first-rate shot of the drama, which they did when *David Gestetner* appeared with her white ensign fluttering. On the shore an elderly English lady missionary, over-come with emotion, is said to have burst into tears and then fainted at the sight.

As the boat crossed the first fall, her stern engine struck a sub-merged rock, which hurled it upwards off its wooden transom. The flaying propeller sliced through the neoprene fabric of the stern compartment, which deflated immediately. Aboard the jet we could see the great raft was being swept out of control into the angry wave towers that we knew must be avoided at all costs. In a second Jon Hamilton had opened the throttle and driven the eighteen-foot boat straight into the pounding mounds of coffee-coloured water.

Mike was in the water, his white crash helmet and red life-jacket showing clearly as he bobbed amongst the flying spray. Our sister jet, driven by Ralph Brown, was already making for him with a scramble-net and Lieutenant Nigel Armitage-Smith was standing by to pull him in. The deafening roar of water and engines drowned all commands: everyone was acting instinctively now. *David Gestetner*'s skipper was trying to pass us a line. His face contorted as he yelled against the din.

Suddenly I heard Ken Mason yell, 'Watch out!' I looked up and saw that an enormous wave had flung the crippled *Gestetner* forward and upward, straight towards us. For a moment she towered above us, riding a fearsome wall of falling white water, and then came crashing down with a great 'ponk', right across us. For a second we were locked together in the tempest, but we managed to wriggle from beneath and circle our quarry once again. This time we succeeded in taking the line and were soon dragging the craft like a stricken whale towards Monkey Island. We were probably the first people ever to reach this large jungle-covered island. The next day, with repairs completed, we set off down river. Rapid followed rapid as we cautiously felt our way through the treacherous waters that gurgled and swirled between the banks of black rock. To get the necessary supplies into the boats meant relays of overland teams working outwards from the capital in our very tired Land-Rovers and a few Toyota trucks. Wildlife was not much in evidence, but on 2 January we did come across some islands literally alive with huge bats. There were thousands of them festooning the trees and when I fired a flare from my signal pistol, the hideous creatures took off and showered us with their excreta. It is interesting that Stanley reported great flocks of birds in this area; I think that in fact what he had seen were these colonies of bats with twelve-inch wingspans. The bats were obviously of value to the Zairois because we could see nets set up on tall poles at the side of the river.

In the days that followed we shot more rapids and avoided the most ferocious waves and water I've ever met. For each, the drill was the same: air reconnaissance by Beaver, then the jets would take the skippers ahead to examine the heaving, inconsistent flood and the swirling whirlpools that went up to thirty yards across. On either side, vertical cliffs of red rock rose for hundreds of feet and fish eagles shrieked their yodelling cries as we passed. Our support teams worked non-stop to get fuel and supplies to us over the deeply-rutted tracks. In my log for Friday 3 January I recorded a typical day's sailing:

On 6 January we reached Isangila, the falls that had forced

Stanley to abandon his boats and march over the mountains towards the sea. Here I decided reluctantly to move the giant rafts overland as far as the Yalala Falls, leaving the jets and the Avon dinghies to tackle the ferocious stream alone. The giant craft simply hadn't got the power to manoeuvre in these rushing currents and boiling water. In no time, one of the dinghies was ripped open from stern to stern on razor-sharp rocks and Jim Masters was injured. It took 900 stitches and a gallon of Araldite to repair the damaged boat. Jim, meanwhile, drank a little J&B and recovered!

It was late afternoon when our jets entered the relatively clear passage that would take us through the terrible Isangila cataract. We were halfway down when I saw two gigantic waves converging on our bows. With a crash they struck simultaneously, hurling the 3,000-pound boat upwards. I fell across Jon Hamilton, knocking him momentarily from the wheel, and out of the corner of my eye I saw Pam almost go over the side. Then as we hit the water again there was another huge wave towering ahead of us. For a moment I thought we were done for. It was a monster. The wall of water smashed over us blotting out daylight but somehow we remained afloat. There was, however, a strange silence; the engine had died. Ahead, a line of black rocks rose like dragon's teeth on the lip of a fall and we were being swept straight towards them. Jon tried desperately to re-start the engine, his face creased with concern. On the third attempt it fired. It only stuttered for a minute, but it was just long enough for us to get into an eddy behind a huge boulder, where we could hold position whilst the electric bilge pumps baled us out.

Finally, even the jets were halted by shallows and reefs at the Inga Rapid, but, with two more short portages and some excellent warping with long ropes, we got the amazing Avon recce boats through to the foot of the biggest obstacle in the entire river, the Yalala Falls. A mile of water boiling over terraces and through jagged rocks of frightening speed greeted us. Meanwhile, our giant rafts had been carried by a Zaire army lorry to within the Crystal Mountains, just as Stanley's men had done, experiencing the same elephant grass, endless rolling hills, ridges and sharp, suet-colour quartz rocks that give these highlands their name. We, too, stumbled and fell on the slippery boulders at the river's edge. Ken Mason suffered a badly ripped arm and I injured my back. Porters, descendants of the people who had helped Stanley, assisted us.

At last we all came to the Falls, where the sappers were already clearing a way for us to carry the giant boats down to the river. For three days we toiled in the blistering heat with pick, spade and crowbar and some highly unstable dynamite to clear the boulders and get the giant rafts to the water.

It was late at night when Pam, Ken and I set out in a Land-Rover with at least two broken springs. In the back were large boxes of sticky, sweating dynamite and a crate of whisky. The vehicle lights didn't work well and, as we motored along the rutted road in the night, Ken began to ask about the dangers of premature initiation. We soon convinced him that our journey was likened to that shown so graphically in the film, *The Wages of Fear*.

'Oh my God,' he said, seizing a bottle of J&B from the back and clutching it between his legs.

'What on earth are you doing?' asked Pam.

'Well, I may as well get drunk and protect my courting tackle at the same time,' rejoined our jovial photographer as we bounced along with our lethal cargo. Nervous tension made us roar with laughter and swig deep gulps from the bottle.

At this point Pam looked very much like a boy, with her hair covered in mud and her shirt in grease. In fact, some Italian engineers whom we had met had referred to her as 'Fred the mechanic'. Earlier in the expedition a chief had greeted her with 'Bonjour, monsieur', but her confidence was restored when we discovered he was almost blind!

Finally, with sixty porters beneath each huge boat, we moved them like giant caterpillars down a 1,000-foot slope to the river. Here we joined up with the Avon dinghies that had been controlled by lines through the surging white water towards us. Now only three rapids barred our way to the sea, but with up to sixteen million gallons per second pouring through a gorge that narrowed the river to a bare 400 yards, the power of the raging water can be imagined. Indeed, the depth here was probably about 140 feet at high water. The river seemed to be alive with great bubbles boiling up from the depths and erupting on the surface. Then as quickly as they came they were replaced by whirlpools and swirling currents.

Our porters, many of them Angolan refugees and some almost

certainly Freedom Fighters, came with gifts of sugar-cane wine and fruit to see us off, but the river was not going to let us get away unscathed yet.

In the final rapid, *La Vision* was momentarily trapped in a whirl-pool, like a cork in a wash tub, being bent downwards and spun round and round with engines screaming. Before I could stop them coming down, Alun Davies's Avon was capsized by a fifteen-foot wave. The upturned boat with its crew of three clinging to it was swept towards a yawning whirlpool. The following recce boat saw the accident and its skipper Neil Rickards, a Royal Marine cor-poral, took his own small craft through the mountains of toss-ing water and managed to get right into the whirlpool and circle around inside it, rather like a motor-cyclist in a 'wall of death' at a fairground. In the centre of this swirling mass was Alun's capsized Avon with its crew of three were still clinging on frantically to the lifeline. By going the same way that the water was revolving, Neil managed to get his craft alongside the stricken boat so that Bob Powell and Somue, one of the ZLOs, could pull the three men to safety. As they left he looked back and was just in time to see the up-turned craft disappear down the vortex. Down river, I was sur-prised a few moments later, when the capsized boat bobbed up from the riverbed beside me. The engine was smashed, the floorboards wrecked and there appeared to be no survivors. But the crew had all been saved thanks to Neil's courage and skill, for which he was later awarded the Queen's Gallantry Medal and made one of Britain's 'Men of the Year'.

Two days later we reached the little seaport of Banana and at dusk our strange fleet, which had set out almost four months before in the centre of Africa, sailed into the setting sun. Basil, in cassock and surplice, held an improvised cross and, beneath the flags of the nations represented in our team, he conducted a simple service. Under our hulls the water heaved gently. Strangely, it no longer tugged and pulled at us; there was no current, for we were now in the Atlantic.

There had been many difficulties in the years that it had taken to plan and execute this expedition. Manpower had been extremely hard to find, money, was almost non-existent and we had a long struggle in the early days persuading our Zaire friends that we were not a bunch of mercenaries. However, in the end it had all been overcome and we had managed to prove Stanley wrong, although we had perhaps been insane to challenge this giant amongst rivers. Stanley, and what he had accomplished, had always been in our minds. In fact, I don't think we ever forgot him and were full of admiration for what he and his force had taken 999 days to do when they had crossed Africa from coast to coast and had ended up with only 115 survivors out of the 350 who had set out almost three years before. No one could appreciate more than we did what this remarkable boy from the workhouse at St Aspeth had achieved.

On our return to Kinshasa we met and talked with President Mobutu about the problems that his country faced. We were able to thank him for the considerable hospitality and kindness that we had received in his land. All he asked of us was that on our return home we should tell people of his hospitality and do what we could to help them to understand Zaire and his difficulties. This I gladly agreed to do, because on no previous expedition had we been received with such wonderful treatment from a ruler, government and people of a country which had not always had much reason to thank white men.

Above all we had had a highly flexible plan. Naturally there had been tensions and there had been the usual vying between science and adventure, but it had worked and that was what counted. Now, when it was all over, there were bound to be those who would knock our success. But I have always found this is largely out of jealousy. I believe we succeeded because of our careful preparation, which had been carried out over a period of four years before we arrived with the main body in Zaire. The logistic support group had achieved an administrative miracle and how our doctors had kept us all so fit is beyond me. In fact, although over half of us did become casualties at one time or another, no one died.

And we had a wonderful team. There were the young, who had been brought up on the traditions of Outward Bound, and the excellent junior NCOs, who had taken on enormous responsibility. There were also fine civilian leaders as well. Naturally people occasionally wanted to scratch out my eyes, but I have always accepted full responsibility on an expedition for everything that goes wrong and I expect people to grumble at me rather than at each other. This helps to keep the team together. Lastly, of course, our equipment had been magnificent. The Beaver aircraft and some of the innovations of the twentieth century had all worked, but of all the pieces of kit at our disposal the most outstanding were the giant inflatable boats that had wobbled their way all those thousands of miles across Africa. And it was primarily down to them that the expedition was later to be awarded the Segrave Trophy for courage, initiative, skill and imagination in pioneering new forms of transport. One of the previous winning craft had been Concorde, capable of cruising at Mach 2; on at least one occasion we had managed twelve miles per hour with the wind behind us!

Of course, the ultimate measures of our success were the medical and scientific results. I am not a scientist but simply, as a Royal Engineer, an 'obstacle-breaker' whose job it was to launch and sustain the experts in their selected areas to the best of my ability. The botanists from Leeds University had worked on the relationship of certain plants to mineral deposits and their work could well have important implications for the developing nations. Our study of the papyrus in Zaire may help developing nations to make use of this raw material for low-grade paper now that the production of newsprint from wood pulp has become so expensive. A means of clearing the river of the choking water hyacinth was suggested to the President during our final interview. Furthermore, Professor Harold Woolhouse, our chief botanist, believed that with more research this protein-rich plant might be used as animal food.

Jeremy Mallinson's conservation-orientated work on the mountain gorilla has contributed to the protection of this rare beast and the fish team's results will certainly add to man's knowledge of fish evolution. The anthropologist and geologists certainly had a field day, whilst the entomologists' work should be of real value in the future understanding of the composition, vertical distribution and richness of the insects of the rain-forest canopy.

After the expedition Harold Woolhouse kindly said, 'We could never have undertaken this without Army support.' However, I felt the operation was only possible because of the expertise, teamwork and mutual respect that the Scientific Exploration Society had built up between civilians and servicemen of many nations. In short, I believe that the whole expedition had been a worthwhile project with a good mixture of science and adventure, showing that there were still plenty of people about with the same healthy contempt for difficulties and dangers such as Stanley and Livingstone had endured.

11

Leadership Training

'And a monster's gobbling up Mr Leggett's goldfish' reported RSM Mansley completing his briefing on the disciplinary matters of the Regiment.

'Better increase the rations on future exercises,' I commented, not believing a word.

'But it's true, Colonel, he's lost 3,000 and we've had a request to help from the Constabulary.' Hank Mansley, a giant of a man with a laugh like a hyena, who had been on the Blue Nile expedition, was now my RSM at the Junior Leaders Regiment at Dover where future Warrant Officers and NCOs for the Royal Engineers were trained.

It transpired that Alf Leggett, a great character who ran a lovely Norman hall as a home for elderly folk, had a lifelong passion for goldfish. After an exciting career in the Royal Navy he had sought more peaceful pursuits in a sleepy Kentish village and was renowned for his success as a fish breeder. He had recently noted a dramatic decrease in his pond's population. A local angling society was consulted. 'Could be a monster perch,' its members said, and set to with rod and line to catch the cannibal. However, in spite of their valiant efforts the goldfish continued to disappear. Alf and a policeman, armed with shotgun, spent the night in a tree, waiting to blast the swine if it surfaced. But although they fired several times, no writhing monster appeared and eventually Alf fell out of the tree.

'Might be an eel,' suggested a professor of biochemistry from the Water Board. 'Or a heron,' said a senior police officer.

Only a handful of goldfish remained when someone mentioned that a lady had emptied her son's tank of tropical fish into a local stream. 'That must be it, then,' said the regulars in the village pub. 'All these mild winters and hot summers we have been having – whatever it is has grown and it's thriving on Alf's fish.' The press, smelling a good story, was quickly on to it. Trade at the village pub increased and, once their gullets were suitably dampened, locals recalled forgotten tales of dark doings dating back to Chaucer. Meanwhile, Alf's former naval chums, reading of his difficulties, began to write in from all over the world. My RSM's uncle lived nearby and told Alf that there was only one thing for it, 'Call in the Royal Engineers!'

The RSM did a recce and reported that the willow-surrounded pond was set in a garden next to some glasshouses.

'A few pounds of plastic underwater would certainly kill anything there,' he said, 'but there is no safe place near enough to the pond from which you can see the demolition on firing.'

'We've got an exercise next week,' I replied. 'We could use one of the ferrets (small armoured cars), get it close to the water's edge and fire the charge electrically from inside the turret.'

As Judith and I swept through the manor gates I was mildly surprised to see a large number of cars. My Adjutant, Peter Enzer, led us across the beautifully mown lawns. Rounding a hedge we came face to face with a tall man in a deerstalker hat clutching a .12 bore.

'Mr Leggett?' I enquired. But before he could answer, we were surrounded by a horde of pressmen. It was later reported that more members of Fleet Street had come to watch the attack on 'Jaws' (as it was instantly nicknamed) than had greeted President Carter on arrival in Britain that same day. Alf had risen to the occasion and provided a splendid lunch, with lashings of booze, to cheer on the reporters and, whilst I questioned him about the monster, the junior Sappers got down to the mucky business of laying the explosive on the pond bed. Spencer Eade, the local Army public relations officer, was smiling gleefully as he strode up and down.

'Must have every national paper in the country here, John,' he enthused.

Whilst the charges were being laid the cameramen jockeyed for position. In the process a TV team crowded onto a small footbridge which, much to the joy of their rivals, collapsed, precipitating the luckless crew into the pond.

Finally, all was ready. The Junior Leader who was to fire the demolition climbed into the armoured car, now being drawn up behind the hedge, its machine-gun pointing menacingly at the muddy water.

'All clear,' came the shout from the sentries and, as the count-down commenced, the cameras were raised. 'Three, two, one, fire.' The roar was barely deadened by the water. Great spouts cascaded high into the sky, much of it drifting down upon us. The only immediate casualty was a duck that happened to be passing overhead and laid an egg in fright. A subdued cheer went up and champagne corks popped. The press, eager for a picture, was delighted when the odd dead minnow was discovered.

'Well, that should have fixed it,' I said, and we strode away for a welcome cup of tea in Alf's kitchen. As we passed a group of old ladies on the lawn I remarked, 'Good heavens, Alf, I should think they must have been scared out of their wits.'

'Stone deaf, all of them,' he winked.

But one old darling reached out and beckoned. 'Mr Leggett,' she wheezed. 'I think I heard something just then.'

Alf bent down and shouted loudly in her ear. 'Don't worry, dear, it was only an atom bomb they've dropped on London.'

'Oh dear! Does that mean I shan't get my paper in the morning?'

Spencer had just put down the telephone. 'Oh well, you can't win them all,' he groaned. 'That was my boss at MoD on the line. He has just told me not to promote the story after all. I had to explain that it was too late, we'd already done it. Apparently there is a programme on telly tonight critical of defence expenditure and he thinks that our story may not give the right image.'

He was right. The report, carried by almost every paper in the country and many overseas and also told and re-told on television and radio, was far from serious. However, it did show boy soldiers having the time of their lives and new recruits flowed in! Luckily for me, a very senior General loved it and later the Prince of Wales asked how on earth it was that the Army managed to lay on such splendid publicity, going on to enquire why it was that the Navy couldn't do the same! Giles drew two splendid cartoons for the *Daily Express* and the next term we had the biggest intake ever in the regiment. Later, a huge perch was discovered, stunned, in a hole in the bank. Amazingly it recovered and now lives quietly in a Kentish reservoir – a rather nice end to a fishy story!

Of course, training is so much more interesting if it is fun, and there could be no doubt that for the fit and motivated youngster the syllabus at Dover was tremendous. We trained on the moors and mountains of Britain and sent boys on Outward Bound courses, of special interest to me as I was now on the Outward Bound Council. I've always been a great believer in the work of this splendid organization, founded on the four pillars laid down by Kurt Hahn: physical fitness, self-reliance, rescue and public service and project work. All this fitted in extremely well with the training of the Junior Leaders.

Meanwhile the SES continued to develop, its list of successful ventures growing each year. Lectures given by members of expeditions were as popular as ever and also served to help raise funds. Dabber and Paddy Davies, who run Associated Speakers, a highly efficient lecture agency, did much to help us organise these talks, as did Barbara Snell, who had another agency.

The world of expeditioning has no hierarchy, no ranks and few prizes. Most explorers are individualists and strongly resent being coordinated by anybody. But to be successful expeditions rely on teamwork and, like a chain, any team is only as strong as its weakest link. And there are risks. In August 1976 an expedition was decimated by the sudden eruption of Mount Sangay in Ecuador. Two died and two of my friends, Jan Iwandziuk and Richard Snailham, were severely injured. It was a miracle that anyone survived.

After Zaire, I found myself being asked to help organise many expeditions. I did this gladly and several of them achieved notable success. Squabbles broke out in some, but usually these were due to inexperience or lack of leadership. Some of the groups even got as far as fighting it out in the press! It was very like the verbal battles between 19th-century explorers. I do not blame the press. In fact, I have a great many friends in Fleet Street, so much so that I have often been accused of showmanship; but I would prefer to call it salesmanship. It doesn't matter how ambitious, worthwhile and well-planned your expedition may be; unless you can sell the idea to someone, you are unlikely to get the support to bring it to fruition. I believe that the two essential qualities of leadership are communication and inspiration. They are particularly applicable to expeditions.

Such was our liaison with the media that I was not altogether surprised to hear that when I was 'kidnapped' for the Thames Television programme *This is your Life*, our detractors fancied the whole thing had been rigged! If they could have known the momentary fear I felt when I found strange people closing in on me and Eamonn Andrews stepping forward to announce in his Irish brogue, 'Excuse me one moment, Colonel, we want you', they might have been more sympathetic. As it was, it was only by chance that I didn't hit him and bolt. When the truth came out I still felt like running, but was assured that many old friends were in the studio having a tremendous party and that I couldn't really walk out on them. The evening was actually the greatest fun. Nobody burst into tears and everyone drank far too much. It was super to have so many chums present, including Charlie Thompson, the colourful local Panamanian who had helped us on the Darien project. He had been flown across the Atlantic especially for the show. Confronted by a beefy Guardia sergeant saying 'You're wanted in Panama City' was the first Charlie knew as he was marched off to El Real jail to await a helicopter.

At Panama airport an Embassy Officer met him. 'Senor Thompson?' enquired the Briton. 'Si,' said Charlie, looking around anxiously for the gallows.

'Do you remember Major Blashford-Snell and a number of Englishmen coming to your village in 1972?' Reluctantly, Charlie admitted that he did. He'd never seen TV and the suggestion that he should fly to London to appear on a show was totally incomprehensible, but anything was better than being garrotted. That afternoon he was issued with a passport and a visa for seventy-two hours in Britain. 'Do you have any clothes?' asked the Embassy official, 'it is rather cold in London in October.'

Barefooted, Charlie had only the patched shorts he had worn for five years, so he was given $20 to buy warmer garments. The money got him a straw hat, some flipflops and a cheap suit but no shirt. Thus clad he arrived at Heathrow. The lady who greeted him later told me that they were almost in London before she realised Charlie didn't speak a word of English and some hurried language lessons followed. I doubt Thames TV realised what they were taking on when they decided to feature the life of an Army explorer! Alas before the show they left Jim, Ernie and sundry other sappers in the Green Room with a table groaning with liquor. The results were predictable but somehow nobody seemed to mind.

The SES has always made a point of including young people in its expeditions. In Zaire we had had three sponsored teenagers – a business student, a police cadet from my home island of Jersey and a river-runner from Colorado – funded by Mr Walter Annenberg, then American Ambassador in London. This proved such a success that it was enthusiastically agreed from then to include such Young Explorers (YEs) on future SES ventures.

Thus we began to plan a series of worthwhile expeditions world-wide. From our meetings with international youth organizations, schools and universities, it had become abundantly clear that many youngsters felt the need to be stretched and challenged more severely than they could ever normally hope to be in modern society. Outward Bound and similar adventure training schemes did their best to satisfy this need and to provide imaginative outlets for natural aggression and excess energy, but for many they did not go far enough.

It was Prince Charles who had pinpointed the underlying cause of the youngsters' frustrations, summing it up in one phrase when he told the House of Lords that what the young were really seeking were 'some of the challenges of war in a peacetime situation'.

It was all still a dream until David Bromhead and other chums in the Royal Regiment of Wales talked to the Prince at a mess dinner. Hearing their tales, he asked to see me. His Royal Highness was especially concerned about the growing numbers of unemployed, bored and listless urban young and said, 'If you can do this for two or three youngsters, why not do it for two or three hundred?' Although momentarily taken aback by the prospect of planning on such a grand scale, I realised that this was simply a logical extension of what we had in mind and would not only broaden the whole outlook of the project but also give it a far greater sense of purpose.

When I returned to Buckingham Palace a few weeks later I had a draft plan for an ambitious round-the-world expedition, which, as it coincided with the 400th anniversary of Sir Francis Drake's great circumnavigation, was to be called Operation Drake. The Prince was fascinated and asked what he could do to help. When I suggested that it would give a tremendous boost if he were to become Patron he readily agreed. Not only would it be a very great honour but also it would endow the project with a prestige and credibility that would encourage the sponsors, on whose financial backing we were totally dependent. Furthermore, it would help to attract young people to take part. Although it was understood that the Prince's association could not be officially announced until the enterprise was financially viable and certain to go ahead, he was kind enough to send a discreet message of support in advance. It read as follows:

'Colonel Blashford-Snell has explained to me the purpose behind 'Operation Drake' and I was most interested by its imaginative and adventurous approach. I hope therefore that it is given a chance to succeed, given all the ghastly problems that exist with raising large sums of money nowadays. From my historical studies I seem to remember Francis Drake managed to elicit some discreet Royal support for his expeditions, but only if the rewards from a little well-planned piracy were forthcoming! Times have changed!'

That message, with its characteristic touch of humour, was the key factor that enabled the Operation to take off.

Our main priority now was to raise the £50,000 needed to launch Drake with any confidence. That kind of sum is hard to come by at the best of times and in a period of recession we reckoned it would be a real battle. In fact, it fell into our laps at the stroke of a pen thanks to the extraordinary generosity of one man.

Mr Walter Annenberg, a renowned philanthropist, noted for his great foresight and imagination, has always found expeditions intriguing. In view of this, it was with a thrill of anticipation that I accepted an invitation to visit him at his home in Palm Springs to tell him all about Operation Drake.

It was quite an experience. I arrived with Judith and daughters, Emma and Victoria, to be met at the airport by a chauffeur-driven limousine that whisked us to his estate on the outskirts of this remarkable desert township, where he and his wife Lee lived with Bob Hope and ex-President Gerald Ford as neighbours. As we passed through the remote-controlled gates, we were impressed by the sheer scale and magnificence of the place, which is really a private golf course with a splendid modern house in the middle. A special guest cottage in the grounds awaited us, and we were provided with a car for transport between there and the main house!

I was just coming out of the shower when Emma rushed in to announce that Mr Annenberg had arrived to see if we were comfortable. I poured him a drink and without any real preamble he said, 'Tell me about this Drake thing – and how much do you need to get it started?' I outlined our plan and added as nonchalantly as possible that we required about £50,000 before we could get under way. He asked if I thought we could really pull off something quite so big, and when I assured him that there was no reason why we should not, providing we could get the finance, he paused for a moment and then said, 'I'm not sure what the exchange rate is at the moment, but if I give you $100,000, will that be all right?'

It was at that moment that Operation Drake became a reality, and from then on it all started happening at a whirlwind pace. My first task on returning to England was to assemble the nucleus of our executive team at our London HQ, which was housed in the Whitehall basement, known as 'Room 5B' or 'the dungeon'. This damp, dark, musty-smelling cellar two floors below ground level was a somewhat dismal place, where daylight never penetrated and the atmosphere was permanently grey. But beggars cannot be choosers.

Among the stalwarts who gathered at this nerve centre was Jim Masters, who had the key role as Head of Logistics and Personnel, which involved the mammoth task of moving hundreds of people and tons of equipment round the world for nothing, or next to nothing. One could not ask for a better man to tackle such a difficult and vital job. I had long respected Jim's ability to get things done. Also from the Blue Nile came Roger Chapman, whilst George Thurston, a tough and determined ex-Royal Marine, gave up a career in the Police Force to join us. Ruth Mindel, a most capable lady, was brought in to head up Procurement and Supplies and another old friend, Val Roberts, agreed to run the office. Andrew Mitchell, a young zoologist came in as Scientific Coordinator and Chris Sainsbury, my photographic expert for the past two years, gave up making films about Junior Soldiers and was appointed Chief Photographer.

There was one more very important post to be filled, and in securing General Sir John Mogg as our Chairman we had a real stroke of great good fortune. The General was initially a little reluctant, pointing out that he was greatly looking forward to a quiet life in his retirement. But he surrendered gracefully to my appeals after I assured him – with an absolutely straight face – that the position would involve no more than two or three meetings a year and a couple of pleasant trips overseas.

Of course, things did not work out quite as I promised and he ended up spending most of his time guiding Operation Drake. Nevertheless, he seemed to enjoy every minute of it. As a former Deputy Supreme Allied Commander, Europe, his international reputation and contacts were formidable and as a respected figure of the highest calibre he brought added prestige to the project. On top of that, he had a rare ability to get on with just about anybody and was also perfectly in tune with the younger generation.

The money was coming in steadily as more and more individuals and companies began to take up sponsorships or to promise support in kind. A major boost came when John Whitney, the energetic Managing Director of Capital Radio, reacted so enthusiastically to the whole idea that he decided to sponsor ten young explorers from the London area as well as giving regular coverage to the expedition.

At this point the Prince of Wales announced officially that he had agreed to be Patron and at the same time promised not only to launch the expedition on the 400th anniversary of the start of Drake's voyage, but also to be at the helm of our flagship when she sailed out of Plymouth a year later. Squadron Leader David Checketts, the Prince's Private Secretary, also became an enthusiastic supporter and formed our Public Relations Sub-Committee. Through him we got our PRO, Beth Barrington-Haynes, who proved to be a tower of strength and became an important member of our expanding HQ.

I felt I was riding a very fast horse in a steeplechase, and as we cleared each fence our confidence grew. However, we had a long way to go before the finishing post, and now the real work of selecting the YEs had started. Following the announcement that anyone aged between seventeen and twenty-five, who was fit, compatible, could speak English and swim could volunteer, 58,000 applied for the 216 YE vacancies originally available.

I modelled the selection test on the Army's Regular Commission Board, and I borrowed a useful volume on discovering personal qualities under stress called *The KGB Handbook*. Basically we had to get candidates wet, cold, hungry, miserable, frightened and furious as fast as possible. We needed people who could work well under adverse conditions.

The tests set up in many lands were devised to show up the candidates' strengths and weaknesses. We hoped that in the end we would have a well-balanced, mixed group. We wanted to be able to put together in the field teams that might include, for example, someone highly intelligent, well-educated and about to enter into one of the professions, along with a young person from a broken home who had possibly been in trouble with the police. We also hoped to include people who were physically disabled. Prima donnas would be rejected, but we were looking for some young adults with leadership potential who would be prepared to place service before self and who would genuinely care about the needs of others.

The batch of sixteen candidates – including three girls – who arrived rather apprehensively for the first selection weekend at St Augustine's Priory, Kent, on a bleak Saturday in February 1978, had no idea what to expect. They had been told simply to report with the kit they felt they would need during a weekend's camping plus a certificate of medical fitness! All they knew for sure was that they would be facing some stiff challenges, both mental and physical.

After a general briefing and a kit inspection to check how sensibly they had prepared for the rigours of the weekend, they were led off into the woods, issued with tents and given half an hour to set up camp. They were then divided into two teams and marched off to Priory Pond for the first test, which had been carefully dreamt up with the sadistic intention of trying to ensure that everybody experienced the maximum discomfort at the earliest possible stage of the proceedings.

They had to imagine they were being pursued through the jungle by terrorists, that one of their number had been badly wounded and was a stretcher case, and that they had just one hour to get themselves and their casualty safely across the crocodile-infested river represented by the pond. They were supplied with a highly unstable canoe with a hole in it and some oil drums, planks and lengths of rope with which to construct a makeshift raft to ferry the heavily-bandaged casualty. We hoped they would fall in and most of them duly obliged! It sent shivers up the spine just to watch them floundering around in the icy water.

The Royal Signals had made some special recordings for me in Borneo but the scream of a Gibbon coming incongruously from the centre of a rhododendron bush, mingled with the squawks of parakeets and other unmistakable sounds of the jungle that issued mysteriously from among the bare winter branches of a Kentish copse did not impress the soaked volunteers. It was snowing by then. 'Bloody brass monkeys if you ask me,' one muttered.

They were given no time to get their circulation going again before being rushed to another location where, having been divided into teams of four, they were to bridge a stream with a structure strong enough to take a Land-Rover. No sooner had this been completed than they were off to a local pool to prove that they could swim 500 yards and then, as exhaustion set in, they were told that they would now be going back to camp for a meal. The sighs of relief soon turned to gasps of anguish when they saw the menu. Hopes of being handed a tasty supper on a plate were cruelly dashed when they were given a freshly-killed, unplucked pigeon and a dead rabbit with its fur still on. If they were lucky, they got a few unappetizing mouthfuls of half-cooked, half-burnt flesh before collapsing cold, wet, tired and still hungry into their sleeping bags.

I told them they could sleep until 0800. Some actually believed me, but, following the KGB's advice, we woke them at 0100 with flashing lights and brass band music and despatched them on a cross-country march to a map reference, where they were warned to expect to deal with some kind of emergency. But on arrival they were informed that it was a false alarm and that they could go back. By the time they had crawled into their sleeping bags once again, they were even more shattered, but still there was no respite.

At 0300 they were woken a second time and sent off to another map reference. This time they found that there actually was a staged emergency and they had to gather their scattered wits sufficiently to deal with it in a sensible fashion.

Now came the test of courage. I wanted to discover how they would behave when scared stiff. Andrew Mitchell pointed out that as everyone is usually frightened of some animal, that's what we should use. I watched the first two candidates as, equipped with bathroom scales and a torch, they searched a darkened upper room in the priory for a 'harmless creature' that they had to catch and weighed. After a few minutes Christine McHugh, a young police-woman, lifted a pile of sacks and leapt backward with a scream. Sliding out from beneath was a twelve-foot python, its tongue flickering in the torchlight.

'Oh my God, I can't touch that. I hate snakes,' she cried.

'Think of your chance-of-a-lifetime,' I urged, so she picked up a cricket bat and tried to steer Monty onto the scales. It didn't work; his head went one way and the tail another. So she took a deep breath, bent down, picked up the writhing serpent and, wrapping it around herself, stood on the bathroom scales. That took guts and she gained her place on Drake.

Next time I changed the act and borrowed a hairy, black tarantula with which we played pass the spider. They all passed, so next I used a gorilla. Candidates were shown a very angry 400-pound mountain gorilla and were told they were being put in the pen with the one that had made him mad – his mate. They were to take her vital statistics with a measuring tape. In came the female, who was actually quite tame, although they did not know this. Her keepers had taught her some tricks and, if she wanted a chocolate biscuit, all she had to do was to put her arms round the nearest human. If you had never faced an amorous lady gorilla this was pretty scary, but worse was to follow. If she didn't get the biscuit quickly it meant you were hiding it in your clothes and this was terrifying!

We had some failures. One night I watched a test at a farm, where two young boys were being briefed by an Army sergeant. 'Right lads, I want you to go into that darkened stable, no torch allowed, feel your way around and identify the animal in there.' After a moment or two there was a loud 'moo' and the boys reported, 'You've got a cow in there.' 'Very observant,' said the sergeant. 'Here's a bucket and a stool, go back and milk it.' A minute later there was a loud clang as the bucket was kicked and a boy rushed out. 'Are you sure it's a cow?' he asked. And when the lights went on, there stood a rather perplexed bullock. For some reason, all the girls passed this test. In fact, as selection process progressed over the ensuing weeks and months we found that, overall, a much higher percentage of women were being accepted.

After the intentionally demoralizing start, the unhappy campers would be plunged into a new series of tests aimed at assessing mental prowess in their state of considerable exhaustion. It was interesting to note that, for many of the youngsters, the prospect of having to get up in front of an audience and speak for three minutes on any chosen subject proved far more gruelling than any of the previous hardships. This, together with various intelligence and observation tests and some shooting, to ensure the candidates could handle weapons safely, rounded off the weekends and the judges then had the task of deciding who should be given places on the expedition.

Our plan was really quite simple. Over a period of two years a large sailing ship would circumnavigate the world westward, via the Panama and Suez canals, carrying around thirty-six YEs at a time and linking up expeditions in Panama, the Galapagos, Fiji, Papua New Guinea, Indonesia, Kenya and the Mediterranean. Every three months the teams of YEs would change so everyone would spend some time both on land and at sea.

Our tasks would include scientific research, environmental work and community aid projects in an adventurous setting; and we would operate in remote areas and difficult terrain. This should encourage the pioneering spirit we sought to foster. At the same time, I needed a staff of experienced experts with the patience of Job and so, through the SES, we recruited dedicated instructors from the Armed Forces, universities and other bodies worldwide.

Originally the flagship was to be the Dulverton Trust's beautiful *Captain Scott*, but then the Sultan of Oman unexpectedly made an offer for the ship that the Trust could not refuse and I suddenly had a problem. We were beginning to get desperate when I heard from my American friend, Allen O'Brien. He had become co-owner of a 150-ton brigantine named *Eye of the Wind* and, having heard about my 'Francis Drake scheme' through the SES Newsletter, wondered whether such a vessel might be of any use to me. Such a timely offer seemed too good to be true. The ship was in Australia and due in England in the summer of 1978 and would then be available. She was not quite as big as we would have liked, but it was our only hope. We wasted no time in arranging a charter.

Eye of the Wind was built in 1911 at a dockyard near Bremen, specifically to ply the round trip from Germany to Argentina to Cornwall and back. Nothing more was heard of her until 1923, when she was bought by a Swedish concern. For the next forty-five years she spent her winters trading cargo in the Baltic and the North Sea and her summers drifting for herring off Iceland. Badly damaged in the late sixties by a fire which broke out while ice-bound, and after being towed back to Gothenburg, she was left there to rot until a syndicate of six enthusiasts found the burnt-out hull, bought and restored her. This they did painstakingly, using church pews, oak panels from a bank, a trawler's compass and old railway sleepers.

Despite all this admirable work by the syndicate – led by Londoner 'Tiger' Timbs and Leslie Reiter, who were to stay on board throughout Operation Drake as Mate and Purser respectively – it became frighteningly clear when we took delivery of the ship in August 1978 that she needed an awful lot doing to her. As well as fitting a new engine, we had to carry out extensive alterations below decks to provide adequate accommodation. In addition, there was an alarmingly long list of less fundamental but equally necessary repairs and refinements.

Gloom and despondency began to set in as it became obvious that, as well as the astronomical costs of carrying out the work, there was no way that it was going to be finished in the few weeks left before we were due to depart. However, Prince Charles had said he would sail her out on 22 October so with enormous help from the Royal Navy and kind sponsors the work went on day and night. Fundraising, too, was non-stop. Frank Taylor, Financial Controller of Esso, had become our Treasurer and kept us on the straight and narrow. Lectures, philatelic covers, book and film rights and thousands of begging letters all played their part.

I have never hesitated to use a pretty face to further a cause, which, however good, will always sound much worthier when charmingly explained by an attractive young lady. 'Blasher's Blondes' or 'Charlie's Angels', as they were variously known, played a vital role in securing sponsorships, goods and services. This gang of beautiful ladies, not always blonde, did a marvellous job of selling the idea of Operation Drake. It was late one evening when Ruth Mindel entered the dungeon looking strangely dishevelled and flushed. Collapsing into a chair, she eyed her laddered tights and reported, 'Well, I've got you 3,500 cans of beef stew and almost got raped in the process!' She was nicknamed 'Rip-off Ruth' ever after.

The list of generous sponsors, many recruited by Prince Charles, grew longer. BP came in with the fuel for the ship and Pan-Am donated many free flights. Multinationals, like Unilever and BAT, were marvellous and almost everywhere Gestetner gave us tremendous backing. Around the world, national committees were also working flat out. In New York, Gordon White at Hanson Trust, with the help of the British Consul, Gordon Booth, did an outstanding job in recruiting and funding some fifty young Americans.

In Australia, Denis Cordner of ICI took up the challenge, whilst Jim Edwards backed us from Nepal and my pal from Zaire, John Chapman-Smith, handled New Zealand. There were also supporters in Canada, Costa Rica, Fiji, Indonesia, West Germany, Hong Kong and Kenya. My old school friend, Adrian Troy, formed a Channel Island committee. We had become a truly international enterprise.

'Well, John, this looks like a splendid party,' smiled Barbara Martinelli, one of Charlie's angelic American blondes, but I had no time to think about my 42nd birthday that bright autumn morning as we awaited the arrival of the Prince of Wales. Cheering, waving crowds lined the waterfront and hundreds more people gathered on Plymouth Hoe to give *Eye of the Wind* a wonderfully emotional send-off as she headed out into the Sound with the Prince at the helm. It was a magnificent sight as the beautiful, white-painted brigantine eased her way gracefully out to sea. Guns fired and warships piped their respects as she passed, while the armada of small boats that escorted her out of harbour whoop-whooped their farewells. From her deck, Capital Radio's David Briggs broadcast a live running commentary on the departure, which to all intents and purposes seemed to get Operation Drake finally under way. Not too many people were aware, I hope, that this was not actually the case.

Like Francis Drake himself, we had got off to a false start. *Eye of the Wind* certainly gave the impression of making a dignified and dramatic exit, but she was actually being towed out to the breakwater by a tug! There, with His Royal Highness at the helm, full sail was set and we appreciated the real beauty of our flagship for the first time. Once Prince Charles had been taken off by launch and whisked away in a helicopter, and when the film and TV cameras had finally stopped rolling and the crowds had dispersed, she was towed back in again. The official excuse was that she had to undergo extensive sea trials before she could actually start the voyage, but the slightly embarrassing truth was that she was far from ready to sail. Her new engine, for which the Prince himself had generously paid half the £11,000 cost, was not yet in running order, and there was still much refitting to be done and equipment to be loaded. It had been a frantic race against time to get her into any sort of fit state, with everybody, including the first batch of YEs who had joined the ship a fortnight before, slaving twelve hours a day, seven days a week. A joke was circulating that it had been cut so fine that there had only been time to paint the side of the ship that would be facing the cameras and the crowds, and the other side had been left untouched! If people laughed a little nervously at that one, it was because it was uncomfortably close to the truth. The deck had certainly not been painted – that chore was not completed until we reached Tenerife.

It would have been a tragedy if we had been forced to postpone the formal departure. For one thing, it is doubtful whether Prince Charles would have been able to fit a later date into his crowded schedule, and that would have been a major disappointment robbing the occasion of much of its significance. Apart from that, it might well have been seen as an ill omen for the expedition. As it turned out, everything went remarkably smoothly.

As *Eye of the Wind* left harbour, the Flag Officer, Plymouth followed in his launch with General Sir John Mogg and the VIPs. We were just beginning to relax a little and breathe a few sighs of relief when I happened to glance at the Admiral and noticed with alarm that his knuckles were whitening as he clutched the brass rail. I followed the line of his stony gaze and experienced an awful sinking feeling as I recognized the Royal Standard fluttering in the breeze. The Royal Navy had most specifically requested that this should not be flown until *Eye of the Wind* was clear of the dockyard, as otherwise naval protocol would require every ship present to parade bands and guards, and since it was a Sunday this would be rather awkward. Not wishing to interfere in any way with the sailors' weekend shore leave, we readily agreed to keep the Standard furled at the masthead until we were out of the dockyard. And yet there it was for all to see, and we had barely left the shore. No sooner had Prince Charles stepped aboard than he asked Captain Patrick Collis, 'Where's my standard, then?' When our skipper explained why it was not being flown, HRH grinned mischievously and said, 'Well, let's break it anyway and see if they have got any bands and guards!'

The Prince's presence made the day a memorable one for everybody, but particularly for the YEs, who were delighted to find him charming, relaxed and informal. From the moment that he took the wheel of the ship with the remark 'All I need now is a parrot!' he was a tremendous hit with them. He chatted to them for over two hours and posed for photographs, showing an obviously genuine interest in what they were about to undertake. In the launch that transported him back to shore I found him bubbling with enthusiasm.

There was one anxious moment at the end. It centred around the provision of special private toilet facilities wherever an official Royal visit is being made and a particularly handsome, prefabricated edifice had duly been erected near the helicopter landing pad. Sure enough, just before boarding the helicopter of the Queen's Flight the Prince decided to use it. An officer jumped forward smartly to open the door, only to find it apparently jammed. Increasingly harder and more frantic pulls failed to shift it. Clearly, it was locked. It emerged later that the attendant, under the impression that if the building was not required when the Prince first arrived then it would not be needed at all, had gone off with the key in his pocket.

When defeat was finally admitted, Prince Charles, who had been observing the proceedings with some amusement, turned to the senior officer present and enquired, 'Do you have a tree, perhaps?'

'I'm sorry, sir,' stammered the officer, indicating a fallen elm nearby, 'I'm afraid we've just cut it down!'

'Oh, never mind,' murmured HRH. And as he turned to board the helicopter he said to the Admiral, 'I hope you find the key.' The Navy did not think it at all funny.

A special service of dedication had been held the previous day at the shore station HMS Drake. During the service the skipper of *Eye of the Wind* called on the congregation to ask for God's blessing on the ship with a time-honoured chant that dates back to the embarkation of the Crusaders in the thirteenth century. Among the prayers was the one written by Francis Drake himself on the day he sailed into Cadiz in 1587. Many of us offered up a few prayers of our own.

Prior to casting off the Prince had given a witty speech that ended with some advice for the YEs. 'I have a feeling,' he said, 'that those who take part in this particular expedition will enjoy themselves, but, at the same time, I expect there will be moments when they will wish that they were back home and had never volunteered for the thing in the first place. All I can say to them on that score is, just stick to it and when you get back you will find that rather like beating your head against a brick wall it's marvellous when it's over.' There were very few people involved with Operation Drake over the next couple of years who did not have occasion to reflect on the truth of those words.

12

Operation Drake

England's economy was in a pretty rocky state in 1577 when a West Country sea captain came up with a plan to set matters right. Basically, this was to plunder the Spanish Main and return with the loot right quickly. Queen Elizabeth not only condoned Frances Drake's proposal but also invested in it to the tune of £10,000.

So, in December that year he set sail from Plymouth with five small ships, wisely not telling the crews the true purpose of his voyage. Had he done so, many would probably have jumped ship. He simply said they were headed for Terra Australia Incognita, or Sydney as it is known today.

Apart from a terrible storm off the Cornish coast, which forced them to return for repairs, all was well until they reached Cape Horn. In the fleet there were two unions, the gentlemen and the seamen, and it was the former who caused the problem by refusing to pull with the latter. Thus Drake, a fair-minded employer, dined with the gentlemen's shop steward, Thomas Doughty. Next morning they took communion together, then Drake hanged him.

At this point two ships fled for home, two sank and Drake was left alone with his 100-ton Flagship *Pelican*. As is sometimes the custom even today when a business venture runs into a spot of bother, Drake changed the name and carried on. Thus *Pelican* became *Golden Hind*, and sailed up the west coast of South America where she met the lumbering Spanish galleons overloaded with treasure. With the aid of his ship's eighteen bronze cannon, Captain Drake relieved the Spaniards of their cargo and, much to the annoyance of their King, headed up America's west coast to return to Plymouth via the north of Canada, a difficult enough feat even today.

Stopped by the ice, *Golden Hind* came ashore to have her hull scraped of barnacles near where San Francisco now lies. Here, the Indians rushed down to the beach but, worshipping white Gods, as many still do in California, they prostrated themselves at Drake's feet. He did nothing to disillusion them and so that they should remember that they were now part of New Albion, or England, he set up an inscribed brass plate in a tree. In its side they placed an Elizabethan sixpence bearing the image of their new ruler. In 1935 a truck driver, proceeding along the freeway stopped to commune with nature and found the plate. But alas the coin had gone.

A prominent member of the Round Earth Society, Drake and his crew headed west and had reached the Celebes, now Indonesia, when in the middle of the night there was a loud crash: *Golden Hind* had hit an uncharted reef. Whilst the Captain fought to save the ship many of the crew took fright and the preacher, with less courage than most naval chaplains, called upon the Almighty, blaming their misfortunes on Master Drake and, in particular, the way he had dealt with the shop steward at Cape Horn.

Meanwhile, the skipper, having thrown overboard the cheaper, heavier trade goods and, finally, eight of his guns, had succeeded in lightening the ship sufficiently for it to drift off the coral and float upright, undamaged, in deep water. He then summoned his men and preached them a long sermon lasting several hours, at the end of which he produced a faded parchment and with a cry of 'Behold I carry the Queen's commission' he shackled the preacher to a hatch and excommunicated him. Perhaps Drake was a mildly autocratic leader, but he was 15,000 miles from head office.

On Monday 26 September 1580, nearly three years after his departure, *Golden Hind* quietly entered Plymouth Sound. Drake reckoned it was Sunday, mysteriously he had lost a day! Knowing he had many enemies at home and having no news of the Queen, they came in unadvertised out of the Channel mist. A lone fisherman, engaged in the usual local activity of looting his neighbour's lobster pots, spotted her first.

'Does the Queen live?' cried the red bearded figure on the stern.

'Aye, Sire, she do and she be well,' came the reply.

'Know you not 'tis I, Francis Drake, returned with North Sea oil in my hold – where the devil are the people of Plymouth?'

'No disrespect, Master Drake, but all those not dying of plague are at church praying they'll not get it.'

Unabashed Drake sent gallopers to London to acquaint the Queen with the glad tidings that he had brought home some £600,000 in booty, certainly the greatest treasure ever to reach England. It is said Her Majesty was exceeding joyful at the news and despatched her auditors to greet them.

So the following year Drake and his ship came up the Thames to Deptford where Queen Elizabeth and her court came aboard. Demanding his sword, she ordered him to kneel. Fearing what she might do with it, Francis Drake rather nervously obeyed, whereupon his monarch passed the sword to the French Ambassador and commanded, 'Knight him.' Thus was cocked the greatest snook possible to the King of Spain.

A beautiful silver replica of the famous sword, specially made for us by Wilkinson's, had been presented to Mr Annenberg, who allowed us to carry it around the world on our ship, and I produced it as I completed the historical briefing (with a little poetic licence) of Drake's voyage.

'We're bound for the Caribbean,' I said, 'where Drake raided the Spanish Main – and where he eventually died of dysentery. So for goodness sake, do watch the hygiene when we get ashore!' I then flew ahead to prepare the way.

Jeremy Groves and his advance party were already clearing an old landing strip at Caledonia Bay, Panama, where we had made some fascinating discoveries on earlier recces. During the Darien expedition of 1971-2 I had flown over to the Atlantic coast to see if there was any evidence of an ill-fated Scots colony that was briefly established there in the 17th century at Fort St George, the construction of which was as far as the colonists got in attempting to realise their dream of creating a township to be called New Edinburgh before being forced to abandon the project by the ravages of malaria and attacks from the Spanish. It was pretty stormy when we reached the sea, but from the air I could recognize the main features that appeared on old maps and knew that somewhere below me lay the graves of several thousand courageous Scots who, in 1698, had defied the King of England in an attempt to gain a Scottish foothold in the New World.

So, four years later, in 1976, I returned with a few pals from the

SES and the Explorers Club, to which I now belonged. Welsh seafarer Tristan Jones said he had met strange white people with names like MacDonald and Robinson lurking in the forest near Punta Escoces and we resolved to investigate.

On arrival we quickly discovered that the supposed lost Scots were in fact albinos or moon people as they are known because their skin burns so badly in the sun that they tend to come out only at night. The San Blas islands, a Cuna stronghold, have a very high proportion of these people, possibly due to inbreeding. They had probably acquired the Scottish surnames as a result of the colony.

Our first task was to try to find Fort St Andrew, so I marched through the coconut groves towards a promontory on which the old Scots maps showed the stronghold to have been located. We found a stream of clear water running from the hills and I felt it should lead to our objective, but the vegetation grew thicker and the brook became a swamp so, moving inland again, I began to hack with my machete. Suddenly the ground dropped away steeply and I stumbled down into a shallow ravine. On either side the undergrowth fell back, revealing a clean-cut channel in the coral. There was no doubt this was the moat of Fort St Andrew.

Vince and Barbara Martinelli, two adventurous New Yorkers, followed the zigzagging ditch. Spoil from the moat had been used to build up ramparts; several bastion positions and a gateway were also apparent. The vertically-sided moat, filled with sea water to a depth of approximately three feet, went right across the neck of the promontory with an entrance to the sea at one end and a mangrove swamp at the other. Searching the rampart, Barbara discovered glazed potsherds while Vince found a small cannonball. Our archaeologist, Gricolio, reckoned it was the type fired from a light cannon, which was probably the heaviest weapon the besieging Spaniards could have dragged through the jungle. Inside the fort there were depressions that might have been wells and a battery position for the guns commanded the harbour entrance. Broken pottery littered the ground everywhere.

But our recce was to have further success. A chance meeting with Father Ned Webster, the American Dean in the Canal Zone, had produced a crop of carefully researched information about the 'Lost City of Acla'. Acla had been built in 1516 by the Spanish Governor of the area, Pedrarias Davila, and was only the second European township to be established anywhere on the American mainland. It was from here that Vasco Nunez de Balboa, the first European ever to gaze upon the Pacific Ocean, later set out across the isthmus, taking with him the dismantled parts of four ships which were to be reassembled on the other side. It was also the place where Balboa met an unjust end when political conspiracy resulted in his being publicly executed in the main plaza.

Later the city declined and disappeared but Ned thought it was near Caledonia Bay. A helpful witch doctor had told us of ruins on a nearby islet and, visiting the tiny outcrop of coral, we did indeed find pottery and bricks. 'Acla is supposed to lie between these two rivers,' I explained, 'and in fact this river is called the Aglatomate.'

'But they must have had a harbour,' said Vince.

'Yes,' I agreed. 'That's the mystery. There's either a cliff, a reef or a mangrove swamp right the way along the coast.'

From the sea we couldn't even identify the two rivers. As we scanned the jungle shoreline with binoculars, the witch doctor said, 'You want go there?'

'Can you get a boat through that reef, Ricardo?'

'Si,' he grunted. 'Es posible.'

Approaching the reef, we could see exposed heads of jagged coral projecting from the boiling surf. Suddenly I saw something that was only visible from very close in-shore. There was a gap in the reef, which almost overlapped itself and, if you knew the way, you could slip safely into a sheltered cove on the far side.

On the palm-fringed beach dozens of Indian dugouts were drawn up whilst the owners harvested the precious coconut in the forest.

'Senor,' said Ricardo, 'there is a wall in the jungle, I see it as a boy.' Ricardo was easily sixty, so I was not too hopeful that he would actually find anything. Nevertheless, we split up, with one party going to the banks of the Aglatomate, whilst the other searched the shore and the Rio Aglaseniqua, the northern river.

Ricardo, Vince and I cut deep into a bamboo thicket, which showed signs of flooding, but we found no walls, nor any evidence of man. Back on the beach we discovered why the rivers had been invisible from the sea: during the dry season a high sandbar extended right across their mouths. However, it was late in the afternoon and I decided that it all looked like a bit of a wild-goose chase. 'We'd better get back,' I said.

'It here somewhere, I know, senor,' grumbled the medicine man.

We were about 200 yards from the boats when I heard the excited chatter of monkeys overhead and paused to watch them leaping through the tall palms. Suddenly a black, furry, feline creature, about twice the size of a domestic cat, leapt out of a tree, hurtled across the path and shot up a palm. It turned out to be a strange mammal called a 'high woods dog'. Ricardo wasn't interested; he'd met a small boy with a dog and was jabbering and pointing excitedly. The boy nodded and pointed. 'He knows, senor,' grinned the sage.

So we retraced our footsteps and then took a side trail leading deeper into the forest. After only a few dozen paces we were standing in a freshly burnt clearing. The boy pointed his machete at a tumbledown pile of stones running from one side of the clearing to the other. Apparently he had been burning the jungle to make space to plant coconuts and had found the wall. I felt a surge of excitement as I called out to the rest of the team. 'Over here, over here, we've found something!'

Dan Osman, our doctor, and I measured the wall. It ran on a magnetic bearing of eighty degrees with an average width of eleven feet and a height of about three. A bastion appeared to project at right angles: between the wall and the sea Gricolio was already finding pottery and, most important, glass. Lines of stones appeared to mark the foundations of buildings.

'What do you think?' I asked our archaeologist.

'I think you have discovered Acla,' he said solemnly.

That night we sat in the sunset, sipping our J &B, being eaten alive by mosquitoes and felt a great glow of contented excitement such as explorers only feel on very special occasions.

It was St George's Day. The rains were approaching so next day we canoed to the island of Mulatudo. Jose, an albino, kindly put us up in his tin-roofed home and even found some beds and sheets. A few beers in the cantina and we were ready for sleep. Jose was smoking a cigarette in a dark corner of his verandah. 'Any mosquitoes?' I enquired. 'No mosquitoes, senor,' he replied and, thankful that I needn't unpack my net, I flopped on to the white sheet and the lumpy mattress. Slipping into oblivion I felt something prick my toe. Assuming it was an insect I kicked out and fell asleep.

The storm broke at 0115 hours and the monsoon rain upon the

tin roof would have woken the dead. Then I realised my bed was wet. Oh hell, I thought, the rain's coming in. As I rose to investigate I felt the call of nature and so, groping for my torch, I stumbled down the external staircase to the evil-smelling loo. The rain had ceased as I ascended again, but my torch revealed something that made me freeze. The stairs were dripping with blood. In six bounds I was in my room and, supposing murder to have been committed, seized my harpoon gun in defence. As I did so something brushed my hair, and, raising my torch beam, I saw a bat flitting around the room. Then the light caught the bed and to my dismay I found it drenched in blood, which, even now, was dripping on to the floor and forming bright red pools. My legs were scarlet from the knees down. 'Ruth,' I hissed through the cubicle wall.

'What is it?' came a sleepy reply.

'You'd better give me a hand. I think I've cut a vein or something,' I whispered. Ruth Mindel padded in.

'Mind where you tread,' I cautioned.

'What on earth...' She stood looking at me in horror.

Dan arrived next. 'Hell, John,' he said, 'what did you do?'

I could remember nothing untoward except the prick in my toe just before I'd fallen asleep. Having cleaned me up Dan looked puzzled.

'I've never seen anyone bleed so much from such a tiny cut!' exclaimed the doctor. 'It's about a quarter of an inch long on your toe.' Then he added, 'Say, is there any history of blood disease in your family?' On being assured that there wasn't, he asked, 'Have you cut yourself recently?'

'Yes,' I replied, 'yesterday on my knuckle.'

I showed him where a normal scab had formed. Dan shrugged and dosing me with antibiotics and plastering up the still bleeding cut, he left me to sleep.

At dawn the room looked like a slaughter-yard and, interestingly, the blood had still not congealed.

'John, I've made some enquiries,' said Dan at breakfast. 'I reckon that bat you saw was a vampire. Apparently the local people are often bitten; and because the creature injects you with a powerful anti-coagulant to make it easier for them to drink your blood, you will bleed profusely,' he explained.

Of course. I should have remembered how our horses had suffered during the Darien crossing. 'There's only a four per cent chance of a bat carrying rabies,' Dan continued, 'but I suggest you start the shots the moment we get back to Panama City.'

Thus in the months that followed I was to undergo no less than three different series of anti-rabies injections, a total of thirty-two jabs in my stomach and backside. By comparison the bite was nothing. I could only hope that the bat got alcohol poisoning from his cup of my blood.

Now, two years later, fifty young explorers from six nations were to investigate these discoveries. To back up our scientific work, *Eye of the Wind* had a fully equipped marine biological laboratory aboard and from here Dr Patricia Holdway directed the programme. They had paused at the Caribbean island of St Vincent to carry out an urgent task with the University of the West Indies.

Mt Soufriére, a fairly active volcano, had not had a major eruption since 1901 but in 1971 and 1972 a lava island had appeared in the crater lake. So our youngsters dragged an Avon 3,500 feet up to its rim in order to float over to the island and assess its flora and fauna and make a thermometric study. They found it was much hotter and more lively than expected and on Christmas Eve beat a hasty retreat to warn the authorities. On Good Friday it erupted with terrifying violence and, had people not been evacuated thanks to the timely warning, there could have been heavy loss of life.

With back-breaking labour, Jim Winter and the advance party cleared an old airstrip at the edge of Caledonia Bay and built a base camp. To get everything ready was a race against time, with over 100 tons of stores having to be shipped from Colon to the Bay by our friends in the Guardia Nacional, but finally it was done, right on schedule.

On 3 January 1979 Piper Robert Little of the Scots Guards cut a magnificent, if slightly incongruous figure, as he stood silhouetted against the palm-fringed headland of Punta Escoces in full ceremonial dress, playing a lament in memory of his ill-fated countrymen of so long ago. It was a moving moment and I reflected that the lonely ghosts of Fort St Andrew must surely have appreciated the haunting sound of the pipes after 280 years.

The arrival of the Young Explorers was the occasion for a surprise visit by General Omar Torrijos, Commander of the Guardia Nacional and Dictator of Panama. Voluble archaeologist Mark

Horton briefed him at length and finally fell silent. The tough General rocked back and forth in his chair, saying nothing but sucking gently at his fat Havana. After several minutes of awkward silence there was a sharp bang and bodyguards hurled themselves into the mud, cocking weapons. Only the Dictator remained unmoved. My youngest daughter, Victoria, had been given a cap pistol for Christmas and there it was, still smoking in her hand. Seeing this, the great man began to laugh, louder and louder until, eventually, his muddy aides picked themselves up and laughed too. 'Little girl,' he said, 'all this is very boring for you, yes?' Victoria nodded. 'Come,' he smiled, 'I'll get you a coconut.' So saying he removed his hat, boots and gun-belt and with astonishing agility shinned up a palm tree and picked her a large coconut which he then opened with a machete and handing it to her, saying, 'It's good, drink.' Everyone cheered and the General strolled off for lunch.

'Who is he?' hissed Victoria.

'Well, he's like the Queen of Panama,' I tried to explain. 'Doesn't look much like a Queen,' she grunted, wandering off with her coconut.

Torrijos was an impressive man and became a good friend of Operation Drake. His personal interest was enormously helpful and ensured the complete support of everyone in Panama. When archaeological excavations in the jungle were threatened by clouds of black fly, mosquitoes and falling coconuts that could kill, General Torrijos flew in a load of protective helmets and gallons of insect repellent and the work continued.

'Mad' Mark Horton worked non-stop to dig up the past. Although distantly related to that Grand Old Man of archaeology, Sir Mortimer Wheeler, he actually reminded most people more of Magnus Pyke. As he waved his arms around and enthused wildly about some point of academic interest, his involvement in his subject was so total that virtually nothing could distract him. This was proved when he was giving our Chairman, General Sir John Mogg, and a party of visitors a guided tour of his excavations at Acla. As Mark rattled on, a long green snake slithered across the track a few feet in front of the General. My hand dropped to my holster but, before I could draw, a Guardia major had his submachine gun up and blasted the beast to oblivion. The shattering noise was still echoing across the bay when, unabated, Mark continued, 'And furthermore ....'

We knew the Scots had lost a supply ship, Olive Branch, which had burned to the waterline and sunk after the ship's cooper had accidentally dropped a lighted candle while tapping brandy from the barrels in the hold, causing an instant inferno. The vessel had carried a mixed cargo, including great quantities of bonnets, Bibles and clay pipes. Knowing it would be an historical treasure house, I got Tony Lonsdale, a very professional magnetometer expert, to accompany us and do a thorough survey. We concentrated our attention on an area close in to the shore on the eastern side of the bay, where it was thought the colony would have had its anchorage. Here, sure enough, readings soon indicated something fairly substantial. When the divers went down and probed in the mud they made contact with wood and coral concretion.

The site was on a steep mud slope that dropped off the edge of the coral reef. At the shallow end there was live coral at a depth of six feet, while at the other end one could go down twenty-five feet before sinking into thick ooze. Underwater visibility was bad at the best of times and became non-existent once this silt was stirred up. Not quite what one expects in the Caribbean! The team used water jets and an air-lift suction pump as well as shovels and buckets to clear glutinous mud, sand and coral fragments. After some considerable time, a piece of timber was prised out and brought to the surface for close examination by a marine archaeologist, who was able to confirm that it definitely came from a sixteenth or seventeenth-century European sailing ship. The next sample provoked even more excitement. It was immediately identifiable as a piece of deck planking and it was badly burned on the underside, while the nail holes were charred right through. We soon realised that we had found a virtually complete ship and the evidence pointed to its being the *Olive Branch*, but it was another three weeks before final, indisputable proof was forthcoming. The breakthrough came when, after much careful probing, the divers uncovered a number of barrels, some of which were still intact. Down on the seabed, they sifted delicately through the silt that clogged the barrels while up above, on David Gestetner, the giant inflatable we had last used in Zaire and that now served as a diving platform, the results of these painstaking labours were awaited with almost breathless anticipation.

The air of tension was further increased by a hair-raising incident. One of the divers, Warrant Officer Marc Moody, was down on the bottom, filling a bucket with silt in zero visibility when he felt someone moving around near him in the dark. There was then a tug on the rope and the heavy pail was snatched away. Marc assumed that it had been hauled in by those up top but when he surfaced he was puzzled to find that this was not the case. Nobody knew anything about it and there was no sign of the bucket.

The disappearance remained a mystery until, shortly afterwards, the Guardia hauled in the fishing nets they had set nearby and there, thrashing around in the mesh, was a number of sharks, including two man-eaters – a five-foot Mako and a ten-foot Hammerhead. It did not take too much imagination to come up with a chilling possibility as to who or what might have stolen the bucket. The divers were understandably a little reluctant to work in the gloomy, pea-soup depths and every time something brushed unexpectedly against them they nearly jumped out of their wet suits. Even the excitement caused by the discovery of the barrels could not entirely take their minds off the spine-tingling thought of what might be nosing around them.

Meanwhile, the contents of several barrels were panned out like gold dust and passed up for examination. The first cask yielded a pronged fork and a few slivers of bone, which suggested that it might have been part of a consignment of salt pork or beef; the next two were empty and the fourth was full of nails. It was the fifth that provided the vital clue in the distinctive shape of three clay pipes that were identical to those found at Fort St Andrew – they even carried the same P and G initials, which, it was irreverently suggested, might stand for Porridge Gobbler.

Back on land, the total success of the historical and archaeological projects was nicely rounded off when Mark's unearthed evidence proved beyond a reasonable doubt that the Lost City of Acla had been rediscovered. By working in this remote, inaccessible spot, largely ignored by archaeologists in the past, we had filled in a few blanks of Panamanian history.

So throughout the dry season, a relative term in Panama, our army of Young Explorers worked on. There was medical research with the Cuna, zoological studies and further historical explorations deep in Darien. One of the most worthwhile projects involved ecological studies of the jungle canopy. Six miles inland a scientific base was established in the primary rainforest. Here, after building a helicopter pad so that equipment and supplies could be airlifted in, Royal Engineers and YEs constructed a unique aerial walkway 100 feet up in the canopy, with observation platforms in each tree top. Botanists, zoologists, entomologists and an ornithologist were thus able to make detailed studies of the ecology. Tropical rainforests are cut down for timber at the rate of fifty acres a minute worldwide, but they do not regenerate. One step in solving the problem is to discover of what they consist and the role played by birds, animals and insects in their pollination biology.

Andrew Mitchell, having worked with me at Dover, knew what sappers could do and this enthusiastic zoologist suggested we construct walkways to investigate this unexplored area – 'where the great trees have their sex lives.' Mick Christy, a very tough engineer, built the construction out of dexion and nylon strapping and arranged an ingenious system of lifts to raise visitors from the ground. The most important of these, General Mogg, marched seven miles through swamp and river and, to everyone's delight, was hoisted aloft to inspect the work. He wore the jungle green uniform in which he had commanded the Commonwealth Brigade in Malaya many years before, but his faithful boots collapsed at the camp so he gave them to a YE, who said he would boil them up if food ran out. It was a pretty remarkable achievement and left everyone, especially the Guardia, who had never met a British General, impressed by his toughness.

However, a few days later when he bade farewell to their senior officers at the Citadel in Panama City, the Guardia surprised him. Lying outside the Guard Room was a huge jaguar on a chain. 'I bet that fellow keeps the prisoners on their toes,' joked our General. 'Oh, yes,' replied a major, 'we put the big cat in one cell and don't feed him for a few days, then we put the prisoner in the next cell. There is a little door in between.' His gold teeth flashed. 'They usually talk!'

Back at the bay we decided it would be appropriate to celebrate Burns' Night. Haggis and copious quantities of J&B scotch were airlifted in and in the warm, moist night we toasted the immortal memory. Piper Little excelled himself as we danced and reeled beneath the stars. Our Panamanian guests were totally confused. Most had thought it a birthday party and came with presents.

Towards midnight a Guardia gunboat sailed in and ran right onto a reef by our jetty. This caused much excitement whilst she was beached. The crew, who it seemed had already dined well, came ashore and the party went on. Towards dawn one of our visitors, an ugly little major, rather the worse for wear, seized my attractive blonde assistant, Sara Everett, and dragged her towards the bushes. Hearing her yell, I grabbed the wretch by his lapels and propelled him towards the sea. However, his pals intervened and apologized.

Later I discovered his name – Emmanuel Noriega!

As the crossroads of the world, this little country housed a great number of interesting folk. At the end of our stay we were holding a meeting of Panamanian YEs in a local hotel. Maps and charts were spread over the floor as we discussed future plans. Suddenly I became aware that a slim little lady in a large hat had come in. With amazing grace, she stepped over the papers and stretched out her hand. 'Hello.' She smiled. 'I just wanted to thank you for having my niece on the expedition.' It was Dame Margot Fonteyn. Her friendship in the years to come was immensely warm and helpful.

Whilst all our land-based activities had gone well we were having major problems with *Eye of the Wind*. On arrival in Colon we needed a new gearbox. Obtaining one and flying it out had almost put us in the red. Now I learned that the anchor chain kept slipping because it was the wrong size for the 'gypsy' around which it wound. The ship was due to sail in a few days when Frank Esson, the new senior watchkeeper, arrived from Britain and achieved a miracle. He carried the 120-pound gypsy as hand baggage on a flight to New Orleans, bought a second-hand chain that fitted it and persuaded a Panama Canal Company ship to carry it to Colon. So *Eye of the Wind* was able to sail through the canal on time.

However, our treasurer was forecasting imminent financial disaster. Back in Britain, General Sir John Mogg bumped into Prince Charles at Badminton and said he hoped he would not end up in the Tower if we went into debt. 'No, you'll probably go to Carmarthaen Castle – that's mine and it's much worse,' replied the Prince of Wales.

From start to finish we lived from hand to mouth and, as inflation alone made a mockery of our original budget estimate of around £650,000, we constantly had to rev up our already frantic fund-raising activities in order to keep up with soaring costs and to stop ourselves slipping back too far into the red.

'Charlie's Angels' and I therefore set to work in America. In New York slow-talking Tulsa oilman John Linehan was an enthusiastic supporter and had spent some time in the jungle with us. He kindly let me use his New York office and provided many very useful introductions. He also helped to drum up a considerable amount of financial backing and threw a party for us that produced more donations. He himself presented me with $5,000 in typically flamboyant fashion, arranging for a radio-controlled jeep to roll to a stop in front of me, whereupon the bonnet lifted automatically to reveal a cheque! At such gatherings we sold, sold, sold and I began to feel like an old gramophone record when the needle became stuck. Whilst the angels were helping a well-fleshed stockbroker to find his wallet, I chatted to a charming young blonde who told me her family was 'into exploring'. Sara was soon to return to London and I would need a new PA, so I suggested my acquaintance might like the job. Just then my host introduced someone else and I learned I had been talking to Margot Hemingway.

Meanwhile the expedition had moved on to Drake's Bay in Costa Rica where we erected a plinth to commemorate Francis Drake's earlier visit. By the time *Eye of the Wind* had reached the Galapagos, the skippers had changed and Mike Kichenside had flown in from Australia to take over the helm.

In the Galapagos the Darwin Research Station urgently needed a female land iguana. They only had males of this endangered creature. After a spirited chase, the youngsters managed to catch a female, which pleased a lot of male land iguanas and saved the species. A hurricane had recently struck Fiji so the ship stopped there and we rebuilt a school. Meanwhile, another financial crisis was looming. In mid-Pacific Tiger Timbs discovered that vibrations in the propeller shaft had almost shaken the props right off. They managed to fix it temporarily, but once in dry dock at Suva, they found a complete new prop shaft was required. 'Fourteen thousand dollars!' I groaned. Then we had an extraordinary stroke of luck. A producer from Columbia Pictures called me. 'We're remaking The Blue Lagoon in Fiji,' he explained. 'Could you possibly hire us your ship for a few days?' 'Certainly,' I replied, 'it will cost $14,000.'

On 5 September 1979 our gleaming white flagship sailed into Lae, Papua New Guinea (PNG). It was a sight no one will ever forget. There was a time when no sailing ship was welcome here. The approach of any such vessel to the reef-bound shores of the island was regarded with suspicion and hatred by the coastal villagers and landing parties could expect to be greeted by a hail of spears and arrows. This was hardly surprising, since, for many years, European visitors had only one use for the wild, remote and exotic land named by the first Portuguese explorers Ihlas de Papuas – Island of the Fuzzy-Haired – and that was as a source of strong young slaves to be carried off and sold on the world's lucrative labour markets.

Attitudes have since changed and *Eye of the Wind* sailed in to a fantastic reception. However, although the people are usually friendly these days, the environment remains as hostile as ever. The island, second largest in the world after Greenland, is shaped like a giant turtle swimming in the South Pacific seas just above the northern tip of Queensland and is divided neatly down the middle by a straight north-south border between the Indonesian territory of West Irian in the west and PNG in the east. It is an untamed tropical wilderness in which soaring mountain peaks rise out of stinking mangrove swamps, mighty rushing rivers gush through plunging rocky gorges and baking arid scrubland gives way to wide delta quagmires. And, overall, it is shrouded in dense, impenetrable jungle, which is why it was still one of the least-explored areas on earth. The inaccessibility of the interior meant that nothing at all was known about it until the first aircraft flew over in the 1920s and existing maps, compiled from aerial photographs still contain blank spaces marked 'Cloud – Relief Data Incomplete', the modem equivalent of mythical creatures, gogs and magogs, with which the old cartographers used to fill the unknown areas that nobody had been able to reach and chart.

It is not just the terrain that makes PNG so inhospitable. The climate and the creepy crawlies – which seem to be bigger, nastier and more plentiful than anywhere else in the world – add further dimensions of discomfort and danger to life outside the few air-conditioned townships. The feverish, steam-heat humidity of the lowlands soon leaves one limp with exhaustion and the catalogue of lethal wildlife includes the world's largest crocodiles, enormous pythons that can break every bone in a full-grown pig's body and then swallow it whole and small snakes just a few inches long with a bite so poisonous that they can cause death within a matter of minutes. There are out-size lizards, scorpions and spiders the size of your fist. Mosquitoes, which, having had three doses of malaria, I regard as the greatest threat of all, are also particularly virulent.

One way and another, it is a real battle against the elements to survive in PNG. Everything stings or bites or causes rashes and infections, and the best that twentieth-century technology can provide in the form of salves, lotions and repellents seem powerless to protect one's skin against continual attack. Your clothes rot and the most rugged boots crack up in half the time it would take anywhere else. Even my pith helmet, which for twelve years had kept me cool, dry and safe from falling coconuts in some of the most God-forsaken corners of the world, finally surrendered to the atmospheric extremes of PNG and sprouted a terrible green mould.

I had always dreamed of leading an expedition here. One place that fascinated me was the Upper Strickland River and, thanks to the help of Gestetner, I had had an opportunity to do an air recce the previous year. I had asked the local Defence Force Commander for his advice. 'That's a really mysterious area,' he said. 'Few have been there and we'd love to know more about it, what the river's like, and the people, the animals and any minerals too.'

I went off to the Defence Force library to see if I could find some air photographs – but there were none. 'Haven't got that far yet,' said the Australian captain. 'It's a hell of a place to fly in.' So, clearly, if we were to tackle this region, we would have to get our own photos.

The river falls 1,000 feet in seventy-five miles and for much of this distance it is enclosed in a deep chasm, the Devil's Race. Low cloud obscures the area for much of the year and thus, even an air recce was unlikely to reveal what secrets lay beneath the swirling mists and the dark green rainforest. But I felt there must be a series of falls, or perhaps just one big fall somewhere along that course. If we were to explore the region we would need to use the river. 'If you get clear weather,' said a bush pilot in Port Moresby, 'it's because of high wind funnelling up the gorge – even the Army planes won't take it. You'll need a real power bird to get you through: if you hit that turbulence, you'll smash right into the rock.' Even if one survived a crash, the chances of being found didn't sound good. And the likely reaction of the tribes of head hunters (who were still thought to exist in remote regions) to an intrusion, let alone the crocodiles, was not very inviting.

Barbara Martinelli was now seconded by Pan-Am as a recce officer on Operation Drake and somehow, as was her way, she managed to borrow a powerful light plane with a first-rate Australian pilot, Noel Frewster. We flew up to Wewak on PNG's north coast to try to make a low-level air reconnaissance of the high-altitude valley of the upper Strickland. Surprisingly, within a day of our arrival, favourable weather was indicated and Noel decided to have a try. Barbara had the still cameras and took the rear seat, whilst I held the Canon eight-millimetre cine in the front and flicked it on to 'slow motion'. The twin-engined Cessna 301, named Olivetti after the company who sponsored it in an air race, was an ideal aircraft for the job and we were soon climbing south into the towering peaks.

At 12,000 feet, we crossed a rocky ridge and winged our way through the crags of this little-known land. Suddenly, Noel pointed. 'Look, it's clearing,' he shouted. Sure enough, ahead of us the clouds were rolling back to reveal an emerald-green valley surrounded by towering cliffs and dark mountains. Barbara's camera was already in operation and as I raised my cine Noel took the Cessna through the valley 1,000 feet above the ground and we got a good view of the river winding its way fairly gently at first and then tumbling over rocky ledges in foaming fury before plunging into the narrow, vertically-sided gorge. I felt the aircraft bank sharply and looked up to see a wall of rock racing past – very close. Blasts of wind shook the Cessna as it twisted and turned through the mountain pass. Noel gripped the controls, his face a study of concentration, beads of sweat running down his cheeks. 'Hold on,' he hissed through the intercom as the nose lifted over a jungle-covered ridge. Our bodies flattened against the seat back as the surge of power took us up, missing the trees by fifty feet. The tumbling brown river had almost disappeared in the dark green foliage which now covered the entire valley bottom and seemed to close over the top of the canyon. Eventually, we emerged from the mountains and saw the endless flat swampland of the lower Strickland ahead.

'That's fine, Noel,' I yelled. 'Can you take us back at low level?' The Australian made a funny face and we reloaded our cameras. The return journey was the most exhilarating flight of my life. Manoeuvring his aircraft like a fighter, Noel hurtled through the great cleft in that dark green wilderness. Barbara and I concentrated on filming, but the gravitational forces on some of the turns were such that my arms felt like lead and I could hardly lift the camera. Cliffs and jungle shot past the wingtips. We saw underground rivers emerging, huge caves, strange trees and then a single rope bridge strung across the river. So someone does live down there, I thought. Even so, there was no other obvious sign of any human habitation. Back at base that night, we celebrated and worked on our reports with enthusiasm, knowing that we now had the vital information that would enable Roger Chapman to tackle this river exploration task.

For the young people this was a wonderland and even to the older folk amongst us, PNG was quite an eye-opener. The local government and people were magnificently kind and the ex-patriots did all they could to help. With their support we built aerial walkways in the jungle canopy, searched for minerals, mapped old wartime trails and combed densely forested mountains for the remains of long lost wartime planes. Our underwater team led by Royal Engineers and RAF divers charted Japanese wartime wrecks, of which there was no shortage. The diving was exhilarating, deep, and once or twice, when sharks appeared, quite nerve-wracking. However, more worrying were the gigantic saltwater crocodiles, or 'salties', some said to reach thirty feet in length, that cruised the shallow lagoons.

Meanwhile Roger, Jim Masters and a foot recce party were preparing to take their Avons down the fearsome Strickland. The going was horrendous, as harsh and inhospitable as one is likely to find anywhere in the world. When not scrambling and hacking up and down almost sheer-sided ridges covered in dense undergrowth, one is picking a careful path across the limestone rock, so sharp-edged that the soles of the toughest boots will be shredded after a few miles. Even seemingly open areas, which appear from the air to be smooth carpets of green turf, usually turn out to be covered in kunai grass fifteen feet high, which is so difficult to cut through that a fit man can be reduced to sweat-soaked exhaustion within a matter of yards.

We had also learned that the interior tribesmen were often extremely primitive and their reactions to outsiders unpredictable. The early patrols had adopted a policy of sending ahead shouters – native guides who would go forward and bellow out advance warning of the party's arrival in the area and call in any tribes in the locality for a meeting. Salt and tobacco would then be handed over as a gesture of friendship and, once the ice had been broken, impressive shooting displays with rifles would be laid on to discourage any hostile notions. Although we were never attacked, we carried arms on the advice of the local Army, but more for protection against 'salties'.

I talked to all our outstations daily on a remarkably reliable radio net. One evening Roger came on loud and clear in great excitement. After telling me that they had been forced to make a hair-raising 3,000 feet climb up the side of Strickland Gorge, he said, 'We've found some people.' Then unusually bad conditions cut him out, but words like 'primitive', 'stone axes' and 'no white men' came through and I knew that they had achieved the ultimate goal in many armchair explorers' minds. Quite simply, he'd bumped into a lost or unknown tribe.

Next morning communications improved and I learned it had taken them nearly ten hours to claw their way to the top. They had to move with the utmost caution, hauling themselves up on vines, roots and the most tenuous handholds in the crumbling rock. By the time they eventually made it, they barely had the strength to rig their hammocks and swallow a hurriedly prepared meal of dehydrated food before flaking out. Then, striking inland in search of a suitable clearing in which to land the planned re-supply helicopter, they picked up an old hunting track and smelt wood-smoke. The patrol immediately crept further along the track until, around a bend, they glimpsed through the trees a small clearing in which stood two, low, rectangular huts, with wisps of blue smoke filtering through the thatched roofs. Then, figures were seen moving about and the sounds of children playing and pigs squealing floated across the forest. No settlements were thought to exist here.

At once Roger sent ahead two of his native Duna bearers – Harirega and Ayape – and when he saw that they received a friendly welcome, he led the rest of the patrol forward into the clearing. As he did so, Ayape pointed towards the man with whom he had been conversing in a strange dialect and when Roger extended his hand, the small bearded fellow grasped it firmly and held on determinedly, clearly not wanting to let go. However, some of the men had seized the pigs and run off, whilst women and children lay down and moaned. There then followed a bizarre four-way conversation, English being translated in Pidgin – the nearest thing to an official language in PNG – so that Harirega could then rephrase the message in Duna for the benefit of Ayape, who was the only one familiar with the dialect spoken by the tribesmen.

In this tortuous way it was established that the village they'd discovered was called Tigaro and that the inhabitants were nomadic Pogaians. There were five families in the group, which numbered fifteen altogether. The man who was hanging on to Roger's hand so affectionately was called Kiwanga, and the chief, who was away working in the village 'gardens' but was due back at sunset, was named Kemba. When he eventually made an appearance, he confirmed that nobody in his small tribe had ever seen a white man before – a fact which seemed to be rather amusingly borne out by the way in which Roger's white team members were subjected to close scrutiny and the occasional curious prod.

The fascination was mutual. Kemba and his people were clearly untouched by modern civilization. Their most sophisticated and prized possessions were two steel axe heads, which they had traded with other tribes in the Bulago Valley, where they had originally been introduced by one of the later Kiap patrols. Otherwise, they had only stone tools and implements and their other possessions were made from natural materials. Barbed or notched arrows of razor-sharp split bamboo were used with six-foot-long hardwood bows for the daily wallaby hunt. Some arrows had three or four prongs for catching birds or fish. The women appeared in the evening, carrying taro and sweet potatoes or 'Kau Kau' in 'bilums', net baskets hung from their heads. They wore only grass skirts, while the men covered themselves with a loin cloth in the front and over their backsides, a banging bunch of 'tanket' leaves known evocatively in Pidgin as 'arsegrass'. Most wore thin armbands, also of bark. Kemba, the chief, sported a necklace of large cowrie shells and a half-moon-shaped 'Kina' shell on his dark chest. They existed on a diet of root crops, grown in their forest 'gardens' augmented with whatever they could hunt down. Their precious domestic pigs were only slaughtered on very special occasions and were otherwise treated with loving care. The women walked around clutching piglets as if they were their own children and apparently even suckled them in emergencies. Men guarded pigs more jealously than their wives and children and a tribesman once told me, 'Women and children very easy to make – pigs more difficult!'

Friendship was further cemented with gifts of salt and tobacco and it was agreed that the patrol would spend the night in the village before clearing a landing-site for the helicopter the next morning. The villagers watched spellbound as my voice came through on the radio from base 350 miles away. Eventually, they grew bolder and fingered everything of metal, glass or plastic with child-like glee. Cigarette lighters and binoculars were considered quite amazing.

My arrival next day in a giant RAAF Chinook brought the Stone Age face to face with the twentieth century in the most spectacular fashion. The idea of a simple supply drop was changed because we decided that the patrol might as well take advantage of the situation and hitch a lift back to the banks of the Strickland. Alas, the stone axes had not cleared the last few feet of tree stumps and landing proved impossible, so we had to remain in the hover as our people struggled aboard. It was one of the most worrying ten minutes of my life, as the huge machine bucked and swayed in the jungle clearing. The 'Lost Tribe' stared in amazement at our monster, which might as well have been a space craft in a city dweller's backyard. Some wept with fear, and were so terrified that they were immobile. When they saw us pull the native carriers onto the open ramp, they thought the great bird was devouring them!

As the Chinook lifted off and rose above the tiny jungle clearing with a deafening roar, the 100 mph downdraught from its twin rotors created a mini-hurricane that raised a swirling cloud of dust and whipped the surrounding foliage into a frenzy of dancing branches and wildly fluttering leaves. Fifteen near-naked brown bodies prostrated themselves on the ground, their hands clamped over their ears, their foreheads pressed to the earth, not daring to look up. As the scene receded, I peered down anxiously at the prone forms and wondered what must be going through their minds. Fifty years previously, when aircraft first arrived in PNG, similar encounters had given rise to the cargo cults among the primitive peoples, who understandably concluded that the strange white men who descended from the skies in the bird-like machines packed with wonderful goods must surely be gods. It was fascinating to speculate about the legends that might grow up around our meeting with Chief Kemba's people.

13

Strange Quests

'There are several accounts of a twenty-foot dragon that walks upright, breathes fire and eats men,' said my visitor. It was said to live in south west PNG and was quite definitely not a 'saltie'! Although it sounded nonsense, the Government was eager to find out if there was any truth in the tale. Having studied the more reliable reports, I decided to mount a search for what would undoubtedly be the longest lizard in the world.

We planned to base the expedition at Masingara, the village of my PNG liaison officer, Somare Jogo, and to include Ian Redmond, a robust young zoologist. Masingara is just up the coast from the provincial capital, Daru, in the area generally considered the most likely haunt for any monster lizard.

Things got off to a suitably dramatic start even before my twenty-strong patrol reached Masingara, when we contrived to get lost in some of the most treacherous waters in the world. The Coral Sea is a wonderfully romantic name for a bit of ocean full of deadly reefs, strong currents and shifting shallows. We never really gave this a second's thought as we set out from Port Moresby, bound for Masingara in the MV *Andewa*, kindly provided by the government. The three-day voyage began well enough. Everybody was sunbathing on the after deck, while dolphins played in the bow wave and large juicy baramundi obligingly swallowed the hooks that we trailed out astern. It was around dusk on the second day that things began to go wrong. There was no sign of the lighthouse, which was a vital landmark, and although we all strained our eyes through the growing darkness it was to no avail. At this point the skipper casually confessed that he never bothered with charts because he was used to sailing in waters that he knew like the back of his hand. Unfortunately, he had to admit that this part of the ocean was quite new to him and he really did not know where we were!

After haphazardly changing course a few times in the hope of finding some identifiable landmark, our position was even more confused. I did have a chart, but it was not a lot of help since we could not pinpoint our location. To make matters worse, the trawler's compass was not working. We were literally going round in circles when Chris Sainsbury, the only real sailor amongst us, suggested that as we were in such dangerous waters it might be a good idea to throw a plumb line overboard just to be on the safe side and this revealed the startling fact that we were over a sandbank with less than two feet to spare! The skipper inched into slightly deeper water before anchoring for the night in the hope that we would be able to get our bearings in the morning, when we would at least be able to see what we were doing. But I feared we were too far south and heading straight for the Great Barrier Reef.

Dawn broke to reveal that the water, which the day before had been the deepest blue, was now a murky, muddy brown, while large clumps of vegetation floated by in the strong current. This gave me the vital clue that we must be somewhere near the wide mouth of the Fly River and enabled us to chart a course that eventually led to Daru.

Whilst the good ship *Andewa* refuelled, I rushed off to find Somare and meet her uncle, Mr Tatty Olewale. OBE, the Premier of the Western Province. We found him at home having lunch and reading from a gigantic leather-bound Bible, whilst his pet parakeet hopped about on his shoulder. The Premier rose to greet us with the words, 'Colonel, it is the Lord who has brought you to us.' After the adventure of the previous night, I was inclined to agree. In no time Mr Olewale summoned his brother, the head postman, who was able to tell us a great deal about Artrellia, as they called the dragon. The Premier wished us well and loaded us with small gifts, before sending us off with his niece, Somare, and a wizened old pilot, to guide us up the rivers.

Next day we anchored off Masingara and marched the half mile inland to Somare's well-ordered home village of traditional stilt supported bamboo huts. There I was ushered by her brother, Seyu, towards a 100-year-old woman, who was the most senior citizen and was said to know more than anyone about the Artrellia, having seen several in her lifetime. The white-haired old lady confirmed many of the things we had already heard: that these creatures grew to over fifteen feet in length; that they often stood on their hind legs and so gave the appearance of dragons or, to our minds, mini dinosaurs; also that they were extremely fierce.

This last point brought much nodding from the village hunters, who made it quite obvious that they treated even the smaller six or seven-footers – which they said were quite common – with the greatest respect. This came as no surprise, since we had already been told of an incident in another village where a captured Artrellia had smashed its way out of a stout cage and killed a large dog, before escaping. Now we learned that the creature's method of hunting was to lie in wait in the trees before dropping onto its victims and tearing them to shreds with its powerful claws. Apart from that, it possessed a very infectious bite as a result of feeding on carrion and this could bring death within a matter of hours. There were plenty of stories of men who had been attacked and killed by the Artrellia.

During the next few days we split into four patrols and combed the surrounding jungle, but, although everyone we met understood immediately when we explained what we were looking for and claimed that they themselves had seen such creatures, the nearest any of us got to a sighting was when local dogs put up something that crashed off heavily through the undergrowth without showing itself. There was a flurry of excitement when we learned that dogs had killed a big lizard, but it turned out to be a three-foot Monitor of a well-known species.

On the Sunday before Christmas I went to matins in the little village church. Singing 'Hark, The Herald Angels Sing' in Pidgin did sound strange, but the sincerity of these simple people was most impressive. Strolling out into the bright sunlight, I paused to talk to the vicar. 'Do you really believe in Artrellia?' I asked. He'd been educated in Australia and I reckoned he would be a sensible man.

'I know he exists. I sometimes wish he didn't, 'cos my people think him's a devil, like an evil spirit,' replied the pastor, 'but him just an animal, bad animal sometime.'

'Well, if we caught one, would it convince your flock that it was no evil spirit?' I asked.

'Sure.' He nodded his head.

'Then how on earth can we do that?'

'Oh, you fellows won't catch him – you makes too much noise tramping around the bush. You needs good hunters,' he stated firmly, adding as an afterthought, 'my choirboys is good hunters.'

'How much to hire the choir?' I asked.

'I needs a new church roof,' smiled the little priest, looking wistfully at the tattered thatch.

'How much will that cost?' I asked.

'Ten dollars,' was his quick reply. However, he suggested that I offer the reward at the village council that evening and in that way I'd get all the hunters helping. Ten dollars (or Kina) would be a month's wage.

'But don't tell dem fellows bout d'reward 'till seven o'clock,' he cautioned, 'cos I wants to leave at five. Oh yes, and can you let me have some shotgun shells?'

Sure enough, the mere mention of money was followed by a mass exodus into the jungle of every able-bodied man, armed with everything from bows and arrows to an antique blunderbuss.

In the meantime, Somare showed us some interesting snakes that had been caught in a nearby swamp. They were almost jet black, more like eels, and apparently quite blind. Their skin lacked scales, but was covered in a mass of tiny pimples. Ian Redmond had never seen anything quite like these reptiles and Alan Bibby, our energetic TV producer, was anxious to film them being caught. 'That is not possible,' said Somare, looking very serious. 'They are only caught by the women at a certain time of year – it is a kind of ritual.'

'Goody, bags I go and catch some,' enthused my jolly PA, Margot Barker.

'I'll go too,' echoed Clare, the adjutant.

'Make sure you bring me a pregnant fully-grown female,' said Ian, with scientific motives in mind.

So we left the all-female expedition to its task.

On arrival at the swamp, Margot noticed the almost naked village ladies plunging into waist-deep mud covered by a thin layer of grass. The women chopped at the grass with bush knives, peeled back the top layer and, feeling around with feet and hands, found a great variety of lungfish, long-necked turtles, lizards and snakes.

They hurled their catches to other ladies who waited on the bank. Margot learned that those on the sidelines were pregnant and were not allowed in the morass 'because they would drive away the mud-dwelling creatures'. Eventually Margot, reduced to battle order of bra and pants, plunged in, causing much consternation because only pregnant ladies wore bras in Masingara. Eventually she felt something rather large squirming past her legs and seized it. Out came a very heavy, fully-grown, black, eyeless snake – almost six feet in length and full of eggs. So Ian got his wish. Margot then sensed another serpent wriggling round her thighs – but this one felt thinner and much more lively. Thrusting her hand back into the mire she grabbed it, or rather it grabbed her, and before she could get it out she was bitten four times by a rather unpleasant diamond-headed snake about three feet long. Luckily, it wasn't poisonous.

Further and further our little ship penetrated up the unmapped rivers. As we were reaching the head of navigation of one stream our writer, Mike Cable, remarked, 'I doubt if any outsiders have ever been up this far.' But then, rounding a bend, to our astonishment we saw ahead a well-kept motor launch moored to the bank. The UN Development Programme flag fluttered at its mast head and a shapely blonde in a bikini was stretched across the hatch. 'Jesus,' breathed Mike, unable to believe his eyes.

The blonde propped herself up on one elbow and said in broad Australian, 'G'day, mates.' I doffed my pith helmet and enquired if she was alone. 'No, Bruce is down below trying to fix the freezer.'

At that point her colleague emerged. 'Strike a bloody light,' said he, eyeing the premier Earl of Scotland (who had joined us on the quest), a British Colonel and sundry others: as unlikely a bunch as you would expect to meet up any tropical river.

'What are you doing here?' we enquired, when Bruce had produced some ice-cold tubes of Fosters.

'A crayfish survey.'

'But there aren't any crayfish here,' said Ian.

'I know mate, but don't tell the UNDP.'

We learned that Bruce recruited his assistant, as the blonde was officially described, by advertising in a Sydney paper for 'Good-looking Sheila required to accompany adventurous male on scientific survey in PNG'. He then spent several weeks interviewing volunteers before taking the selected lady back with him for the next season. It sounded like a good way to spend a few years.

Next morning Clare radioed to report that the vicar had managed to shoot a big lizard somewhere deep in the forest and was on his way back to Masingara with it. We returned at full speed and, by the time we arrived, a large crowd had already gathered around a strange-looking creature that was lying at their feet, roped to a bamboo pole. 'It's still alive,' muttered Mike Cable. Chris Sainsbury's cameras were already clicking as I handed the ten-Kina bill to the vicar, who assured me that this was Artrellia. Its dark green skin was flecked with yellow spots and its square head housed a set of needle-like teeth. The eyes twitched malevolently as it tried to squeeze itself out of the vines binding it to the pole, but the most impressive part of its anatomy were the claws. At the end of its short thick legs were enormous, black scimitars, quite out of proportion with the rest of its body. The tail was long and thin and twice the length of the body. I noticed the village dogs kept well away from the dying beast with its terrible talons. The mouth and tongue gave a red/yellow effect. 'Fire,' said the priest, and I saw at once how the legend of a fire-breathing dragon might have been started by the effect of the tongue darting in and out in sunlight.

Ian pushed in the hypodermic and Artrellia passed quietly into death. As soon as it was safe to handle, measurements were taken. It was no dragon, but, even so, it was still a pretty fearsome looking specimen at just over six feet from head to tail. Once Ian had performed his postmortem, he was able to confirm that it was only a youngster, which left plenty of room for speculation about what size an overgrown adult might reach. Meanwhile, a small patrol that had been keeping vigil beside a remote water hole, which we had been told was a favourite haunt of the creatures, came back with reports that they had seen several quite sizeable specimens coming to drink at night, but had been unable to get near enough to photograph them in the dark.

We did catch a glimpse of one monster with a head like a horse peering over a fallen log in the first light of day. Ian also made several sightings of pretty impressive adult lizards up to twelve feet in length. From our specimen, we knew that Artrellia was indeed Salvador's Monitor (*Varanus salvadori*), but no one had dreamed of the size to which these killers can grow. I was not surprised for in these little known tropical forests there are many tales of giant reptiles.

During our reconnaissance in 1978 we had come across a rather macabre, and well-documented story of an incident in Sulawesi.

The *Indonesian Times* had reported that a farmer from Ongka Malino village at the foot of Mount Tinombala in Central Sulawesi, had been eaten by a twenty-foot python. The snake could not move because of its distended stomach. Monty, our own python used in the selection test, was thirteen feet long: I made a note to increase the accident insurance!

While the thought of coming face to face with a fifteen-foot lizard may be somewhat alarming, I doubt whether it would be quite so disconcerting as a run-in with an angry fifty-foot sperm whale, the most alarming experience I had during the entire expedition. It happened as I was aboard *Eye of the Wind*, after visiting our underwater team. A school of some forty whales was sighted, many of them leaping awesomely clear of the water, and we decided to get closer in order to film them. So, using an Avon, we approached to within thirty yards and, not wanting to disturb them, cut the engine. We got some excellent photos and were heading back to the ship when we saw three whales nearby and decided to get one last close-up. Frank Esson had volunteered to handle the engine. Now he shut it off and we paddled gently towards the leviathans. I was filming with my eight-millimetre cine, which has a zoom lens, when I saw a gigantic tail rise out of the leaden sea, then fall and disappear with a great splash. Then, as I adjusted the zoom, a dorsal fin appeared, coming straight at us. 'Shall I start the engine?' asked Frank calmly. But I was concentrating on filming and, looking through the view-finder, felt strangely detached from the world around me. The dorsal fin came on. 'Shouldn't I start the engine?' shouted Frank, and, without waiting for an answer, he did. It was just as well because by now the bull whale's massive head was right beneath us and beginning to rise. The 'dorsal fin' was still fifty feet away. All we had seen was the fluke of its tail! Luckily the motor fired first time and we shot off its head and away, pursued for a short distance by the huge creature, its cavernous jaws and rows of molars rising in a ghastly scissor-like movement behind us. A second more and we would have been lifted out of the water and probably smashed to death by his tail. We were very happy to find ourselves back aboard *Eye of the Wind*, where the crew had enjoyed a grandstand view of the drama and thought it extremely funny.

On 22 January 1980 when our ship reached the island of Sulawesi, the advance party was already there and, thanks to an RAF airlift of stores from PNG, the base was ready. The pattern of our activities here was different from the other land phases. Instead of being spread over a variety of unrelated projects, our efforts were concentrated almost exclusively on a single grand purpose: the preparation of a detailed and comprehensive management plan for the proposed nature reserve at Morowali. The inspiration for this came from ex-sapper John Blower, an old friend from Blue Nile days, who headed the National Parks Development Project. He had drawn my attention to the fact that the Indonesian government had an enlightened attitude towards conservation and proposed to make five per cent of the country's entire land area into nature reserves and national parks. The one at Morowali was ready to go ahead as soon as the 2,000 square mile jungle wilderness in the southeast of the island had been surveyed and a proper plan produced, a daunting task, since the region was largely unmapped and unexplored. A project that promised to mix research, exploration and adventure in such a worthwhile way was very much in keeping with the SES's objectives. Furthermore, Andrew Mitchell pointed out that Sulawesi was of paramount zoological interest since it lies on the Wallace Line, the watershed of animal life that separates Asia from Australia in the evolutionary process.

But I had foreseen that at this point I would need to spend time in London raising funds and planning ahead so, after consultations with John Blower and the Indonesian authorities, I asked Derek Jackson to lead the phase. All his logistic skills would be needed here.

Back in Room 5B, Jim, George, Val, Beth and many others were labouring away, but we were all growing a little tired. Apart from the Drake work, I had an army job, rewriting the military 'bible', *Training for War*, which was somehow completed over the two years of the operation by my writing on planes and in every spare second. I wondered how many MoD authors had written about jungle warfare when actually sitting in one!

In the meantime, Judith and I had bought a charming sixteenth-century cottage in the village of Box, near Bath. 'The Old Dairy' was conveniently near the Royal School, where Emma and Victoria were following in their mother's footsteps. I was sad that my supportive parents had now died, but although my in-laws, Lal and Tommie Sherman, must have thought their daughter crazy to put up with my extraordinary lifestyle, they backed me to the hilt. It was as well because these were worrying times. Raising money was a nightmare and those at the front did not always appreciate that we simply did not have a crock of gold.

However, the Prince of Wales was elated by the success of the project and was already encouraging us to do it all again! Indeed, his enthusiasm, interest and help with the fund-raising did much to keep us going. Michael Colborne, the Prince's secretary, was one of our greatest supporters and his quiet, sensible counsel was of enormous value.

Once the Sulawesi phase was completed successfully, we pressed on to Africa. When I first heard about the mysterious 'Lost World' of the Masai tribesmen that was supposed to exist at a volcanic crater less than thirty miles from Nairobi, I dismissed the idea with a cynical chuckle. I felt sure that somebody was trying to pull my leg. Either way, I was not about to announce a dramatic attempt to conquer the last remaining piece of unexplored territory in East Africa when the location was actually to be found within an easy Sunday afternoon drive of the Kenyan capital.

However, Gordon Davies of the Wildlife Planning Unit assured me that, although the outer crater of Susua was a popular spot, there was an inner crater that was far less accessible and within that was an unexplored plateau. 'I ought to know,' he said, 'I led the last expedition that tried and although we reached the top of the plateau, we were forced to turn back by the incredibly hard going and the lack of water. There was no way we could have gone any further. All other attempts have failed for the same reason. You'll need to build up stocks of water on the plateau or find some secret source if you're to explore it. Why don't you go and have a look for yourself – then you'll see the problem. It will be very useful to us if you can do it.' Gordon went on to tell me of strange lava caves that led outwards from the inner crater. It all sounded intriguing. If no one's been there, goodness knows what we might find, I thought as I drove back to Nairobi.

As soon as I set eyes on the place, I understood exactly why it had remained so effectively cut off. It was possible to get four-wheel-drive vehicles up inside the outer crater of what was effectively a volcano within a volcano. However, a rocky and at times almost sheer-sided gorge, 1,000 feet across at its narrowest point and about 750 feet deep, separated the central uplifted raft of land from the rim of the inner crater like a gigantic dry moat of a huge castle. To get down into it and up the other side would require mountaineering techniques. On top of that, the terrain was murderous – jumbled lava rocks and boulders the size of houses, with treacherous crevasses in between, wicked thorn bushes that tear you to shreds if you are not careful and spear cactus with sharp, poison-bearing spikes, just like bayonets. And not a drop of surface water anywhere. A strange fact struck me. The central plateau and its moat was a mass of dark green vegetation, in stark contrast with the surrounding area, which was covered with thin yellow grass. Yet apart from the steam vents, the place was bone dry – or was it? Was there perhaps some huge underground reservoir? Could this untrodden land hide some unknown species? An air recce revealed a strange conical feature on the southern side of the plateau that towered above the moat. On the summit were rocks that looked unusually regular, giving the appearance of being man-made. We nicknamed it the 'Temple'. Could it be an ancient centre of ritual worship?

It was necessary to establish some kind of supply line across the gorge and the only feasible method of doing this was to rig up an aerial ropeway of tensioned steel wire on which a cable car could be suspended. But even if we could find a steel cable long enough, there was still the considerable problem of how to get it up there when there was at least a mile of boulder-strewn lava field between the point beyond which Land-Rovers could not go and the edge of the crater. A 1,000-foot wire wound on a drum would weigh nearly a ton and it would be impossible to carry or roll it over such rugged ground. Apart from that, I wondered how we were going to keep the advance party supplied with water once they started hacking their way across the plateau. In the kind of conditions and temperatures they would be encountering, each man would require at least a gallon per day, maybe more, and there was no chance of their carrying sufficient quantities with them as they went.

After an air reconnaissance with our local chairman, John Sutton, we decided to go ahead. If it seemed like Mission Impossible, well, really tough challenges were just what we were supposed to be looking for. The Kenya Army could provide the explosives necessary to blast a path through the lava field along which we could roll the cable drum to the crater's edge and to dig anchorages for the ropeway. Amongst our stores were cargo parachutes which could be used for water drops onto the plateau from the Beaver aircraft that had been flown out to join us from Britain by veteran Army Air

Corps pilots Mike Badger and Mike Sommerton-Rayner, the 'Biggles Outfit' as they were affectionately dubbed. As the preparations went ahead, including the setting up of a base camp, excitement and enthusiasm mounted. Gordon needed information on fauna, flora, water sources, caves, tracks – indeed, everything there was to know about the area that would help to turn Susua into a unique wilderness reserve.

We decided to tackle the problem on two fronts: first there was to be the direct assault onto the central plateau across the moat. Later, we would explore the extensive lava tubes, a cave system close to the surface on the eastern side of the inner crater. I wondered if the strange long passages led up to the centre of the volcano.

There was a slight hiccup in our plans when the company supplying the cable confessed they had made a mistake and that the longest section they had extended only to 750 feet. However, a solution to that problem was found when Kenya Railways then managed to splice two steel cables. John Leach, a highly experienced Warrant Officer in the Royal Engineers, took charge of the ropeway project and we dynamited a path through the lava, but it took a full ten-hour day of heaving, sweating and straining by our entire twenty-strong work-force to manhandle the heavy cable drum up to the edge of the crater. To make anchorages for either end of the ropeway, we blasted two narrow trenches, one each side of the gorge. In them we buried the trunks of cedar trees to act as anchors for the cable, which had to be dragged by hand down into the moat and across to the other side before being tensioned. A team of the toughest YEs available helped John with this exhausting and potentially dangerous task. On one occasion, the cable, which had become snagged, suddenly sprang free, hurling a youngster aside and catapulting another who was holding it fifteen feet into the air. Luckily, he managed to hang on as the cable bounced him about above the rocks.

Everyone worked to get the stores and explosives over the moat Even our treasurer, ex-sapper John Hines, who was no spring chicken, was pressed into service. Barbara Martinelli, who had given up her holiday to rejoin the Operation, almost didn't go home when a football-sized boulder broke away from the top of the gorge and came crashing down the near-vertical slope. I heard a scream of 'Look out,' and flattened myself against the side. Several small chippings struck my shoulders and with a crunch, crunch, crunch, a fifty-pound lump shot past a few inches from my face. To my horror, I saw it heading straight for Barbara, who was clinging to the fixed rope 100 feet beneath me. It was a miracle that it missed her.

Once the cable had been rigged and the first water cans and equipment were sent over on the little trolley, the exploration began. Through the long hot days we toiled to hack a way forward across the plateau. The going was far worse than we'd imagined from our air recce. Huge chunks of rock lay scattered across the broken ground, covered in a sharp, barnacle-like lichen that slashed fingers and knees. In between the giant boulders, the deep ravines caused more hardship and, everywhere, thorn trees and spear cactus threatened to catch the unwary. Once or twice we saw a much-feared death adder, one of East Africa's most deadly serpents. 'Don't think much of this place – it's just like I imagine hell to be,' commented my Devon driver, Corporal Richardson, who compared everything with his native Exmoor.

At times it was, indeed, very like an inferno. We were over 6,000 feet above the sea and at night the temperature plummeted to frost level. At dawn, we stood outside our tents sipping scalding tea and shivering, watching the steam vents on the plateau puffing their vapour into the clear air. Then, as the sun came up, the dry yellow grassland of the outer crater began to shimmer with heat and sweat pumped from our pores to stream down our bodies. Only the graceful movement of the giraffe to their feeding ground and the bobbing flight of the gazelle reminded us that this was Africa.

Our scientists spent the next two weeks carrying out a thorough survey of the flora and fauna on what Ian Redmond described as 'a unique ecological island'. Leaving the comfort of our base camp, the teams picked their way through the lava field, down into the moat and up onto the waterless plateau into a completely different world. The one fear that bothered me was that of a casualty on the plateau. How on earth can we get an injured man back to base, I thought. Thus, when Gordon Davis's son, Ben, went down with violent stomach pains and diarrhoea, I ordered up the strongest medicine we could get. The plateau was no place for an epidemic of the runs.

In the outer crater, there were scattered Masai villages, where Barbara and Judith did their best to help with some first aid and medicine for the children. The people knew little about the plateau, for the Masai, courageous hunters that they were, would not go onto that land of spirits. We still wondered about the 'Temple' and each day brought our cutting teams nearer to it.

Our underground survey concentrated on the subterranean passages that had been created when the volcano erupted. The red-hot lava had spilled over and run down the mountainside. As the outside surface of this molten tide cooled and solidified, the inner core continued to flow, thereby creating hollow underground tubes that opened at intervals into large caverns. The network of passages, ranging in diameter from eighteen inches to thirty feet, was estimated to extend over five miles. Once used as a hide-out by Mau Mau terrorists, there were now plans to turn them into a tourist attraction and it was with this in mind that some of the YEs helped local cave experts John Arkle and Jim Simon to survey and map the tunnel system.

John, an ex-soldier living in Mombasa, had one hair-raising experience when he and Jim penetrated far into the network. They had just wriggled their way through a long section of tunnel that was only eighteen inches high when they burst through into a large chamber. A shaft of sunlight was pouring through a small hole in the roof creating a pool of warmth on the floor of the cave in which was lying, fast asleep, an enormous fifteen-foot python. The two men tiptoed past and continued on their way up the next section of tunnel, which turned out to be a dead end, and when they came back, the snake was nowhere to be seen. There was only one way it could have gone – down the eighteen-inch-high passage along which they had no option but to crawl. Their hearts were in their mouths as they inched forward, expecting to see at any moment the shadowy outline of the huge reptile rear up out of the gloom into the light cast by their lamps. In fact, they never did catch up with it, but John admits that the prospect of coming face to face with the huge serpent in such nightmarishly claustrophobic circumstances still makes his flesh crawl.

The system was an eerie place, full of strange shapes of solidi-fied lava, some twisted like great ropes, others forming platforms at the sides of the passages and giving the tunnels the appearance of an underground railway station. Stalactites of lava hung from the roof on which musical notes could be rung. In one cavern we found the skeleton of a bull rhino. A gaping hole in the roof told the tale of its end and reminded us not to drive our Land-Rover carelessly through the bush above the passages. On another occasion, we discovered fresh leopard prints in the dust; they were going in, so we decided to go out!

Meanwhile, up on the plateau the battle continued and flying low in the Beaver I saw something very odd. As Mike Badger swung the powerful plane over the cedar trees we came to a big clearing. We were looking for suitable parachute dropping zones and, as I glanced down, I saw an extraordinary animal. It was rather like an antelope, with a flash of white above the tail. My immediate reaction was to say 'waterbuck', but such a creature would hardly be likely to be living on a waterless plateau. Whatever, it was a biggish animal and it would need water. Later we were to discover other large mammals on the raft.

One day we came face to face with a group of approximately forty olive baboons on the track. Initially they showed no fear of us, probably because we were the first humans they had encountered. They appeared inquisitive and our yelling and shouting did nothing to make them move. Suddenly, they seemed to feel threatened and two large males rushed at us with teeth bared. We had machetes, but no guns and the odds of getting away without injury were slim. Luckily, the two animals stopped short and, deciding not to push our luck, we retreated back several hundred yards, hoping that they would move along in their own time. We then tried throwing stones to scare them away, but soon discovered they could do this too! It was an hour before they moved off. In fact, many of the female baboons acted in a strangely carnal manner towards us. Perhaps they thought we were rather attractive apes.

Hopes that the fiction of Conan Doyle's Lost World might come true with the discovery of weird and wonderful creatures, marooned there since prehistoric times, were not fulfilled. But the fact that there was a considerable amount of wildlife in this waterless zone was a puzzle in itself. The only source was from the steam vents, which were clearly visible at dawn, but which, later in the day, as the temperature rose, were barely to be seen. Early one morning as I rested atop a large boulder near one of the vents, my eye caught a movement below. A rock hyrax, a small rabbit-like creature with short ears, emerged from a crevice and crept up to a stone on the edge of the vent. Its nose twitching in the sulphur fumes, it began to lick up the condensed moisture. So, smaller creatures could survive. But what about the large animals? While the survey path was being cut, I began to seek for a pool, which I felt must be somewhere amongst the jumbled rock. However, Susua did not intend to give up her secrets easily and, after several abortive searches, I returned to base camp, battered, bruised and full of thorns. The mystery remains to be solved.

The oddest thing about the place was that whenever I was moving alone on the plateau I always had the feeling of being watched. I think it had something to do with the terrain, the huge rocks and boulders behind which it was easy to imagine all sorts of things lying in wait, and the many unexplained noises. It was quite common to hear a sudden crashing in the undergrowth without being able to see anything. The strangest noise of all was the ghostly whistling that was most noticeable at dusk. However, we discovered that this came from the acacia trees that play host to a particular type of ant which nests in ball-like growths on the branches. These are full of holes made by the ants and wind blowing through them created the whistling.

It was desperately hard work to carry water forward from the head of the aerial ropeway. Using plastic sheets, we managed to collect a few pints of the precious liquid from the steam vents, but this was not nearly enough. However, by now, the Beaver was able to parachute water to us.

With the YEs to help him, Ian Redmond had been able to make several transects, noting the variety of animals and plants. The results were particularly interesting as the inner area of Susua has been effectively cut off from outside influences since it was created. After several weeks of back-breaking toil, these tough young people had blazed an eight-foot-wide trail for a distance of two miles, from one side of the plateau to the other and up to its highest point at 6,850 feet, where the Kenyan flag was ceremonially raised. It then took three and a half hours to scramble back along the path that had been cleared, an indication of just how thick and impenetrable the virgin terrain had been. Rather disappointingly, the 'Temple' turned out to be a natural feature. It was just a huge steam vent topped by unusually rectangular rocks, although it might easily have been used for Masai initiation rites.

Meanwhile our teams were excavating old Islamic ports under the direction of Mark Horton, still rushing about everywhere waving his arms. Around the great emerald Lake Turkana camel patrols were highly popular, whilst Ernie Durey of Darien fame built a magnificent 300-foot bridge at the Ark Lodge and we dug cattle dips and counted game from hot air balloons in the Masai Mara. Scientific studies were carried out in conjunction with the National Museums and everything was going rather well until, tragically, two YEs, Andrew Maara from Kenya and Richard Hopkins of Britain, died in separate motor accidents. For me, this was a great sadness as I had always hoped to get through the venture without a fatal casualty, but alas the statistics were against us.

The Kenyan phase ended with a fascinating study of a giant cavern inside Mount Elgon, an extinct volcano on the Uganda border. It was that was said to be inhabited by elephants! Sixty years before, a farmer called Renshaw Mitford-Barbeton had entered Kitium Cave and got a very nasty shock. Having edged cautiously through the wide, low, letterbox-shaped entrance, he then penetrated right to the back of the 750-foot-deep cavern, crawling over fallen boulders, inching past narrow crevasses and skirting dark pools into which water dripped with echoing plops. It was as he prepared to make his way back out again that he suddenly realised with a start that he had company. He heard them long before he saw them – heavy, shuffling footsteps, a strange flapping noise and some terrifyingly loud huffing and puffing. There was also a sound that seemed to him like the rumbling of giant stomachs. His mind boggled. Whoever or whatever they were, they had him trapped in the dead-end cave. He strained his eyes into the darkness beyond the range of his lamp and then gasped in amazement as he eventually managed to make out a group of huge shadowy forms in the gloom. It was a herd of elephants.

Mitford-Barbeton escaped unhurt when, after an hour that must have seemed to him like an eternity, the elephants left. However, we were to discover that his confrontation was no chance meeting, since the herds regularly visited the cave: they had beaten a well-worn path to the entrance. But why they should want to go out of their way to squeeze themselves into this one particularly inaccessible cavern had remained a mystery for many years – an even greater mystery than the legendary Elephants' Graveyard. Part of the problem was that it was impossible to see what they were doing in the darkness, and lights would scare them off and possibly start a stampede.

When Gordon Davies took John Sutton, Judith and me to Mount Elgon, we first checked very carefully to make sure that the cave was uninhabited and then posted an armed game guard at the entrance before we ventured in. Following the beams of our head torches, we were soon deep underground when an appalling stench hit us, the unmistakable smell of decaying flesh. On peering into a crevasse, we saw the cause. There, ten feet down, lay the putrefying carcass of a baby elephant, which had obviously stumbled to its death in the darkness. We pressed on, our lamps startling thousands of fruit bats that were hanging from the roof, so much so that they showered us with their droppings! Finally, we came to the pools, surrounded by recent elephant manure and then we looked up and saw what attracted the great beasts.

All over the walls and roof were tusk marks – they had been mining salt. 'What an incredible story,' said John. 'Salt-mining elephants. It must be unique.' But it wasn't only elephants, for at much lower levels and in small side tunnels, I found the marks of wild pig, antelope and giant forest hog. Analysis of the minerals showed that it contained mirabilite, which has a mild purgative effect and probably helped the beasts' digestion. Clearly we were dealing with highly intelligent animals. Gordon felt that viewing facilities could be provided for tourists by cutting a path up to the entrance and constructing an observation platform. We agreed to do this and also to carry out a survey of the cave itself to find out more about the frequency and duration of the elephants' visits. There was one thing about the cave of the elephants that still mystified me. I'd noted with an engineer's interest that the roof appeared to be supported by a single pillar, about twenty feet thick, but made of the same mineral salt as the walls. There were tusk marks on it, but very old ones. No fresh mining. Very strange and it posed a question. Did the elephants, who after all are great engineers, know they must maintain this vital roof support, or was it pure chance? I like to think they did, for sadly some while later when a film team, encouraged by the SES, was making a documentary about Kitium, an earthquake collapsed the pillar and part of the roof fell in, trapping an elephant. A very courageous Kenyan warden went inside and shot the crippled beast, risking bringing the entire roof down on top of himself.

By now *Eye of the Wind* was sailing north up the Red Sea – or, at least, trying to do so against the most appalling head winds. John Hines, our tireless supporter, had gone ahead to Egypt to co-ordinate plans for a small task there and to clear the ship for transit through the Suez Canal. Unable at first to locate the vessel, he borrowed a MiG fighter from the Egyptian Air Force and roared past our flagship a few minutes later, but no one aboard realised it was that 'our man in Cairo' who was 'buzzing' them.

I was waiting for her at Alassio on Italy's Mediterranean coast, where she was to rendezvous with the Goodyear airship *Europa* and the Beaver for the last – and visually most spectacular – of our scientific projects. This was a unique experiment that involved taking simultaneous pollution samples from the sea and the air in and above the Gulf of Genoa, where the build-up of toxic trace metals in particular had been causing concern. The experiment, for which a sailing ship was perfectly suited since it would not itself add to the pollution, was to be carried out in cooperation with the UN Environment Programme as part of the Mediterranean Pollution Monitoring and Research Project.

Andrew, Barbara and I were to coordinate the experiment. The weather was appalling, but in the late afternoon the sky began to clear and I saw *Europa* approaching from the sea like an attacking zeppelin. The tubby silver 'cigar' looked really menacing as she flew low under the rain clouds and I felt that we were going back in time. The appearance of the high-winged Beaver, piloted by the two Mikes, added to this impression, and when dawn came, there to complete the picture was *Eye of the Wind* resting at anchor on a mirror-like sea 200 yards off the beach.

I felt slightly out of place standing there in desert uniform with a radio, whilst bikini-clad holiday-makers strolled by, but everything went like clockwork and even the weather turned out just the way we needed it for the four-day exercise, which developed into a marvellously colourful and exciting international occasion.

We had thrilling moments, too, as the Beaver, with its leather helmeted crew, would seek for the slow-flying *Europa* in the broken cumulus. Approaching from the south one afternoon, we saw the airship disappear into a bank of cloud some miles ahead and followed. 'Christ, where's she gone?' muttered Mike Somerton-Raynor as visibility dropped. The wings shuddered as he pushed through the cotton wool and then broke out. 'My God, she's turned back,' he yelled, pulling the Beaver's nose up and we roared over the great silver hull. In the cupola I saw Barbara's anxious face look up in surprise.

Our conferences in the hotel bar, our slightly luxurious 'base camp', were a hoot as the boffins of various nationalities discussed the research. 'Where do I find the Arno River?' asked Mike Badger at one briefing. 'You bomba da Italy alla de war and you ask now where is Arno....' exploded Professor Aristeo Renzoni of Siena.

On *Eye of the Wind* an oceanographer from the Saclant Research Centre at La Spezia studied temperature profiles across the Gulf using expendable bathythermographs, which relayed information from below the surface of the water to instruments aboard. Up above, samples showed levels of atmospheric mercury contamination to be 280 times higher over Genoa than other non-industrial areas of the coastline. The airship proved a perfect craft for collecting the samples, being able to float over potential pollution hotspots whilst special instruments 'sniffed' the air.

This brief episode was one of the highlights of Operation Drake. Everyone was struck by the great spirit of international co-operation, the tremendous energy that was put into co-ordinating a complex operation and the feeling that something really worthwhile had been achieved. And there was a bonus in that the dramatic newspaper and television pictures that flashed round the world showing *Europa* hovering above *Eye of the Wind* gripped the public imagination and did much to boost our image. The airship and the brigantine even featured on the set of special stamps issued in Jersey to commemorate the operation.

On 13 December 1980, shortly before noon, *Eye of the Wind* passed under Tower Bridge, with Kenyan YE Mwingi Japan at the helm, to mark the end of the great adventure. It was a wonderfully colourful and exciting occasion for the tens of thousands who lined the banks of the river and packed into St Katherine's Dock to witness the homecoming and a very moving moment for the many youngsters from earlier phases who had made the pilgrimage from as far away as New Zealand to be in at the finish and to be reunited with the friends made during their time with the expedition. As the ship covered the last few hundred yards of the 36,000 miles she had logged altogether during her two years away, Capital Radio's David Briggs broadcast a live commentary from a vantage point, halfway up the mainmast, while all around him the crew lined the yardarms. A flotilla of small boats and a fly-past by the Beaver and an RAF Hercules added an extra bit of theatre and helped to ensure that the enterprise closed on a dramatic note. At precisely 12.25 pm *Eye of the Wind* docked, to be greeted by the Lord Mayor. It was all over.

For the YEs who brought her home, the excitement was high to the very end. After stopping off at Guernsey and Jersey, where thanks to Adrian Troy's committee they were given a fantastic welcome, they then encountered some of the worst weather of all, as a force eleven gale blew up, and, for six hours continuously, the anemometer was off the clock as the winds topped seventy mph. However, as our Australian Chairman, Rugby star Denis Cordner, who had made a special flight to the Channel Islands to join the ship for the final leg, said, 'I wouldn't have missed it for the world.'

My former CO, Brigadier Tony Landale, had organised the whole of St Katherine's Dock into a massive exhibition with the ship at its centre and it was here, next day, that Prince Charles came to meet the YEs and our supporters. At the end our Patron said Operation Drake was the sort of 'crazy expedition' that the British were particularly good at organizing, and went on:

> We have it somehow in our national make-up, the ability to withstand with an amazing degree of good humour, the most appalling conditions. The fact that on this occasion it was combined with scientific research and social projects showed the host countries that the British were keen on helping generally throughout the world. It can have done nothing but produce more good will and favourable reactions.

One of the elderly skilled craftsmen who serviced the ship was waiting to see me at Room 5B. 'It's about this 'ere invite,' he grumbled. 'You've asked me and the missus to meet the Prince of Wales.'

'Yes, of course,' I replied, 'I do hope you'll come.'

'But she's not my missus, we was never married,' he moaned. 'Well I'm sure....' I started to say.

'Oh no, that wouldn't do,' he chipped in, 'I'm going to take her out and marry her today.' And so he did, giving us one other little success for the venture!

14

Nothing Ventured, Nothing Gained

Nineteen-Eighty-One was not a happy year for Britain's inner cities. As dole queues lengthened the crowds of unemployed, frustrated and restless young grew and finally, on a warm summer's night, violence erupted on the streets. The police should not have been taken by surprise, for many of us associated with youth had warned of the explosive situation. At Prince Charles' suggestion, Sergeant Major David Taylor and I had spent an evening with the Rastafarians in Wandsworth.

'You from the Fuzz?' hissed a dreadlocked West Indian.

'These guys is in the Army,' said his pal.

'What you do there?' spat the questioner, pushing his face closer to mine.

'We kill people,' said the Sergeant Major quietly.

There was a short pause then a roar of laughter, 'Why Man, that's great – have a drink.'

Then they told us a long tale of strained race relations and inter-tribal strife. When I suggested they go to Kingston-on-Thames for a job with British Aerospace, I was regarded as an idiot. 'You'd never get back to Wandsworth with your pay packet. You got to pass right through Red Tigers or the Black Hand,' they confided. Indeed, it seemed parts of Britain were becoming rather like PNG.

General Mogg passed our report to the Home Secretary but, by the time it was acknowledged, Brixton, St Paul's, Bristol, and Toxteth were burning. Many former YEs now involved in Youth work did their best to restore peace, but the scars of that terrible summer were deep.

It was a Friday afternoon when the Director of Army Training rang me. 'John, what do you know of the proposal for a Youth Adventure Training Unit?' he enquired.

This was a paper exercise being carried out at the insistence of the Government, desperately seeking a solution to urban unrest. Like so many plans that circulate in Whitehall, it would be considered and later scrapped. The staff, with their long experience of fatuous ideas, had not taken it too seriously. 'Well, General, I believe it's a plan to take young civilians off the city streets and give them a new direction in life through a few weeks' outdoor activities under military experts,' I said, glad that I could recall the brief, and added, 'Frankly, its unworkable.'

My boss raised his eyebrows. 'Well, maybe you can do something with it, because you are going to command this outfit. The Secretary of State, Mr John Nott, will see you on Monday. Have a good weekend.'

I rushed back to the office and shouted, 'No one goes home, meeting in ten minutes. Margot, get the files on that ruddy Army Youth Scheme,' and we got down to work. On Monday the Secretary of State smiled hesitantly. 'It's terribly important that this should succeed. If there is anything you need, just ask. You will be backed to the hilt.'

'How is all this to be paid for? I enquired.

John Nott, like all cautious politicians, considered his answer carefully. 'Let the costs lie where they fall,' he said, and I repeated this to everyone who asked me. I was not over-pleased to be given command of this new enterprise. Nevertheless, I was determined to make the best of what seemed to be an impossible task to achieve in one year.

So it was that I took over the massive eighteenth-century Fort George, near Inverness. It had been built after the last battle on British soil to keep the rebellious Scots in order. It seemed appropriate and was convenient to reach the Highlands for some really tough exercises. Recruiting 180 of the Army's top adventure trainers and assembling a fleet of vehicles, plus our dear old Beaver, I moved north with Judith and Max, the labrador.

The Fort George Volunteers, as we were named, took as their motto 'Nothing ventured, nothing gained'. When the doors opened in May 1982 and the first of 2,500 teenagers trooped in, the paint was still wet.

The Prince of Wales at once took an interest, as did the press. We quickly became a political hot potato. However, I had Chris Sainsbury and several of the Drake team to help, plus an energetic new PA named Sally Harris, who typed like a machine gun. To my surprise, the scheme was a success and I learnt much about the needs of modern youth. I saw that the longer people were unemployed, the longer they were likely to remain so. It was a frightening statistic that in 1983 there were over 7.5 million Britons aged between seventeen and twenty-four and, of these, some 1.2 million were without work. Not only did they lack jobs, they were without any direction to their lives and, it seemed, any will to find one. Was this a product of the swinging sixties? Old values were being questioned, youngsters were reared with looser family ties and parental discipline had slackened. Perhaps the sixties had swung too far. At Fort George the young showed they wanted challenges and inspiration, and during each group's two-week stay at that bleak establishment I saw a great change in them.

To help keep the Highlands tidy we got the volunteers to collect rubbish wherever they went and especially on the summit of Ben Nevis, Britain's highest peak. Never having climbed the mountain myself, I took Judith and Max to inspect the clean up. There is an old pony track and normally it is possible to walk up. However, on this particular day heavy snow had fallen and white-out conditions were setting in. Our rescue team was positioned halfway up and here I met one of the instructors.

'We've called the young off,' he said. 'It's getting a little tricky on top, but it you'd like to go on, Colonel, I'll come with you.'

On the pony track we exchanged greetings with four elderly gentlemen clad in heavy anoraks. A gale was blowing as we neared the summit but, to my horror, I saw a plastic bag with its contents spilling over into the fresh snow. 'The little swine,' I roared into the wind. 'We send them to clean up and they chuck their rations all over the place. Is it muesli or porridge?' I asked, as we tasted it.

'I'm not sure,' replied the instructor, 'seems a bit gritty.' Max sniffed it, but it was not to his liking. So I scooped up the mess and carried it home. Later, when we saw the rescue team again, they asked if we'd met the four gentlemen on the hill. I nodded.

'Did they tell you what they'd been doing?' asked the Sergeant. He went on. 'You see, their father was a famous mountaineer in these parts; he died last week and they had been up to scatter his ashes.' 'If he tasted all right, he must have been a Gordon,' commented RSM MacDonald on our return to the Fort.

One cannot live in the Highlands without being aware of Nessie or the Loch Ness Monster. A few years before, when planning an army exercise, I had gone to Loch Morar and while attempting to rent a field for the base had met some extraordinary folk.

The air in the bar was heavy with tobacco smoke and the delightful aroma of malt whisky as we stood in a corner watching the dying sun sinking behind the Island of Rhum. 'Excuse me one moment,' said Adrian Shine through his dense red beard, as a thin man with a ruddy, weather-beaten face touched him on the sleeve. Tim Dinsdale, Corporal Thomas and I continued our conversation whilst Adrian talked intently with the newcomer at the other end of the room. A few moments later, our bearded friend returned and, with suitably furtive glances, spoke in a low voice, 'There's been a sighting,' he said, adding quickly, 'this afternoon – near the Chapel.'

I was faintly amused and they sensed it. 'I expect you think we've set this up especially for you,' said Tim, but I could tell from his expression that he hadn't and I felt that these people were deadly earnest and quite sincere. Already I knew that the Loch Morar Expedition was a serious attempt to solve one of the world's greatest mysteries and that this group of engineers and scientists were not the sort of people to gamble their meagre resources on something that they thought was a hoax or a myth.

'This man lives beside the loch, not far from here,' said Adrian, a tinge of excitement in his voice. 'Apparently, his wife and children watched a big hump moving about for several hours this afternoon, and he's agreed to allow us to question them.'

Although the hour was late, it was still daylight in this remote corner of the West Highlands and we set off at once for their lonely cottage. The lady who opened the door was worried and nervous and welcomed us as if ushering in guests to a funeral. Her children sat or stood in the parlour where a low fire glowed in the hearth. They seemed stunned and overawed, but tea and cake were produced and then expert monster investigator Tim Dinsdale and the expedition leader, Adrian, began their questioning.

The woman told her story, quite firmly and without a trace of emotion. She had been gardening in front of the cottage at about

2 pm; it was a fine clear day and the surface of the loch, some 200 yards away, was still. Suddenly, she heard a splash and, imagining it to be wild duck alighting, looked up, but what she saw left her speechless and clutching the hoe for support. About 200 yards out into Loch Morar, and therefore around 400 yards from where she stood, was a great dark hump. 'It looked about this high,' she said, indicating with her hands a vertical distance of about three feet. Then, full of fear, she did what every mother would do – called out to her children. They came running and saw it; the girls ran behind the house in terror, but the little boy, a tough lad, whom I guessed to be about twelve, seized a garden fork and raced to the shore. However, whatever it was, took no notice of them. The amazing part of the story was how, for almost three hours, the thing submerged, surfaced, and darted hither and thither 'as if it were trying to catch fish.' Eventually it headed off up the loch, leaving a big wake.

Tim questioned her with great tact, but with an insistence on detail. She'd lived there for fourteen years and had never seen anything like this before. The frightened woman knew the difference between salmon leaping, otters playing, ducks landing, floating logs, patches of weed and upturned boats. This bore no resemblance to any of these. She kept saying, 'it was just like a whale.'

How do you know what a whale looks like?' asked Tim. 'Because I'm the daughter of a fisherman,' was the instant reply. Tim made her repeat the story – but her recall was faultless and except for the size of the one or two dimensions, her son's description confirmed it in every detail.

Sitting in the old armchair in the comer of that small sitting room, I had no part in the proceedings, but was fascinated. When we arrived, the woman had asked us all what we did and made us swear that none of us were from the press. The thought of any publicity was totally abhorrent to her. This, I learned later, was because of a local superstition that says Morag, as Nessie's cousin, the Loch Morar monster is known, was the harbinger of death, and this was confirmed by the sinking of HMS *Hood* during World War II, with many local men in her crew. It was said that on that fateful day, Morag had been seen rising from the dark peat-stained waters. Ever since then, its appearance had been regarded as an omen of ill fortune.

It was midnight when Tim switched off his tape recorder and

– we all stood up, thanked the woman and her family for their kindness and patience and strolled out into the twilight. In June, darkness only lasts for an hour or two this far north. The surface of the loch was still, nothing moved. There was not even a ripple. How on earth could so large a beast inhabit a few square miles of water and remain unknown to science? But I had seen people interrogated and I knew that liars usually have a motive. I could see no reason for these simple folk to lie and I was quite convinced that they had been describing accurately whatever it was they'd seen. Many explorers claim that it's curiosity that drives them on, and I feel that this is an important motivating force in my life. Thus this mystery has always intrigued me. Later I discussed it at length with a fervent believer, Sir Peter Scott.

Adrian Shine had already made an important advance by establishing the existence of a food chain in the Loch, perhaps sufficient to support a large beast. The SES has always tried to support serious investigations, so I called my friend at Goodyear, Phyllis Angliss, who earned the nickname 'Philatelic Phyllis' by marketing hundreds of special covers bearing the airship stamp from the special Operation Drake set issued by the Jersey post office to help fund the expedition.

By the time *Europa* appeared over Inverness Airport, a whole series of experiments had been organised. The youngsters of the Fort George Volunteers were delighted with the idea of a spot of monster hunting from an airship and we had assembled an impressive array of scientists. Adrian brought his 1907 Humber sailing barge to do sonar surveys, whilst Chris Sainsbury came along to film it and eccentric artist, Bob Williamson, produced a 1930 Puss Moth monoplane.

The weather looked promising on 2 June as *Europa* came obediently to her mast at Dalcross. Broadly speaking, the programme was to do two flights a day, dividing the time between the scientific research and surveillance over Loch Ness. As I knew from Alassio, airship flying is the perfect way to travel. The great bulbous creatures are relatively quiet; there's plenty of room in the cabin and not even seat-belts to restrict you. Visibility is marvellous and if you want extra air, you just open a window. With a top speed of around 50 mph, *Europa* usually cruised at 30 mph. Although she could climb to 8,500 ft, the pilots preferred to operate under 3,000 ft. She could cover 500 miles without landing, but as there was no lavatory aboard, you would be pretty cross-legged by then!

As part of the scientific studies, the dispersal of sewage from Inverness into the Beauly Firth was studied by the Highland River Purification Board, who had red dye poured into the outfall and, from the airship, we then photographed its movement on the ebb and flood tide. To us laymen, it seemed to show that it all flowed back to Inverness when the tide turned! 'Good for the salmon,' commented Chris, who was filming the experiment from Bob's Puss Moth.

Other scientists experimented with some very sensitive photographic and video equipment fitted on *Europa* and, clambering into the eight-seat cabin of the massive craft, I sat up front with Enzo, the pilot, with whom I'd flown in Italy. We pushed the aerial of the Army radio out through the open window so I could talk to my mobile HQ and also to Adrian on his barge.

Richard Snailham took the cine camera and climbed in next with the scientists and their heat scanner. There was just time to brief the team on their areas of observation before we slipped gently from the mast and, with our engines ticking over, were walked to the take-off position. Then, with an effortless roar, the twin engines pushed us up at a steep angle into the blue sky.

We rose majestically and headed for Loch Ness. The engines, sounding like a well-tuned motorcycle, purred away astern. We approached the pewter water of the loch and moved down to rendezvous with the sonar barge. The familiar sight of Urquhart Castle, the sun lighting up its crumbled ramparts, appeared ahead. Several motor coaches had brought dozens of tourists to swarm over the ruin. 'They've got a bonus today,' said Richard.

The barge was already on station and, as we circled, Adrian opened the throttle and began to creep along beneath us. Down in the spacious hold, the scientists and operators scanned the screens as the sonar probed the depths. In the half-light, the steady stream of red, yellow and green blips passed by like a slow-moving rainbow. Once, a tremor of excitement went through the crew as a huge blip appeared.

'Side echo,' muttered Adrian, ignoring it and scanning on. Up above, we in *Europa* all longed to see a long, dark, leathery neck, or a massive hump emerge dramatically from the surface, but nothing

Operation Drake's flagship,
Eye of the Wind, off Jersey.
(*Jersey Evening Post*)

Monster hunting: the airship
Europa over Urquhart Castle,
Loch Ness, with the sonar
barge below.

Young explorers in the swamps of Panama. (*Chris Sainsbury*)

Barbara Price (Martinelli)
a very effective recce office
on many expeditions.

The flying trapeze on the walls of Fort George. (*Chris Sainsbury*)

During a visit to the Fort George Volunteers in 1982, HRH The Prince of Wales takes a ride in the Avon Searider, now being used as a fast inshore rescue craft. (*Chris Sainsbury*)

OPERATION RALEIGH, 1985
Sir Walter Raleigh, flagship of Operation Raleigh, and the expedition's
brigantine *Zebu* rendezvous off the Turks and Caicos Islands. (*SES*)

Venturers constructing the Canadian sub-igloo off Grand Bahama. (*SES*)

Shaving in the snow with Silva's compass mirror on the slopes of
Mt Xixabangma, Tibet, 1987.

With some of my greatest allies: (*left to right*) General Sir John Mogg, Ambassador and Mrs Walter Annenberg, and Graham Walker. (*ORPL*)

An Executive Expedition: the microlight sets out on a dawn recce in the Kalahari. (*Daily Telegraph*)

Raja Gaj, king elephant, 11'3" at the shoulders, browsing quietly near the Karnali.

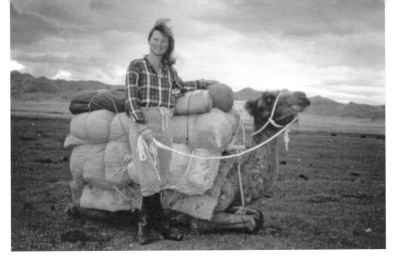

Ann Tweedy Savage with her camel, Basil, west of Khovd. (*Ian Robinson*)

American banker Pamela Stephany with my pal Nokhoijhav near
Mt Somboros.

Victoria and Julian fly away in t[...]
Royal Engineer balloon 'Sapper[...]
after their wedding.

Actress Rula Lenska in Nep[...]
with elephant Chan Chan
Kali.

Airlifted from Mongolia:
Lindsay Griffin with a shatter[...]
leg in the helicopter with (lef[...]
Richard Snailham and Dr Ja[...]
Kemmis.
(*SES*)

happened and our joint patrol continued. Several times, we dived down to examine unusual shapes in the water, but they were just sediment. 'High wind is bad for us,' said Enzo, as he swung the great silver craft around over Fort Augustus and headed home up the loch into the freshening breeze. With engines droning, the airship slid over the rippling waters 500 feet below. By the time the white-walled cottages of Dores appeared on our port bow, the wind had gone but as we began to climb over the Caledonian Canal we saw trouble ahead. Visible beyond the swaying mooring lines that dangled from our nose was a rising grey wall that stretched from the treetops into the sky – a bank of mist rolling in from the North Sea, brought by the easterly breeze. I could see from Enzo's expression that he was none too happy. Behind me, Richard looked up from his notes and raised an eyebrow. The scientists peered out into the swirling cotton wool as the mist began to envelope us and the engine note changed as we slowed. Enzo pulled the vertical elevator wheel back and the mooring lines swung in to meet us as our bulbous nose rose. The *Europa* was probing forward through the dense banks of fog at a few miles an hour. Our radio was dead; we were too far from control and Inverness Airport was now closed, but we could just hear Goodyear's base station as Enzo searched for the landing ground. It's a weird feeling to fly in mist in an airship. With windows open and the billowing vapour drifting past, I quite expected to hear a foghorn. Suddenly, to my amazement, we were level with a seagull, which overtook this monster of the skies and flew on unconcerned. 'I believe we're over the Moray Firth,' said the pilot and we dropped lower until a patch of dark green conifer forest showed briefly below. Even the trees were wreathed in white mist. 'Blimey – it's down to ground level,' muttered someone. Navigating by beacon, we knew that the airfield must be near and so we crawled forward, a few hundred feet above Inverness-shire.

We were almost on the airfield when the cloud base lifted a little and we saw the grass-edged runways. Enzo heaved the great wheel forward and our nose dipped towards the red-and-white mooring mast. Already, the ground crew was running through the long grass to seize the bowlines and guide us to the coupling. The engines gave one last triumphant roar and died. 'Phew,' said Richard. 'Quite exciting, yes?' said Enzo.

The next day was to be our last and Nessie had coyly refused to be enticed to the surface, or even within sonar range.

At 1455 hours on 7 June, I was manning our control radio in bright sunshine at Urquhart Castle, whilst *Europa* made her final sweep up the loch above the barge. It was a warm afternoon. Sally Harris had produced a good bottle of cold white wine for lunch and I was feeling that, even if we didn't see Nessie, it had been an enjoyable little expedition. Suddenly, I heard Adrian's voice in my headphones. 'Hello Zero, this is One – Contact. Over.'

'They've got a sonar target,' I yelled to Chris, whose cine camera was in action nearby. Already, a steady stream of bearings was being sent out from the barge to the airship. We could hear the higher revs of *Europa*'s engines as she closed rapidly with the barge.

By now, we could see the airship and the barge together, about a mile southwest of the Castle. The huge silver craft hovered 250 feet up, just ahead of the barge. Tim Dinsdale was on the edge of his seat, peering down, but he knew from an experiment we'd made with a submerged dustbin lid that whatever it was would have to be within three metres of the surface to be visible. In the twilight below decks the signallers tried to hold the contact in the sonar's beam. 'It was like chasing a bat on a dark night with a flashlight,' they said. For thirty minutes they kept it there, whilst it moved around the barge in a 300-yard diameter circle and, at one time, Adrian got his vessel within sixty-six yards. The horizontal display showed the target to be between forty and fifty feet below the surface, then it vanished out of range just as suddenly as it had appeared. Tim saw nothing, which at least showed it wasn't a huge bubble of gas, or a decomposing log rising from the loch bed.

We were elated and Adrian went on to get a total of thirteen major sonar contacts that year. The expedition taught us a great deal about Nessie-hunting, and we were greatly encouraged by the results. I feel that this is a very complex problem; however, by bringing together leading experts and the latest scientific techniques and equipment, we'd made an important advance. I firmly believe there is a case to answer at Loch Ness and not all those who claim to have seen something strange there can be branded as liars or alcoholics.

After the airship had departed, the *Daily Star* telephoned to ask if we'd like to try a hot-air balloon over the loch. Adrian and I had talked about this as a possible aerial observation post and I was delighted to give it a try. Greenall Whitley, a well-known brewery, kindly lent two balloons and we prepared to make the first such crossing of Loch Ness. It was all a bit of a spoof, but the volunteers had some tethered flights and it would be interesting to see how powerless aircraft got on over the loch. The plan was for the wind from the north to take us out over Castle Urquhart when we should pick up the southwest breeze to blow us along the water to the eastern end of the loch.

At dawn a cheer went up as we ascended, a union jack fluttering from the basket. It was rather like going up in a lift. Beneath, I could see Mike Gambier running after us, waving his arms and shouting. The chase Land-Rover keys were still in my pocket! I tied them to my handkerchief and dropped them, but they fell into a huge gorse bush. Mike muttered a dreadful oath. There was hardly a breath of wind as our propane gas burners sent their fiery blast into the envelope and it took twenty minutes for us to cover the two miles across the water. To demonstrate the control that was possible, our pilot touched down in mid-loch and we drifted along on the surface of the water for a few minutes before rising up again. 'How about the southwest wind?' I enquired.

The pilot looked anxious. 'There doesn't seem to be any,' he confessed, 'and we have not enough gas to get us over the mountain.'

We were drifting quite fast into some pretty inhospitable-looking hills and so we returned to the water again to get Adrian to tow us a short distance with a launch. When he released us we were opposite a convenient clearing. However, as we cleared the low fir trees beside a road we needed help on the ground and I threw down the drag rope, shouting and at a small tent that shared the clearing with a camper wagon, 'Could you grab our line, please?' The tent flap opened and an attractive, scantily dressed French girl stepped out and looked round to see where the voice had come from. For a moment she saw nothing. In the meantime, a rather older Scotsman in loosely tied striped pyjamas had emerged from the camper, rubbing his eyes and then they both saw our balloon and ran to take the dangling rope. At this point, striped pyjamas' wife, in nightie and curlers, stuck her head out of the camper window, failed to see us but found her beloved jumping about with a lightly clad blonde. French boyfriend then crawled out of the tent and, still on hands and knees, gaped in astonishment at the unbelievable scene. A nasty international incident was only avoided by the necessity for all to pull like mad to get us down safely. Suddenly the girl seemed to remember she was topless and let go, whereupon the balloon rose again lifting the Scotsman up with it. 'Hold on,' I yelled and they all pulled again. This time we landed and the balloon started to collapse across the small country road. At that moment a milk float rounded the bend and in its effort to avoid 'Greenall Whitley Beer' went into the ditch. The press, whose own balloon had landed rather more successfully nearby, then appeared and I left the scene of devastation as quickly as possible.

Despite the Falkland war, our support did not dry up and the Fort George scheme was indeed a great success. When the enterprise ended I was asked to find a number of volunteers to be interviewed by the London press; amazingly, I couldn't find any in London who were still unemployed. Eventually a few took time off work to be interviewed and nearly all of them made the point that they had got jobs because of the self-confidence gained on the course.

As I had tramped the Highlands with the volunteers I had time to reflect on the lessons learned from Operation Drake. Some of the youngsters had been disappointed that their expedition was not as vigorous as the selection process, but clearly it would have been impractical, and also unfair on the slightly less aggressively daring souls, to turn every activity into a make-or-break challenge. The YEs had ranged from hard-bitten Zimbabweans, fresh from fighting in the guerrilla war, to teenage English secretaries who had never been away from home. So it was impossible to please everyone all the time. However, the maturity and capabilities shown by many of them did surprise me and, with the wisdom of hindsight, I regret that we were not able to give them more responsibility. The older ones, certainly, could have coped very happily with it. Furthermore, they objected to being called 'Young' explorers – only those over thirty want to be called young! Only one homesick youngster out of 414 gave up!

From the point of view of communications, I owed a great deal to the Royal Signals and the companies who loaned the sets. I do not believe that any expedition has ever had such widespread links that worked so well under such adverse circumstances. To carry a briefcase-sized radio that operated on a rechargeable dry battery and with an aerial that one simply threw into a tree, and yet know that wherever we were one could usually speak to Room 5B, was very comforting.

I was also pleasantly astonished by the number of scientific discoveries that were made. Even in my most wildly optimistic moments I had never anticipated that there would be so many important breakthroughs in zoology, biology and archaeology. It just goes to show what you can do when you have a lot of highly motivated young people with good eyes and strong legs. However, we had often needed field laboratories as well.

The gloomy atmosphere of 5B was not conducive to inspired and efficient work, and yet our team, which led a mole-like existence in the cellar, soldiered on superbly. They were the ones who had to deal with the crises, absorb the bad news and fight the endless, desperate battle for funds without seeing much of the fun at the front end. Inevitably, the strain sometimes showed and I often noticed, when in the field and on top of the world because things were going well, how glum the voices sounded over the radio from Whitehall. Their only consolation was the satisfaction of knowing that without them none of it could have happened. We could have done with a few more expert sailors at HQ. I do not think that those of us on land really understood all the problems faced by the flagship and, equally, I suspect that Mike Kichenside did not really appreciate just how difficult things were when viewed from the dungeon. Perhaps Prince Charles was thinking of the fund raising when he summed up expeditions as being like banging one's head against a brick wall – and that is as true for the organisers as it is for those taking part.

In November 1979 I was based in Papua New Guinea. The rain had stopped but the heavy night air was no cooler. As I walked up the steps of our wooden office, the radio operator was scribbling messages that crackled through from England. He looked up as I entered. 'George Thurston's on, says he'd like to speak to you.'

Slipping on the earphones, I heard George's distant voice.

Never a man to waste words, he came straight to the point. 'I had breakfast with our Patron this morning.'

'Good Lord,' I said, 'Have we done something terrible?'

'Far from it. The Prince is rather pleased with progress and thinks we should do it all again on a bigger scale.'

I took a deep breath and sat down.

Later that night, sitting on the verandah and sharing a Scotch with my old schoolfriend, Nigel Porteous, I told him of the message. He said, 'Well, you'll need a bigger, faster ship.'

I listened intently while Nigel, a master mariner, put forward his ideas for a larger scale operation with a motor vessel as its flagship. Drake, Sir Walter Raleigh's cousin, had been a fiercely nationalistic privateer. Raleigh was more of an internationalist, who tried to settle a society in a New World. It was felt that the new expedition should be named after him and, by starting in 1984, it would commemorate the 400th anniversary of the founding of English-speaking America in what is now North Carolina. Prince Charles liked the name, so Operation Raleigh it was, and with the Prince as Patron, the new and greater machine ground into action.

The aim was, quite simply, to develop leadership potential in young people through their experience of the expeditions. Our hope was that they would return home to give service to others. Having witnessed the inner city riots, it was clear to me that young leaders had a far better chance of communicating with the underprivileged than older counsellors or the police. Each 'venturer', as the youngsters came to be called, would spend approximately three months in the field. Weather charts dictated that we should go west and an invitation from Sir Jack Hayward to visit the Bahamas for our first expedition proved irresistible. But our first port-of-call would be in New York and on to the very site where Raleigh's colonists had landed in 1584, then south to the Caribbean, Central and South America before crossing the Pacific to Australasia.

The scientists were fascinated by what Indonesia had had to offer and we wanted to break new ground in Japan and Tibet. There were also interesting possibilities in Pakistan. Africa, of course, could not be missed from the route of any worldwide expedition, and after that we planned to spend time in South America before returning to Britain five years later, via the wastes of Arctic Canada.

Before anything could be set in motion we needed considerable financial backing. Once again our good friend Walter Annenberg stepped into the breach and provided the necessary seed money. The next essential was a dedicated, hardworking staff that could not expect much remuneration, and a team of experts to advise us on setting up an international venture. Thanks to the generosity of IBM, a giant computer was installed in the London HQ to programme finance, logistics and venturer selection.

A worldwide recruiting and selection system was set up to find young people, aged between seventeen and twenty-five, who were fit, compatible, spoke English (for safety reasons) and could swim well. They also needed to have leadership abilities and a willingness to place service to others before self. We planned to select a total of 1,000 venturers. There was a danger that Raleigh might become an expedition for the elite and, to offset this, our selection procedure in Britain was consciously designed to help the less privileged, who lacked only the opportunity to reach their potential. As on Operation Drake, this process included an interview and, for the finalists, a weekend in the wilderness, where they were put through their paces under adverse conditions.

Publicizing Operation Raleigh in Britain began with a special television programme in which Prince Charles interviewed three ex-members of Operation Drake. His Royal Highness then called for volunteers. Candidates were advised to apply to any branch of the Trustee Savings Bank, the only bank with branches in every part of the United Kingdom.

As with any non-profit making organization, fund-raising was vital to our success. Although our commercial director, David King, and his friends in the City were striving to raise as much sponsorship as possible, the venturers themselves would help to fund the expedition. We calculated that if 4,000 young people brought in $5000 each, the expedition would have $20 million to spend over four years.

Applications poured in and the selection process went into full swing. Once again, eager youngsters faced the giant python in darkened rooms, handled hairy tarantulas and were made wet, cold, hungry, frightened and furious by turns so that we could discover just how well they would get on together. We also found many large companies prepared to send employees with us as part of their personal development policy.

Two vessels were acquired to support the enterprise. Our search for a sail training ship led us to discover the brigantine *Zebu*. She had begun life in a small, busy Swedish shipyard in 1938 and spent the next thirty-five years carrying cargoes across the Baltic. During World War II she smuggled arms for resistance movements and refugees. In 1980 she had foundered in a severe storm in the Channel Islands and then a young couple, Nick and Jane Broughton, bought her and *Zebu*'s new life began. We found our support ship in Hull. A 1,900-tonne former factory vessel, built in West Germany in 1965, she had been converted into a North Sea oil exploration vessel, equipped with submersibles. She still retained the distinctive features of a stern trawler and the massive A-frame across her afterdeck, originally used to haul nets up a sloping stern ramp, could lift mini-subs. Her cavernous hold could stock expedition supplies and the former submarine base could be converted to house landing craft. Owned by J. Marr & Sons of Hull, it was Hull City Council and the Department of the Environment who bought her for us. Her new name became *Sir Walter Raleigh* or *SWR* for short. Many companies offered to help equip her and a refit committee was formed in Hull under the driving force of Councillor Jim Mulgrove. The people of the city soon took the ship to their hearts, no one more so than Alan Marr, the enthusiastic Chairman of J. Marr & Sons. I invited Mike Kichenside to join us again and captain the ship.

As the United States committee had been allocated forty per cent of the venturer places, I paid particular attention to their problems. The determination and persistence of Ann Smith and Mark Bensen in North Carolina held Operation Raleigh USA together, and around the globe other marvellous friends gave up their time to help. On the operational front we were desperately short of qualified staff. Encouraged by the Prince of Wales, the US Defence Secretary, Caspar Weinberger, kindly agreed to second members of the American armed forces. Australia, New Zealand. Panama and Portugal followed suit.

In January 1984 the Prime Minister, The Rt. Hon. Margaret Thatcher, was our guest of honour at a luncheon organised by David King. Mrs Thatcher and her husband, Denis, became keen supporters. It was thanks to Denis Thatcher's powers of persuasion that many oil companies helped finance the running costs of the flagship. Whilst David worked flat out at the fund raising, I concentrated on expedition planning and logistics. The lights in our HQ, now at London's St Katherine's Dock, were rarely out.

There were local difficulties in approaching the proposed host countries for various projects. All the liaison and reconnaissance teams who toured the world did sterling work but I found that, in dealing with the US in particular, the greatest difficulty was getting the inhabitants of one state to cooperate with those of another.

I made many visits to Texas, where Prince Charles had played polo and had sown the seeds of the idea for Operation Raleigh. On one trip I arrived to be given complimentary accommodation in a luxury downtown hotel. I had been flying all day and was tired. The thought of dinner with thirty guests was distracting, so, as I was ushered to my penthouse suite by the proud manager, it was not easy to demonstrate an appropriate amount of enthusiasm. He rushed about singing the praises of the hifi, the TV, the fridge full of champagne, the four-poster bed and other accessories that, had I been paying for it, would have cost me $400 per night! Finally, there came the tour of the bathroom, by which time I was barely awake. The taps were golden and there was even a golden razor; but the only device that really intrigued me appeared to be called the 'gazooza'. The manager eventually backed out, smiling, and I was left with the four-poster bed, the champagne, the fruit and the 'gazooza'.

Now cursing the forthcoming dinner, I undressed and was heading for the shower when I decided that the 'gazooza' might make an interesting alternative. Bottles of perfumed bath essence were at hand and, vaguely remembering the manager's instructions, I climbed into the empty bath and anointed myself with one of these pungent preparations. It seemed the next move was to turn on a golden tap on the wall, which I did. There were a few seconds delay, during which time I gazed about in anticipation. I didn't have long to wait. Without warning, jets of icy cold water erupted from at least six points, some of which unfortunately were directly beneath me. Immediately the bath oil, with which I was covered, produced a swirling mass of bubbles. Unable to withstand one particular jet that was giving me an involuntary enema, I tried to escape only to be struck in the face by another geyser. The water was now painfully hot and the steam level had increased to such a degree that I could no longer find any means to turn the confounded thing off. By a Herculean effort I slithered over the edge of the bath, but attempts at standing were thwarted by the bath oil and I fell flat on my back. Whilst lying winded in this ridiculous posture, I perceived a charming black maid in her sixties peering at me through the steam.

'You gotta problem, sir?' she enquired.

'Turn the bloody thing off, please!' I cried.

By now the entire room was one gigantic bubble bath and I was slipping and sliding around the floor like a stranded sea lion. The maid calmly pressed a well-concealed button and handed me a towel. I glanced at my watch and realised that within ten minutes I had to be making a major speech to an elite Houston audience. As I muttered some heartfelt thanks my heroine left, saying, 'Yessir, those jacuzzi can be mighty dangerous – you'd never get me in one.' James Bond films thrive on such scenes.

Whilst raising support in Australia, David King and I visited many schools. At Scotch College in Perth we were accommodated in a room off a boys' dormitory, the pupils all being on holiday. Following a splendid dinner with the headmaster, we returned to our quarters and I tried to make a credit card call on a school phone to Britain. It was imperative that I get through, but the telephone had no number on it and although I was using a valid credit card, the operator simply refused to connect me unless I gave her the number from which I was speaking. In desperation I cried. 'What would you do in a real emergency. Suppose an airliner dropped on this place?' After several minutes' pleading and explaining who I was and that I must speak to the Ministry of Defence in London, she very reluctantly connected me.

Back in the room. David was already in bed when I returned, ranting about the Australian telephone system. I was about to turn out the light when the door burst open and the room filled with burly policemen. Seeing two middle-aged gentlemen tucked up in the boys' room, they looked rather surprised.

'Well now,' said a bull of a sergeant who was carrying a shotgun. 'Which one of you lovely geezers claims he's Colonel John Blashford-Snell?'

'That's me,' I retorted.

'I don't suppose you have an MoD Identity Card by any chance,' he rasped sarcastically. I produced it and he looked perplexed. 'Blimey,' he said to his colleague. 'I do believe it is him.' 'And who is this then?' he asked pointing at David, who passed an impressive little blue folder over.

'Superintendent King, Interpol,' he stammered.

'Gentlemen, I'm very sorry to bother you. There seems to be some misunderstanding,' and they were gone.

'The old card comes in useful sometimes,' yawned David, who had indeed been a police officer. Next day we learned a lunatic was at large in Perth and had murdered several people. He often disguised himself as a serviceman! The telephone operator had alerted the police. I often wonder what on earth the Australian Coppers' report must have said!

As D-Day approached there was one little problem that no one seemed able to solve. The Prince had mentioned it to a defence minister; generals had muttered about it in the Rag; and Judith reminded me of it daily. Who was to look after my salary? Four and a half years was rather too long for the hard-pressed Finance branch at the MoD to pay a colonel whilst on an expedition. Raleigh simply couldn't afford it. When I was preparing to sell my house, a staff officer called me. 'We've just had a memo from 10 Downing Street,' he told me. 'It just says: "Blashford-Snell, pay him".'

On 4th September 1984, Her Royal Highness Princess Alexandra won everyone's hearts when she commissioned the ship in bright sunshine. We were almost ready.

Zebu was the first to depart and on 11 October 1984 she sailed from Tower Pier, London, with arch sea-goon Sir Harry Secombe at the helm for a few minutes. Aboard were sixteen venturers and nine professional crew members under the watchful eye of Captain Peter Masters. 'America next stop,' cried Sir Harry as her square sails filled and she left for the open sea and four years of adventure.

Meanwhile, in Hull, field director Charlie Daniel, with whom I had shared exciting times in Oman, was working his teams around the clock to have *SWR* ready for departure on 13 November. By the dawn of that day miracles had been achieved and the Prince of Wales gave us a wonderful send-off. To the cheers of a large crowd, *Sir Walter Raleigh* sailed for New York by way of the Channel Islands. As with Operation Drake, it was a close-run thing. Even as the Prince was speaking to the crowds from the upper deck, welding was in progress on the other side of the ship!

15

Operation Raleigh

New York gave us a great welcome, and, thanks to the Prince of Wales being interviewed by Barbara Walters on her *Twenty-Twenty* TV show, eleven million Americans heard all about the operation. The phone lines to our US office in Raleigh, North Carolina, were jammed.

The North Atlantic in November is no place for fair weather sailors and it had been a crossing few would ever forget. Four hundred miles out from Britain the sea was spectacular and, as the ship rolled and pitched, spume blew off the wave tops in the biting wind. The course was taking her straight into the seas, so that she surfed down one roller then came to an almost complete shuddering stop as the bow vanished into the next in a cloud of spray with fifty-foot waves breaking right over her. Suddenly a particularly violent roll hurled one of our two landing craft off its rails in the stern hangar. The situation was serious: about eleven tons of craft with two Suzuki vehicles on its deck was being swung around like a toy. The chains that had held it in place had come loose and had to be tensioned before any serious damage was done. After several hours most of the movement had been controlled using blocks, and it was safe to reach the chains between the two craft without running the risk of being crushed to death. Later, when the weather abated, came the task of jacking the trolley back up onto its rails. Later the third Officer, Chris Mahoney, went off forward to the heads and suddenly rushed back into the mess and grabbed the fire extinguisher. He had been steadying himself when the ship rolled and had burnt his hand on the bulkhead; all the clothes in the drying room had caught fire after a waterproof fell on top of the heater. The plastic clothing was giving off acrid fumes and the heat was intense. Nearby cabins were evacuated and it took two extinguishers to get the blaze under control.

Next day the disasters continued. Charlie Nicklin and Ted Seymour were doubling up all the wires and chains on the landing craft after the emergency job the previous night. Conditions in the hangar deck were uncomfortable, with the freezing wind howling around and water splashing across the deck. Matters were made worse by the fact that the massive hydraulically operated stern gates were not completely closed. Using a crowbar, Ted was holding them together while Charlie attempted to lash them securely. With the movement of the ship this was proving difficult, and suddenly an ear-piercing scream filled the hangar deck. Charlie had got his thumb caught between the gates and they slammed shut completely squashing it. Jane Dunbar, the ship's Orcadian doctor, had the unpleasant task of stitching the stump together. A fuel leak was only stopped by Charlie Daniel and a muscular Territorial Army lass, Cathy Davies, lying on their backs in several inches of oil and water in the bilges to remove a pipe.

Another fault was repaired in New York, while in harbour, with the festive season in full swing, Chase Manhattan, one of our enthusiastic sponsors, held their Christmas party on board and many members of the Explorers' Club came along. We all felt rather proud of the SES's Scientific Exploration Ship.

Rolling banks of freezing fog greeted us on arrival in North Carolina where a banner read 'Welcome Sir Walter, you're only 400 years late', but the Southern hospitality and the bonanza of gifts, including four twenty-one foot Carolina skiffs, more than made up for the weather.

It was now time to start the land operations and after a quick call at Miami to pick up incoming Venturers we sailed into Grand Bahama Harbour to be met by 'Union Jack' Hayward and his Port Manager, John Hinchliffe. The sky was blue and the sun shone as we got down to a host of scientific and conservation projects on land and underwater.

We were joined by a group of American juvenile delinquents from an organisation called Vision Quest. My colleagues thought I'd taken leave of my senses when I invited these young criminals to join us, but it was an amazing success. They arrived aboard the

Vision Quest's schooner *Western Union* and were quickly integrated into our team, helping to create a new national park. Most of them had suffered as a result of child abuse and responded very favourably to kindness and understanding. Our Venturers became their big brothers and sisters.

The main underwater project in the Bahamas was a coral reef survey on which we tested an amazing sub-igloo, a clear perspex underwater house, kindly loaned to us by our Canadian chairman and leading diving expert, Dr Joe MacInnes. Eight feet in diameter, this air-filled sphere enabled up to three divers to swap information on the seabed. We assembled Iggy in fifty feet of water off Grand Bahama, the main problem being that it needed nine tons of ballast to hold it down. Mark Bensen solved that by rummaging around the island for some old car engines to cut up. They made our smart igloo look a bit unsightly, but they did the trick and Iggy proved a fascinating and useful addition to our equipment. It provided a few surprises, too. Early one morning two divers went down to prepare for the day's activities and found to their surprise that Iggy was already occupied; staring out at them was a large barracuda. The American Venturer, by graphic demonstration, urged on his British Colleague to grab the fish by its tail and pull it out, 'See, like that, easy.' To his utter astonishment, he did, and got away with it. The barracuda then promptly chased the American!

But there were also hazards above the surface. We had with us a Recce Section of the Royal Scots Dragoon Guards led by David Allfrey, a most resourceful officer. One of his corporals was strolling quietly back to his quarters, having enjoyed a convivial evening in a waterside bar, when he was set upon by three thugs armed with knives. In spite of his short stature he was immensely strong and possessed a high qualification in martial arts. Experience in the back streets of Glasgow had fitted him well for such an encounter, but even I was surprised when the local police phoned to say they had arrested him for causing grievous bodily harm to three peace-loving Bahamians. It later transpired that when the first robber had attacked, the NCO had seized him by the ankles and used him as a club to down the others. Then he had knocked on the door of an expatriate's house and asked if he might telephone the police so that his assailants, none of whom could walk, might be retrieved from the roadway. However, the Bahamas were overrun with drug smugglers and there were several occasions when I thought *SWR*'s well-stocked armoury might come in handy.

Our flagship proved her worth when conducting amphibious operations. The Merseyside County Council had built us two robust water jet powered landing craft, *Prince William* and *Prince Henry*, and they gave us the capability to land stores over beaches. Two Avon seariders could cope with really heavy weather and we also had a fleet of alloy assault boats, inflatables and skiffs.

On 31 December 1984 we were landing a party on the reef strewn shore of Cat Island. Although the sun was bright, a heavy swell was running and each roller threatened to slam the landing craft up against the ship's hull. Most of the Tac HQ staff were also helmsmen, as were the ship's officers, so we took turns at driving the boats. It was really exhilarating and everyone came back wet and smiling. I adored handling the seariders and apparently reminded everyone of 'Mr Toad'. Although everything went surprisingly smoothly, despite the swell, unloading proved a slow process. As the day wore on it became clear the job wouldn't be finished before dark, so a lithesome, bikini-clad Venturer was commissioned as a mobile, nubile lighthouse. Given a flashlight, she was sent to stand on the rocky headland to guide craft in. At 2130 hours the wind freshened. It was imperative that the flagship sailed at dawn to make the next rendezvous so the message went to the party ashore: 'Sorry – you've had your lot – see you in a month.'

'OK. We'll manage,' they sent back, 'and, by the way, Happy New Year.'

We had quite forgotten it was New Year's Eve, and had also quite forgotten about the mobile, nubile lighthouse, still flashing away from the headland. However, Charlie Daniel, gallant as ever, took the big searider, *St George*, and went in to collect the poor girl, who was frozen stiff and very hungry. As she waded out to the boat, a water snake slithered across her feet! Oh, well, at least it was a little different from the London solicitors' office where she usually worked. After that, the New Year was well and truly celebrated, many times over, as it occurred in all the home countries of those present. Amazingly, the ship stayed on course and I took the opportunity to telephone our World President, Walter Annenberg, in California, via satellite, and exchanged greetings with the guests at his party, which included the President of the United States!

Meanwhile, having taken a southerly route across, *Zebu* was now supporting a diving team searching for lost treasure ships in the Turks and Caicos. It was hoped a major discovery would boost the economy of these impoverished islands. With them was Keith Jessop, who had gained fame and become a millionaire after his successful recovery of the gold from HMS *Edinburgh*, sunk off the coast of Russia in 1942. Keith, whose treasure hunting company had a contract with the local government, was to direct the search for wrecks along the south side of the Caicos Bank.

A great cheer went up from *Zebu* as *SWR* sailed into the anchorage. It was only on rare occasions that the two vessels met. Led by Barry Moss, who had been with me on Operation Drake in Kenya, the Turks and Caicos expedition was very successful. The divers found no fewer than fourteen wrecks. Although none carried gold, they did discover one cargo of copper coins and numerous cannon and also salvaged a complete fifteen-foot USAF target plane that bore the interesting but, as it turned out, totally untrue legend: 'Finder Will Be Rewarded!'

The scientific research had gone well. There had been some interesting caving, the old Militia building on Grand Turk had been renovated and a basketball court for the locals had been constructed at Bottle Creek. A large supply of sports equipment, collected in Britain, had been presented to the local high school and it was obvious that the expedition had made quite an impact on this little community. I was especially pleased that things had gone so well as this was our first major Raleigh expedition to be led by an ex-Young Explorer. There had been a great many difficulties for Barry to overcome, not least avoiding complications caused by drug trafficking in the islands. As we left, we heard that the Chief Minister and several colleagues had been arrested in Miami for drug-related offences!

Thanks to Dr Armand Hammer, Occidental Petroleum had kindly offered to bunker the ship if we called in at Galveston and thus a few weeks later we enjoyed a brief visit to Texas. The hospitality was overwhelming and when we docked, Charlie Daniel, who had flown ahead, was there to greet us with lorries loaded with provisions and an escort of long-limbed ladies.

Our next series of expeditions were in Belize and Honduras. Once again *SWR* was invaluable in supporting the land based teams, but Mike Kichenside had already warned me that it would be a tricky operation at the entrance to the Black River on the infamous Mosquito Coast. As far back as the 1700s the Black River bar had garnered for itself a reputation as a graveyard. In 1732 a handful of English colonists had tried to establish themselves here. A small British enclave on an otherwise Hispanic coast, the ill-fated colony had twice been burned and then finally abandoned. I stared across the line of breakers to where the shore lay, a thin swathe of jungle pressed beneath a sky of leaden grey.

We anchored around 3 pm. It had taken us some time to locate the narrow break in the bar that marked the lagoon entrance. Guiding ourselves in by the smoke of an unseen village, we spotted the two bright orange panel markers set up by our advance party. Having been here on an earlier recce, I took an Avon searider to gauge the strength of the surf and land a small beach team who would provide shore support and radio communication during the unloading. It was a rough trip, but the boat handled well, climbing high over the top of one wave to slam down into the trough of the next. We rode the surf for the last 200 yards, a muddied green surge crested in dirty white. Through the spume of the breakers I could make out brown sand to our starboard, and to port the unbroken green of mangrove. The lagoon entrance remained hidden until we were almost on top of it. We burst over the bar, scattering spray and found ourselves suddenly in quiet water. On either side the mangroves fell away to reveal clearings of palm and fruit trees and in the centre of each was a thatched-roofed hut. I turned the bow in towards one of these clearings where our advance party stood waiting. The Avon nosed in beside a row of dugouts, beaching on a narrow strip of sand that fronted the clearing and we stepped ashore onto the Mosquito Coast.

Still strewn with half-buried cannon, Fort Wellington had been built back in 1748 to command the entrance to the lagoon and protect the infant British colony from Spanish attack. After the last Britons left in 1786, it was re-christened Fuerte de la Purisima Concepcion and re-armed to defend the newly-formed Spanish settlement. Its guns, however, stood silently pointing out to sea at 2 am on the morning of 24 September 1800, when hostile Indians, under their leader General Tempest, swept out of the jungle, putting the town to the torch and massacring all but a handful of its inhabitants. It was this blood-soaked patch of ground that thirty Venturers from America, Britain, Hong Kong, Japan and Oman were to call home for the next three months.

Light was fading rapidly and there seemed little chance of our getting any stores ashore before dark. In Central America the gentle twilight of more northerly latitudes is replaced by a swift and violent sunset sliding into starlit blackness. The advance party fell asleep to the mingled roar of the howler monkeys and the surf.

For centuries rumours had circulated of a 'Lost White City' hidden deep within the mountainous jungles of Mosquita, one of the many El Dorados that haunted the early Conquistadors and lured so many of them to their deaths. Cuidad Blanca had been the subject of search and speculation for the last 400 years and local legends spoke of it lying somewhere in the 16,000 square miles of wilderness that lay over the mountains to the southeast of the expedition's camp. Our archaeologist maintained a healthy degree of scepticism, doubting that a white-walled city of palaces and temples could still exist, undiscovered, even in so remote a region. Yet even he was eager to see what ruins, if any, lay on the far side of the mountains. So a seven-member patrol set off upriver in search of 'the last great lost city of the Americas'.

They never found it. Instead, their searches revealed something in many ways more impressive. When they staggered back into base camp they brought with them reports of not one but a series of ruins, stretching from the coast to the uplands. This was to be our first indication that the Black River/Rio Paulaya region, long ignored as an archaeological backwater, had been the home of a sophisticated pre-Columbian culture similar in many respects to that of the neighbouring Maya. Experiences previously unimaginable – a patrol stumbling into a green-lit jungle clearing to face a massive stone altar and a girl wakened in the middle of the night by a puma brushing against her hammock – became everyday occurrences. They were not, however, without their price. The damp heat of the rain forest brought on jungle rot, tiny blisters that with time spread into open sores three to four inches across. Insects were a hazard too. On the coast the major problem proved to be jiggers, small flea-like animals, which burrow into the skin of the foot to lay eggs. The only effective means of removing them was to make an incision next to the white, pea-sized egg sack and then squeeze.

But in the interior the botflies were the real menace. They lay their eggs on the proboscis of mosquitos so that they can then be injected by the mosquito into a host. Once beneath the skin the tiny larva, whose head is built on the same lines as the bit of an oil drill, forces its way deeper and deeper and begins to swell until it is about the size of a maggot. We found that the only way to remove them was to smear the area with Vaseline and cover it with adhesive tape. Starved of oxygen, the larva backs out of the wound and can be drawn painfully the rest of the way.

Red-bearded Mark O'Shea, our eccentric Irish herpetologist, attracted considerable attention from the 'locals' due to his penchant for slithering under the raised floors of the local houses in search of boa constrictors. One afternoon I took him by boat into the mangroves at the edge of the lagoon. Suddenly he let out a whoop and scrambled up a tree. On the top branch two eight-foot black and yellow snakes were entwined in matrimonial bliss. Rudely interrupting, Mark seized one and dropped it down into the boat beside me, where it hissed with rage. By now the second reptile had bitten our intrepid hunter several times. However, he returned, triumphantly proclaiming his catch as 'thunder and lightening' snakes that were 'only mildly venomous'.

The archaeological and scientific work went well. We explored the former British colony of Roatan. *Zebu* was assisting this archaeological and diving project and we encouraged venturers to undertake community tasks. One young lady, a member of our Royal Family, was to hit the headlines later in life, but whilst with Operation Raleigh she was a deeply caring and hard-working girl. Marina Ogilvy decided that the little town of Coxens Hole should be cleaned up, so she painted a collection of empty oil drums blue and white and put on a message in Spanish exhorting the people to make use of her improvised rubbish bins. When I came to see her work I was met by the Mayor, in dark suit and bowler hat. Strangely, no great improvement resulted and I asked the Mayor why the rubbish was not being put in the bins. 'Well, sir,' he replied, 'see, dey is Royal trashcans and we is ordinary folk.'

In the operations centre on the ship we often heard the radio traffic of other vessels in the area. Off Black River we picked up an unusual language that seemed to be booming through from a large banana boat lying nearby and apparently talking to a station in the jungle.

'What's that?' I asked a linguist on our staff.

'Russian,' she said without looking up from the charts.

A few days later *SWR* sailed for Costa Rica to support another expedition. Having a day in hand. Mike Kichenside dropped anchor for a spot of diving at Edinburgh reef, a series of coral out-crops off the coast. Later, US military intelligence asked me if I could shed any light on a strange incident. A Nicaraguan gunboat had gone tearing out to the Edinburgh Reef to intercept what they believed to be a CIA ship, but the Hondurans, in whose territory the reef lies, were alerted to this incursion by 'spy in the sky' satel-lite. They despatched fighter aircraft and sank the gunboat. Check-ing the dates, I realised that we must have been the 'CIA Ship'.

In Costa Rica we were in a more peaceful area and I visited a science camp where one of our aerial walkways was being con-structed in the forest canopy of a wildlife reserve. Even snakes were protected here. A venturer who adored reptiles had a live *fer-de-lance* that he had rescued when it was about to be decapitated by a local. He had been keeping the snake in the British Airways day-sack with which all venturers had been issued. Alas, he could not remember which one was his! Eventually, however, the right bag was discov-ered and I took a long-range glance at the creature coiled therein. The previous week, the venturer had witnessed a Costa Rican for-estry worker, bitten by one of these potential killers, neutralize the effects of the venom by drinking an infusion made from the leaves of a local bush. Now our scientists were collecting samples of the plant in hope of isolating its medicinal properties. At another site a similar *fer-de-lance*, when not gazing libidinously at a coil of the expedition's electric cable, insisted on escorting senior research officers to the loo, which they found a trifle off-putting!

Keith Hamylton-Jones, who led this expedition, was a former British Ambassador in the country. When I visited him in San Jose, his HQ was packed with venturers, so one afternoon we sought the peace and quiet of a nightclub to hold a meeting to discuss the science programme. Maps were spread across the tables and the scientists presented their problems. The proprietor brought beer and we became absorbed with the conservation of the rainforest. Time went by and when the club opened, topless bar girls wan-dered over to see what it was that so distracted four bronzed explorers. Growing weary, the ladies chose to sit on the laps of several of my colleagues. When I asked one of our number if he could, in simple biological terms, describe the importance of his research programme, he sighed, 'Just look at those nipples.' The meeting was then adjourned.

Another expedition had returned to Caledonia Bay, where, with great skill, Mike edged *SWR* in between the reefs to anchor clear of the sandfly and mosquito-ridden shore. There were some old buildings on the airstrip and two Panamanian soldiers had come ahead to clean out the vegetation. But to my horror I found that the walls had been knocked flat, leaving the expedition homeless. 'You blithering idiots,' I tried to say in Spanish, 'all we wanted you to do was tidy the place up.'

The men looked grave and waving their arms cried, 'Boom, boom!'

Eventually an interpreter arrived and explained, 'They're trying to tell you a big earthquake collapsed the buildings yesterday.'

More work on *Olive Branch* brought up bones from the salt beef barrels that the Cuna thought were human and this nearly caused a major upset. We also lifted three cannon onto *SWR* and decided to take one back to the Panama Museum. As we chipped away at the coral encrustations, there was a loud hissing and the unmistakable stench of gunpowder. We backed away, as, with a 'poop', a cannon ball appeared at the end of the barrel. The release of pressure on the breach when the gun was raised from a depth of thirty feet had caused it to be forced forward.

At Acla we discovered the foundations of a circular tower that is believed to be the oldest European stone structure yet unearthed on the American mainland and this caused international interest. I was preparing to take the British Ambassador, Terry Steggle, and some friends down to see this when an emergency message flashed through to the Ops Centre. Michael Williams, a British venturer, had been sliding down a grass slope on a Colombian island when he had pitched over a ledge and gone headfirst into a rock, sustaining terrible injuries. General Jack Galvin, the region's US Commander, was a good friend of General Mogg's and, thankfully, he had instructed his staff to give us every support, so when I called for a Medevac, a USAF C130 loaded with doctors was on its way in minutes. Meanwhile Terry handled the diplomatic clearances required to fly a British casualty from a Colombian island to Panama in an American aircraft.

Initially the first aid administered by his colleagues kept him alive until the Colombian emergency services could take over, but as we stood around the flagship radio, I saw our senior medical officer, Jane Dunbar, was looking grim. 'He hasn't much of a chance,' she confided, as our US Navy radio officer recorded the details of Michael's deteriorating condition. We needed a top brain surgeon if Michael were to live. I remembered meeting one at a Kiwanis Club lunch and called my pal, Billy St Malo, who raced out in his speedboat to collect the man from a holiday island and got him to the airfield just as the C130 touched down. It was this timely rescue and the skill of the Panamanian surgeon, still in his shorts, that saved Michael's life.

For our next phase, both ships passed through the Panama Canal, *Zebu* sailing on to Hawaii and *SWR* to Peru, where she arrived just as a customs strike was starting. The result was that all the rations and stores were held in bond. Nevertheless, we gave them fifty cents per venturer per day and told them to get on with the projects. Living off the land, they achieved miracles of improvisation and, after several months, when the food was eventually released, the up-country teams said, 'Don't send it. We're enjoying the challenge.'

A new team of US servicemen arrived and amongst them was a Yeoman of Signals. 'You're just the chap to sort out my UHF problems,' I said as he put down his bags. He looked a little blank and, knowing there were often different nomenclatures used by our nations, I explained the difficulties with our Ultra High Frequency ship-to-aircraft radio. He still looked puzzled so I said, 'Well, I expect you will be used to much more sophisticated equipment in the US Navy.'

'I don't use any of this gear,' he said slowly.

'What do you use?' I asked.

'Flags,' he replied.

So now I was without a Chief Signaller, but he made a good public relations officer.

Originally I'd planned only three expeditions in Chile, but after seeing the excellent opportunities open to us amid the mountains and fjords of the south, this was extended to four. However, due to the severity of the southern winter, our first three-month expedition was to take place in Chile's northern regions, an area which surely must rank among the world's wonders. Soaring volcanoes, stark lava fields and huge, rolling dunes make a startling contrast to a seemingly endless desert. The immense Atacama stretches for over 600 miles, with many vast areas where it has never rained in recorded history.

Alas, our first Chilean phase threatened to begin badly. Many of the proposed projects never materialized or fell through only days before the expedition's arrival. Perhaps the Chilean committee had expected too much of us, coming, as they saw it, from a host of relatively wealthy nations. There were other problems. The country is divided into twelve regions, each virtually self-governing, and we soon discovered that arrangements made in Santiago are not always effective 1,500 miles away. Planning ahead in South American countries doesn't always ensure the expected end result, and we were confronted daily with what came to be called the 'South American factor'.

Thankfully, the problem of our providing suitable tasks was solved by the National Park Organization, who, having a surfeit of work and a very tight budget, welcomed our offer of labour with open arms and stepped in at the last moment with new projects throughout Chile. Our expedition extended for almost 1,000 miles, covering sixteen project sites, and the barren, almost uninhabited, northern wasteland made the distances seem even greater. Furthermore, to the discomfort of several venturers who'd brought clothes designed for perhaps more predictable desert weather, the Atacama was freezing cold.

By now *SWR* was anchored off the small port of Mejillones, with a mixed crew of British Army, Portuguese, and US Navy personnel, plus our splendid merchant seamen. Wide beaches and spectacular rock formations stretched along a coast that reverberated to the roar of explosions as the local dynamite factory tested its wares. Oddly, these blasts seemed to have no effect on the pelicans whirling sleepily and endlessly above the ship in the clear, cold air. Fat sea lions barked at our divers, seeming to invite them in for a swim, so they were delighted when we started on an oceanographic survey of the bay, clearly under the impression that the supply of human playmates had been laid on for their benefit.

The flagship was due a refit and, working ahead of us as usual,

David Allfrey had discovered that at Puerto Montt in Southern Chile there was a shipyard where labour costs were $1 per man per day. Thus I set up Tac HQ in a rented house in Antofagasta and despatched *SWR* south. Nick Horne, my highly efficient Operations Officer, linked us by radio to the expeditions in Peru, Bolivia and Northern Chile, so the work started. I had arranged to pre-dump material for the projects and David Allfrey's Scottish soldiers went around depositing the necessary rations and equipment. Speaking Spanish in thick Glaswegian accents, they had left strict instructions with one particular mayor and a local cafe owner, in whose store they left everything, that 'on pain of death' they were not to mention to anyone the whereabouts of the kit, except, of course, to people like themselves.

Three weeks later a group, under the leadership of an Australian Army officer, arrived to begin their project and collect the stores. Despite enquiries in best Sydney Spanish, no one in the village would admit to any knowledge of them. Not surprisingly, frantic messages flashed across Chile and, believing that everything had been stolen, I contacted the regional commander. Troops were despatched forthwith, police ordered to investigate, and the entire village was subjected to a veritable inquisition. At last the stores were discovered, exactly where the recce team had left them.

'Se Escosia say we are to tell no one,' explained the perplexed mayor, 'except people like them – and they were very fierce men.'

Many centuries ago the remote desert oasis of San Pedro de Atacama had been the centre of a flourishing Paleolithic civilization based within impressive rock fortresses built upon the steep mountains that almost completely encircle the green valley. Thousands of ancient graves scattered throughout the hills were beginning to yield their secrets. An extraordinary museum, set up by the late Father Gustave Le Paige, contains numerous mummies, skulls, stone-age tools, jewellery, weapons and wood carvings. The mummies, many with their hair intact, were found still clad in their fine burial clothes.

Directed by local archaeologists, we helped with the excavations and in fifteen days recovered twenty-nine pre-Colombian mummies, many perfectly preserved. It was fascinating work. Discoveries included the graves of important warriors, buried with their weapons and a llama, presumably as food for the afterlife. Some men carried a pouch of drug-taking implements on their belts! One of our most extraordinary finds was a large basket containing an earthenware pot which, when opened, held a cake at least 1,500 years old. Later we were to explore nineteenth-century battlefields, where the arid, salty soil had preserved the dead exactly as they had been buried in their uniforms. However, there were also lethal relics of earlier border wars and poorly marked minefields were a constant hazard if one strayed from a well-used track.

In September 1985 we moved south down the enormously long, thin country to rejoin *SWR*. Chilean lakeland is one of the least spoilt places on earth. Stretching for hundreds of miles, scores of emerald lakes glitter amidst beautiful mountains. This is a land of snow-capped volcanoes, deep woodland meadows and small peaceful villages. There are flowers by the acre, great pine forests and awe-inspiring waterfalls. Puerto Montt, capital of the region, lies on a flat plain beside Reloncavi Bay, overlooked by the perfect cone of the Orsono Volcano. Here our flagship lay at anchor, already swarming with eager Chilean workers, hammering, scraping, painting and welding.

The next expedition, still under New Zealand SAS Major Stuart Grey, had its HQ a further 400 miles south at the sprawling frontier city of Coyhaique, capital of Chile's eleventh and least known region. Referred to locally as the 'End of the Earth', the wild, untamed beauty of Chile's Austral zone is breathtaking, a rugged extravagance of nature. Blue glaciers, mirror-black lakes, snowfields, ragged rows of mountain ranges and volcanoes join a seemingly endless coast of bays, channels, inlets, fjords and islands. Flying high above this splendid wilderness, I saw few traces of man – just a lone track, perhaps, and maybe an isolated Indian hut or fishing village. This was real frontier country, as the American West must once have been. Over a third of all Chile lies here, yet this immense wilderness holds less than three per cent of its population. The incredible terrain, the weather and the miles of uninhabited land offered us wonderful opportunity for adventure. Situated at the northern tip of the Patagonian Icefield, the massive glacier of San Rafael, isolated and wild, provided an awesome setting for one of our southerly projects. The only building amidst this wilderness was an abandoned hotel offering a spectacular view of the glacier but left empty by the lack of visitors and this became one of our bases.

Following their successful project with us in Panama, Dr Harry Brown came again from California with his SEE International ophthalmic team to operate on cataract victims. Thanks to Charlie Daniel's excellent work in Santiago, the customs passed through the nineteen boxes of medical equipment without comment and within a few days the team were hard at work in the expedition area. With co-operation from a local Chilean opthalmic surgeon and assisted by venturers, Harry and his colleagues set about their sight-restoring mission. In four days of intensive surgery, often working for sixteen hours at a stretch, they gave back sight to seventeen people and provided hundreds of pairs of free spectacles to poor people who would never normally have such a service. It was a rewarding feeling to be part of such a humane project.

There were some strange incidents. One ninety-year-old gentleman was led back to bed after his cataract operation by an attractive American venturer, Linda Walters. As soon as he was between the sheets he muttered something, leapt up, grabbed Linda and gave her a smacking great kiss. Not understanding Spanish, she asked someone whether he was trying to express his thanks for the operation.

'Oh no,' said a Chilean nurse, 'he just likes pretty girls and now he can see them again.' An elderly lady examined by Harry's wife Baillie was found to be wearing spectacles fitted with plain glass. She cheerfully confessed they did her no good – she simply wore them because she wanted to follow the trend!

After one session I showed a video film I had made of this intricate micro-surgery to the crew, but the sight of it in Technicolor was too much for all but the most hardened. However, the Chileans really appreciated our assistance and all the tasks being done for the impoverished pioneers of this challenging land and we received much hospitality. Knowing I enjoyed shooting, the locals invited me on a boar hunt, saying that if I would provide the weapons, they would find horses and hounds. So it was that Pablo Calderon, our liaison officer, and I flew to an isolated, but beautiful lakeside community known as Lago Verde.

The mayor, a twenty-five-year-old graduate of Santiago University, accommodated us in his simple wooden cottage and everyone gathered to admire the rifles and shotguns I had brought along. I could have sold my .357 Smith & Wesson revolver for a huge price. That night a pre-hunt party was held in the village hall. Apparently

I was the first Briton they had seen and, whilst some of the loveliest ladies I have ever met flirted outrageously with me, the men folk toasted Mrs Thatcher and suggested all sorts of horrors they would like to inflict on General Galtieri. By 4 am few were sober, and as we were to start at dawn I slipped away to prepare the guns.

To my astonishment the hunt did assemble roughly on time. Sad, shaggy horses with sheepskin saddle cloths stood in the drizzle as we mounted up. A pack of ferocious dogs skulked around us, snapping and snarling. The carabineros and I dished out weapons and ammunition and then we were off, looking for all the world like a John Wayne posse. A hundred yards beyond the last house a lone goose flew over our heads and with a roar like the opening barrages of El Alamein the Chileans discharged everything they had at it, from the saddle. Chaos ensued as their terrified mounts reared and bolted, some depositing their riders amongst the hounds that tore round in circles biting each other in the absence of anything else to kill. It was a pure miracle that no one was shot.

Once the hunters had caught their horses and the dogs had been lashed into silence we reassembled. It was quite clear that our ideas on hunting did not correspond, so via Pablo I delivered a short speech praising their spirit and courage and recommending some weapon training.

'But in England you hunt with the horse and the dog,' they argued.

'Yes, but not with the gun too,' I explained. 'We shoot on foot.'

'Chileans go nowhere on foot,' retorted an old sage.

However, we progressed and by noon had shot a couple of ducks, two hares and one of the hounds.

'Now we eat,' cried the Mayor as we flopped down beneath some convenient firs to sip mate tea and drink litres of heavy red wine, which had been held in great green demi-johns on the packhorses. The mayor's groom had plucked the ducks as he rode and roasted them with commendable speed. In the early evening we sighted a boar and, with a fusilade of shots, the field galloped after it. Pablo and I decided pursuit was pointless and dangerous and walked our horses to the night stop. One by one the hunters came in, scratched to blazes by the thorn and with a host of tales. The pig, clearly a jet-propelled monster, had finally eluded them but not before it had charged them all in succession, or so the stories went. That night we ate the hare and drank more red wine around the fire whilst a vaquero mournfully strummed his guitar.

My hangover the next morning was not improved by riding into a low branch and being knocked off my horse, to howls of mirth from my colleagues. For several days we rode through brush and bamboo, higher and higher into the Andes, and then suddenly we came to a clearing across which stretched an old wire cattle fence. The expedition dismounted and, lining the fence, urinated with great relish across it. Clearly this was a custom, perhaps Chilean hunters always pee over fences, as waggoners in England would relieve themselves on the wheel of their cart, I thought. 'That's an interesting ritual,' I remarked as Pablo remounted.

'It is not a ritual,' replied my swarthy pal, 'we do that out of respect to you, Englishman. Over the fence is Argentina.'

By now Raleigh's finances were at a low ebb. In setting up the Operation we had taken bids from all countries wishing to participate. Australia had asked to send 240 venturers, Oman 100, and the United States committees, not unreasonably, had said they would like to bid for 1,500. Now, fourteen months into the venture, it was a different story. For a wide variety of perfectly understandable reasons, many of our national committees had not been able to fill their quotas, and although our expenditure was well within budget our income was falling far behind. Every possible measure had been taken to bridge the gap and we had raised the UK quota from 375 per year to 660 in the first twelve months. But there is only so much cash in dear old Britain and we simply could not generate any more funded venturers from home.

Zebu had ably supported the expedition in Hawaii, where an active volcano had rather dramatised events and our plans were well-advanced in the Pacific and Australasia. Whilst we were winning the battle at the front, we urgently needed support at the rear, and so Charlie Daniel and I returned to Britain to spend the first part of 1986 supporting our overworked CHQ.

On a boiling hot Christmas Day the venturers of the second Chilean expedition poured onto the flagship for a momentous party. Fit, happy and confident, with new-found friends and a host of tales to tell, they'd soon be on their way home. With the day drawing to a close, an American pastor joined me in conducting a carol service on deck. I managed to distract his eyes from the bow where some scandalous female venturers were sunbathing topless. In the service we took the theme of peace on earth and recited Sir Francis Drake's prayer:

> O Lord God, when thou givest to thy servants to endeavour any great matter, grant us to know that it is not the beginning but the continuing of the same unto the end, until it be thoroughly finished, which yieldeth the true glory: through him who for the finishing of thy work laid down his life, our Redeemer Jesus Christ. Amen.

As the last carol died away across the sunlit blue waters, I was reminded that this was just the end of Operation Raleigh's beginning. There were still three years to run and many, many more young people around the world to take up the challenge.

16

•

Around the World

'Never fear my boys, we'll all go to hell together.'

These words of encouragement, growled by HMS *Pandora*'s master of arms early one August morning in 1791, were almost the last that the imprisoned mutineers from the *Bounty* ever heard. But as the ship that held the captives began to sink to her grave on the Great Barrier Reef, the boatswain's mate opened the wooden cell and most of the men scrambled out and plunged into the foaming ocean.

This great saga of the sea had begun in 1787 when HMS *Bounty* was sent to Tahiti to collect breadfruit plants for the growing slave population in the Caribbean. Finding the attractions of the Tahitian ladies greater than service under the infamous Captain William Bligh, the British sailors seized the ship and started the most notorious mutiny in naval history.

Led by Fletcher Christian, the mutineers put Bligh and eighteen loyal crew into an open boat off the island of Tonga. Then they sailed back to Tahiti, where the 'pirates' rejoined their ladies, many of whom were pregnant. However, Christian, with eight shipmates and a number of local men and women, sailed to Pitcairn, an uninhabited island, which, he knew, was wrongly marked on the charts. Their chances of ever being found were slight, but they set fire to the ship as a precaution and, as far as the world knew, it had simply disappeared.

Perhaps maligned as a leader of men, Captain Bligh was, however, an acknowledged master of the sea. Set adrift in an open boat, he and his crew reached Timor in forty-one days, having navigated *Bounty*'s tiny launch 3,618 nautical miles through terrible seas and

– 308 –

the Great Barrier Reef. Their bold sea run is still a record. On return to England, Bligh acquainted their Lordships of the Admiralty with the news of his ship's fate. They were not amused. Meanwhile, Fletcher Christian's paradise had soured. Quarrels with the Polynesians led to blows and all save two sailors were killed By 1808, when the first ship called at Pitcairn, only one Englishman was alive to tell the tale, kept company by a large 'family' of women and the descendants of shipmates. These were the founders of the colony that exists to this day, and to whom our flagship, *Sir Walter Raleigh*, brought much-needed supplies and fuel in August 1986. It was a strange fact that as our gleaming 2,000-ton exploration vessel rode at anchor in the turquoise seas of the tropical isle, she was linked through history to the wreck of the *Bounty* eight fathoms below, since the home port of both ships was the city of Hull.

In 1790 the Royal Navy had come to investigate the *Bounty*'s disappearance. HMS *Pandora*, a twenty-four-gun frigate captained by Edward Edwards, arrived at Tahiti in November and found the fourteen mutineers foolish enough to have remained in their love nest. They were dragged aboard *Pandora*, clapped in irons and incarcerated on deck in a hastily created wooden cell, called *Pandora*'s box, with only two small gratings, secured by bolts. The heat was so intense that the sweat 'ran in streams to the scuppers and soon produced maggots .... ' They had little chance to bid fond farewells to their women and children who stood in canoes holding their babies aloft, howling with grief as the man-of-war sailed for England and the inevitable courts martial. The only sign of *Bounty* was an anchor that Captain Edwards hauled aboard as evidence.

It was late in the day. Sailing for home on a westerly course, *Pandora* sought a passage through the Great Barrier Reef near what is today Cape York. She struck the knife-edged coral wall hard, hurling crew and captives alike onto the deck. During the frantic effort to save her, two of the ship's pumps broke: she sank at sunrise at a spot now known as *Pandora*'s Entrance. Thirty-one sailors and four of the mutineers drowned in the Coral Sea. The ninety-nine survivors, including ten mutineers, swam to a nearby bay where they erected sailcloth tents against the relentless sun. The mutineers had no such luxury. Their skins were lily white from five months' confinement in *Pandora*'s Box: without protection they would die agonizing deaths.

Midshipman Peter Haywood, one of the prisoners later to be pardoned, recorded, 'We had to bury ourselves up to the neck in the burning sand which scorched the skin entirely off our bodies...' The hapless band that had survived the relentless forces of the sea and sun had yet another test ahead. Like Bligh, the sailors managed to row to Timor and eventually reached England. Some of them need not have bothered. Six mutineers were condemned: three were hanged at the yardarm.

Pandora rested under the waves until 1977 when Australians Ben Cropp and Steve Comm, aided by RAAF anti-submarine aircraft using an aerial magnetometer, located the wreck in only thirty metres of water. The local museum's Curator of Marine Archaeology, Ron Coleman, followed up the discovery and soon well-preserved artefacts were brought to the surface, including the surgeon's watch. One of the earliest timepieces to have a second hand and a stopwatch control, it has now been restored to near working order.

In 1986 a larger expedition was planned to visit the historic wreck. A large support vessel with a recompression chamber was needed for the forty divers who would take part and Nigel Porteous, now our Queensland Chairman, suggested that we co-operate with the museum in this exciting venture. Whilst *Sir Walter Raleigh* had been crossing the Pacific I had flown ahead to set up my Tac HQ in the bush near Cairns and it was here that Charlie Daniel, Nick Horne and I pored over the charts. Mike Kichenside was handing over as skipper to Tommy Smith of Brisbane, who knew the reef pretty well and we had a very experienced mate, New Zealander John Parsloe. *SWR* was the perfect vessel for the job. The six-week expedition would provide information of great value for our hospitable Australian friends, and at the same time offer some really advanced diving for ex-venturers.

The crew, which included young men and women from Operation Raleigh and US and Royal Australian Navy personnel, needed all their skills for the challenging project. *Zebu* could support the expedition with sixteen venturers and nine crew, while back in Cairns Nick and my superb adjutant, Major Hawk Freeman, organised seaplanes to resupply the expedition. Again, we experienced the unstinting generosity and enthusiasm of Cairns, with a great many companies and individuals donating supplies.

Back in England our Advisory Council, fighting for funds, feared this expedition would break the bank. My protestations about covering the cost through the museum's fee and local sponsorship were to no avail. Even when I pointed out that it would be cheaper than keeping the ship in port, I received little encouragement. It was the old problem of a committee on the far side of the world not fully appreciating the situation. However, *Sir Walter Raleigh*'s owners were the SES who were ultimately responsible for the whole operation. The Operation Raleigh Council was simply an advisory body and, having secured the backing of the SES for this project, I had no option but to ignore the advisors. It did not make me very popular, but the enterprise went ahead, fully sponsored in Australia, as I had promised.

Charlie started the *Pandora* project whilst I handled the rest of Raleigh by radio from Tac HQ. We had a large team preparing to fly to New Zealand and there was much clearing up to be done following the Queensland expedition. However, eventually Peta and I dragged ourselves away from our desks and squeezed into a tiny single-engined 'push me-pull you' seaplane. Skimming over the dun-brown coast, we headed out across a vast expanse of turquoise sea for the small white dot on the edge of the reef. We hit the water with a fearful crash and waves came right over the canopy so that for a moment I thought we'd gone straight under, but several crashes and bounces later we came to a halt beside the ship. On board there was sad news. The previous night, the ship's popular Able Seaman, Neil Carmichael, from the Isle of Lewis, Scotland, had disappeared whilst on anchor watch. The weather was calm and warm and the ship was stationary. In spite of intensive searching, no trace of him was found and it can only be assumed that he fell overboard whilst attempting to adjust a mooring line of a boat secured astern. The tragedy will always remain a mystery.

We had relocated the wreck and work was in full swing when I dived next day, but as we were preparing to go down from one of the large inflatable tenders there was a bump. Something nudged us. This was odd as we were in open water. I glanced up and my jaw dropped, for only thirty feet away a huge dorsal fin was moving slowly towards us. 'Look,' I hissed in alarm, whereupon Jasmina Hilton, one of our diving instructors, cried excitedly, 'It's a whale shark', leapt into the water, grabbed the fin and went off for a free ride. Nellie, as we christened her, was twenty feet long and massive.

She visited us frequently and often nudged the grey Avons, perhaps thinking they were potential mates. We had no worries about this harmless monster, but there were plenty of other much more dangerous predators around to keep us on our toes. A school of 'bronze whalers' gave me a bad turn in relatively shallow water and I must confess a shark is the one creature that really makes my hair stand on end.

Pandora is 'the most significant wreck in the southern hemisphere', according to archaeologist Dr Margaret Rule, Research Director of the Mary Rose Trust. A museum officer added, 'We are only scratching the surface of this remarkable wreck, which will give us an unrivalled collection of late eighteenth-century naval artefacts and much more information about shipboard life of the period.' Certainly it was clear that *Pandora*'s officers had been enthusiastic collectors, for stone implements, wooden clubs, cowrie shells and carved fishing lures were found in abundance, one of the finest collections of datable ethnographic material in the world. Captain Edwards' underwater cabin also yielded historical treasure. Parts of sextants, hourglasses and what appeared to be a complete flint-lock pistol were brought to the surface. Soon *Sir Walter Raleigh*'s deck was covered with bottles, plates, wine glasses and even a stone water purifier. Human bones were also found, the sad remains of the thirty-five who met their deaths when *Pandora* sank in the Coral Sea. On the seabed was the *Bounty*'s anchor, which was to have been used in evidence, and there was also the massive galley stove, sitting square on the foredeck area. Here, sailors would once have dipped for lumps of salt pork and now a large moray eel stood guard.

We also took the opportunity to study the wildlife of the sand cays in this remote area for the Queensland Parks and Wildlife Service. Jasmina and I joined a group of venturers counting green turtles and booby birds on one cay. As the sun set, massive lumbering turtles heaved themselves out of the ocean, like amphibious tanks, and came ashore to lay their eggs, having to complete the task and be back in the water by dawn to avoid being cooked in their shells by the intense heat. Their wanderings disturbed the colonies of booby birds, who wheeled and screamed above us all night. We counted hundreds of turtles on this tiny islet alone and watched as, exhausted, they dragged themselves back to sea to brave the sharks waiting for weaklings in the shallows.

The publicity resulting from the *Pandora* project was immensely helpful and did much to show the Australians that we were not just a group of 'poms' out for ourselves.

From my base at Cairns we supported expeditions in PNG and the Solomon Islands. Perhaps it was just as well that Colonel John Swanston, a senior Army doctor, led the PNG expedition. Sickness had not been a great problem so far, but in the tropics the toll began to rise in spite of all the medical precautions. Ann Tweedy, a charming and most accomplished American writer, had joined us in Chile to help with the writing of the Raleigh books. Ann was a great friend to us all, spreading good cheer wherever she went and, in a most unassuming way, integrating herself into every group she visited.

When I visited PNG I found a wide-ranging medical programme in progress, with the SEE team restoring sight and Professor Conrad Gorinsky using teams of venturers to collect data on traditional medicines. They recorded over 500 remedies. Some would undoubtedly save lives in the future, but the ingredients were enough to make a high street chemist nervous: ants, bark, soil and fungus were all part of the bottomless reserve of biological treasures. I was told that red and black ants crushed together release something like formaldehyde to relieve fevers. There was also a riverside plant, a relative of the iris, whose root helps to cure diarrhoea and stomach problems; and a tree bark that makes an excellent anaesthetic, good for everything from toothache to a night's sleep.

In the Solomons Youth Worker David Parker was leading another expedition that also carried out medical work and, in addition, built a very useful Red Cross Centre. As I set off to visit them the news was grim. Over 100 people had died in a savage cyclone and more than 100,000 were homeless. In three days of wanton destruction, Namu's winds had reached 100 knots. The jungle had been ripped from the hills and entire villages torn apart. International response was immediate. The venturers on Guadacanal, one of the hardest-hit islands, had immediately joined the relief effort. Their tireless work very probably saved lives and as I reached David's base camp, the island postman rushed in with a telegram. It was addressed to David Parker, 'The Leader, Operation Raleigh, Gizo Red Cross, Solomon Islands', and read: 'Please convey my best wishes to the local community and my congratulations to all members of the team on their good work.' The telegram was signed simply, 'Charles, Patron'. This was just one of the many encouraging messages and letters that the Prince of Wales sent to us in the field.

As *SWR* went in to Brisbane for her annual refit we commenced operations in New Zealand, where I was able to see our youngsters doing great things for the National Park Authority. Under the direction of my friend, polar explorer Charlie Burton, and, later, Tony Walton, the venturers built trails, bridges, and huts amongst the beautiful lakeland of South Island. I had selected the area following an earlier visit to see the place in which my parents had started their married life. Now, it was now especially pleasing to see the results. One of the staff was Falklands hero Simon Weston, who led a conservation task on a remote island, trying to trap rats that threatened the rare kakapo. Simon had been with the Welsh Guards aboard the *Sir Galahad* when the ship was hit by Argentine bombs and he was left terribly burned on his face and hands. Nevertheless, this courageous soldier had decided 'life was for living' and volunteered as a signaller on Operation Raleigh. He was a great inspiration to the other staff and venturers.

Meanwhile, another group was busy in Tasmania and I arrived there at Christmas, their height of summer, and staggered off in a quite unseasonal snowstorm to find a team working on Cradle Mountain. As night approached, I realised we were not going to reach the venturers' camp that day, and I was thankful to see an emergency hut ahead, a welcome shelter from the storm. As we entered, Joel Schmiedeke, my new and cheerful USAF adjutant, did a classic house search worthy of any private eye. He didn't have far to look. In one room was a large sleeping bag, inside which there were signs of movement. Joel poked it cautiously and the heads of a honeymoon couple emerged.

'G'day,' said the man. Joel asked if he'd mind sharing the nuptial bedroom with four weary travellers. 'Make yourselves at home, mate,' grunted the Aussie, disappearing back into the bag. Twelve hours later the pair were still inside and had not once left their cocoon.

'What stamina these Australians have,' remarked Rodrigo Noreiga, our Chilean mountaineer, admiringly.

Next day we trudged on and saw wallabies hopping about unhindered by the snow. Australia is a strange and wonderful land!

We always included disabled youngsters among the venturers and in Victoria one young man in a wheelchair complained to me that the axles had rusted badly. I passed his complaint on to the manufacturers, who were mystified but sent out replacements. A year later I saw some photographs of this lad in his chair, forty feet under-water, doing a marine biological survey! No wonder the axles rusted.

Many of our tasks were aimed at helping Aboriginal communities and there were some especially interesting conversations between our black youths and the Aborigines. Seated around a fire beside Lake Tyers, Victoria, one evening the leader of the community talked with a black British university graduate. 'Tell me,' said Chief Murray Bull, 'is there much good grazing land in Manchester?' After some thought and a sip from his tin of Fosters, the young man replied, 'It's getting in short supply.'

The chief pondered on this and then commented, 'I suppose the white folk took it.' More deep thought until the venturer replied, 'Yes, you could say that, but we call them the city council.'

These unsophisticated folk have many problems, especially with their children. It isn't heroin, coke or pot that Aborigine parents worry about, it's petrol sniffing. Cheap and readily available, petrol can be sucked from the tank of a car, outboard or even a lawn-mower. The short-term effects are dizziness, violence and addiction. The long-term effects are brain damage and death. At the same time, alcoholism is a widespread problem among the Aborigines, often leading to more violence, homelessness and early death.

Paula Urschel, an energetic American from the SES team, conceived the idea of a counselling programme after she and I talked to the Aborigines in Western Australia. In July 1987, with blessing of the Australian Government, she returned to the Northern Territories under the auspices of Raleigh with her team of paramedics. One volunteer was an old friend of mine, Eric Niemi, a biology teacher with many years of experience in counselling young people, who had also been with us in Panama and Costa Rica. The other two were counsellors for young people and families suffering from addiction. Both American Indians, they had seen their own tribes suffer many of the same problems the Aborigines now face. The situation is fraught with political and emotional issues. Too often, for example, the addictions of any people in the world are regarded as a feature of their personalities. Our aim was to work with the Council for Alcohol Programme Services and the skilled team at the Gordon Symons Centre near Darwin, where we hoped to take an active counselling role and to exchange ideas.

During the summer months Paula's group lived in villages and towns and 'went bush' for weeks on end in the remote areas. They would be the first to recognize how limited their help could be, given the enormity of the problem. But help they did, and their contribution could stem the growth of the addiction in a few cases. Without such assistance there is a widespread fear that the twin addictions of petrol and alcohol will not be defeated, and that 30,000 years of 'the dreaming' could evaporate with this generation. It was a wonderful sight to see a Red Indian in full headdress discussing the problem with a war-painted Aborigine chief!

Thanks to some marvellous fund raising by Walter and Lee Annenberg, our financial situation was looking healthier. However, to help keep us on the straight and narrow I was most fortunate to get the help of Tony Nowell, formerly Managing Director of Guinness, Malaysia, on secondment. He usually wore a rosy smile and did not look much like an accountant, but by golly he was good. I also had a new Chief of Staff, Geoff Straw, a highly efficient former Fusilier who took on the running of the CHQ. Political events and wars in Sri Lanka, the Persian Gulf and India had necessitated drastic changes in the sea-going programme and as most of the remaining expeditions were inland it was decided that once *Sir Walter Raleigh* had completed her Australian tasks she return home a year earlier than originally planned, sailing back via West Africa. *Zebu*, however, which was heavily committed to sail training, would continue. Venturers were still pouring in and in 1987 we had projects in Australia, Malaysia, Japan, Indonesia and again in Chile. *Sir Walter Raleigh*, resplendent in a new coat of paint, swept majestically into Fremantle Harbour. Along the quays, boats were gathering for the world's greatest yacht race, the America's Cup.

The starting-gun also signalled the imminent beginning of *Sir Walter Raleigh*'s voyage home. For the run, Tommy Smith handed over to his friend, Captain John Fisher, Scottish-born but long of Adelaide. Adrian Turner, the purser, who had sailed from London aboard *Zebu* at the beginning of Raleigh, was one of the many former Venturers in the crew. Indeed, we kept finding our 'family' growing. Raleigh was becoming a way of life! Steaming out of Fremantle Harbour on a hot, dry day in March, the ship's horn sounded a final thank-you and farewell to Australia. Ahead were the infamous Roaring Forties, notorious for its storms, grey beards and freak waves. The fronts thundered across the south of the Indian Ocean from Cape Horn with nothing to stop them. As if in defiance of the sea, the ceremonial ship's bell in the Prince of Wales bar rang vigorously as she pitched and rolled. Some of the most seasoned sailors felt uneasy and almost all were sick, but they need not have feared, for even in a sixty knot gale the stout vessel took the sea in her stride.

Sailing via Capetown and St Helena, to pave the way for *Zebu*'s visit, *SWR* came to Sierra Leone to join in the little country's bi-centennial celebrations. Richard Snailham and I spent a few days investigating the interior with a view to future expeditions, but after a humid night in a dilapidated rest-house, with a nest or cobras for company, I had to admit there really wasn't much left to explore here.

On the afternoon of 19 June, *Sir Walter Raleigh*, as freshly painted and powdered as her sixteenth-century namesake, sailed into the inner harbour of St Helier, Jersey, and to a huge welcome at the pier. From there it was on to Guernsey, through the North Sea to Lowestoft and finally, the Humber estuary. In three years the grand ship had done 43,143 nautical miles and made 117 ports of call without one serious breakdown, quite an achievement for any twenty-two-year-old, and a great tribute to those who maintained her. The anchor was weighed for the last time on 30 June at 7.30 am. The ship then made her way upstream to the dock basin of Hull, where HRH The Duke of Gloucester, a member of the Scientific Exploration Society, came to welcome her home.

The City Council and hundreds of friends, families and expeditioners were on the quayside cheering and shouting congratulations. As *Sir Walter Raleigh* sailed majestically into dock, British Aerospace jets wheeled and dived overhead and the twin cannons boomed a final salute. I felt a little sad but rather proud and when, a few months later, we sold her for a very good price everyone was happy.

For twelve years SES had been planning an expedition to Tibet, a project that had originally been part of the Raleigh programme.

But in 1986, when all was gloom and doom at CHQ, some of my colleagues felt it might prove too costly, so although it encompassed Raleigh's aims I ran it directly under the auspices of the Society. I hoped in this way to remove a source of aggravation, for I felt that a rift was growing between those who wanted Raleigh to be a youth development programme and the explorers who sought to use challenging expeditions to promote leadership in young people. Thus I left the show in Geoff Straw's capable hands and headed for Tibet.

We had wanted to raft the Bramaputra, but the Chinese required a million dollar fee. 'We just want to run it, not buy it,' remarked Sapper Colonel, Henry Day, who had been negotiating with the Chinese on our behalf. In the end we settled for a cheaper option – an expedition to Mt Xixabangma, which, at 26,000 feet, is the world's thirteenth highest mountain. It is also the greatest Himalayan peak within China, of which Tibet is part. Sharing borders with Bhutan, India and Nepal, it is a mysterious land of awesome mountains, deserts and lakes. For centuries Tibet has been shrouded in secrecy and closed to outsiders, but by 1984 the 'Roof of the World' was opened to foreigners.

We set out in September 1987, at the end of the monsoon, when there is normally little snow below 16,000 feet. Our team of thirty-four was drawn from four countries. Two tough and resourceful American ladies, nurse Paula Urschel and banker Pamela Stephany, were members of previous Raleigh expeditions. The British contingent consisted of soldiers, scientists and climbers, some of whom were also Raleigh veterans. Imperial Chemical Industries (ICI) became our major sponsor and sent a young executive, Ivan Hui, from their Hong Kong office. Speaking Mandarin, he was to prove a valuable member of the expedition. The Swires Group also backed us, and sponsored Chuhg Kin Man, an experienced Hong Kong mountaineer who proved to be another asset on the language front. Through the efforts of our chief scientist, Dr Henry Osmaston, The Chinese Academy of Science provided two scientists. An interpreter, liaison officer and Tibetan driver also joined us from the Chinese Mountaineering Association. One of our goals was the encouragement of Himalayan mountaineering, and Henry Day selected ten young aspirants to join his team and gain experience of climbing at higher altitudes.

The science group also included three young researchers, plus a newly-qualified nurse, my twenty-three year-old daughter, Emma. As patrons, we had our good friends General Sir John Mogg and Eric Hotung. Indeed, it was Eric's generosity that made it all possible. No one could pronounce Xixabangma (Shisha-bangma), so we code-named it Jade Venture. On 11 September we began our long trek from Kathmandu to Tibet. The heavy monsoon had caused serious landslides along the Friendship Highway linking Nepal to China and the road was impassable by vehicle for some thirty-two kilometres before the Chinese border.

Most of us acclimatized to the altitude by marching northwards over the mountains. British mountaineer Julian Freeman-Attwood, together with Lance-Corporals John House and Jim Kimber and with the help of 178 porters, carried four tons of stores up the valley of the Bhote Kosi. I met them winding their way over the landslides. Each man bore a large box with the label 'Jade Venture' and an ICI logo.

Filing up a narrow mountain path, we came upon some American tourists who watched the procession with interest.

'Tell me, sir,' said the elderly gentleman. 'What's ICKY?' 'ICKY?' I replied, somewhat puzzled.

'Yeah. I.C.I. on each box.'

I quickly explained that ICI manufactured, amongst other things, fertilisers and explosives.

'Looks as if you've enough to fertilise the whole of China and then blow it up,' retorted the American.

At that point John House walked past carrying a team lance, which is used to drill holes for scientific measurements in glaciers. The evil-looking lance bore a strong resemblance to a weapon from Star Wars. On it the words 'Made by British Aerospace', who also manufacture missiles, were clearly visible. To contribute to the confusion, John wore a T-shirt inscribed 'Jade Venture – the Empire Strikes Back'.

'I get it,' the American winked. 'The CIA has companies like ICKY. Good luck to you, young fellow.'

Perspiration poured off us as we continued the climb up the high, steep slopes, picking off tenacious leeches that dropped from every tree, bush and shrub. It was a fit, lean group that finally reached Tibet.

The climbing and scientific groups had got to Tibet at about the same time. However, once across the border there were more land-slides and, at Zhangmu, we were narrowly missed by a rockfall. No sooner had we traversed a slope than boulders the size of houses came crashing down the mountain. Thirteen people had already been killed at this spot. We now understand why our interpreter, Wei Jian Kong, kept crying 'Hully! Hully!' Gratefully we clambered aboard a sturdy lorry, which, in spite of its obsolete design, was to prove a reliable runner in the weeks ahead. Glad to be off our feet, we happily endured the drizzle as the open truck wound its way through the precipitous gorges once known to caravan traders as 'The Gates of Hell'.

Far below us the rapids of the River Po roared a greeting as the cold, white water tumbled from the great glaciers of the Himalayas to the plains of India. At the little town of Nyalam, old stone build-ings and tin sheds provided a backdrop to the partly-built hotel at the junction of two rivers. Now at 12,000 feet, we puffed and panted as we set up camp in the icy wind.

From here Henry Day would start his climbers on the twenty-mile march to their base at 16,000 feet. After long negotiations, a train of yaks was assembled to carry the stores, and later even diminutive donkeys were used. Waving off the climbers, the aca-demic team turned its attention to the job ahead. It was, to say the least, ambitious. With our Tibetan driver, Basna, and his faithful old truck we set out to investigate the archaeology, botany, ecology, geology and zoology on the northern side of the mountain. We still felt the effect of altitude, but the scenery made us equally breath-less. Army composite rations yielding 4,000 calories a day kept our energy levels high.

On our way up the mountain we paused at a small monastery some nine kilometres north of Nyalam. A serious young monk ush-ered us into a low-ceilinged cave, which, some 900 years before, had housed one of Tibet's best-loved religious masters, the poet Milarepa. Like many Tibetan monasteries, it was destroyed dur-ing the 1966 Cultural Revolution but has since been rebuilt with Chinese Government funds. Dr John Davies, an old Raleigh hand, advised me on our altitude stops and at 14,000 feet we paused at the village of Yalan. A low hill ahead was crowned with ruins. 'Ah! A lost city,' joked Pamela. We camped by the road and were soon surrounded by grubby, grinning children.

Scanning the pictures in my wildlife books, the children claimed to have seen wolves, bears, wild goats, blue sheep, snow leopards and even the Yeti. Our diminutive guests departed as the sun dropped behind the hills and the temperature followed suit.

The next day we explored and mapped the ruins of what appeared to be a fortified monastery. The massive walls had suffered fearful destruction about which the villagers knew nothing, except that it had happened long ago. Checking historical records, we guessed the monastery had been a victim of King Langdarme, who tried unsuccessfully to eradicate Buddhism some 1,100 years ago.

The Lalung Leh pass at 17,000 feet marks the limit of the South Asian monsoon. At the top we had breathtaking views of the snow-clad Himalayan range. Next we passed into a wasteland of dry, gravelly hills and soon came to the barren Tibetan plateau. A vast landscape of windswept grasslands and desert stretched between snow-capped mountains.

Settlements in the region are few and far between. The inhabitants of this rugged land are self-reliant nomads. Their homes are sturdy tents, warmed by dung stoves, and herds of goats, sheep and yaks surround the camps. At Lake Paiku we saw convoys of yaks, like troops of tanks, advancing across the arid plateau. The lead beasts flew red flags, religious rather than political symbols. On the plain were wild asses, gazelles, woolly hares and what appeared to be a fierce crossbreed of wolf and dog. Moving about the region, our studies continued in an area where few foreigners have been. The sun shone and at midday the temperature usually reached 70°F. Henry Osmaston, who at sixty-five was one of the fittest of the team, and Jonathan Cook, a young geologist, even managed a swim in the chilly waters.

Henry and the research assistants took several yaks and moved to the remote Dasuo glacier that flows north from Xixabangma. At 20,000 feet they discovered fantastic ice pyramids over 150 feet high, standing in rows like huge dragons' teeth. These strange formations are only found on the north side of the Himalayas and the Karakoram mountains and these were the largest Henry had ever seen. He also discovered some extraordinary, and as yet totally unexplained, footprints in the snow. Unlike those of a bear, and closer to a human foot, the prints disappeared into the vastness of Tibet. There was no sign of the creature that had made them, but the scientist captured the intriguing tracks on film.

We also needed yaks for the next part of the expedition up the south-eastern side of Xixabangma. Overnight their price doubled! Clearly, they must be the most profitable cattle in the world. Although yaks appear to be large, clumsy creatures, they move with surprising grace, trotting quickly on their dainty hooves up the narrow trails, their flowing hair waving in the breeze. Said to be the most efficient, all-purpose animal in the world, they provide their owners with butter, meat and milk, as well as wool, clothes and tentage. Their dung dries quickly in the sun and is used as fuel and building material, but they can be ill-tempered and obstinate. I noted the caution with which their handlers approached their sharply pointed horns. In our train were also several dzo. A cross between yak and domestic cattle, the dzo is smaller, but carries the same load as its big brother.

As we plodded up a gently sloping valley, the pace was that of a pleasant, easy walk, giving us time to enjoy the magnificent scenery and observe our surroundings. The whistles of the herdsmen steering their beasts became for us the strange music of the mountains.

In the early afternoon we reached a major obstacle. A huge moraine rose 1,400 feet above a fast-flowing river. We were already at 14,000 feet and, in the thin air, it took us an hour of puffing up an ill-defined path to reach the cairn, bedecked with prayer flags, at the top. Beyond the crest lay the intermediate base and we camped amongst piles of ration boxes, the emergency store. Next day, after a steady climb through boulder fields, we reached Henry Day's main base, with its yellow tents nestling among the rocks in the shadow of the mountain. At 16,500 feet and only some five miles from the summit, this was to be our home, too.

On 17 October lead climbers Luke Hughes and Stephen Venables, were already part way up the virgin east face of Xixabangma, which rose at a sixty-five degree angle from the glacier below. Mean while, John Davies and I used the lightweight Avon inflatable to begin a hydrographic survey of the clear, cold lake at 16,952 feet above sea level.

'You'll be dead in a couple of minutes if you fall in,' said John cheerfully as we launched the craft. Later we discovered that we had unwittingly established the world altitude record for rowing a boat! Everything was going rather well. The climbers were making good progress and Jonathan's geological specimens and botanist Clare Roberts' plant collection were increasing rapidly. We had also spotted several clusters of blood-red garnets. The rest of us concentrated on studying the wildlife, including the tiny tailless rodents that we fondly called Tibetan mice.

Our only link with the outside world, the BBC, brought news of a hurricane in Britain, but our minds were on our own weather as ominous dark clouds swept up from Nepal. As dusk fell the temperature registered below 0°F and the first flakes of snow began to swirl about the tents. Later that night the storm struck and raged for the next thirty-six hours. It was bitterly cold and pitch black inside our little tent. Emma's breathing was laboured and rapid. I, too, was having difficulty. Is it the altitude, I wondered, but we had been above 16,000 feet for several weeks and were fully acclimatized. Reluctantly pulling my arm from the warm sleeping bag, I rolled down my glove and glanced at the faint luminous dial of my wristwatch. It was 0300. Funny, I thought, it's very quiet outside, no wind. My shoulder touched the tent wall: it was solid. Not just frozen stiff as usual, but as solid as concrete. I remembered that it had been snowing lightly as we turned in. Now we were virtually entombed.

'We've got to get out. Get dressed quickly!' I shouted.

'Oh, Father, why must you always do things at three o'clock in the morning?' came my daughter's sleepy reply.

There was no time to be lost. Pulling on thick socks, over-trousers, boots, balaclava and over-gloves, I turned to the entrance. The tent door was frozen solid too and it took several strong pulls to open the zip. A wall of snow cascaded inwards. Now we heard the wind and, digging through the snow with our mess tins, cleared a way to fresh air. My torch beam reflected off the flakes driven horizontal by the fury of the storm. Nearby I heard cries and laughter, but in the blizzard I could see nothing. Suddenly in a brilliant blue flash of lightning, I saw that the girls' tent had collapsed. With amazing good humour, they staggered to the more robust army mess shelter. In base camp everyone dug to save tents and stores, whilst on the slopes of the mountain the climbers kept a wary vigil for the ever-present threat of an avalanche.

Camp Two was totally buried and the precious video camera and much of our best film were lost. At 20,600 feet, four mountaineers were marooned for three days. Our advance science camp was cut off on a distant glacier. The deep snow, shortage of fuel and the fact that no yaks could possibly reach us, soon changed the expedition into a battle for survival. The mountaineers evacuated most of their camps and Henry Osmaston's party had an epic escape from their glacier in what was, by now, a full-scale blizzard. They were lucky to reach base camp with only mild frostbite.

To make matters worse, a petrol stove exploded in our mess tent and Annabel Huxley, a member of the science group, and I were only saved from serious burns by the rapid action of Paula and Emma, who hurled us, flaming, into a snowdrift. Our demi-paradise had become a freezing hell. Eventually the storm passed and, as the sun shone, temperatures rose again. However, we now had to contend with a six-foot blanket of soft snow. We'd have given much for a pair of skis in our retreat! As the sun swung past, we trudged along a high ridge now tipped with a razor edge of blown snow. Claire, weighing only 100 pounds, was carrying a seventy-pound pack. She would never abandon the botanical specimens. I've seldom met such an uncomplaining, resolute person.

A French climber coming up from Nyalam warned us that another storm was predicted. We radioed this news to Henry Day and wondered how on earth they would get out in even more snow. Near intermediate base, we again met leading Polish climber, Wojtek Kurtyka, and his friend, Halina Sickaj, whom we had first encountered in Nyalam. These marvellous people shared their ninety-three per cent proof 'mountain tea', a greatly appreciated brew.

I listened to the BBC, and the news of the stock market crashing a world away, and then stepped outside to gaze one last time at the moonlit landscape. Scanning the mountain face before me I saw something move. It looked like a couple of foxes, but at dawn Wojtek showed me fresh wolf tracks. Finally reaching the town, we learned of the tragedy caused by the blizzard. People had frozen to death in buses trapped in the high passes on the Lhasa road; villagers had died of hypothermia; and several expeditions had lost men in avalanches. A group of Tibetans, watching us hobble in, shook their heads in amazement that we had survived our stay on Gosainthan, the Sanskrit name for Xixabangma. It means 'The Abode of God'.

We had only to reach Kathmandu. The road along which we had driven forty days before was blocked in a hundred places by landslides and the twenty-five-mile walk through the 'Gates of Hell' was littered with mud, rocks, trees and tangled telephone wires. It was after dark when Wei Jian Kong and I, our frostnipped feet hurting like hell, stumbled into a hut on the outskirts of Zhangmu. There we found Emma and Jonathan, who provided a welcome dish of noodles. Refreshed, we traversed the worst landslide of all, guided by a drunken Tibetan and a fading pencil torch.

'If we could see where we were going, I don't think we'd do this,' I remarked, as we scrambled over the loose rubble and around cascading waterfalls.

After a night in a dormitory at the local hotel, we crossed the frontier into Nepal. Disappointed tourists waited in vain for permission to enter Tibet, for following the Lhasa riots, foreigners were banned once more. Chinese hostility seemed to be displayed by the roar of a nearby explosion that sent rocks flying around us. Our newly-acquired Nepalese porters dropped the baggage and fled for their lives, whilst we sheltered beneath our packs and prayed that the Chinese Army engineers would cease blasting.

Another long march and a few lifts later we reached Kathmandu, where my old friends, Jim and Belinda Edwards, took us in and provided a wonderful feast. I needed it. I had lost twenty-six pounds.

On the mountain Henry Day's team had gone back up the east face. Stephen and Luke came tantalizingly close to the summit, but were turned back at 23,950 feet by strong winds. The team had spent the night out in temperatures of minus 32°F, sheltering in a snow cave – without sleeping bags. Although the summit remained unconquered, the climbers did complete a new route up the eastern face and had succeeded in reaching the 23,950-foot summit of Pungpa Ri.

It had been an epic expedition in itself. The yaks never did reach the base camp and all our heavy equipment was cached in the hope that it might be collected the following spring, but we never returned and I guess the Tibetans did very well out of us! The successes in both mountaineering and science, and the close liaison with the Chinese Academy of Science, boded well for future cooperation. Miraculously, everyone got home safely, although several had frostbite.

Feeling very fit, I went on to visit the Raleigh expedition in Pakistan that my former PA, Sue Farrington, had done much to set up. Veteran explorer, David Bromhead, was in charge here and Ann Tweedy was gathering material for the Raleigh books. It was proving a tough expedition and, as I arrived, David was sorting out the little problem of a Japanese girl having her bottom pinched by a frisky Pakistani. It almost resulted in his being stoned to death!

The plan was for the whole operation to end in April 1989 but by 1988 many thought the operation too successful to close. I was due to return to full-time military duty and the SES Council, although rejoicing in the success, had grown weary of the endless fund raising and inevitable petty squabbles that always seem to occur when large numbers of unpaid volunteers become passionately involved in an ambitious project. A study was commissioned to examine the best way forward, but suddenly we found that a group with support from a large American company was, in effect, trying to stage a takeover bid. Unfortunately, those representing them were too heavy-handed and battlelines were immediately drawn. The press generally sided with us, 'the little chaps', and sadly the Prince of Wales himself became drawn into the dispute. Had the SES Council been approached in a different manner, I feel we would happily have agreed to hand over Raleigh, but the certain way to stir the British is to threaten them and this resulted in an unseemly conflict. The opposition eventually backed away and we decided on the future.

With some gentle persuasion from the Government, which had invested considerably in our scheme for Inner City youngsters, the MoD agreed to my remaining on loan to Raleigh until the end of my military service, provided I did some school and university lectures to aid recruiting. This suited me well, but I knew the venture would continue to need sound business management after Tony Nowell and our other commercial helpers left. The SES debated the issue and decided that the best answer was to set up a separate charitable body to take over. I had got to know Graham Walker, an astute and charming Northern businessman, who had backed the British entry for the America's Cup races in Australia. A somewhat shy man, he was extremely good with youngsters and was, indeed, truly young at heart himself and also very successful. Graham accepted the challenge and formed the Raleigh Trust and I agreed to stay on, at least until the end of my army career.

Entering this next phase, we needed new areas to explore and I began to call my chums around the world. Peter and Val Enzer encouraged me to consider Zimbabwe, whilst Brigadier Joe Singh, now Chief of Staff of the Guyana Defence Force, was eager for us to go there. Cameroons had long been in mind, and there was still plenty to do in Chile and Pakistan. An expedition in Alaska helped to clean up after the Valdez oil spill and our Canadian committee ran a fine project in the Arctic. We even organised a small expedition in Britain, providing community aid. Portugal, our oldest ally, hosted another and no fewer than three expeditions took place in Kenya. Furthermore, the Iron Curtain was looking shaky and I began to work on plans for Siberia and, encouraged by Lord Glenarthur, then Minister of State, we also considered Mongolia. In line with our sea-going tradition, we had used the Jubilee Sailing Trust's *Lord Nelson* to carry the venturers to and from the Bahamas, where Tony Walton ran more projects. The return of *Lord Nelson* fitted in well with the end of phase one.

On Monday morning, 3 April, the sun was just beginning to penetrate the grey clouds as Vic Rudge, our stalwart Hampshire Co-ordinator, and I climbed aboard the launch to greet the ship. Beneath the towering cranes lining the quayside, a crowd of well-wishers waited in the chilly breeze. Ahead, silhouetted against the distant horizon, was the tall ship. Her masts stood out like church spires amongst the squat container vessels ploughing furrows up the Channel. Her rigging was alive with venturers, furling the sails; it was a scene that could have happened a hundred years ago. Three hundred metres from the dock, her cannon boomed seven times in stentorian salute. Flis Bowden, our movements officer, in her Territorial Army role, answered with the shore gun as cheers rang out; sirens blared and welcoming banners waved in the wind. The press swarmed over the vessel and Vic had arranged a splendid reception with the backing of the Mayor of Southampton. Another ship had come home.

Next day, an exhibition of our artists' work was opened at the National Army Museum by the Minister for the Arts. Another guest was the great explorer Wilfred Thesiger, who had assisted us in Kenya. He viewed a portrait of himself, done by one of our venturers, with approval. It was a great tribute to the efforts of our Art Director, Ley Kenyon, who worked tirelessly to get his protégés into the remotest parts of the world, where they painted and sketched in jungles and swamps, often with only the stub of a candle for light.

The art show was just one of the events with which we celebrated the end of the first stage of Raleigh and the beginning of the next. Four days later, over 3,000 venturers, international representatives and supporters piled into London's Royal Albert Hall for a grand re-union, organised by Geoff Straw and Bill Bellars. Peruvian venturer Sandra Echegaray Samanez spoke on John Dunn's popular BBC radio programme and our press office excelled itself, fielding interviews across the country. As evening drew in, people from many lands arrived at the Albert Hall. Some wore black tie, others sported expedition T-shirts and jeans and a number of two-legged lions were seen being chased by gorillas. Knightsbridge had never seen the like. Tony Walton, just back from Zimbabwe, acted as Master-of-Ceremonies, our padre, Olympic canoeist Basil Pratt, said prayers, and against the din in the cavernous hall, I reviewed the progress of the 'Raven Rations Survivors' Club'. Graham Walker, our new Chairman, spoke of his hopes for the future and read a congratulatory message from Prince Charles. A multi-projector audiovisual show splashed across the screen; afterwards the party dissolved into splendid informality.

General Sir John and Lady Mogg were in the thick of the disco dancing. Everyone scoured the circular maze of the hall's corridors looking for companions who had come from as far away as Pakistan, Australia and Singapore. Hawk Freeman flew in from Colorado and Clive Barrow arrived straight off the plane, still covered in the dust of Kenya. In the programme was a glowing tribute from Prime Minister Margaret Thatcher, who had given consistent and enthusiastic support. It was a night no one present will ever forget, a night that made us recall the achievements of this extraordinary band.

Of course, we had encountered a host of problems during the previous four years. The venturers faced their own trials in trying to raise funds for their expeditions, but few of them knew the battles fought by CHQ and the international committees to maintain the vital cash flow. Sending expeditions to the ends of the earth often means long and costly negotiations with governments, expensive reconnaissance trips and the necessary boats, trucks, rations, tents, and equipment. If, as sometimes happens, political conflicts force us to cancel arrangements, a great deal of time and money will have been spent for naught. Then there is the cost of insurance, of recruitment and selection tests, and expenditure on research, communications, rent and wages raises the bills to alarming proportions. With careful economic planning, however, we had managed to use a bit more black ink than red, and it was time to look ahead.

More and more venturers were sponsored by their companies, convinced that the challenge of strenuous tasks and demanding projects would prove a good investment. Thanks to Sir Peter Morrison's powers of persuasion, large numbers of young were sponsored by the nationalised industries. The success of the inner-city venturers had led the British government to send members of the Youth Training Scheme out with us, although this meant increased instruction and guidance by the staff. One group of industrialists told me that they judged a young person's time with us as the equivalent of holding a university degree: 'Many people have paper qualifications, but very few have practical experience of group management, problem solving, teamwork and tackling projects under difficult circumstances. We know that all the men and women who have been on Raleigh have that experience.' Without a doubt, throwing together young people of different backgrounds, colours and creeds before they have developed any unshakeable prejudice does much to foster international understanding.

In maintaining our global links, it was necessary to take care that words in one English-speaking country were not misinterpreted in another. I received some very funny looks when, during a TV broadcast in Raleigh, North Carolina, I talked about 'venturers humping their rucksacks over the hills.' In another instance, I remember the Lord Mayor of Hull missing a step or two as he danced with American Jenny Bond who casually remarked that the North Carolinians 'so enjoy shagging that they hold contests for it.' Apparently 'shagging' is a dance common to their coastal regions.

But everyone understood the broader language of the goals of Operation Raleigh – the development of leadership and character. People from all over the world shared hardships and returned to their own countries to help the disabled, the sick, the elderly and the unemployed. They are all answering the final challenge of Drake and Raleigh: 'What can you give back to your community?'

As our numbers grew, it became necessary to give more guidance to those returning from the rigours of expedition life. Roberta Howlett produced a booklet entitled 'Been There ... Done That ... What Now?' In particular, we formed a close association with the Duke of Edinburgh Award Scheme, which operates all over the world and which recognises various levels of achievement attained by young people. This kind of follow-up is vital, and it is good to see how many venturer support groups have been established by the young people themselves. The overwhelming enthusiasm to help others generated by Raleigh expeditions is equally strong in other parts of the world. I have seen it as I tramped through the heather to see Venture Scotland's bothy – a remote hut in the Highlands. I saw it again as I watched venturers launch their hot-air balloon *Spirit of Kitty Hawk*, on a stormy night in North Carolina. The young lions were beginning to lead the pride.

17

New Directions

'Look out!' cried the startled accountant as the tusker bore down on us. Needing no further bidding, the chairman, the doctor, the banker, the journalist and I plunged through the bush. Happily, the elephant lost interest and left us, adrenalin pumping, to draw breath and laugh at our headlong flight.

This was just one of the many experiences indelibly stamped on the memories of the twenty-four members of Operation Raleigh's first executive expedition, ranging in age from twenty-seven to sixty-nine, when they volunteered to spend four weeks in southern Africa on the aptly named 'Kalahari Quest'. Irreverently nick-named 'the wrinklies' by the seventeen to twenty-five-year-olds who usually took part in our expeditions, these mature explorers were to experience the same thrills that made Raleigh so memorable for the young.

The scheme came about because venturers returning to their companies found their superiors did not appreciate what they had done during their expeditions, nor how the experience might fit them for greater responsibility. So they suggested executives should see them in action in the field. 'Fine,' said the sponsors, 'but we need to give them the sort of experience offered to younger people. We want something to stimulate and re-motivate them and pro-vide opportunities to develop teamwork, decision making, problem solving, innovative and creative thinking, planning, controlling and time management, and, above all, to give them confidence in their own abilities.'

Professor John Adair, my colleague from the days of the Sealed Knot, and one of the world's foremost experts on leadership in management, believed the Raleigh experience could do all of this. He suggested that by taking executives overseas to face challenging projects, we could provide the cloak of excellence in management training while doing much to overcome the day-to-day stress and pressure of the commercial world.

Thus the Executive Expedition was launched. Within hours a secretary rang to ask if we would take her chairman to the North Pole for a year.

We picked a team from varying occupations, skills and backgrounds, from Britain, Botswana, Ireland, France and the United States and from companies including the Bank of Boston, British Gas, ICI, Guinness and Vickers Medical Division. Compatibility is vital on expeditions and, to check this, applicants had to endure an assessment weekend at Sherborne Castle, Dorset, Sir Walter Raleigh's former home.

Final briefings over and kit issued, we boarded a British Airways flight for Gaborone, capital of Botswana. Each executive had a particular role. Eleanor Rogers, company secretary of News International, was the botanist, while Jerry Shively, formerly chief executive of Johnson Wax, was in charge of video filming and canoeing.

Our Botswana chairman, Louis Nchindo of Anglo-American, enthusiastically welcomed the team, delighted that so many top business people should be visiting his country, which, as big as France, is still little known outside Africa. Then, guided by author and Kalahari expert Mike Main, we set off to seek new archaeological sites and study the fauna and flora of the country. By dusk on day one, our column of land cruisers had reached Kubu, a crescent-shaped rocky island about a kilometre long situated in the Makgadikgadi Pans. This vast ancient lake bed was the setting for Wilbur Smith's bestseller *Sunbird*. Here we made camp, assembled the microlight that had been towed up from Johannesburg and then settled to watch the flaming red sun sink behind the grotesque baobab trees that stood sentinel on this lonely shore of a sea that dried up long ago. It was like sitting on the beach waiting for the tide to come in, but that had not happened for 1,500 years. Mike said of this place, 'None will forget the deep-rooted and tranquil magic of that extraordinary island, lodged like a pearl on the shore of a limitless sea, where the land and sky at evening merge, inseparable, into a symphony of muted colours. To stand here, on the rim of Botswana nature's palette, is to stand on the edge of another planet – stark, simple, silent and beautiful beyond words.' No soul was untouched. At this site, directed by Tom Huffman, Professor of Archaeology at Witwatersrand University, and Alec Campbell, who had been director of Botswana Museum, we mapped an ancient walled enclosure and examined over two hundred strange cairns. Tom postulated that the cairns could have been schools at which boys were initiated into manhood and taught how to farm, fight and hunt, before entering regiments. But rumours of another ruin nearby prompted us to dispatch Philip Welch and his microlight, with Alec riding piggyback, on a dawn mission. The sun had hardly risen when they were back with the exciting news of significant ruined walls, around a metre high, enclosing some seven hectares at the edge of the pan. Arriving at this new site we found pottery scattered everywhere and discovered a cowrie shell that had originated in the Indian Ocean, probably carried here as currency. Ruins of buildings in the enclosure and the absence of cairns fascinated Tom who had studied the Zimbabwean Empire for over twenty years. He believed that the walls were of thirteenth-century origin and once belonged to this empire. Was this another lost circumcision centre or the remains of a once important city? We shall have to await future excavation to learn more.

The next task lay on Botswana's western frontier. Jon Foulds, chairman of the Halifax Building Society, led his team to the Tsodilo Hills and managed to locate some previously undiscovered rock paintings. Meanwhile, the rest of us drove many dusty miles westward to explore caves near the Namibian frontier in search of more archaeological sites. Vast colonies of bats inhabit these caverns, which were discovered in 1932 and are said to be the lair of leopards and the site of a great treasure hidden by an early settler. Sadly, we made no dramatic finds, and yet to sit in the total silence and darkness of the caves was a thought-provoking experience. After a day's exploration in the baking sun, there was little time for rest, with meals to prepare, punctures to repair, reports to write and equipment to service. However, a bottle of specially brewed, extra-strong original Irish Guinness, even if a trifle warm, did much to restore our health. Entertainments officer Eamon Murphy, Dublin sales manager for Guinness, kept us well supplied. Indeed, because some bottles had broken in the trucks, we were literally awash with it! Rations were canned or dried, supplemented with fresh beef and delicious local sausage. Several of us became addicted to the tough, salty biltong made of dried buffalo meat, which we sliced and chewed like gum.

The nights were often bitterly cold and insurance company chairman, Robert Rose, woke on several mornings with frost on his woolly hat. However, we did have one splendid hot water bottle in Mike Main's enchanting Jack Russell, although Pamela Stephany said that a dog's cold nose worming its way into her sleeping bag felt rather like a mamba! Travelling across the Kalahari, ancient baobab trees, on which early explorers had carved their names and had used as post boxes, were among the few landmarks available to us. However, navigation was no problem as John Lyons, a New York electronics engineer, had brought along a new device, known as a Magellan, which used four satellites to determine its position within three metres. Another useful item of twentieth-century technology was a Pilkington image intensifier, with which we could see in the dark and count game at night. Some of our fresh meat had gone rotten and we put it out as hyena bait and then sat to watch with this device. After a short time Helen Foulds exclaimed, 'I can see something moving. It's large and white.'

'Where, where?' we questioned.

'Oh, but I think it's Jerry,' she exclaimed. Indeed it was, for he had taken his shovel and sought privacy to commune with nature in the darkness. Such are the problems of squatting, even a hundred yards away, when the camp has one of these infernal machines!

The final phase took the expedition into the Okavango Delta, where the moist air revived us after the dry, dusty Kalahari. Crocodiles and hippos shared the waterways, moving noisily among the papyrus reeds, while the great fish eagle's yodelling call echoed overhead. Our muscles ached from the effort of canoeing, and blistered hands bore testimony to the roughness of the homemade paddles, but Eamon had thoughtfully deposited a supply of 'six-packs' in shallow water so that we could refresh ourselves with a cool Guinness. Later on we overheard two Australians in a bar in Maun saying, 'Unbelievable – haven't had a beer for days and we reached down beside the boat and there was a bottle of Guinness – bloody amazing.'

Whether on foot among big game or being poled silently through the reed beds in dugouts, our trip was a journey through another world, and the final supper at the Victoria Falls in Zimbabwe completed the magic.

Writing to me afterwards, John Campbell, our management trainer, said:

The scale of everything you undertake is so much bigger on an expedition to a remote place, the distances are longer, the scenery more magnificent, the flora and fauna more exotic, the very timelessness of it. And so it is with the experience. There is no doubt that management development using the outdoors is immensely successful in Britain – mine and other companies can testify to this. But there is something very different about doing the same work in the wide, open spaces of the Kalahari, perhaps reviewing the day under a baobab tree, or examining leadership styles after some key decisions around a camp fire in the Okavango Delta. The reality of the situations, the need for decision and the interplay between people is inescapable. There is no hotel room to retire to in comfort and hide away, there is just the reality that tomorrow is another day when tasks have to be completed and the journey continued. So from a management development viewpoint it is an exhilarating environment in which to work. People do learn, do discover new resources in themselves, and new perspectives on a wide range of issues. It is not an experience from which people return unmoved. In many ways it is this personal quest which participants will value most on reflection, the fact that they have had a good opportunity to reconsider their priorities and recharge their batteries and all this on top of examining their leadership, decision-making and interpersonal skills.

The impact on the individuals was certainly profound and they returned home thoughtful, re-motivated and in many cases, suffering post-expedition blues, but clearly the concept worked. So I decided to repeat it in another land.

In 1987, on my way to Tibet, I lunched with friends in Kathmandu.

'It's said there's a mammoth-like beast living in a remote stretch of jungle alongside the Karnali River,' smiled John Edwards, filling my glass with ice cold beer.

'Rubbish, they're extinct,' I retorted.

'Of course, but something big is frightening the pants off the people and messing up their crops,' said John.

'Get a few facts and we might have a look for your giant one day,' I laughed.

Three years later, a bubbly young lady who had been with me on Operation Drake, burst into my London office. 'I took this a couple of months ago from a canoe on the Karnali,' announced Sarah Bamfylde proudly, handing me a photograph of what appeared to be a very fat bull elephant with a massive bump on his head and a heavy, bearded tail.

Experts could not explain the bump. Some thought it might be a tumour resulting from a bullet wound, but all felt the subject worth investigation. Thus began the Karnali Quest, with the next team of executives going to Nepal in 1991 and, travelling by river, foot and elephant, carrying out valuable scientific work. But although giant footprints were seen in the jungle, we found no mammoth-like monsters. However, reliable witnesses convinced me that a large beast did exist in the remote Bardia forest.

The map legend reads:

- Footpath
- Vehicle tracks
- Metallic road
- **X** Giant elephants discovered
- Forest

Map labels: Karnali River, Chisipani, Birendronagor (Surket), Royal Bardia wildlife Reserve, Bheri River, Babai River, NEPAL, INDIA, Kathmandu, Nepalgung, Miles, N, 0 10 20

We therefore returned in 1992, flying into Kathmandu with high hopes. Seven members of the original group had been joined by seven newcomers, with ages ranging between twenty-eight and fifty-five, again with a wide variety of professions. Chief Inspector David Warren of the Humberside Constabulary was the ornithologist, whilst Rod Barnes, landlord of the *Jolly Woodman* at Burnham, was studying the rare Ganges River dolphin, and Sheena Cox, who managed Our Price Record shops in London, was researching the flora. Everyone had different responsibilities and John Hunt, General Manager of Marks and Spencer in Belfast, was to make a video film and specialise in elephants. He trained by running the New York marathon! With luck, we might catch a glimpse of the strange beast, but I was not relying totally on luck and had arranged for trackers to scour the area for weeks before we arrived. Our work was also to take in a wide-ranging survey of fauna and flora for the Natural History Museum and the Nepalese Wild Life Department, so there would be plenty to do.

Tiger Mountain, a company noted for its conservation interest and expertise in handling clients who wanted to climb Everest, had the arrangements in hand when we stepped off our plane. We were to fulfil one of my ambitions, to explore the little known Karnali River Gorges with Avon inflatables en route to the remote forest, and forty porters had already carried the boats over the mountains. Two days later and 200 miles westward we de-bussed and started the long trek to the Karnali canyon. Climbing up and down the foothills for three days got us much fitter. The route was mapped, discoveries recorded and the bird list grew longer as inspector Warren's binoculars picked up our feathered friends. However, there was apprehension as we approached the river. It had never been navigated at low water, when the rapids would be obstructed by huge boulders. 'It may be technically more difficult, but the force should be down,' confided Megh Ale, our chief boatman, as we sipped Kukri rum by the campfire. Even he seemed concerned. Few of our team had ever been rafting, but all could swim!

We hit big water on the first morning and, hearing the roar of the cataracts, checked helmets and life jackets, digging our feet under thwarts. 'Paddle together,' screamed the helmsman as the Avons slid down the slope into the wall of towering waves. Freezing glacier water cascaded over us as we bounced through foaming torrents. The exhilaration was tremendous and tension gave way to joy as, wet but unscathed, we hit rapid after rapid. The gorges reminded me of the Blue Nile and I hoped there were no bandits. One especially dangerous obstacle forced us to disembark and lower our craft, unmanned, on lines, but in eight days we navigated sixty-eight cataracts, charted the river and caught fish both for science and the pot, as well as counting birds, crocodiles and mammals; but still no sign of giant elephants.

We were the first foreigners to enter several villages, but everywhere we were greeted by smiling people. Perhaps this was due to the locally grown marijuana, but they were jolly friendly. One declining tribe, the Raji, had until recently been hunter gatherers, believing it taboo to grow crops, but sadly deforestation had forced them to become labourers. With pitiful thanks they accepted our gifts of biscuits and salt and told us they had heard of great creatures in the jungle to the south. I wondered if they meant rhino or something larger. On 7 March a huge fish-eating crocodile watched us cruise out of the last great gorge into the jungle covered valley and, as the sun set, we found five lovely ladies awaiting us on the bank. Honey Blossom and her sister, Luksmi, had come with three younger elephants to carry us on the next phase of the quest. With raised trunks they trumpeted a welcome. In the days ahead we would come to love these lumbering jumbos as they transported us through the dark forest. Whatever we found, they must face the danger with us. Tents up and steaming mugs of tea served, we sat in the warm evening listening to the news from the trackers who had been working ahead.

'Only last night tulu hatti, big elephant, destroyed a banana plantation two hours from here,' reported Pradeep Rana, the naturalist who was to direct the hunt.

'How big?' asked Zimbabwean company chairman, John Cochran.

'The foot prints are very large, you must see for yourself,' said Pradeep.

'I'll go,' volunteered the enthusiastic Marks and Spencer man.

'Any snakes?' enquired our red-headed Irish herpetologist, Mark O'Shea.

'Too cold right now, perhaps a little later,' the Nepalese assured him. Mark looked sad; he lived for snakes!

That night I slept fitfully, constantly awoken by Honey Blossom's insistent calls. 'God, what a noisy beast.' My dreams were little comfort. There was something massive, something malignant, perhaps even supernatural, always lurking just beyond vision in the dense vegetation. I wondered what on earth the next day would bring. Perhaps Honey Blossom was having nightmares too.

Clutching his tape measure, John Hunt left at dawn and, moving through the dripping grass, soon picked up fresh tiger spoor and the track of a large rhino. Then his Nepali tracker pointed out a vast circular print in the mud. 'Tulu hatti,' he hissed. It was very fresh and water oozed into the impression as they measured the diameter.

'Twenty-one inches, multiply by six for the shoulder height ... wow, that's ten foot six.' whispered John, calculating the size of the beast by a tested formula. 'A very big elephant.' The Asian elephant is smaller than its African cousin, the largest is thought to have reached eleven feet one inch. Cows grow to around eight feet and can weigh a little over four tons. Most bulls have tusks, which can exceed nine feet, whereas cows do not, although they can grow short tusks.

In the dark next morning, festooned with binoculars and cameras, we hauled ourselves up our jumbo's tails into the stout wooden howdahs – three explorers, a tracker and the phanit, or driver, to each beast. Our mounts breakfasted on balls of grass filled with saffron rice, which they stole from a canvas-covered pile. As we climbed aboard, their great brown eyes watched patiently. 'Why is it that the largest and strongest animal on earth willingly takes orders from mere men?' we asked, knowing that a flick of the trunk could break our backs. There is a strange bond of respect, even love, between man and elephant, but I knew that Luksmi had broken her phanit's back with her trunk when he had been operating on her foot some years before.

Moving at around two miles-per-hour we entered the cuckoo grass. Twenty-foot stalks brushed passed, brightly coloured birds dipped from tree to tree and spotted deer scampered away as our unstoppable transport plodded forward. At the river, the ladies pushed down the bank, then, tucking in their hind legs, slid gracefully down on their bottoms. Like five fat cruisers in line ahead, they entered the swirling water; leaning into the current, feeling the way forward, they had no difficulty with the crossing. Elephants love water. Walking further on, someone dropped a lens cap. The jumbo picked it up with her trunk and passed it back. We began to wonder who was in charge.

A flash of orange was all we saw as the tiger left the last of its kill and, with a defiant snarl, loped away through the reeds, but our hearts beat faster. 'They'll never believe this in the Tottenham Court Road,' said a lady manager from London, the beating of her heart almost echoing through the forest. Only a week before the ladies had surrounded a tiger on a kill and in a couple of bounds the cat had clawed its way up an elephant's trunk. The surprised phanit hit it over the head with his stick and it leapt off. Asian elephants are thought to respond to orders in Hindi, which sometimes causes problems for the Nepalese. A young elephant was on a training trip in Bardie with Pradeep Rana when they came across a large tiger, which then charged. The phanit gave what he thought was the appropriate command and to his horror the elephant sat down. However the tiger skidded to a halt, looked rather puzzled, and stalked off.

We picked up the previous day's tracks and headed into the mist that still hung amongst the sal trees at the forest edge. Suddenly, the ladies stopped. Their ears came forward like parabolic reflectors and the deep rumbling purr of elephants' communication by low frequency sound began. There was something ahead of us. Our eyes strained into the thin mist. Our sharp-eyed policeman saw it first.

'Look,' he muttered, pointing forward. I saw nothing, then the grey background I had assumed was sky beyond the trees began to move. It looked like an enormous pile of rocks was sliding silently through the forest, then a huge creature emerged. Its great domed head, heavy tusks and bulbous body gave it the appearance of a fat old gentleman, with spare tyres and double chin. A thick, serpent-like trunk sought our scent. No one spoke, but our elephants trembled and our cameras clicked. 'My God,' gasped John Cochrane, as I reloaded my Canon (camera not gun!). Looking up, I could scarcely believe my eyes. A second grey mountain was moving into view, even more massive than the first, his enormous tusks curved upwards and his huge head carrying an even higher dome. 'What on earth is it?' whispered someone.

'Mammoth?' suggested another softly. And I could see how that legend had grown up. It was as if one had been seeking the Yeti and had suddenly met it face-to-face, but this chap weighed at least six tons.

'He's in *musth*, we must be careful,' warned Pradeep, indicating the yellow discharge running down the big bull's face from a gland behind the eye. Knowing that this condition makes even domestic elephants extremely dangerous, we backed away.

Flapping their ears, the ghostly apparitions approached, pausing only to pluck some choice branch or seize a trunkful of grass. The giants were fifty yards away and our mounts were shaking with fear. They, too, had never seen anything like this before, but the phanits spoke gently, coaxing them to retreat slowly across a dry riverbed. However, we wanted good, clear pictures, so we returned and found the monsters feeding in a shady copse. To tempt them out, Chan Chan Kali, a sexy young thing, was persuaded to trumpet to the bulls. 'A mating call,' exclaimed Pradeep.

'I hope not,' commented John Davies, our medical officer. But the shrill cry, which would have woken the dead, had no effect. 'Just our luck to find a gay elephant,' mused my assistant, Sally Cox.

Measurements of the footprints showed Raja Gaj or King Elephant, as our trackers named the big fellow, to be approximately eleven-foot-three and eleven-foot-six at the shoulder, whilst Kancha, the youngest beast, was around ten-foot-six. I knew they must be amongst the largest Asian elephants ever discovered, but could not explain their strange shape, nor why they existed in this remote valley.

For ten days we followed them, sometimes meeting in dense jungle and other times in the tall grass along the river. We stalked each other in a slow moving game of cat and mouse. Gradually they seemed to become more interested in the ladies and came to meet us when we approached. Did they realise there were humans there, too? One day even the girls forgot this when Luksmi suddenly lost patience with a younger elephant, charging her and butting her, much to the alarm of the riders. The great bulls looked on as the two trumpeting females thundered through the bush. They seemed to say 'what on earth are you silly women playing at?' But for most of the time they regarded us with amused indifference, although, when they were together, Kancha acted as an escort and forced us away. At other times they would show off, dusting themselves with clouds of dirt or wrenching over stout trees. There were rumours of a third bull but we did not see him, nor for that matter any cows. That remained a mystery, but with a six hundred square miles of forest, who knew what was there.

The BBC World Service news had just ended and I had closed my eyes when Pradeep started beating on my tent. 'Come quickly, John. Raja Gaj is here,' he hissed.

'In the camp?' I exclaimed, wrapping on a sarong and grabbing a torch.

On the moonlit path to the elephant lines I found the boys agitated and frightened.

'Big elephant has taken Honey Blossom', wailed one.

Sure enough her tethering chains were broken and I knew she could not do that herself. How on earth could a six-ton kidnapper walk undetected into a camp of forty people, I asked myself as we set out to find her? Just inside the forest I shone my flashlight on a black mass and called softly, 'Come along, Honey Blossom, be a good girl.'

The black mass turned and I found myself facing two enormous curved tusks. Thirty feet away stood Raja Gaj. His piggy eyes reflected the light, then, ears forward, he came shambling at me in a deliberate charge. But as I flicked off the torch, he stopped. Elephants have poor sight and I was downwind of him. Quietly, Rod Barnes pushed an image intensifier into my shaking hands. Now able to see in the dark, we stood silently watching him in the green electronic light as he tried to locate us. His long thick trunk sniffed the air. I could see Honey Blossom just beyond the tusker. 'Get everyone among the boulders by the river for safety,' I whispered to Rod as the phanits advanced with torches of burning grass. For a moment the raider stood and I thought he would charge again, but then, with a snort, he wheeled and, pushing over a two-foot thick tree as if it were a matchstick, disappeared into the darkness. Before Honey Blossom could follow, her phanit climbed up her tail and onto her shoulders, driving her back to camp. A disappointed lady and a brave man! I returned to the campfire, looking ridiculous in sarong and flip flops, and poured myself a stiff scotch.

Our work continued. Mark found his beloved snakes and collected an impressive fifteen-foot python, a beautiful black and rather lethal cobra and other highly dangerous reptiles, all to be released after study, measurement and the milking of venom. The bird list reached 200 observed specimens and Rod saw his dolphins.

John Davies, our doctor, who had accompanied me on many expeditions, was noted for his dry wit, shaggy dog stories and quiet professionalism. This time most of his patients were animals. A large python, nibbled by a tiger, was stitched up whilst it writhed in Chris Burke's firm grip, and then we had a really big casualty.

Chan Chan, our foxy lady, held up her foot, as a dog will lift a paw with a thorn in it. 'John,' I called, 'we've got an interesting little job for you.' Lying the young elephant down, her phanit pointed to a bamboo spike, deeply buried in the sole of her right foot. Clearly it was going to be extremely difficult to dig out. However, whilst her handler sat on Chan Chan's head and whispered soothing words into her great ear, John set to work. 'The forceps are no good,' said the doc. 'I need some pliers.' Luckily my Swiss penknife, the one essential item that comes everywhere with me, includes a small pair of pliers, and using this, he pulled at the splinter. Chan Chan curled up her trunk as one may grip the arms of a dentist's chair and great salty tears ran down her cheeks. She was in considerable pain. As John worked, I watched that coiled trunk anxiously, knowing what Luksmi had done to her keeper during a similar operation. A blow from this iron-hard muscle could easily kill. At last, the four-inch spike was out and John cleaned the pliers. The patient stood up and tested her foot. Well-satisfied and grateful, she put out her trunk and stroked the doctor's back. Tears came to our eyes. However, on the last day, Kancha, the smaller tusker, suddenly emerged from the jungle and charged Pradeep's Land-Rover, just to remind us that not all elephants are friendly.

Our success was entirely due to the Nepalese, who live with and love the elephants and wild beasts of the forest. Their Hindu God, Ganesh, is said to be reincarnated in the elephant and we prayed that this would ensure their protection from poachers, but the size of that ivory is a great temptation for an impoverished peasant with a hungry family.

When news of our discovery reached the outside world, there was immediate interest and John Hunt's film was shown by CNN worldwide television. Raja Gaj was thought to be around fifty, and Kancha in his late thirties. Elephants can live to be seventy, so they were not old and the reason for the massive size and strange shape is still under discussion. Some suggest they are survivors of a herd that has existed in isolation for many years and may be mutants, the result of inbreeding. Other experts urged a survey of the surviving wild elephants of Nepal. However, the speculation about their very existence was over and our thoughts turned to the possibility of perhaps we arranging for some female elephants to be introduced. Otherwise these great bulls might be condemned to a sterile existence and their genes never passed on.

Back in Kathmandu I found ele-experts Iain and Oria Douglas Hamilton on their way home from the Tokyo CITES conference at which the contentious question of the sale of ivory had featured. They had gone to Bardia and found only dung and footprints: the enormous grey ghosts had disappeared again into the vast forest. Perhaps our executive explorers were just lucky, or maybe they had used their initiative and enterprise to solve a problem far from the boardroom. But I knew we must preserve these unique creatures before some ivory-hungry poacher killed them.

So it was that when I returned to Britain I sought support from my friends in conservation. Hardly had I started when a fax arrived from Peter Byrne, hunter turned animal defender, who for some years had been protecting another large elephant some 100 miles further west. He wrote to tell me how, shortly after we left the area, this huge elephant, heavily in *musth*, had left a reserve and, doubtless in great pain, had wandered into a populated area. The locals, resettled hill people, do not understand large wild animals and when their dogs attacked the intruder, he panicked, crashing through the settlement and killing three villagers and several buffalo. According to a witness, the giant tusker had speared a bull buffalo from its back to its chest, hurling it fifty yards, before returning to his herd in the sanctuary of the reserve. The outcry can be imagined, but realising it would be tragic if this awful accident were to lead to the destruction of these noble creatures, I asked friends of the King of Nepal to help. He did and the tusker was spared. At the same time, SES set up a fund for a detailed study and we began to plan our return.

Preparing for our third visit to Nepal in 1993, it was clear that we needed some expert help and it was through Iain Douglas-Hamilton that we were fortunate to acquire the volunteer services of Chris Thouless, a zoologist who had been working with the Kenya Wildlife Service. Chris was clearly made of the right stuff, having shown exceptional courage in dealing with an ugly situation that had developed while he was taking part in an operation in Kenya to dart wild elephants with anaesthetic before tagging them with transmitters to track their movements.

The Zoological Society of London were funding the project and had sent out Miss Alexandra Dixon to assist Chris in fitting a radio collar to a suitable elephant. Guided by a spotter plane, the scientists left their vehicles and approached a herd on foot. They had gone about seven hundred yards when Chris suddenly spotted that there were small calves with the adults and, knowing that this would make the herd very protective, ordered an immediate, quiet retreat. However, a thunderstorm was approaching and as he and the team backed away the wind changed and the herd picked up their scent. The elephants immediately became highly agitated. The team, still three hundred yards from their trucks, realised the imminent danger and ran for cover. At this point the massive matriarch charged and, singling out Miss Dixon, began to gain ground on the fleeing woman. Screaming with fury the beast came on at a frightening speed, its trunk waving. When the matriarch was almost on top of her, Alexandra swerved sideways, but in doing so slid on the slippery earth and fell. In a second the elephant was over her and before she could struggle to her feet it tried to kneel on her. Rolling into a ball she spun this way and that, desperately trying to avoid the raging creature. Chris had done his best to distract the animal by shouting and waving his arms, but it was no good, and to his horror he saw the matriarch kneel down to get at Alexandra. There was a sickening crunch as one great tusk went into her hip and another struck her calf. Then the maddened beast seized the stricken woman in its trunk and held her aloft before dashing her to the ground. As the helpless victim struck the earth, the elephant lowered its massive forehead and attempted to crush her to death. Bellowing and trumpeting, the rest of the herd closed in.

Chris thought Alexandra must be dead, but then he heard her screams as the trunk entwined around her and, ignoring the risk to himself, he rushed forward, yelling like a banshee to distract the killer. It had no effect. His only weapons were his fists and with these the zoologist hammered at the elephant's head, striking with frenzied might. 'I hit it with my fist between the eyes to try and grab its attention. Of course I was scared, but it was all I could think of doing,' Chris was reported as saying. At that moment a game ranger fired his rifle over the enraged animal. This did the trick and as the elephant backed off, Chris picked up the shattered woman and bore her to safety. Amazingly, Alexandra survived the attack. Ian Douglas-Hamilton reckoned it was one of the bravest acts he had ever known. Chris had saved her life, and for his selfless determination and conspicuous courage, he was awarded the Queen's Gallantry Medal. He sounded like a very useful person to have with us.

If handled with respect, most wild animals are peaceful enough and elephants are one of the most beloved of creatures. Some people, including myself, are crazy about them and thus I was not surprised to read the application to join the expedition from Sue Hillard, a fingerprint officer with the Merseyside police. Sue adored elephants and spent much time visiting those in Chester Zoo. I felt she could be useful in tracking the bulls by helping to identify the different footprints.

Another of the applicants was a lady who had been in the army for twenty-two years and described herself as being 'very fit and keen to go to Nepal'. Over the phone, she told me of her love for cats and how she longed to see a tiger. I was to lecture at a boys' school near Blackpool the following week and we agreed to meet. Arriving a little later than planned, I found the audience already seated. As the headmaster made the introductory remarks, I scanned the serried ranks of rosy-cheeked lads and spotted amongst them a slightly built lady with silver hair, clutching a large string bag. It had to be Miss 'Bimbo' Coleman. 'What branch of the Army were you in?' I asked over tea after the talk. 'The Royal Military Police,' came the proud reply. 'What is the most frightening thing that has ever happened to you?' I enquired. 'When my D-ring stuck at three thousand feet,' said Bimbo without batting an eyelid. 'You mean you are a freefall parachutist?' I gasped. She smiled and produced her certificates. 'And an Outward Bound instructor, canoeist, skier; and until my mother died recently at ninety, we used to go camping together at weekends.' Recovering my composure, I asked what job she had done since leaving the forces. Apparently she had been driving a gritter lorry for the local council – and was a member of the local cat club. She could see that I was finding it difficult to accept this. 'I thought that you might like to speak to my old commanding officers,' she smiled, passing me a list of names and addresses. Judith, my wife, had also been in the Women's Royal Army Corps, so she called her former colleagues. They confirmed everything that this remarkable lady had told me, adding, 'She's a terrible practical joker – beware!' So, in accepting this grand character, I made her promise, 'No practical jokes – at least not with tigers.' We appointed her the expedition quartermaster.

A good photographer would be essential on the expedition and at our office Christmas party I managed to recruit Nick Wilcox-Brown, the photographer for our local 'freebie', the *Blackmore Vale Magazine*. He had been helping us in his spare time and I had admired his pictures of steeplechasers. After the second glass of mulled wine I said, 'Why don't you come to Nepal and photograph giant elephants?' He almost collapsed, but next morning rang to ask if I'd been serious. And so it was that he ended his career with the *Blackmore Vale* and embarked on a new life as a most successful freelancer.

The expedition, the third of what were to be eleven visits to Bardia, went pretty well although we did not establish the origins of the giant mammoth-like tuskers and it was several years before we eventually located their herd, complete with cows and calves.

Without doubt the most exciting moments came when a Royal Bengal tiger made an appearance. Near the end of the project Bimbo came over to me as we relaxed by the campfire. 'I've one complaint,' she said. 'I'm the only one who has not seen a tiger. What am I going to tell my friends in the cat club?'

'Tomorrow, Bimbo, bring your elephant alongside mine and if we come across a tiger we'll stop for you to get a photo,' I promised, downing my Scotch.

Riding out at dawn I should have been alerted by the alarm call of the deer, quickly taken up by a peacock, but my attention was focused on changing the film in my camera. We were moving through five-foot ferns when, with a blood-curdling growl, a large tiger sprang from beneath Honey Blossom's feet. The old girl trumpeted and raged, but stood her ground as the orange-and-black form of a big male bounced away through the cover. 'He's carrying a kill,' said Chris. Sure enough he had a spotted deer in his powerful jaws. 'It won't go far,' hissed Pradeep as we set off in pursuit. As predicted, the tiger soon sought refuge in a small copse and lay down, breathing heavily. With practised drill, the elephants formed a ring. Bimbo and her mount were in the best position and for several minutes had a clear view of a truly magnificent Royal Bengal tiger at the edge of the trees. They were very privileged, as many more humans are seen by tigers than ever glimpse these magnificent but elusive creatures. Cameras clicked and from where I was placed I could just see its tail beginning to twitch from side to side. 'Looks agitated,' muttered Pradeep. 'We'd better leave him in peace,' I started to say. Before I could finish there was a shattering roar and I saw its back legs working like pistons as the predator hurled itself at Bimbo's elephant. Seeing the cat coming, the elephant, squealing and trumpeting, turned to face the charge. Her trunk flailed as the tiger dodged and stopped its rush a few feet from the ex-gritter driver from Yorkshire. Then, still trumpeting, the young elephant turned and gave chase, almost tipping off the gallant Bimbo. Our herd was in full cry as we rounded the wood. 'Are you all right, Bimbo?' I shouted. 'Yes, thank you,' she replied serenely, looking like Queen Victoria. 'But that pussy should definitely have a collar!' Later, I heard that the tiger's teeth had only been a couple of feet from Bimbo's leg. It took several minutes for everyone to stop chattering like excited children and for the adrenaline to die down. 'There's not a lot of room here,' shouted our doctor, who had also been on Bimbo's elephant, so I invited him to join me on Honey Blossom. Climbing aboard, he confided that the real reason for wanting to change was that when the tiger had charged, Bimbo had grabbed his trousers and got so excited she'd almost pulled them off. 'I'm worried what might happen if we meet another one,' he murmured.

Amazingly, I was the only casualty on our elephant quests, although my injury was no fault of Honey Blossom's. As a cameraman, I was sitting directly behind the phanit, which necessitated holding on to the corner posts of the howdah as it swayed from side to side. At times, the movement is pretty violent and one has to grip hard. By the end of one expedition, I had lost the feeling in the end of a finger on my right hand and could hardly feel the camera button. Dr John Davies had a look and diagnosed carpal tunnel syndrome. 'Bricklayers get it and if it doesn't get better you'll need to have an operation to free the trapped nerve,' he explained. Back in Britain, a surgeon in our local hospital set to work. 'How did you do this?' he enquired as I submitted myself to his knife under local anaesthetic. 'Riding a galloping elephant' I replied. He looked mildly surprised as he sliced open my palm. With my arm in a sling, it made a great story at dinner parties.

The following year, the lovely actress Rula Lenska joined us for what was becoming an annual visit to Bardia and she later worked with me on the book *Mammoth Hunt* and a TV film about the expeditions. Rula, a most enthusiastic conservationist, did much to help draw attention to the need for wildlife conservation in Bardia and indeed elsewhere in the world. On her second trip with us, the *Daily Mirror* sent a reporter and photographer. 'We've only got a week to get the story and photograph the king of the elephants,' the reporter pointed out. 'Can't guarantee that,' I grunted as we headed into some dense bush. But our trackers had done well and a few minutes later the earth shook as many tons of Raja Gaj raised himself from a short nap. Clouds of grey dust wafted off the huge body as he extended his massive trunk to Honey Blossom. 'My God, its prehistoric' muttered the reporter. 'How close are we?' 'About thirty feet,' I whispered. 'It will be fifteen for my readers,' he replied. We left the old boy to enjoy his breakfast.

By the time of the 1994 expedition, Professor Adrian Lister, a leading expert on the Asian elephant, had become part of our team and in 1997 we at last discovered a herd of cow elephants and their calves in Bardia, exhibiting great domed heads similar to the giant bulls. Raja Gaj proved to be elusive; his tracks, a few hours old, showed that he was on his own (he was in *musth*), but some members of the team encountered the king's guardian, Kancha, also in *musth*, when they were returning to camp by vehicle one evening. He was extremely aggressive and would not let the vehicle past, so they radioed for assistance and Kancha was eventually driven back into the forest.

To assist with identifying and tracking the wild elephants, Sue Hilliard's system of scanning their footprints into a computer was proving a much friendlier method than fitting them with radio collars, which is both expensive and stressful to the animals. Each footprint is measured and photographed and it is thought that the variation between elephants' footprints is so great that there is essentially no limit to the system.

On this expedition we found ourselves in the midst of a most unusual concentration of tiger. Dinner had just finished when a series of deep roars reverberated through the forest. It was clearly a tiger fight. Or they could be just mating; tigers make similar noises at the height of passion! However, next day we had a group going out on foot to view birds so I decided to sweep the area of fifteen-foot elephant grass from which the roaring seemed to originate. Taking five of our jumbos, we entered the towering grass. Everything was obscured by the tall stems and nothing moved, not even a bird called. Then, with no warning, the largest tiger I'd ever seen rose up right in front of my elephant, Laxmi Kali. Roaring its head off, with teeth bared, the tiger reared up on its hind legs. I saw the huge paws striking out, the claws like a handful of carving knives. Laxmi Kali shrieked, lashing out with her trunk and the snarling cat rolled to one side and disappeared.

Almost at once Nick Turner came on the walkie-talkie. 'There's a bloody great tiger beside us,' he yelled.

'Take a photo of it and let's get clear,' I retorted.

Nick did just that, but better still, Sheila Sulley, riding with Nick, captured the encounter on video film, complete with roars!

Then to our astonishment, the tiger, whom we later named Snow White, sat down in an open patch as if nothing had happened. 'He must have a kill near here,' said our Nepalese guide Ram Din. So, leaving three elephants to watch Snow White, we back-tracked to the site of the initial confrontation. Taking quite a risk, Shakali, another guide, climbed down from Laxmi Kali and, along with Ram Din, searched the ground. They made an extraordinary discovery. In an area of flattened grass, splattered with blood and fur, lay the paws and head of a tigress. Snow White appeared to have torn the female apart and eaten her. No one I knew had ever come across such a case of a tiger killing and devouring another full grown adult.

Carrying the grizzly remains back to camp, we took them to the tent of Andrew Mitchell, our zoologist, who was having a lie-in. His wife, Laura, woke him, holding the skull up to the bed whilst we made a low roar. Andrew opened his eyes, focused and yelled. Only the previous day he had almost fallen off his elephant into the jaws of a tiger whilst he was making a recording for the BBC. Later, Snow White killed a local woman and was said to have then been captured by the Wildlife Department and taken to Kathmandu Zoo; a sad end.

Throughout our expeditions in Bardia we became aware of the damage caused by wild elephants to villages around the reserve. One village, in particular, suffered badly and, as a result, was putting out poison to kill Raja Gaj and his herd.

To win the hearts and minds of the villagers, we always took them gifts, including the first computer for their school and reading glasses. Our doctors and dentists treated patients and to show the children that not all elephants were wicked, we got them to ride our domestic jumbos and play football!

In 2012 I took my three grandchildren, aged 9-14, plus six other youngsters on a family expedition, which they loved, especially the bathing of their elephants in the river at the end of the day. We had several exciting encounters, although when an angry tigress charged our elephant, my grandson Jack grabbed my arm, saying,

'I don't want to be eaten, Grandpa'.

Adrian Lister successfully obtained DNA from wild elephant dung that showed these giants were not, in fact, mammoth, but there was an interesting comparison with the skull of an ancient elephant named *Elephas hysudricus*, which he found in a Kathmandu Museum. The study of these distinctively giant beasts continue and in 2012 we found almost fifty wild elephants in Bardia, although, sadly, Raja Gaj had disappeared.

Back in 1991, at around the time of the first Bardia expedition, I had also turned my attention northwards to the curtain that was rising on the Soviet Union. As peristroika spread in the late 1980s, leading to the collapse of the Soviet Union and the end of the Cold War, new and exciting challenges opened up in Siberia, a land I had doubted I would ever see unless as a prisoner-of war, and after some correspondence with interested Russians, I flew out to investigate the possibilities. Aeroflot had kindly provided me with a first class seat and I felt like a member of the presidium as we winged our way over the endless forest and steppe. Sensing that a meal was about to be served, I lowered my tray table from the back of the seat in front. It flopped down on a broken hinge, refusing to stay upright. Pressure on the call button produced the stewardess, one of Russia's leading lady weight-lifters by the look of her, who glowered at the offending table and then with a flash of inspiration, grunted 'moment' and headed for the galley. 'Ah! Gone to fetch her toolbox,' I thought. A few minutes later she returned, wrenched the table back into its fold away position, put a bottle of warm champagne on the seat beside me and commanded, 'Drink.' Perhaps that was the answer to all problems in Russia! Our meal finally arrived; two doorstep-thick slices of bread separated by a thin smear of fish paste, wrapped in cling film. My neighbour, who appeared to be an important official, inspected his sandwich with the care of a connoisseur, then rang for the weight-lifter to whom he indicated that there was something amiss. Seizing the plate, she stamped off towards the economy section. I watched, fascinated, as she plucked a plate from a red-faced peasant woman, peeled the sandwich apart, nodded in satisfaction, exchanged it for the official's meal and marched back. All seemed happy, although the peasant looked a little sad. I had discovered one of the differences between First Class and Economy travel on Aeroflot; in First Class you get butter in sandwiches, in Economy you do not.

At Irkutsk I was greeted by our new committee and treated to a whistle-stop tour of the region. One evening I was left to my own devices and, following their directions, decided to join a dinner party in a beer cellar. My hosts were holidaying East Europeans. No one spoke English, but with the help of a dictionary we managed to communicate. The menu included a dish from each country represented at the dinner, but, sadly, because they only learned I was coming at a late hour, it had not been possible to include an English course. However, by way of making up for this the hosts pointed to the buxom waitresses at the far side of the restaurant and explained that they had found some T-Shirts bearing 'English children's songs'. 'Ah,' I remarked, 'nursery rhymes.' As the waitresses approached I saw that a cartoon was emblazoned on their ample bosoms. To my astonishment the caption read: 'AIDS KILLS, DON'T BE SILLY, GET THAT CONDOM ON YOUR WILLIE.' Apparently a free issue from the World Health Organization!

18

In the Hoofprints of Ghengis Khan

'Welcome to Mongolia, Colonel,' said the almond-eyed beauty in the black leather mini-skirt as she brushed aside a lock of long black hair that hung over one eye. 'I am here to look after you, my name is Minjin,' (which means Beaver) she smiled. My God, I thought, this must be a KGB trap. But there was no opportunity to flee as my damnably attractive escort lead me out of the airport to the waiting Volga. Somewhere from behind came the rest of the greeting team, including Sean Hinton, a young musicologist, who was to become my most valued adviser over the next two years.

Travelling into Ulan Bator, Minjin briefed me in perfect but somewhat Victorian English.

'Where did you study my language?' I asked.

'In Moscow. I do hope it is correct.' I assured her that it was, although perhaps just a little quaint. 'Oh, the tapes were very old,' she replied.

By two that afternoon I had explained what Operation Raleigh was all about to a dozen Mongols and was repeating it for the Minister of Education. The planning for this expedition had begun eighteen months previously when a Mongolian Government delegation had visited London seeking closer ties with Britain. After almost seventy years of Soviet domination, Mongolia, landlocked and sandwiched between Russia and China, was likely to become truly independent. However, the departure of 400,000 Soviet troops and the probable withdrawal of Russian aid was going to cause immense problems in a land roughly the size of Western Europe, with a population of only two million and few natural resources. The Mongols needed new friends.

Slightly to my surprise, the Minister appreciated the value of hordes of Raleigh venturers invading his country and suggested we fly to the most remote aimag, or province, to see if we could carry out a series of community aid and conservation tasks there. Thus, Minjin, Sean and I found ourselves jostling to get aboard a well-used Mongolian Airlines (MIAT) Antonov 24 airliner. The seats were utility and not designed for fifteen-stone Colonels, but we were soon winging westward over the rolling sands of the Gobi. Frozen lakes and snow-capped mountains passed beneath. The other passengers stared at us with mild curiosity. My neighbour, a small lad, picked his nose thoughtfully and watched everything I did.

At Khovd, bright sun and a bitter wind greeted our arrival. On the tarmac a short, smiling gentleman advanced and introduced himself as Mr Terbish, rector of the local Pedagogical Institute. He was to be our host and later to represent Operation Raleigh in the region. Here the arid Gobi desert meets the Altai Mountains. In the far northwest, the Tavan Bogd range extends across the border with China, Mongolia and Russia. The highest peak, Mt Huiten (15,300 feet), dominates an area of alpine magnificence. The sharp ridges of the mountains with their eternal snowscapes are the birthplace of glittering glaciers leading down to sparkling emerald lakes.

Khovd city, with some 20,000 Mongols, Kazakhs and other racial groups, is the capital of the aimag. Apart from the government building and a colourful theatre the place was drab and dilapidated. Warmed by a bowl of boiled mutton and some soggy rice in the hotel, we began the long round of briefings. We explained about Raleigh, and local officials outlined their own needs, including medical help, the construction of refuge huts for travellers, bridges, biological studies and, above all, English teachers.

Within a few hours I was ready to see something of the countryside and so over the desert we bounced in an old Russian jeep with a singing driver. I quickly realised I was in an area that few, if any, westerners had ever visited. There were unclimbed peaks, unnavigated rivers and tales of wildmen. By 11am next day I'd seen enough to know that this was certainly a place for an expedition, but it would be no picnic.

The only transport would be the short, sturdy Mongolian horse and the heavily-built Bactrian camel, a double-humped, ill-tempered beast whose disposition is not improved by the wooden nose peg inserted through its nostrils to which strings are attached for steering. The horses' saddles would also be a problem. Made of wood and designed to fit a small dwarf, they would cause grave discomfort and perhaps serious injury to the average European male. We decided to seek venturers with small bottoms who could ride well. A few 'jeeps' and trucks might be available and the ancient biplane at Khovd airport was said to be airworthy.

The Altai rise from the desert to over 14,000 feet. Armagu (13,200 feet), Tsasan-Sume, Irvis Tag and many unnamed summits tower upwards above the source of large rivers including the Khovd, one of Mongolia's longest. The mountain lakes offer a quiet retreat for numerous varieties of birds, including swan, geese and other waterfowl, whilst golden eagle, buzzard and kite glide above.

Although it was now cold and dry', Terbish told me that when the rains came in the summer, the desert would turn green, providing lush pasture for the cattle, goats, horses, sheep and yak of the nomadic people. Being a biologist, he was eager to tell me of the wildlife, which included the vigorous mountain sheep or argali, the wild goat or yangir, and even the rare snow leopard. Wolves, he explained, were known to attack domestic animals and there were also bear and deer in the region. Being far from the moderating influence of the oceans, surrounded by mountains and situated at a relatively high altitude, Mongolia has a climate of extremes that can produce severe unpredictable weather, as we were to discover.

Mongolian food is traditional and has remained unchanged for centuries. Meat, occasionally beef or more usually mutton, is the main dish. It is boiled as small pieces and served with rice imported from China. Nomads have no time to grow vegetables and we were told that 'grass is for horses, meat is for men'. The fat is considered the best part and guests are given generous portions and expected to down great lumps of it with relish. 'Talkh', a tasty bread, and 'Arul', a hard yellow cheese made from camel, cow, goat, or sheep's milk, are also par of the regular diet. I could see our western-trained stomachs might have a few problems. Mongols drink salted, milky tea or 'suun chai' by the gallon. It contains more cow or yak milk than tea and, very often, a large dollop of rancid butter is added as a delicacy. Apart from staples such as flour, rice and tea, which are purchased whenever they happen to pass through a town, the nomadic families produce most of their food from their own herds, just as their ancestors did in the time of Genghis Khan. To my taste, the diet, which is the same for all meals, is exceedingly bland and I knew we would need to bring our own spices and dried vegetables. 'Airak', or 'Kumiss', fermented mare's milk with a slight almond flavour, is the principal alcoholic drink. However, it has a very low alcohol content, which cannot be said of the vodka!

Back in Ulan Bator, the Minister gave his approval for a full-scale expedition in 1992, but, meanwhile, the country was in turmoil and great crowds gathered in Suha Bator Square demanding democracy. It was an eerie experience, standing amongst them and facing the lines of unarmed soldiers that were guarding the Parliament and wondering if tanks were waiting in the side streets. The orderliness of the mass demonstration was most impressive. A crowd of some 12,000 people sat quietly in the square with banners displayed, whilst a big bass drum beat a remorseless thump, thump, thump, like some giant clock ticking away metronomically. Hour after hour, day after day, the crowd came to sit and stare at the Parliament. Was this what brought down the walls of Jericho?

The Russians in our hotel were obviously worried. Early one morning, I found myself awaiting our battered Volga on the steps and beside me stood a bemedalled Soviet General, impatiently looking for his vehicle. Our car was approaching when the Russian moved forward and I feared he was about to take it.

'I think that's our car, General,' I said.

The great man spun round. 'Ah, English, how do you know I'm a General?'

'Because I'm a British Army Colonel,' I retorted.

'At the Embassy, I think?' he said inquiringly.

'No, actually I'm with the Ministry of Defence in London.'

'So what are you doing in Mongolia?'

'Planning an operation, General,' I replied, but his car had arrived and, as his aides swept him away, he gave me a long, penetrating look. Heaven knows what he told the KGB!

My final job was to set up a local committee and we were fortunate in getting Mr Ch Ganbold as Chairman and the backing of his Peace and Friendship Organization.

Back in London, I set about fund-raising for the expedition and thanks to my friend, financial journalist Lorna Bourke, obtained some very valuable help from the Save and Prosper Group, which enabled us to buy Mongolian tents and saddles. Meanwhile Richard Branson had set up a scheme on his Virgin Airways to collect passengers' loose change at the end of flights and with this we financed the TB vaccination programme.

The following year, Pamela Stephany, British businessman Brian Henslow, Sean and I did a complete recce of the northern part of the region, whilst Ann Tweedy and another team examined the southern area. Recruiting was going well with lots of small bottoms, mainly girls, applying.

In the mountains, there were tantalising tales of almas or the yeti. The male was said to be six to nine feet tall and the females five to six feet. Heads were somewhat pointed and the body covered in reddish grey hair. We were told that the creature walked upright and had enormously powerful back legs, allowing it to leap up to three feet vertically from a standing start. The footprint, similar to a human's, is often larger and wider. The body shape is that of a heavily-built human and females are said to have pendant breasts, which, it was said, they toss over their shoulders when they run! It seems they are afraid of water, but not fire. There are stories of almas being found asleep in gers – the circular felt-lined tents built around a wooden lattice-work frame in which the nomadic Mongolians live – or warming themselves by abandoned fires. There are also tales of them kidnapping children and of female almas kidnapping male hunters, whom they then rape! Generally, they seem to be very shy and usually run away from man. Although they do not appear to speak, they are said to emit a high-pitched squeak or shrill cry.

Reports of almas in western Mongolia are more numerous than in most areas of the world where they are alleged to exist and there are many who readily admit to having seen them. I learned that since my last visit an almas was said to have been seen in the Khovd River Gorge, but fled when called to by hunters. Although it may be a myth, the existence of the almas is very much part of Mongolian folklore and a number of eminent Soviet and local scientists have spent much time and effort researching the mystery. The morning after a discussion with some nomads in the mountains, I was shaving, stripped to the waist, and some local children, watching in fascination, pointed at the hair on my chest and cried 'almas'.

There followed a year's planning in Britain where, ably assisted by my super PA, Sally Cox, and Sean Hinton, we set up the first major western expedition to Mongolia for over fifty years. Sir Bob Reid kindly offered the help of British Rail, but the collapse of the USSR and the problems of getting a multinational group down the Trans-Siberian Railway curtailed our plan to go out by train. This was a great shame as I'd quite looked forward to going up to the ticket office at Victoria and demanding, 'One hundred-and-twenty single tickets to Ulan Bator, please.'

The advance party flew out in April 1992 under the leadership of my second-in-command, Squadron Leader George Baber, RAF. Containers of everything we needed had been sent out by sea to China and thence by rail to Ulan Bator. George's first task was to get these forty tons of stores and rations across the Gobi to Khovd and then to set up a base camp. Corporal Tony Martin, a Commando Sapper, soon had five Mongolian Army trucks loaded and, with three other British NCOS, set off on a thousand-mile drive. The Mongol drivers reckoned to stop at every ger en route for vodka, women and song. That they managed to reach Khovd in five days was a miracle and a fine example of the leadership qualities of British NCOs.

When Sally and I arrived with the main body of the staff in May, George had a splendid tented camp set up at the foot of the Altai

Mountains, beside the shallow Buyant River. It was still cool and the wind would whip up sandstorms and even play havoc with a sturdy ger.

The Mongolian economy was meanwhile deteriorating at an alarming rate. Food and fuel were rationed and construction materials were like gold dust. However, Mick Ponting, our vet, had procured a herd of horses and several camels, Sean had borrowed a battered old Russian GAZ jeep and George had an agreement for the hire of the Antonov biplane. The local telephone company, to our amazement, produced a radiophone that could link us to the outside world.

Simon Hamilton, formerly of the Kalahari Quest, was our treasurer and had spent four months begging for goods in Britain and as a result our store ger was filled with gifts, including some home-brewed beer and wine-making kits from Boots. As local drinks only consisted of Vodka and fermented mare's milk, these were especially welcome.

I went back to Ulan Bator to collect the venturers, sixty-six from abroad and twenty from within Mongolia. I also met Gerald Brown, the Anglican Archdeacon for the enormous area from Oslo to Ulan Bator. He needed no persuasion to accompany us and hold a Whitsuntide service in the field. This must certainly have been the first Anglican service ever held in that remote region.

Whilst in the capital I had tried to buy some frying pans and spent hours going from one under-stocked shop to another. At last, one assistant claimed she had what I needed, but, strangely, she brought back a trumpet. She looked so disappointed when I declined that I gave her the equivalent of the few pence that she asked and roused the camp with badly-played reveilles thereafter.

The flight to Khovd with MIAT was quite an eye-opener for the young. We had chartered the plane, so we got on first, then the stand-by passengers were loaded into the luggage bay Next, small children were passed around to sit on our knees and, finally, a few strap hangers came aboard to stand in the aisle all the way. The loo was out of commission, so, after two hours, we landed at a settlement, aptly named Moron, where everyone tumbled out to relieve themselves on the grass before flying on to Khovd.

To prepare the venturers for the expedition, George had organised a week's training in everything from river crossing to Mongol etiquette. So, schooled in local niceties and on how to survive in this stark land, our teams deployed. We organised the expedition into seven groups and the Field HQ (FHQ). Between six and twelve venturers made up each group, along with a small number of staff. Although we used a motley collection of old Russian trucks to deploy the teams, the only permanent vehicle on the expedition was an ancient and unreliable 'jeep' at FHQ. Horses and camels were used almost everywhere, as was Shank's pony!

The tasks included river exploration by Avon inflatables, fauna and flora studies by horse-borne parties and a scientific team on the vast Black Lake. There was also a 220-foot suspension footbridge and a refuge hut to be constructed. Two medical teams would administer community medicine and handle the vaccination programme as well as eye operations. In the high mountains, at the junction of the Chinese, Mongolian and Russian borders, the mountaineers aimed to climb new peaks and study the animals and plants. Our final report, named the Wainwright study after a famous British Lake District guide, was to include as much information as possible about the area, its people, fauna and flora. I was very conscious that being the first westerners in the area, we had a great opportunity for real exploration, as well as helping the people of the area. The way the Mongolian economy was deteriorating, it could be a long while before others came here and, when they did, our work would be invaluable. At the same time, I felt we were privileged to be here and must make a point of respecting the local culture and traditions.

Each group was named after an appropriate historical figure. So we had Tenzing (mountaineers), Drake (The Black Lake), Brunel (Bridge builders), Genghis (the horse team), Livingstone and Nightingale (medical) and Nelson (the river explorers). All were linked to FHQ by radio.

Food was rationed and in short supply and we guarded our stocks with an armed policeman, for whom the local police chief charged us $11-per-week, of which we gathered that the constable himself received only four! As the situation grew more desperate, there was a marked increase in violence and we suffered several robberies. Sadly Mongolia was no longer a place where you could rely on the honesty of the locals. We had brought vegetable seeds from Britain and I dug a small plot outside my tent and labelled it 'The Garden of Eden'. As a lady of easy virtue who helped in the camp assisted with the digging, some joker had added, 'dug by the whores of Babylon'. To keep down the rodents in the ration store, I encouraged a stray black cat to adopt us and named him 'Cooking Fat' after Ann Tweedy's ginger feline in Britain.

The Mongolian Army had kindly lent us some marquees but, for the most part, our camp consisted of the traditional gers, The Buyant river flowed within a few metres and provided water, which we boiled and sterilised most religiously. From his office at the Pedagogical Institute eight kilometres away, the good Terbish and the local government did all they could to support us with the province's limited resources.

On 13 June the teams deployed. Tenzing headed for the heights of Tavan Bodg, whilst Tony Martin led his merry band to the mosquito-infested lake. The horses of Genghis, and one rather reluctant camel named Basil, went northwards to the Khovd River gorge and White Table mountain. Tan Chi Chiu and Richard Tan, our energetic Singaporean military doctors, trucked southwards over the mountains to Bulgan Sum, leaving Dr David Clayton's team to screen cataract patients in the Khovd area.

The rafters motored to join the upper reaches of the Khovd River that would take them into the great gorge, and Mick Christy's Brunel team, the nearest group to FHQ, trotted off to their bridge site in fine style. Suddenly, Base Camp was very quiet, the sun shone and the temperature began to rise. I planted my vegetables, issued strict instructions on the watering and drove out to watch the river explorers descend the cataract at the bottom of the Khovd River gorge. When I had first seen this placid river in 1991, I had no idea that it contained such a formidable set of rapids. For 600 yards a torrent of foaming white water rushes out of the canyon. The powerful stoppers and 'holes' are a real challenge for even experienced rafters, but there are no major obstructions and a vehicle track ran along the bank. It was therefore an ideal setting for the venturers to experience the thrills of the exhilarating sport we had pioneered with our Avons on the Blue Nile. However, there were spills as well.

White water expert Mark Herriott took the first boat down and the other two followed. Screaming with excitement, the paddlers fought against the tossing, tugging waves that towered around them.

'So far the Khovd has been a bit of a doddle,' remarked Rob Leppard from Croydon, 'but this is the real stuff, with big water roaring around you, flinging your neoprene craft about like a cork in a tempest.'

'Like riding a wild roller craft,' said Su-Ann Lim from Singapore.

The last raft, helmed by Mike Metcalfe, a tough and popular Geordie, had just started down when it hit a huge standing wave that catapulted it over, flipping the crew into the racing foam.

'I thought I was drowning as I spun round and round under water – it was terrifying,' said a shaken teenager when I talked to her later. That evening, as the cliffs of the gorge turned scarlet in the sunset, I relaxed, catching plentiful Arctic char that swam in the turbulent waters before joining the venturers for a fish supper under the stars. Tsogt, a young Mongolian, had brought his guitar and played Beatles' favourites learnt entirely from listening to the BBC. What an experience this was for all of us, but especially the young. One day they would tell their grandchildren how they were the first westerners in Outer Mongolia. Ann Tweedy had her tent up by the river and, sharing a plastic mug of Scotch, we talked of Aberdeenshire, the reconnaissance trips and the years of effort that had gone into making this particular dream come true. High above us, the Argali rams fought for possession of ewes, their great horns crashing together with a sound like rifle shots. It was another world.

A complaining Basil woke me at dawn. Camels have an extraordinary vocabulary and the ability to express it at both ends of the body. The goretex bivvy bag had kept me warm and dry and within minutes I was downing hot sweet tea before scouting ahead to find the route for Mick Ponting's horse-mounted group that was to ascend the mountains on its wildlife survey. A day and a half later we reached the hidden valley Pam that I had found the previous year. But now it was later in the season and scores of gers dotted this Shangri-la. Herdsmen came galloping, eager to see the strangers.

Some hours later we rode to a ridge at 10,000 feet to view a huge corniche, where Mount Somboros' snowfield dropped into a vertically-sided glacial valley. Returning to camp, a rider thundered towards me. Topol, my solid bay, plodded on and I paid little attention to the newcomer. But he raced straight at us and with a great cry of 'John', flung his arms about my neck, almost dragging me from the saddle. It was Nokhoijav, head of a family of Oh-ulds, who had befriended me on my last visit. He begged me to come to his ger, but the hour was late and, instead, we persuaded him to accompany us to our camp, where a 'hot rock' supper was being prepared by other locals. So, whilst we drank tea, a whole sheep was chopped up and placed in a large milk churn full of heated stones. The evening grew cold as we pressed the chunks of fatty mutton to our lips and, through one overworked interpreter, told each other of our lives since we had last met.

Nokhoijav's family were well. The herd had multiplied and, through his radio, he had learned of the dramatic events in Moscow and Ulan Bator. He had known we would return, it was a good omen he confided: now all would improve in Mongolia. Why, we had even brought the vet that we had talked of and medicines, too. It was just as well because one of the nomad's horses had been savagely mauled by wolves and, next day, all Mick's skills were called upon to save it. Later, seated on low stools, we lunched in Nokhoijav's ger. The whole family was there and it was a great reunion, but, alas, Ann, photographer Ian Robinson and I had to go back to the plains. As leader of such a large enterprise, there was never time to linger, but I promised to return.

As the expedition progressed, the Mongolian economy declined further and by Naadam, the three days of national celebration in July, the situation had become extremely difficult. Fuel was in such short supply that MIAT had ceased its internal flights. With great difficulty, we managed to get Harry Brown's surgical eye team in and out of Khovd. However it was worth the effort for they restored sight to sixty-three people and did much other good work. Ann just got back to Ulan Bator and Richard Snailham, who was to take over as writer, only just made it. With him came his wife, Chris, a trauma doctor, who was to prove invaluable.

At Naadam it began to rain, but we entered into the spirit of the games, with venturers taking part in the archery and wrestling, although with little success. The twenty-five-mile horserace started hours later and we spent a damp day in the desert awaiting its finish. When the bedraggled horses and their exhausted young jockeys cantered in it was something of an anti-climax.

Bob Rose and John Lyons, who had been with me in the Kalahari, somehow got themselves to Khovd, but as they arrived a real drama hit us.

I'd just finished watering my vegetable garden when the dreaded words came crackling over the radio from Tavan Bogd. 'There's been an accident.' Julian Freeman-Attwood's tense voice gave me the facts. Lindsay Griffin, one of Britain's finest climbers, was moving through a boulder field as they returned from a visit to the summit of Mt Huiten when, without warning, a huge granite rock had toppled over, pinning him to the ground and mangling his left leg.

His colleagues, Julian and American Ed Webster, had descended by a different route and were already cooking a meal at their tent. Lindsay was alone and unconscious. When he came to, the top of the trapped leg had turned purple and gone numb. To restore the flow of blood, the climber managed to drag a rope from his rucksack and lasso a higher rock, thus creating a sort of pulley system that enabled him to raise the rock a fraction of an inch. As the pressure was reduced the blood flowed back into the shattered limb, but with that came excruciating pain.

Back at the tent it was now 1830 hours. The accident had happened at around 1500. Puzzled by Lindsay's long absence, the other two retraced their route, looking for him. But it was not until 2000 that, hearing faint cries, they eventually found him. It took three more laborious hours of work with elaborate pulley systems to shift the boulder and haul the stricken man out. His leg was pulped, with multiple compound fractures. For the next fifteen hours they struggled in darkness to descend 1,000 feet to a flat area where Julian thought a helicopter could land. Here they put him in a tent by a stream and, leaving him with rations and painkillers, set off to get help.

It took all the next day and most of the following night, struggling over snow-covered crevasses and a glacier, to reach their base and the vital radio. They had been going for fifty-one hours, without sleep and little food.

'Can you get a helicopter as quickly as possible?' pleaded Julian.

'Leave it to us. Get some sleep and I'll call you in three hours,' I told him, wondering where on earth I'd find a helicopter that could reach Lindsay before his wound, the wolves or the cold overcame him, alone on the mountain.

Sean was already phoning the Ministry of Defence in Ulan Bator when George brought in the detailed maps. After five minutes' scrutiny we looked at each other and I said, 'My God, they've carried him down into China.'

'The Army says that they have helicopters but there is no fuel west of the capital,' reported Sean.

'See if MIAT can help,' I snapped.

'But John, there's no fuel.'

'OK, but give them a call anyway,' I retorted.

'Then it's the Antonov Two,' said George, referring to the ancient Soviet biplane that stood in the airstrip. I knew it could land at Bayan Olgiy, some seventy-five miles east of Mt Huiten. From here a truck could carry a rescue team to the base of the mountain. Then, with luck, it would be two days' march to Lindsay. There was fuel for the old plane and, although it was a forlorn hope, we despatched some eager venturer climbers along with Army medic Andy Herrod, and Jan Kennis, a Belgian surgeon.

Sean burst in, as he always did. 'It's MIAT,' he cried. 'They've called to say there is a chopper and they reckon they can get fuel, but,' he lowered his eyes, 'it will cost US$26,000.'

Sally interjected. 'The insurance company will cover that.' 'Send it.' I said, praying it would get there in time.

It was next day before the huge MIL 8 transport helicopter reached Khovd and George, his airforce interest aroused, was there. However, it quickly became apparent that MIAT's information about fuel was incorrect. There was none in Khovd. So the pilot, Captain Nyamaagiin Jambaldorj, and I dashed off to see the Premier. Mongolian bureaucracy grinds slowly and it is not easy to burst in on even a provincial Premier at short notice. However, within a quarter of an hour we were explaining our predicament to the heavily-built official. Nyamaagiin and our liaison officer, Chuluumbaatar, spoke quickly. They knew what to ask for so did not waste time interpreting for my benefit. At last, the Premier nodded gravely and, sending for the keeper of the strategic fuel stocks, the city's last emergency reserve, he generously released a ton. However, it was 4pm before it had been trucked to the airport and the helicopter was airborne.

Meanwhile, Sally was arranging an ambulance jet with SOS Services in Hong Kong and Bob Rose, himself a pilot, was investigating our local airport's navigational beacons, whilst in Ulan Bator the British Embassy was seeking clearance for this unprecedented flight. I had sent George and Sean with the helicopter, plus Chris Snailham as the doctor and Richard, her husband, who himself had once fallen 1,640 feet down a mountain in Ecuador and knew what it was like to be rescued. Another team of venturer climbers went as stretcher bearers. There was nothing else we could do but pray.

Every hour's delay increased the risk of infection and the possible loss of Lindsay's leg. Lying alone in his tent, he sipped water from the stream, swallowed pain killers, but ate nothing. He never really expected to see a helicopter. When the MIL 8 thundered over the base camp ger, the biplane party, who had marched non-stop, was just about to start up the awful Potanine glacier. 'Here comes the school bus,' yelled Ed, as the bulky machine, quite unsuited for mountain rescue, lumbered into sight. Leaping aboard, he guided it to Lindsay's tent, some ten miles' distant, at an altitude of 10,800 feet. In the thin air, this was the extreme limit for the groaning, juddering chopper, but somehow Nyamaagiin coaxed it upward. At 12,800 feet, the flaying rotor carried them over the col and they saw the blue tent on a ledge just below the crest. Still too heavy and too high to hover, the captain made five attempts to roll land onto the ledge, but each time the boulders defeated him. He eventually dropped the rescuers two miles away. But as they set out for Lindsay, the aircraft whirled away. I wonder where he's going, thought George, as he raced for the tent. Inside Lindsay greeted them and consoled our stalwart RAF officer on the disappearance of his helicopter.

Night was coming as the team dragged Lindsay to a clearer patch of land and waited. There was no sign of the helicopter. At the base camp Julian was almost frantic with worry. What could have happened? Had they crashed? The consequences were too awful to contemplate. At FHQ, Bob opened a bottle of special vodka. 'I think we all need a little drink,' he said as we crouched by the radio.

At 2100 to George's intense relief, he heard the heavy throb of the aircraft returning. The pilot had to jettison more weight, so he had flown to a lower altitude, landed and, to save fuel, had shut down his engines whilst he allowed time for the casualty to be moved. Then, after restarting, he had removed the heavy batteries and returned. With Lindsay safely aboard, he collected his batteries. It was all an incredible act, balancing weight and fuel and overcoming altitude and the advancing darkness to snatch the horribly injured man from what we now knew must be Chinese territory.

As the 'school bus' landed at Bayan Olgiy airstrip, the engines cut: they were out of fuel and no more was available. Commandeering a van, the medics rushed Lindsay to the local hospital. The only operating table was the hospital director's desk and there, working with Swiss Army penknives, Chris and Jan cut away at tattered clothing and near rotting flesh. Bone was sticking through the skin as they operated.

'Splints?' asked Chris.

The Mongol nurse shook her head sadly. 'No splints.'

'Not to worry,' grinned Sean, hacking up the director's filing cabinet with a pickaxe.

Back at the strip they found the chopper connected by a hose to an Aeroflot airliner that was collecting emigrating Kazahks. Nyamaagiin had swopped five bottles of vodka for 100 gallons of fuel, which would get him to Khovd.

A great grin spread across Lindsay's emaciated face as I stepped aboard. 'Sorry about all this,' he muttered, 'but John, I have something very important to tell you.' As we waited for the Lear Jet from SAS Services Hong Kong, he told me how, up in the mountains, he had caught sight of a large auburn-coloured creature that seemed to walk upright. His sighting had taken place not far from where Julian had spotted some strange tracks, quite unlike those of snow leopard or bear, that appeared to have been made by a biped.

It was late July before I could visit Tavan Bogd myself and see the extraordinary Alpine scenery, quite unlike anywhere else I had been in Mongolia. Few outsiders had seen these incredible mountains before our expedition and, as we rode through the swirling mist on our shaggy ponies, I found it difficult to imagine any large creature living in this land of snow, ice and swamps.

However, on 10 June, Julian, his colleague Ed Webster and Lindsay had crossed the vast Potanine Glacier and put up a camp near the Alexandroff Glacier, 500 yards from a charming little peak named Snow Church that rose on the Chinese border. The next day, snow and wind prevented climbing, but the following morning the weather cleared and they set out for the north face of the mountain. Suddenly, they became aware that someone or something had been there before them, for only 250 yards from the tents, they saw a strange set of tracks. Pointing out the detail on the ground, Julian told me the story.

'Looking to the east, we could see the tracks had come over a col and down onto our Alexandroff Glacier, right across its head between our tents and Mount Snow Church, and finally over the col into China. In the crisp morning light we could see roughly a mile of tracks,' he explained. 'We first thought they were made by a bear, but the configuration was oddly in groups of three and ridged up slightly on one side. We wondered if it could be a biped, walking on two feet and touching the snow with one hand.'

We knew these tracks must have been made between 2000 hours and 0600, otherwise fresh snow would have obliterated them.

'Most mysterious,' said Richard Snailham, as we climbed the steep grassy slope behind Julian's ger to examine the spot where Lindsay's sighting of a creature had occurred. The Terbishes came too and, being biologists, took an interest in the plant life. Pulling up a bunch of small red flowers, Mrs Terbish said, 'We use this for coughs.' Funny, I thought, as we wandered amongst the rocks, looking at the ground – someone's been here before, picking these plants and also the wild garlic. But we found no tracks on that bare hillside. Gazing north into Russia and west to China, I shook my head. A few years ago I could not imagine, even in my wildest dreams, being here, especially as a British Army officer. How the world had changed! Now even the almas seems possible!

On returning to Britain, Daphne Hills, a zoologist at the Natural History Museum, kindly examined the evidence for me and felt confident that the tracks were those of a quadruped, almost certainly a carnivore. She said, 'Mammal tracks differ according to gait and speed; when using certain gaits, an individual's hind foot will be placed in the same position as a preceding forepaw, leaving only a single mark for both feet. This is very common and results in various unexpected combinations of footmarks. This phenomenon is seen in at least three carnivore families and, looking at examples of the tracks, a wolverine seems the most likely culprit.' However, I could find no record of the existence of wolverine in the Altai, although they are known around Lake Baikal. But in this little explored region, who knows? Without more evidence, one can only guess.

By chance I was able to investigate a sighting in the Khovd River gorge, where, in April 1991, an almas had been seen by two men. One of these, Gansukh, was my driver for a while and gave me a convincing account of a biped, approximately eighteen-foot tall, covered with reddish hair. Ann Tweedy was able to obtain the negatives of the photographs of the footprints it left. They were size sixteen!

Gansukh, a taciturn, dour man was a hunter of some repute. He had seen the creature walking and running 500 yards away and knew it was not a bear. 'Never did it move on four feet,' he said seriously, as he dictated his account slowly and deliberately to me. However, when Ann tried to tape his tale for the BBC World Service, he clammed up. 'I cannot speak more,' he insisted 'It is a state secret. We have been forbidden to talk of it.'

Our own scientific research was concentrated on the Black Lake, where Tony Martin's troops struggled to study the prolific birdlife beset by swarms of mosquitoes. Visiting the teams in battered old 'jeeps', Richard and I had some incredible journeys, and throughout the region venturers had many lucky escapes when crossing rivers swollen by unusually heavy rain.

The country had now completely exhausted its stocks of aviation spirit and as there were no MIATS internal air flights, the only one way to get back to the capital was to travel by lorry, 1,000 miles over the desert. Whilst preparation went ahead, the Brunel group completed their bridge and, taking the Khovd Commissioner with us, we went off to open it. Named Irons Bridge in recognition of a kind donation from the actor, Jeremy Irons, it looked very fine when we arrived at the site. Speeches were delivered and ubiquitous vodka bottles produced by the Commissioner, who drank rather a lot of it! Then Ian Robinson wanted a group photograph, so he arranged the team across the span, including Mick Ponting and his horse, Caesar.

As our guest of honour was now a little unsteady on his feet, I kept him at the end, which was just as well. Suddenly there was a sharp crack; a locally-made clamp had given way and one of the main wire cables ran through the anchorage. The decking tilted over, venturers grabbed the handrail and Caesar performed a graceful leap off the bridge onto the bank as if he did it every day. But poor Ian, festooned with cameras, did a backwards somersault into the river. The Commissioner made another speech, saying it was no one's fault and that such things often happened in Mongolia. Ian poured the water from his cameras and Mick Christy cursed the local clamp manufacturer. It says something for Mandy Grey, the young British Rail engineer who had directed the building, that she just bit her lip and said calmly, 'OK, let's get it repaired.' Ten days later, whilst the rest of us were motoring across the Gobi, she and her team finished the job and managed to get seats on the last plane out of Khovd.

The convoy worked well, although I had to run it in a military style. Tony Martin acted as Sergeant Major and at our regular 'comfort stops' yelled, 'Girls to the left, boys to the right.' The Mongols always got this wrong, which caused some consternation. At night we made a tight circle of trucks and slept within. Sentries watched for prowling robbers, but the six-day journey was largely uneventful until we reached Karakorum, site of a famous city built in 1220 by the great Khans. By 1586 it had been ravaged by Chinese armies and a monastery built on the site and it was this that we had stopped to see.

Camping in low trees by a river, we visited the magnificent temples and shrines, many of which are being restored. The sky grew black and then the howling wind brought clouds of swirling sand, closely followed by torrential rain, thunder and lightning. Sheltering in a temple entrance, I heard a different sound, 'Rump, rump, rump', then an indistinct whisper followed after several seconds by a 'Crump, crump, crump' overhead.

'What on earth's that?' I asked one of our Mongolian Army captains.

'Thunder,' he replied.

Then, as the rain fell in rods, it came again. From my days in the anti-aircraft regiment I knew the sound of guns. 'That was artillery,' I protested.

'No John, just thunder,' my friend insisted.

Back at camp the noises came again, but this time it was louder and I could hear bits of shrapnel falling in the trees.

'Get under the trucks.' I cried.

Everyone thought I had gone mad until Royal Engineer Corporal Paul Hardon drove in. 'You won't believe this,' he said 'but there's a load of civvies firing bloody great ack-ack guns skyward at the edge of a wheat field back there. Are we under attack?'

Back in Ulan Bator I told the tale to our Mongolian Defence Department friends and asked if they had an artillery unit at Karakorum.

'Oh no,' said the Colonel, 'those are the weather guns. They shoot chemicals at the clouds to prevent hail forming and destroying the crops. That is an important farming area.' As the hungry people of the capital fought for bread it was easy to see how vital the success of Mongolia's sparse agriculture will be in the future.

By contrast two days of packing and partying gave the venturers a splendid send-off. The reception laid on by our most supportive Ambassador, Tony Morey, and wife, Agni, at the residence will never be forgotten by the young. 'I never knew the British were so jolly,' commented Sylvie Jonckeau, our delightful French member. Tears poured down many a face as the international venturers bade farewell to their Mongolian colleagues at the railway station. They had shared much over the past ten weeks and, for most, the world would never seem the same again. As the well-laden train pulled out, heading across the Gobi for Beijing, we waved frantically and my thirty-three-tugrik trumpet sounded for the last time. Sean and I were left with a sad group of young Mongols, standing in the drizzle. The perilous state of their country's economy does not bode well for their future. I wondered if we were right to have given them a glimpse of a lifestyle beyond their reach, but hopefully it will encourage them to use the western advice and help to full advantage.

In Suhbaatar Square, by the statue of the national hero, an old Mongol was trying to sell a pair of fox cubs, but there was something odd about them. They were huge. Sensing my interest, my interpreter said, 'Wolves. They use them for guard dogs in the city. There is much crime now.'

What an extraordinary country. I'm sure there is much more to discover here, and hopefully, one day, I shall return to the land of Genghis Khan.

Epilogue

At the end of 1991 I retired from the Army. We had bought a farm house in the friendly village of Motcombe, near Shaftesbury where we established a base for overseas expeditions. It was here, on a sunny April day that the great Royal Engineer balloon rose from a grassy field. A cheer went up, but this time I was on the ground, waving. Victoria, our younger daughter, waved back and hurled her bouquet, which was neatly caught by her bridesmaid, Cara. Julian Matthews, my new son-in-law, wearing an old family flying helmet, saluted from the basket as they drifted away across the Dorset countryside. The post-wedding party, with chariot racing and tug of war contests, went on into the small hours and when Judith and I sank into bed the disco beat was still pounding from the marquee. 'Youth is a state of mind,' she groaned. But it had been a memorable day.

I think that it was this event, even more than my retirement from the Army a few months earlier, that signalled a new beginning to me. For almost forty years my job has really been to build teams to tackle arduous tasks, overcome obstacles and solve problems. Those who have taken part were at times tired, hungry, cold and wet, or hot, thirsty and covered in sores. Sometimes they have no idea what is happening around them or where they are going. This is when the strength and flaws of character will show. So, to head the various groups, I have always looked for people who I believed would go on leading under the worst conditions. Such men and women need to possess unusual ability and understanding in order to knit together a team, which, in turn, must have confidence in its leader. I therefore feel that, although one should not ignore setbacks, if one is seen to despair, group morale will deteriorate rapidly. I strongly believe that expedition officers must display cheerful, reasoned optimism and, by their enduring courage, be ready to press on when lesser men might falter.

The selection process is terribly important. To find out if someone possesses courage, I first try to discover if they have fear. For one who does not fear can have no courage: they do not need it. Such folk do exist and can be frightening company, often leading their comrades to take unnecessary risks.

Next, I want to see if the candidate has willpower, because I believe that in very many cases courage is simply resolute willpower. But as well as sheer physical courage, there is the moral variety, the sort that will lead one to make an unpopular decision or stake all on your own judgement. Strangely, those who appear to possess unbounded bravery do not always display moral courage. On the other hand, I have never known a person who has moral courage to be found wanting in the face of physical danger. The Duke of Wellington's advice to leaders to be 'cool in crisis and decisive in action' still holds good. Being a leader is a lonely business and all too often one's own thoughts are of little comfort when there is no one around to boost one's confidence. Those who lack confidence in their own abilities tend to be oversensitive to criticism.

On an expedition I occasionally find myself listening to two internal voices, perhaps representing two sides of my personality. One complains and moans, urging me to rest, to turn back or take the easy way out; fortunately, the other is more forceful and able to suggest alternatives when plans fail. This voice tells me to cheer up and keep going. At times of crisis, I have witnessed a confrontation between the two personalities in my dreams. Sometimes the image is so vivid that the different courses of action advocated are played out as if on a TV screen. I have even found it possible to replay the scene, sometimes on a different night. At one time, I thought I must be going round the bend until I met a very normal sort of chap who had exactly the same sort of experiences under stress.

Team members must also be selected carefully. I usually look for people who are cheerful, compatible, unselfish and tolerant. Both mental and physical toughness are important, but a person who tends to be over-competitive can be very disruptive.

Loyalty to the leadership and to the aim of the expedition is vital, but under stress and strain there is always the person who will grumble and knock the system. This is inevitable. Indeed, they may need to criticize in an effort to satisfy their ego and restore their own self-confidence. Whatever the reason, anyone who disintegrates the group under stress is a bad influence and should be removed at the earliest opportunity, before they infect others.

I have always gone to great lengths to build up the team's pride in its achievements so that it becomes self-motivating. My greatest mistakes in man-management have been when I have failed to sack someone, usually because I've been too soft-hearted. But there are a few around who have never forgiven me for removing them when they transgressed.

The difficulty facing the overall leader is to select the people with the right characteristics, but the system used on Raleigh has proved most successful for both young and old.

Unfortunately, expeditions attract prima donnas. Although a confounded nuisance on a prolonged venture, they are fairly easy to spot. Their vanity and self-interest usually give them away. On the rare occasion when I have met such characters, I have found that they are often bad mixers, or they will usurp the leadership and can become quite irrational. In extreme cases they can become rather exhibitionistic and complain bitterly of persecution if they do not get their own way. Masochists sometimes join hoping for the opportunity to prove themselves. Being an idle chap who believes that any bloody fool can be uncomfortable if that's their wont, I also regard such people as a potential danger to a team.

I have found that political and religious extremists, or for that matter anyone with very strong views, can cause friction. But I have absolutely no doubt that faith can help one to overcome difficulties. My own view of religion is that it is best described as a bank account, into which one must pay regularly so that in times of need you can withdraw. But you cannot arrogantly demand to cash a cheque when you need a miracle: it is very much up to the 'bank manager' to decide on the timing and amount of his support, although one hopes that he might be better disposed to assist if one maintains a credit balance. Of course, not all explorers believe in a god, and I have known many who claim to be atheists or agnostics. Whether someone has or has not got a religion only really concerns their selection for an expedition in that it is quite useful to know if you have to bury them! Even so, whenever possible I encourage simple services to be held on Sundays. Apart from being appreciated by some members, I feel it has moral value and helps us to retain a sense of time. Congregation numbers are usually poor at the start of an expedition, but increase in proportion to the tension. There are few atheists before a battle!

For many years I was against taking girls with us. I felt that, human nature being what it is, they would be an unwelcome distraction and would not really pull their full weight. However, I soon discovered that there were many advantages to having women members. In Darien, for instances, there were five girls in the team and they showed themselves to be mentally as tough or even tougher than the men and I found that their inbuilt capacity for survival more than made up for their limited physical strength.

As far as sexual distraction is concerned, it is a question of selecting your ladies carefully. They know most men, and explorers particularly, tend to be a red-blooded lot, but in the end it is the female who calls the tune and if you have the right sort of women, they will keep even the most ardent suitor at bay until the task in hand is completed. On Drake and Raleigh the number of girls wishing to take part surprised us and, today, I see no reason why women should not fill all roles on expeditions. They tend to be more caring and sympathetic and are useful listeners on those occasions when worried men might want to pour out their troubles. But one of their greatest assets is that they add tone. Men are often inspired by the women's good example and are far less likely to be petty when they are around.

Over the years the expeditions with which I've been involved have raised well over £20 million. It is never easy, but I would recommend all aspiring leaders to cultivate those vital qualities of communication and the ability to inspire, for without these one will never sell the project nor persuade others to follow. Broadcasting, lecturing and writing are all tools of the explorer's trade, but it is one's moral standards, integrity and expertise that will win the respect of the team.

Explorers tend to be conservationists and there are few tasks more urgent than the protection of the environment, the tropical forests, wildlife and the oceans. The search for traditional remedies for disease awaiting discovery is another tantalizing subject. I can assure those who fear they have been born too late that there is still plenty left to do as the technology advances. We can now dive deeper into the oceans and spend longer in space and the inflatable river boat, which we helped the Avon Rubber Company to develop, has opened up whole new areas.

As far as I, personally, am concerned, it is curiosity that drives me on. I have no particular desire to conquer a peak or to be the first man to complete some particular feat. Although I must confess that even if the challenge is not of primary importance, I still derive satisfaction from striving 'to seek, to find' without yielding. But it is the quest for the unknown that is paramount. Therefore, I believe that I am justified in using every possible aid to achieve the aim and solve the problem. I know it has been said that, given the huge amount of equipment, manpower and technical expertise available to us, it is hardly surprising that SES has got through where others have failed. But I am not in the exploring game to find out something about myself or to compete with others, and do not feel compelled to obey any self-imposed rules for physical challenges.

However, one must remember that expeditions may endanger your health. And for the novice, the experience can be an introduction to negative aspects of one's personality easily suppressed in normal daily life, although with appropriate counselling and support, this can be a journey of self-discovery, leading to increased self-confidence and a more enlightened attitude to others.

Seasoned adventurers recognize a condition I call post-expedition blues, the symptoms of which are similar to bereavement. This is triggered by the loss of one's new-found 'family' of expedition friends and suddenly being cut off from the excitement on return home. A routine and a mundane lifestyle can aggravate the condition and for many it is cured only by involvement in another challenge. Explorers also face isolation from family and colleagues, who have no concept of their intense experiences: they are often perplexed by the indifferent response to their stories and, as a result, the explorer may end up silent and withdrawn. The envy and resentment of the uninitiated, who imagine that one has been on a jolly picnic or simply suffered some self-inflicted masochism, is also common. The advice of Dr John Davies, with whom I have been on many trips, is to spend several days enquiring about the day-to-day problems that have occurred in their absence, before slowly beginning to recount their experiences.

Operation Raleigh had been the culmination of many years' work by thousands of people and in spite of all the battles to keep it going I had, for the most part, enjoyed it immensely. Under the new Trust it will live on, but I felt it needed different skills to sustain it as a permanent body. Like Kipling's explorer when the railway comes up from behind, it is time to move on. I had achieved my aim and must press forward to the next horizon. So I handed the reins to Jamie Robertson-Macleod, who had served the cause since the start and had plenty of experience of raising sponsorship. I left him with a good team of administrators and expedition leaders and turned my attention to my first love, exploration.

Julian Matthews, his enthusiasm fired by an upbringing in the Rhodesian bush and his experience on Raleigh in Guyana, had caught my disease and, with several like-minded friends, we formed Discovery Expeditions to cater for the growing number of older folk now seeking challenges and worthwhile endeavours in remote areas.

I could not leave the youth scene completely, however, and I continue to try to help the young, especially the really deeply underprivileged in whom the spirit of adventure has yet to be instilled or redirected.

Whenever I need to remind myself that 'Youth is a state of mind', I read Kipling's poem:

> 'There's no sense in going further – it's the edge of cultivation.'
> So they said, and I believed it – broke my land and sowed my crop -
> Built my barns and strung my fences in the little border station Tucked away
>   below the foothills where the trails run out and stop:
> Till a voice, as bad as Conscience, rang interminable changes On one everlast-
>   ing Whisper day and night repeated – so:
> 'Something hidden. Go and find it. Go and look behind the Ranges - 'Some-
>   thing lost behind the Ranges. Lost and waiting for you. Go!'

Index

INDEX

INDEX

INDEX